CHINA POLICY FOR THE NEXT DECADE

China Policy For The Next Decade

Report Of The Atlantic Council's Committee On China Policy

U. Alexis Johnson
Chairman

George R. Packard
Rapporteur

Alfred D. Wilhelm, Jr.
Project Director

with *Foreword* by Kenneth Rush

 Oelgeschlager, Gunn & Hain, Publishers, Inc.
Boston, MA

Published in 1984 by Oelgeschlager, Gunn & Hain, Publishers, Inc., for the Atlantic Council of the United States.

International Standard Book Number: 0-89946-179-4
0-89946-182-4 (paperback)

Library of Congress Catalog Card Number: 83-23785

Printed in the U.S.A.

Library of Congress Cataloging in Publication Data

Main entry under title:

China policy for the next decade.

Bibliography: p.
Includes index.
1. United States—Foreign relations—China—
Addresses, essays, lectures. 2. China—Foreign relations—United States—Addresses, essays, lectures. I. Johnson, U. Alexis (Ural Alexis), 1908–   . II. Packard, George R. II. Wilhelm, Alfred D. IV. Atlantic Council's Committee on China Policy.
El83.8.C5C5356   1984   327.73051   83-23785

ISBN 0-89946-179-4
0-89946-182-4 (paperback)

Contents

Foreword

Two of the truly historical events of the past decade were the visit to China by President Nixon in February 1972 and President Carter's establishment of formal diplomatic relations with the People's Republic of China on January 1, 1979, while simultaneously withdrawing diplomatic recognition from the Government of the Republic of China.

The effects of this dramatic shift in the relationship between the world's most populous country, which not only had a managed economy but previously had a defense alliance with the Soviet Union, and the world's greatest free economy, were not confined to China and the United States. The strategic effects on Europe, the Middle East, and Asia were immediately obvious and again demonstrated that in the modern world "Atlantic" and "Pacific" do not live unto themselves but that we all live in one interdependent world.

It thus seemed appropriate that the Atlantic Council should seek to look at China policy not just from the standpoint of our two countries, but also from the standpoint of our allies in Western Europe, Canada, Japan, Australia, New Zealand, Korea, and Southeast Asia. In the United States the heightened American awareness of China was reinforced by a growing interest within the Administration, the Congress, and the general public in the future of this relationship. It is against this background that on December 9, 1980, the Directors of the Council approved undertaking the project. The hope was that the project would be able to define for the United States a policy that the American public, the Executive, and the Congress could endorse, and that our friends and allies would support as contributing to global stability and their their own security.

U. Alexis Johnson, who chaired the Council's earlier project on the Common Security Interests of Japan, the United States, and NATO, agreed to chair a Committee for this project that would include not only American members, but also membership from Japan, Korea, and Europe. The concept was that participation in some form would be sought from an appropriate institution in the People's Republic of China. This was successfully accomplished in two visits by the members of the Committee to Beijing, as was consultation with the authorities on Taiwan. In neither case was concurrence sought to the text of the Committee's report, but rather there were full discussions designed to assure that their points of view were adequately presented.

I was pleased that Dr. Masamichi Inoki, president of the Japanese Research Institute for Peace and Security, agreed to serve on the Committee, and members of his Institute participated in its work. The Council is honored that the Institute will publish the text of the Report in Japanese.

I was also pleased that Mr. Philippe Deshormes, secretary general of the North Atlantic Assembly, served on the Committee and participated in one of its visits to Beijing.

I hope the Council can continue the valuable relationships that the Working Group established with the Chinese Academy of Social Sciences in Beijing, and the Institute for International Affairs in Taipei. We also look forward to continuing to work with the Institute of Foreign Affairs in Seoul.

On behalf of the Board of Directors I want to congratulate the chairman, Ambassador Johnson; the rapporteur, Dean George Packard; the project director, Alfred Wilhelm; and all the distinguished members of the China Policy Committee on their outstanding contribution to a better understanding of an important area of the world and its relationship to the security and well-being of the West.

While no member of the Committee can be charged with responsibility for every word of the Policy Paper, it does seek to reflect the consensus that emerged from the discussions and correspondence. Our Committee worked hard to produce from diverse experience and divergent points of view this collegial "white paper" and the related studies contained in this book. Given the breadth of the issues, we take satisfaction in having concluded the work with substantial consensus on the part of the members.

The project has been made possible, as are all Atlantic Council projects, by the support of U.S. corporations, foundations, labor unions, and individuals. We especially thank the U.S. Department of State, the U.S. Information Agency, the BankAmerica Foundation, the McDonnell Douglas Foundation, the Pennzoil Corporation, and TexasGulf, Incorporated. We particularly appreciate the help provided by Sanford N. McDonnell, Chairman of the McDonnell Douglas Corporation. The views and findings contained in the Policy Paper are those of the China Policy Committee. Each of the related studies is the responsibility of the individual author. These studies and the policy paper represent the views of the authors and the China Policy Committee, respectively, and should not be construed as official U.S. Government positions, unless so designated by other official documentation.

Only by free and informed discussion of our world problems can we hope to find the solutions that history demands of us. It is in that spirit that I commend this study to the U.S. government and the Congress for action and to the interested public for study and debate.

Kenneth Rush
Chairman
Atlantic Council of the United States

Preface

As Kenneth Rush has noted, it is more than two years since the Atlantic Council decided to undertake a study on future U.S. policy toward China from the perspective of the United States and its European and Asian allies.

When invited to be chairman of the project, I was reluctant because of my memories of the highly divisive and emotional effects of our China policy on the American body politic, and the past frequent extreme swings in the policies of the People's Republic of China (PRC) itself, which complicated the task of looking into the future. Although I was in no sense a scholar of China or Chinese, I had, however, had a long association with the country from the period before World War II when I was assigned to posts in North China and Manchuria when those areas were occupied by Japan, up through the post-war period when I was State Department "action officer" on the Korean War and armistice negotiations from 1950 to 1953, coordinator of our delegations to both the Korean and Indochina Conference of 1954 which were attended by the PRC, and from 1954 to 1957 conducting the bilateral "Ambassadorial Level Talks" at Geneva with a representative of the PRC. I thus had a strong interest in and direct appreciation of the importance of our relations with China. When George Packard, with whom I had worked on the Japan project for the Atlantic Council, agreed to be rapporteur, and Alfred Wilhelm, a Chinese scholar on detail to the Council as a senior fellow from the Department of Defense, agreed to be the project director, I capitulated.

I was determined that the Committee should be representative of the broad spectrum of opinions on China, and my original approaches were based on this principle. On this I found that those willing and anxious to contribute to the project exceeded my expectations, eventually totalling fifty-eight. To assure a responsible Japanese input, my longtime friend Dr. Masamichi Inoki agreed to be a member of the group, as did Philippe Deshormes, secretary general of the North Atlantic Assembly, to represent a European view.

At the first meeting of the Committee on January 19, 1982, we discussed an outline for the project and assigned authors to write twenty-five working papers. It was agreed that each paper would be discussed in meetings of the Committee and that while the authors would be free to make any changes they desired in the light of those discussions, the author would remain solely responsible for its content. Moreover, the papers and the discussion would be used by the rapporteur as the basis for the Policy Paper, which would seek to represent an agreed consensus of the Committee. It is my considered view, as well as that of many others, that the individual papers, as presented in this volume, constitute the greatest single collection of scholarship on China that has yet been published.

At the outset I stressed to the Committee that the Policy Paper would not simply represent the "common denominator," but that it would be a meaningful and incisive document that should have consequences for the policies of concerned governments. I also stressed that the proposed consultations in Beijing and Taipei did not have the objective of arriving at agreed positions with either, but rather of understanding and accurately representing their points of view.

Seven formal meetings of the Committee were held, and there were numerous conversations, conferences, and exchanges of correspondence with individual members. Contrary to my fears, instead of generating sharp controversy, the papers and discussions resulted in a degree of consensus that I could not have anticipated when the project was initiated.

During the study various members of the Committee and I made two visits to Beijing, one of six days in the spring of 1982, and the other of three days in the spring of 1983. In Beijing, our host was His Excellency Huan Xiang, vice president of the Chinese Academy of Social Sciences, but we also met with the Institute of Contemporary International Relations, the Chinese People's Institute of Foreign Affairs, the Institute of International Studies, members of the Foreign Ministry, and members of the American Embassy staff including Ambassador Hummel.

In each case, we visited Taipei where we met with the Institute for International Relations, as well as with the prime minister, other government officials, James Lilly, the director of the American Institute on Taiwan, members of his staff, the American Chamber of Commerce, and local Taiwan officials.

On both trips we visited the prime minister and other senior Japanese officials in Tokyo, Dr. Inoki and other members of the Research Institute for Peace and Security, of which he is president, as well as with Ambassador Mansfield and members of his staff.

On both trips we also visited Hong Kong, where we met with a group of American, British, and Chinese observers of the PRC organized by the Hong Kong Forum on Asia and the Pacific, under the chairmanship of Professor Kenneth Chern of Hong Kong University. We met as well with American businessmen, local publishers and press correspondents, government officials, and American Consel General Levin and members of his staff.

On the first trip to Beijing, we also visited Bangkok, Singapore, and Manila, where we met with senior government officials and community leaders, American Ambassadors Dean and Armacost, and American Embassy staffs. On the second trip we visited Seoul, where we met with the Foreign Ministry's Institute of Foreign Affairs, as well as with senior Korean officials, Ambassador Walker, and members of the Embassy staff. The reasons for the success of our visit in Korea and the sources of many valuable insights into the future of Sino–Korean relations were Dr. Pyong-choon Hahm, Secretary General to the President of the Republic of Korea and a member of the China Policy Committee, and Foreign Minister Lee Bum Suk. Both of these men were tragically killed on October 8, 1983, in the bombing during President Chun's visit to Burma. These were great men whom we will all miss.

Finally, we arranged to meet in Brussels with a group of European China scholars, NATO and European community officials, and appropriate European parliamentarians, under the auspices of the North Atlantic Assembly.

After each of these consultations, I circulated to members of the Committee a "Trip Report" and thus sought to assure that our work took into consideration the broad spectrum of viewpoints in the area.

On June 6 a final Committee meeting was held to discuss the latest draft of the Policy Paper. The penultimate draft was circulated to members of the Committee on June 30 for comment or concurrence. George Packard, Alfred Wilhelm, and I have carefully reviewed all comments and incorporated the many excellent suggestions that were submitted. Others of substantive importance that we did not feel able to incorporate have been included as footnotes. Thus, while no member of the Committee can be charged with responsibility for every word of the Policy Paper, it does seek to reflect the consensus that emerged from the discussions and correspondence among a diverse and bipartisan group of informed Americans and their foreign colleagues.

I am profoundly grateful to the members of the Committee who contributed so much time and talent in the papers they have submitted, as well as the other members who have acted as reviewers of those papers, and all who have participated so fully and thoughtfully in the task of the Committee. I am also deeply grateful to the scores of foreign officials and scholars, as well as American officials abroad who contributed their time and wisdom. Finally, I should note my thanks to the many officials in Washington who have been so patient with the importuning of myself and other members of the Committee for information.

I hope that this study will commend itself to all those in the U.S. Government concerned with the future of our relations with China, as well as to those in Tokyo, Beijing, Taipei, Seoul, and our associates in the ASEAN, ANZUS, and NATO capitals.

U. Alexis Johnson
Chairman
Committee on China Policy

Editor's Notes

The Atlantic Council's Committee on China Policy and the individual authors of this study have attempted the very difficult task of predicting policy decisions over the next decade in the United States and the PRC and in many of the countries affected by the nature of the relationship between these two countries. Predictions are at best educated guesses considering the large number of different outcomes that are possible from the interaction of just a few variables. Although each author is familiar with the historical record of each country, general attitudes therein, and how its various systems function, the specific outcomes of any policy decision cannot be foreseen. Most have attempted consequently to develop outer parameters, based on essential facts, within which to analyze various options and prospects; they are at best cautious about the results.

The authors hope that the reader will not attempt to judge the probable reaction of a foreign decisionmaker based on the reader's own approach to decisionmaking. Assuming that others will make the same decision about a given set of data as oneself has been an historic source of misunderstandings. Each nation has its own assumptions, style, and needs based on distinctive experiences with geography, political philosophies and culture, and on history.

Attempting to look ten years into the future through the lenses of more than a score of different nations has thus been a challenge, especially considering the wide range of attitudes about U.S.–PRC relations that the members of the committee brought to the project. Within a reasonable range of possible developments, the committee has arrived at a series of policy recommendations they feel are in the best interest of the United States in its relationship with the People's Republic of China over the next decade.

George R. Packard
Alfred D. Wilhelm

Members Of The Committee
On China Policy

Chairman

U. Alexis Johnson, Director, Atlantic Council; former Under Secretary of State, U.S. Ambassador to Japan, Thailand, and Czechoslovakia, and Chief, U.S. Delegation to SALT

Rapporteur

George R. Packard, Dean, School of Advanced International Studies, Johns Hopkins University; former Deputy Director, Woodrow Wilson International Center for Scholars, Smithsonian Institution

Project Director

Alfred D. Wilhelm, Jr., Senior Fellow, Atlantic Council; China scholar

Members

A. Doak Barnett, Member of the Board, National Committee on U.S.– China Relations; Professor of Chinese Studies, School of Advanced International Studies, Johns Hopkins University

Ralph N. Clough, East Asian Scholar; former Fellow, Asia Society

Terry Deibel, Professor, National War College

Philippe Deshormes, Secretary General, North Atlantic Assembly (Brussels)

Job Dittberner, Director, Institutional and Political Affairs, North Atlantic Assembly (Brussels)

Russell E. Dougherty, Executive Director, Air Force Association; former Commander-in-Chief, SAC and Chief of Staff, SHAPE

John K. Emmerson, Senior Research Fellow, Hoover Institute on War, Revolution, and Peace, Stanford University

Carl W. Ford, Jr., Professional Staff Member, Senate Foreign Relations Committee

Henry H. Fowler, Chairman, International Division, Goldman Sachs & Co.; former Secretary of the Treasury

Ellen L. Frost, Director, Government Programs, Westinghouse Electric Corporation; former Deputy Assistant Secretary of Defense

Curt Gasteyger, Director, Programme for Strategic and International Security Studies, The Graduate Institute of International Studies (Geneva)

Jeffrey Gayner, Counselor for International Affairs, The Heritage Foundation

William H. Gleysteen, Jr., Director, Asia Society; former U.S. Ambassador to Korea

Andrew J. Goodpaster, former Superintendent, U.S. Military Academy; former Supreme Allied Commander, Europe

John E. Gray, Chairman, International Energy Associates Limited

Pyong-choon Hahm, * Secretary General to the President of the Republic of Korea; former Professor of Law, Yonsei University (Seoul); former Korean Ambassador to the United States

Harry Harding, Senior Fellow, Foreign Policy Studies Program, The Brookings Institution; former Professor of Political Science, Stanford University

Eric W. Hayden, Vice President, Economic and Strategic Planning, Bank of America Asia Limited (Tokyo)

Martin J. Hillenbrand, Dean Rusk Professor of International Relations, University of Georgia; former Director General, Atlantic Institute for International Affairs (Paris) and U.S. Ambassador to the Federal Republic of Germany

Harold C. Hinton, Professor of Political Science, Institute for Sino-Soviet Studies, George Washington University

David S. Holland, Senior Vice President, Exploration, Pennzoil Exploration and Production Company

William G. Hyland, Senior Associate, Carnegie Endowment for International Peace; Editor Designate, *Foreign Affairs*

Masamichi Inoki, President, Research Institute for Peace and Security (Tokyo)

Thomas Kahn, Special Assistant to the President, AFL-CIO

Franklin D. Kramer, Partner, Shea and Gardner

Winston Lord, President, Council on Foreign Relations; former Assistant Secretary of State

David E. McGiffert, Partner, Covington and Burling; former Assistant Secretary of Defense for International Security Affairs

James W. Morley, Director, East Asian Institute, Columbia University

*Participated in the work of the Committee in a personal capacity, and not as a representative of his Government.

Richard Nations, Correspondent, *Far Eastern Economic Review*

*Hisahiko Okazaki,** Minister; former Director General for Foreign Relations, Japanese Defense Agency (Tokyo)

Jan S. Prybyla, Professor of Economics, The Pennsylvania State University

Christopher H. Phillips, President, National Council for U.S.–China Trade

James Reardon-Anderson, East Asian Librarian, Columbia University; former Professor of Asian Studies, School of Advanced International Studies, Johns Hopkins University

Thomas W. Robinson, Sun Yat-sen Professor, Georgetown School of Foreign Service; former Professor, National War College

Rainer Rupp, Economic Directorate, NATO Headquarters (Brussels)

Nathaniel Samuels, Advisory Director, Lehman Kuhn Loeb Inc.

Robert A. Scalapino, Professor of Political Science, University of California (Berkeley); Member, National Committee on U.S.–China Relations

Brent Scowcroft, Lt. General, U.S. Air Force (retired); former Assistant to the President for National Security Affairs

Raymond Philip Shafer, Chairman, National Committee on United States-China Relations; Partner,

Coopers and Lybrand; former Governor of Pennsylvania

*Gaston J. Sigur,*** Director, Institute for Sino-Soviet Studies, George Washington University

Richard H. Solomon, Head, Social Science Department, Rand Corporation; former Staff Member (China), National Security Council

Helmut Sonnenfeldt, Guest Scholar, The Brookings Institution; former Counselor, Department of State

Douglas T. Stuart, Director, University of Southern California School of International Relations (Munich); NATO Fellow

Leonard Sullivan, Jr., Defense policy consultant, System Planning Corporation; former Assistant Secretary of Defense

Robert G. Sutter, Specialist in Asian Affairs, Congressional Research Service, Library of Congress

Gregory G. Tallas, Vice President, The First National Bank of Chicago

William T. Tow, Professor, University of Southern California School of International Relations (Munich); NATO Fellow

Philip H. Trezise, Senior Fellow, The Brookings Institution; former U.S. Ambassador to OECD

Leonard Unger, Professor, The Fletcher School of Law and Diplomacy, Tufts University; former U.S. Ambassador to Taiwan

**Served on the Committee until he accepted a position on the National Security Council Staff.

Roy Werner, Corporate Director, Policy Research, Northrop Corporation

Allen S. Whiting, Professor, University of Arizona

Mike Witunski, Corporate Staff Vice President, McDonnell Douglas Corporation

Joseph J. Wolf, Rapporteur, Atlantic Council's Committee on NATO; former Minister, U.S. Delegation to NATO

EX OFFICIO MEMBERS

Theodore C. Achilles, Vice Chairman, Atlantic Council

Joseph W. Harned, Deputy Director General, Atlantic Council

Kenneth Rush, Chairman, Atlantic Council

Francis O. Wilcox, Director General, Atlantic Council

Project Assistants

Eliane Lomax, Atlantic Council
Robert Means, Atlantic Council

Student Intern

Rosemary Brennan, Temple University and Nankai University (Tianjin)

PART I

The Policy Paper

Chapter 1

The Policy Paper: China Policy for the Next Decade

Atlantic Council Committee on China Policy

George R. Packard, Rapporteur*

INTRODUCTION

Relations between the American and Chinese peoples have, from the beginning, been marked by turbulence and surprises on both sides of a deep cultural, historical, and political chasm.

From an American perspective, our "sentimental imperialists" of the nineteenth century—the missionaries, businessmen, soldiers, and adventurers who served as pioneers and shapers of our images of the Chinese people—gave us a tradition of unrealistic, even romantic expectations about China—expectations that in the first half of the twentieth century led us to conceive of China as a great power, a potentially democratic and even a Christian nation, a vast untapped market, a fighting comrade in arms during our war with Japan and a grateful recipient of American science, technology, and culture. Our "manifest destiny," it was thought, would carry us westward across the Pacific, bringing progress and enlightenment to the largest nation on earth, along with satisfactions to the benefactor.

Not even a shooting war with the Chinese on the Korean Peninsula in 1950 could, as it turned out, entirely eradicate our nostalgia for a

*Dean, School of Advanced International Studies, Johns Hopkins University.

past we had imagined for ourselves and the Chinese. Despite the tensions that persisted over Taiwan, Vietnam, and other Southeast Asian insurgencies, despite their embrace of the Soviet Union and Mao's communism, despite two decades of vitriolic denunciation of each other, a national outpouring of sentimental affection for the Chinese attended the arrival of President Nixon in Beijing in 1972—an event that rivaled Neil Armstrong's step onto the moon and even surprised the president himself, who had long been aware of a powerful attachment on the part of some Americans to the government on Taiwan.

In the decade that followed, the relationship grew in fits and starts, with exchanges of scientific and cultural delegations, private and public citizens, high level government visitors, students and scholars, athletic teams, journalists, trade missions, consular outposts, and finally full normalization of relations on January 1, 1979—all against a background of professions of warm friendship. A major impetus for this new rapprochement was, of course, our shared perception of a growing global threat from the military power of the Soviet Union, particularly in Asia and the western Pacific, which tended to mute our dispute over the future of Taiwan.

Throughout this decade, and in fact throughout our entire history of dealing with each other, there was no period that could be called "normal"—no time of equilibrium from which to measure aberrations. Thus, today, the task of planning a stable and predictable posture for the decade ahead remains elusive.

It now appears that some of the euphoria has worn off the relationship and that each side views the other with some caution. The Chinese have moved toward a more assertive nationalism, which calls for independence from the two superpowers, and as part of this posture, they seem to be moving somewhat closer to an intermediate position between the United States and the USSR, though they are still in important aspects closer to Washington than to Moscow. They have resumed attacks on U.S. "hegemonism," a term recently reserved for the Soviets, and have been engaging in negotiations with the Soviets.

Given the volatility of this relationship and the complexity of foreign and domestic forces that drive it forward, can a projection of likely developments and a set of policy recommendations for the coming decade be anything more than an exercise in futility?

The Atlantic Council's China Policy Committee believes that, from an analysis of the record of the recent past, with all its fluctuations, we can form a more accurate understanding of where we stand today and can make some cautious estimates of where we are headed over the coming decade, realizing fully that there may be surprises ahead.

The Committee believes that the United States government needs a clearly articulated concept of the American national interest with respect to the People's Republic of China—a concept that goes beyond the more narrow common security interests that have nurtured the relationship for the past decade, a concept that can lead to longer term policies aimed at producing certain outcomes more desirable than other outcomes, and a concept that makes sense to our Western and Asian allies. The Committee does not wish to overstate the effect the United States can have upon either the domestic or foreign policies of China. What is clear, however, is that the roller-coaster diplomacy of earlier years, with its secrecy, sudden shifts, jolts to friends and allies, and *ad hoc* reactive solutions to deep-seated and intractable issues, will not suffice for the decade that lies ahead.

Although there are areas of common interest yet to be explored, it should be recognized that there are very real limits to the commonality of Chinese and American interests. It will be important during the coming decade for the two countries to seek to identify and act on additional areas of common interest, particularly in the Third World (where they exist) and frankly discuss those areas in which the policies of the PRC and United States are or can become adversarial. Nonetheless, to the extent that China can be influenced by our actions and policy, the Committee feels that the United States should encourage development of China's latent national potential within our preferred framework of norms of international conduct.

The Committee agrees with the views of many of our allies and friends worldwide that the American approach to China has been more emotional than pragmatic. It urges a more realistic premise that would recognize China's constructive geopolitical role. The Committee agrees that China is a very large and very distinct political and cultural entity capable of an increasingly influential role in world affairs, particularly as a stabilizing element in both the regional and global correlation of forces—not as a client of the United States or of the Soviet Union but as a secure and independent power in its own right.

We should view China as a nonaligned state in a complex balance-of-power system that is emerging in Asia and, to a degree, globally. As such, China will be an independent actor and one that, for reasons of both ideology and national interest, will not in the foreseeable future have a relationship with the United States comparable to that which the United States has with Japan or Great Britain. But the United States and China can have a mutually beneficial economic and cultural relationship and can cooperate on certain political, strategic, and diplomatic issues. To this end, the United States needs to approach China with much less emotion—and much more hard-headed realism—than we have mustered in the past.

China's emergence onto the world stage over the past decade has, in fact, been a strong tribute to the quality and maturity of its current leadership, which has recognized the importance of stability to China's development. Where it might have pressed recriminations against earlier isolation by the United States, it has maintained and encouraged a productive dialogue. Where it might have exacerbated tensions on the Korean peninsula, it has acted as a stabilizing force. Where it might have strained Japanese–U.S. relations, it has in fact helped to improve them. Where it might have caused further strife in Southeast Asia, its endorsement of ASEAN has served to raise stability and confidence in that increasingly important region of the Pacific. Where it might have been a disruptive influence in the United Nations, it has acted independently but responsibly. Where it might have chosen to trade outside Western economic institutions, it is steadily expanding its involvement in the economic infrastructure of the industrialized nations. Where it might have overextended its credit on overambitious modernization plans, it has scaled back its aspirations to coincide with its modest economic means. Where it might have turned to more extreme measures to undermine Taiwan's economy and physical security, it has not done so.

While China could have mortgaged its future on highly sophisticated Western weaponry, it has scrutinized its options but resisted exaggerating its needs or its capabilities. While it has tested its right of access to the full gamut of Western commercial technology, it has not ignored the peculiar demands of its manpower-intensive resource base. While its political ideology is incompatible with the majority of the countries with which it deals, it has demonstrated a pragmatic ability to compartmentalize its relations on separate "party-to-party, state-to-state, and people-to-people" levels. Those who seek to treat China as an inanimate counterweight in the balance of superpower military force fail to grasp the larger perspective of China's potentially positive contributions in the overall "correlation of world forces." It remains to be seen how much China's and America's political and ideological differences will inhibit our collective abilities to assist constructively in their national growth.

The Committee stresses the importance of recognizing and encouraging the current convergence of common Sino–American interests, while openly acknowledging specific areas of different or conflicting interests and leaving substantial room for modified relations as future world events unfold and expose common threats and opportunities. For instance, we appear to share strong common interests in constraining

Soviet expansion and in developing stronger economic ties throughout the Western Alliance. We are interested in exploring with China common interests in the United Nations and the Third World. But we surely do not share a common political ideology, and the United States would doubtless seek to resist the spread of Communist regimes elsewhere in Asia or the Third World. We do believe that China should be— if it is not already—militarily strong enough to deter, or at least to attach a high cost to, intimidation of China by the Soviet Union and further Vietnamese expansion into Southeast Asia.

What is needed is a steady, cool appraisal of our interests, a clear understanding of where those interests converge with or diverge from those of the Chinese, a break from the romantic notions of inevitable harmony or hostility that have plagued us in the past, and the construction, where possible, of a sound long-term relationship based on our national interests in the context of our global commitments.

What follows, then, is an examination of the current state of bilateral relations between the United States and China, a projection of the most likely objectives and options that will enhance the relationship and further our common interests over the next ten years, a survey of the prospective and likely interaction of other key actors who might influence the relationship, a discussion of how the United States can best coordinate its policies to satisfy the interests and allay the anxieties of its Western friends and allies (Japan, Korea, and the ASEAN nations) and to avoid complicating the Taiwan issue, and finally, some conclusions and policy recommendations for the future that can commend themselves to a majority of the American people and to the U.S. government.

COMMON INTERESTS OF THE UNITED STATES AND ITS FRIENDS AND ALLIES

The United States and its friends and allies in Western Europe and Asia share an interest in pursuing closer relations with the People's Republic of China, particularly insofar as such closer relations result in economic progress for a China that is contributing to the peace and stability of Asia.

In the first decade of improved U.S.–PRC relations, both sides placed a heavy emphasis on shifting the strategic balance of power toward a more effective alignment vis-à-vis the Soviet Union, which was seen as a common threat. Many of our European and Asian allies and friends did not fully share in this appraisal and worried openly that the U.S.– PRC rapprochement could lead toward a military relationship that the Soviet Union would view as excessively hostile or threatening. They feared that this trend, if it continued, would prove destructive to the process of détente with the Soviet Union, which had blossomed in the 1970s.

Now, as we enter the second decade of improved relations, there is an historic opportunity to shift the emphasis away from such divisive issues and toward the goal of China's economic growth within international economic institutions and legal frameworks. The time has come for the United States, working in close concert with Beijing and with our friends and allies, to seize this common opportunity, both in our interest and in the interest of the Chinese.

An economically growing, secure, and modernizing China can be an important trading partner, a stable counterweight to the Soviet Union, and a valuable contributor to peace and stability in Asia and the world. A weak, vulnerable, unstable China, on the other hand, could offer a tempting target that would invite aggression.

Our European and Asian allies and friends have generally welcomed the relaxation of tension between the United States and the PRC, and all of them share the view that an improvement in economic, cultural, and political relations with Beijing is in the common interest. Most West Europeans and Japanese believe that a Chinese leadership that succeeds in solving its most pressing economic problems, and makes progress in economic development, is less likely to pose major challenges to the international community in the years ahead than a leadership that fails and encounters mounting domestic problems. Within the limits of their respective national policies, these governments are prepared to assist China economically through trade and investment and the transfer of technology.

To give effect to this general policy of encouraging Chinese economic development will not be easy. The United States and its allies may find themselves competing or taking different views on questions of trade, finance, and technology transfer. China will undoubtedly seek an allocation of economic aid from the World Bank's International Development Agency (IDA), which will result in a diminishing flow of aid to other developing nations. This will result in pressure on developed nations, particularly the United States, to increase its subscriptions and contributions to IDA. As part of its campaign against Taiwan, Beijing may again seek the expulsion of Taiwan from the Asian Development Bank. There will continue to be discord on such questions as whether or not to liberalize import and export controls for China. Such liberalizations will generate domestic pressures as well as pressures from our allies.

Despite these difficulties, it behooves the United States and its allies to make every effort to work together to establish concerted policies that will have long-range benefits for themselves and the Chinese. For example, we can encourage more effective and realistic planning and project management in China. Joint efforts can and should be undertaken to ensure that adequate feasibility studies and planning are carried out for projects to be supported by government financing. We should encourage the PRC to continue to develop its legal framework for handling trade, patents, trademarks, economic, financial, and other related matters and to assist China's development of quality control, management, accounting, legal, financial, and other sound business practices, for everyone's benefit. As China's worldwide commerce grows, it is in all of our interests to encourage China to integrate more fully as a member of the world economic community by joining the General Agreement on Trade and Tariffs (GATT) and participating in world intellectual property conventions. There should be continuing consultations among the United States, its allies, and China on decisions that will affect China's exports, with a view to avoiding protectionism directed against China wherever possible.

While there are certain to be disagreements on these matters, the fundamental emphasis must be placed on the critical need to broaden our economic relationship with China and to do what is necessary to ensure that the PRC will continue to devote its energies to peaceful growth and modernization in a peaceful, supportive environment in Asia.

EVOLUTION OF U.S.–PRC RELATIONS IN THE DECADE AHEAD

Recent Background

The decade from the Shanghai Communiqué of February 1972 to the Joint Communiqué of August 17, 1982, saw a radical improvement in relations between the United States and the PRC, but it left unresolved the single issue that, with the exception of the Korean War, had created the most tension between them, namely, the status and future of Taiwan. From the standpoint of the leadership in Beijing, their stated fundamental national goal—reunification—will require at least the minimum step that Taiwan acknowledge their sovereignty. These leaders hold that the United States is responsible for frustrating their goal of completing the civil war which began in the 1920s.

The diplomacy of the past decade brought some gains for Beijing, to be sure. In the Shanghai Communiqué, the United States made a concession by "acknowledging that all Chinese on either side of the Taiwan Strait maintain that there is but one China and that Taiwan is part of China," and adding that the United States "does not challenge that position." But the United States did not then nor has it since explicitly recognized or denied PRC sovereignty over Taiwan.

The United States in the Shanghai Communiqué reaffirmed its "interest in the peaceful settlement of the Taiwan question by the Chinese themselves," and stated that "with that prospect in mind," the United States "affirms the ultimate objective of the withdrawal of all U.S. forces" from the island and would "progressively reduce them . . . as tension in the area diminishes."

When relations were normalized (January 1, 1979), the United States made further concessions by recognizing the PRC and stating that it "acknowledges the Chinese position that there is but one China and Taiwan is a part of China." Washington agreed to end formal diplomatic relations with the Republic of China, terminate its defense treaty with it, and withdraw all its military forces from the island. (In fact, all U.S. military forces had long since been withdrawn from the island.) But the United States stated that it would "maintain commercial, cultural, and other [unofficial] relations" with Taiwan, and that it "expects that the Taiwan issue will be settled peacefully by the Chinese themselves." Four months later, the U.S. Congress insisted on reinforcing our relationship with Taiwan by its overwhelming vote in favor of the Taiwan Relations Act.

Under the Taiwan Relations Act (TRA) of April 1979, which appeared genuinely to disturb the PRC leadership, the United States formally declared that it would make available to Taiwan "arms of a defensive character" and asserted that the United States itself should "maintain the capacity . . . to resist any resort to force or other forms of coercion" threatening to Taiwan's security or its "social or economic system." In FY 1979 and 1980, U.S. foreign military sales to Taiwan averaged more than half a billion dollars a year.

The Chinese had tacitly agreed to defer the issue of arms sales to Taiwan, while publicly making clear their unalterable opposition in the long run to such sales. However, a number of events, including the increase in dollar value of military sales following the passage of the TRA, resulted in the matter becoming a contentious issue within the Chinese political leadership. Some leaders appeared to take the long view that normalization would bring about a gradual reduction of U.S. arms support for Taiwan and a willingness on the part of Taiwan leaders to negotiate a final settlement, while others apparently argued that continuation of such sales could lead to the permanent separation of Taiwan from the Mainland.

In any event, normalization in 1979 brought a new surge of contacts and exchanges between the two countries and, as tensions between the United States and the Soviet Union rose following the Soviet invasion of Afghanistan in December 1979, it was natural that the question of military cooperation with the PRC would arise. Within the U.S. government, some argued for military sales and assistance to the PRC to the grounds that "the enemy of my enemy is my friend" and that such gestures, besides strengthening Chinese armed forces and cementing the relationship with the Chinese, would also have a symbolic value in sending warning signals to the Soviets. A series of U.S. decisions, first by the Carter administration in 1980 and then by the Reagan administration in 1981, authorized sales of "dual-use technology of possible military use," and then authorized sales of nonlethal military support equipment. There were also press reports in 1981 to the effect that the United States and China had, in 1980, begun joint operation of two stations in northwest China to monitor Soviet missile tests, using American technology and Chinese personnel.

The next major effort by the United States to broaden U.S.–China ties in the military-security field came during June 1981, when Secretary of State Alexander Haig visited Beijing. It was announced then that Washington had decided to remove China from the list of prohibited destinations for munitions control purposes, thus opening up for the first time the possibility of American sales of lethal military equipment to China, the precise list of which would be determined on a case-by-case basis. Subsequently, a Chinese mission with a shopping list was planned for by the fall of 1981.

Others within and outside the U.S. government questioned whether such sales were in the long term U.S. national interest. The various offers seemed based on ad hoc, unrelated decisions, often prompted by "trip-book diplomacy" (i.e., the need for each American visitor to Beijing to bring some new concession or expansion of the relationship in order to maintain "momentum" in consolidating the relationship). Other American offers came in response to particular Soviet activities, such as the "discovery" of the Soviet brigade in Cuba or the Soviet invasion of Afghanistan. Questions were raised about the Chinese capacity to use advanced technology effectively and whether these moves were needlessly provocative of the Soviet Union, adding fuel to its paranoia about a two-front war arising from a Chinese–American threat to its eastern flank.

In 1980 and 1981, intense debate occurred within the U.S. government over the possible sale of the FX advanced aircraft to Taiwan (either the F-5G or F-16/J79). Beijing vehemently opposed such a move and threatened to downgrade diplomatic relations if it were made. In January 1982, the Chinese were informed in Beijing that the United States would *not* sell the FX to Taiwan but that it *would* permit continued coproduction in Taiwan of the less advanced F-5E—the principal aircraft in Taiwan's air force—and would approve a sizeable sale of military spare parts to Taiwan. Subsequently, the Congress was notified of the intended sale of $60 million in spare parts.

Meanwhile, in the latter part of 1981, the Chinese shifted to a tougher line and, broadening the issue from the FX to all arms sales, demanded that the United States set qualitative, quantitative, and time limits on *all* arms sales to Taiwan. At about the same time, they dropped their earlier interest in sending a military purchasing mission to the United States. By early 1983, however, the PRC was negotiating through U.S. commercial channels for the purchase of the Hawk and Tow missiles, two items on their 1981 list.

Beijing also stepped up its campaign for peaceful reunification, offering a nine-point plan on September 30, 1981, under which Taiwan could "enjoy a high degree of autonomy as a special administrative region," and it could "retain its armed forces." Under the plan, "the central government will not interfere with local affairs on Taiwan," and "Taiwan's current socio-economic system will remain unchanged, so will its way of life and its economic and cultural relations with foreign countries." The PRC plan promised that there would be no encroachment on private property rights or foreign investment in Taiwan. Industrialists and businessmen in Taiwan could "invest and engage in various economic undertakings on the Mainland," with their legal rights, interests, and profits "guaranteed." Taiwan's leader promptly denounced the plan as a trick. Observers pointed out that if Taipei accepted the PRC's offer, including PRC sovereignty over the island, there was no assurance that Beijing would live up to its promises and guarantees. Indeed, the case of the Chinese rule of Tibet was less than reassuring on this score.

A long internal debate within the U.S. government and intense negotiations with the Chinese led to a compromise agreement on the issue of arms for Taiwan. In a joint communiqué on August 17, 1982, Beijing cited its intention to strive for a peaceful solution to the Taiwan question, stressing that this was a "fundamental policy." The United States, reaffirming its earlier recognition of the PRC as the sole legal government of China and acknowledging the Chinese position that there is but one China and Taiwan is a part of China, stated that "it does not seek to carry out a long-term policy of arms sales to Taiwan, that its arms sales to Taiwan will not exceed, either in qualitative or in quantitative terms, the level of those supplied in recent years, . . . and that it intends to reduce gradually its sales of arms to Taiwan, leading over a period of time to a final resolution." The United States linked its commitment to a continuation of efforts by the PRC to reach a peaceful solution.

Simultaneous with the issuance of the communiqué, each side offered interpretations which foreshadowed future disputes. A Chinese spokesman asserted on August 17 that the "final resolution" of the arms sale issue referred to in the communiqué "certainly implies that the U.S. arms sales to Taiwan must be completely terminated over a period of time." Meanwhile, President Reagan stated, "We have paid particular attention to the needs and interests of the people of Taiwan." He added, "My longstanding friendship and deep concern for their well-being is steadfast and unchanged." Several prominent Senators, concerned about the future of Taiwan, denounced the communiqué.

In February 1983 the PRC pointed out, as proof that the United States will not honor the communiqué, the U.S. sale of sixty-six obsolescent F-104s from the Federal Republic of Germany to Taiwan. Even more troubling to the Chinese was President Reagan's February 26 interpretation of the communiqué in a response to his conservative critics right after Secretary Schultz's return from Beijing. He said that "If the day ever comes that those two [the PRC and Taiwan] can get together and become one China, in a peaceful manner, then there wouldn't be any need for arms sales to Taiwan." This statement seemed to link PRC settlement with Taiwan to a particular course of Chinese behavior, a linkage that the PRC denounced as unacceptable. It seems clear that the issue will continue to fester also as a domestic political controversy both in Beijing and in Washington.

Meanwhile, Beijing seemed to be shifting its balance somewhat between the two superpowers. This became apparent as early as 1980 when the Chinese, probably for domestic political reasons, took a different stand from the United States on the Polish Solidarity movement and on several other international events. In a speech to the Twelfth Congress of the Communist party on September 1, 1982, Chairman Hu Yaobang asserted that both Washington and Moscow were bent on "global domination" and portrayed China as seeking to unite with the Third World to "upset the strategic plans of the superpowers." This was a marked shift from the earlier Chinese statements that the Soviet hegemonism represented the greatest threat to world peace.

There are several possible explanations for this shift. It is possible that the Chinese leadership now feels it has wrung as many benefits as it can from the rapprochement with Washington for the time being and that it can exact more concessions from both sides only by taking the middle ground and bargaining. It may appear that, as a political reality, it has pushed Washington as far as it can on the Taiwan issue. It may also seem that the Soviets, bogged down in their problems in Poland, Afghanistan, and elsewhere, and facing a succession problem as well as enormous economic difficulties at home, represent less of a threat and that efforts to enhance the American counterweight are consequently less urgent than promoting ties with the Third World. The Chinese also have feared they were becoming too closely associated with the United States—with the danger that they would be perceived as a status quo power. Domestically there were conservative factions that feared that the doctrinal purity of the party was being diluted.

Yet in mid-1983, despite continuing differences over the August 17 communiqué, problems with the textile quotas (later resolved) and railroad bonds, and the PRC's decision to cancel part of this year's schedule of cultural and sport exchanges with the United States following the granting of political asylum to the Chinese tennis star Hu Na by the United States, the United States and China were continuing trade and keeping their doors open to each other along a broad range of cultural, educational, scientific, technological, and military fronts. They were also preparing to explore (through major investments by U.S. oil companies) China's offshore oil potential and were planning visits by the U.S. secretary of defense and the PRC foreign minister. It also seemed clear, however, that Taiwan would remain, as it had for thirty-three years, an important divisive issue.

Evolution of Policy in China

It should be stated at the outset that any effort to predict events involving the United States and China for a decade in the future is extraordinarily difficult. One needs only to look back at the past decade, with its totally unexpected developments, to be awed by the task. Our knowledge of events and movements in China, especially in the vast hinterland away from the capital and urbanized coastal areas, remains fragmentary and is not likely to improve substantially. In addition, the variables within the bilateral relationship and outside it (among the key actors such as the Soviet Union, Japan, the nations of Southeast Asia, and the Koreas) and the tide of events within Taiwan itself (which cannot be taken as a mere pawn in the game) tend to be so numerous as to defy comprehensive analysis.

The committee has concluded, nevertheless, that history can teach how to identify more and less successful policies and that, based on certain likely trends, there are better and worse ways to manage the process of making and implementing policy toward specific outcomes and away from known risks. However foolhardy it may seem to attempt to predict the future of this relationship, the failure to make the effort could lead to policies that would be contrary to the national interests of all concerned.

The PRC has emerged from the catastrophic upheavals of the Cultural Revolution and its aftermath (1966–1976) and the experimentation with radical socialism to a period of consolidation and cautious reform under the leadership of Party Vice Chairman Deng Xiaoping and a pragmatic group of followers who appear, at least for now, to be tightening their grip on the Communist party, the People's Liberation Army, and the bureaucracy. Major reforms are underway to recover from the irrational policies of Mao's late years. A program for modernizing agriculture, industry, science and technology, and the army has been launched. The "cult of personality" in leadership style is being abolished. With the help of foreign training, higher education is being revitalized. Older bureaucrats are gradually being retired. Leaders of the Cultural Revolution appear to have been eased out of key positions in all areas. One cannot be sure how much longer Deng Xiaoping (born in 1904) will remain in charge, but he has apparently succeeded in placing younger colleagues in key positions where he hopes they will remain after his death.

Economic Policy: The critical determinant will probably be the performance of the Chinese economy under the new leadership. Most experts agree that China has enough energy resources and mineral wealth to achieve economic modernization and become an industrial giant, albeit with a low per capita income. It is not so certain that their basic system of central control and planned allocation of resources— transplanted with some adaptations from the Soviet system in the mid-1950s—can overcome enormous obstacles, including the mistakes of the Maoist era. After three decades of major economic development programs, the Chinese economy today remains underdeveloped, with low per capita GNP (around $300 in 1982), low productivity in labor, a large share of the labor force engaged in agricultural production, and an economy in which the process of capital accumulation and technological innovation fails to produce significant and sustained increases in standards of living or in labor productivity. Despite some pockets of advanced development, China will in the aggregate remain over the next decade and probably into the next century an underdeveloped economy. Although favorable growth rates have been achieved over the past three decades, these may not be sustainable over the next decade for Chinese labor productivity has seriously declined during this period and is declining today. The current Chinese leadership appears to have understood this dilemma and is clearly searching for a new development strategy and policies that can offer a better hope of success. They explicitly admit that, in the next decade, their economic strategies and policies will be aimed at correcting the ills inherited from the past rather than trying to sustain the unrealistic growth target rates of the past three decades.

In the short run, the Chinese must deal with an economic system crippled by tremendous waste and inefficiencies arising from inappropriate allocation of resources and inappropriate management. By investing too much in heavy industry (the Soviet model), the Chinese have failed so far to build an appropriate capital and manpower base that will sustain rapid growth in the future. Neglect of agriculture, transportation, urban development (especially housing), energy, consumer goods, and construction materials has led to serious imbalances and bottlenecks, threatening growth even in the favored sectors. Neglect of agriculture, for example, has meant, at least until recently, a failure to increase per capita consumption among the 80 percent of the Chinese population in rural areas—a fact that has obvious political ramifications.

Another immediate problem facing China's economic planners is that under the Maoist principle of self-sufficiency, foreign trade had been regarded as a necessary evil, and this had meant that China had foregone significant economic benefits made possible by international specialization in production. China's present leaders are currently pursuing a more open economic strategy, but it is not clear if they will succeed, nor how they will find the means to pay for the large increase in imports that economic development requires.

The Maoist principle of self-sufficiency also led to significant restrictions on the borrowing of modern technology from abroad and excessive reliance on the development of an indigenous technological base. The question of whether Chinese leadership can overcome this bias and create a means of keeping pace with technological development abroad lies at the heart of whether economic modernization will be possible in China. Again, it seems that the post-Mao leadership intends to change course and to seek to import a substantial amount of new technology.

Certainly the Chinese have shown their interest in progressing toward assimilation of higher technology by sending thousands of their brightest students for prolonged periods of advanced study in the United States, western Europe, and Japan. When these foreign-trained students return to the PRC they will create pockets of competence in a variety of fields.

Another problem of the past three decades has been the wild fluctuations in levels of investment, aggravated by political struggle between competing factions of the party. These have produced alternating periods of "great leaps" followed by retrenchments which have produced considerable waste and inefficiency, and it is by no means certain that the Chinese leadership coalition has reached a political equilibrium that will allow for stable policies over the next decade.

Management inefficiencies also became worse over the past three decades, and China's leadership faces the enormous problem in the next decade of creating an institutional/organizational framework in various enterprises, decisionmaking groundrules, and an incentive system to reverse the current downward trend in total factory productivity.

Current Chinese leadership seems aware of these problems and has adopted an "Eight Character Program" aimed at "readjusting, restructuring, consolidating, and improving" the economy. Among the reforms is a call for an increase in the level of technology effectively used in production, both by facilitating and increasing the borrowing of modern technology from abroad and spreading it more widely throughout the economy.

The committee believes that the current leadership has made a rational analysis of China's economic problems in the modern era and is adopting pragmatic policies for dealing with them. The United States has an obvious interest in the success of China's modernization efforts. An economically progressing Chinese nation with a stable government in control of its own population is eminently desirable. The alternatives—failure to make progress toward modernization and political stability or the rebirth of regionalism and the catastrophic breakup of China into warring units and factions—would bring serious instability to Asia and to the world. Although there is a limit to what the United States can do to support current economic trends in China, those few things that can be done should be done. Specifically, the provision of technology for peaceful purposes in energy, light and heavy industry, and agriculture—technology suited to the conditions of an underdeveloped economy and technology specifically requested by the Chinese—should be made available whenever possible. Educational opportunities and vocational training, where sought by the Chinese, should be offered. Advances in science, medicine, and agricultural technology, where helpful and applicable, should be made available to them on the same basis as to other friendly, nonaligned, developing countries.

Even if the Chinese leaders adopt the wisest conceivable policies and receive the maximum help from the United States and other foreign nations, they must grapple with population and food problems of a magnitude never before encountered on this planet, problems that cannot possibly be "solved" within the decade under consideration or even in the twentieth century. Though the Chinese statistics indicate that they have brought population growth down from an annual rate of 2.4 percent (1952–1957) to 1.3 percent (1975–1981), current demographic facts make further decreases extremely difficult. Their population to-day of about a billion is almost twice as large as in the early 1950s, while the cultivated area is slightly smaller and more than 70 percent of the labor force is still engaged in agriculture. The implications are horrendous. There will be massive unemployment or underemploy-ment—more than 100 million surplus laborers in the countryside by the end of the twentieth century according to preliminary Chinese es-timates—as well as massive increases in demand for consumer goods, especially food. Pressure to migrate to the cities will result in either Draconian methods to prevent such migration or massive unemploy-ment in the urban areas. The leadership will be faced with rising expec-tations for increases in per capita consumption, especially food and housing. It will be under intense pressure to adopt a more rigid birth control program, which will increase discontent in the countryside and which may or may not be effective.

The challenge facing the leadership will be to introduce technology that increases output (and which is *labor-using,* not labor-saving) throughout the agricultural sector. To meet the challenge, modest gains in consumption must also be achieved, and unprecedented methods for increasing employment discovered. Policies for reducing inequalities between the richer provinces and the poorer must be found. While the situation is not hopeless, it does seem to indicate that China's earlier plans of becoming a strong, rapidly modernizing nation by the 1980s cannot be achieved even in the best of conditions. It also raises serious problem for political leaders.

Domestic Political Policy: Given the complex of grave problems the leadership faces, it is also virtually impossible to predict with any confidence future political developments in China and their effect upon foreign policy and U.S.–Chinese relations. Three possible scenarios are:

1. A continuation of the present situation, with current leaders and their like-minded successors exercising maximum efforts to mod-ernize through pragmatic policies, leading to modest economic progress despite huge difficulties. China would remain relatively open to international influences as a condition of modernization and would move only marginally toward the Soviet Union, while maintaining fairly close ties with the United States.
2. Internal factional disputes, economic failures, foreign setbacks and weakness, with the danger of war abroad and revolution at home, would present the party leaders with crisis after crisis, leading to the weakening of central control and the emergence of varying degrees of regional independence.

3. Faced with setbacks in their effort to modernize and in their foreign policies, the party would turn to repression, harsh discipline, and "internal remedialism" in the bureaucracy, and recentralization in politics and economics. The ideologues would defeat the technician-managers. A new charismatic strongman could arise (supported by disgruntled sectors of the military) and impose a kind of bureaucratic Stalinism on the country. New Maoist-style campaigns would be launched. Relations with the United States probably would be cut back, as China possibly moved closer to the Soviet Union. Security and stability would be threatened in Asia.

These are, of course, only three of a large number of possible scenarios, whose precise dimensions are impossible to predict. It is possible to imagine dynamic alternation among them or a combination. While the current administration has demonstrated a high degree of consistency and stability and the first scenario today appears to be the most likely, none of the above nor other possibilities can be ruled out. Some implications for U.S. policymakers are evident. Stable political leadership committed to modernization through rational, pragmatic policies is desirable. The use of their resources for economic development rather than military might is also desirable. A foreign posture that permits the introduction of much-needed technology from the West will assist the process of modernization. Concentration on domestic goals rather than adventures abroad is sensible. Nonetheless, the danger of less favorable political developments that would be totally beyond our control and that could arise almost without warning, should be kept in mind at all times.

Foreign Policy: Chinese foreign policy goals will of course be affected by the economic and political factors cited above, but they will almost certainly be built upon four main aims leading toward becoming a major power: the achievement of security, development toward modernization, independence, and reunification. Security requires the avoidance of a disastrous war with either the United States or the Soviet Union that could wreck all current plans. A part of this aim would be the maintenance of a favorable balance of power in Asia. Modernization would seem to require (although some Chinese leaders may have different ideas on this) the maintenance of some minimum level of relations with the United States and the West in order to have access to technology, capital, and management know-how. This requirement need not prevent improvement of state-to-state relations with the Soviet Union, and in fact it is likely that the PRC may move further toward an independent position between Moscow and Washington, tactically continuing to shift its balance between them in order to increase its leverage with each of the superpowers. This movement will of course be vitally affected by the policies of the Soviet Union and the United States toward China and toward each other.

Finally, China will seek to assume a strong voice among the nations of the Third World as a means of enhancing its international role while preserving its independence from each of the superpowers. It may well also seek closer ties with Japan and Western Europe for the same reason. It is not at all certain that the Third World, with its numerous and shifting power centers, is prepared to accept Chinese leadership, however, nor that China can afford costly aid ventures merely for prestige.

The selective use of assertive nationalistic themes to unify the Chinese people behind the government's policies will enhance the possibility of achieving the other three goals. Taiwan, Hong Kong, and other possible irridentist claims are specific objectives whose value as instruments of foreign policy may exceed their intrinsic importance.

Defense Policy: In the mid-1960s, the Soviets began a buildup along the Sino–Soviet border that, by 1968, posed a serious threat in the eyes of China's leadership. This threat undoubtedly began to cause the Chinese leadership to see the Soviet Union as a threat increasingly surpassing that posed by the United States. By the early 1970s, Zhou Enlai had begun to speak of the Chinese second strike threat to the Soviet Union, thereby producing an element of stabilization in the Sino–Soviet conflict. To reduce the likelihood of war, however, additional efforts were needed.

As calculated in Beijing, the development of the relationship between the PRC and the United States over the past decade helped to diminish the likelihood of a Sino–Soviet war. Pressure from within the PRC for rapid, large-scale modernization of the People's Liberation Army (PLA) to deal with the Soviet threat has correspondingly decreased. With the United States playing a helpful strategic role and the perception of a diminished Soviet threat, China's leaders have been able to deflect many of the demands on scarce national resources for expensive foreign and domestic weapon systems and to direct those resources to the building of China's economic infrastructure. Investments in such long-neglected areas as the PRC's transportation and communication infrastructure and in China's ability to absorb and proliferate new technologies will greatly enhance the PRC's ability to become an independent major power after the next decade.

Deterrence of a Soviet attack is increasingly only partly attributable to the role of the United States. Chinese advances in strategic nuclear weapons have played on Soviet fears of war on Soviet soil, enhancing the credibility of the PRC's retaliatory capability. Soviet experiences in Afghanistan and Chinese experiences in Vietnam have made both more appreciative of the complications involved in a "people's war." Despite the PLA's relative deficiencies in the equipment and doctrines of the modern battlefield, continuing improvements in organization, training, and the acquisition of selected equipment, coupled with a better appreciation of the strengths of China's physical features (vast territory and population, dispersed industries), cultural legacy, and historical experiences have enhanced the confidence of China's leaders in their own ability to cope, in however costly a manner, with a Soviet attack.

With their somewhat enhanced image of China's ability to defend against a Soviet attack short of a third world war, China's leaders are focusing more attention on China's role in a general war. Under such conditions, Soviet concern about the possibility of strategic cooperation between the PRC and the United States and NATO will be important. Through the next decade, therefore, the Soviet Union should not be allowed to overlook the possibility of China as a possible second front with which the Soviets might have to deal in any conflict.

The United States and the PRC will, over the coming decade, be required to balance their need for geopolitical cooperation against the great reluctance by China to allow cooperation to appear as dependence, much less as a cooperative defense or alliance effort. Technology transfers will be sought, as in recent commercial negotiations, but purchases of equipment to upgrade significant conventional forces will be minimal. Relations that will enhance the PLA and the U.S.–PRC strategic relationship without giving high capital investments will be cautiously sought.

Evolution of Policy in the United States

The United States entered into its current period of rapprochement with the PRC in 1971 based on its calculation of regional and global balances of power. The Sino–Soviet split shifted the world balance of power in a favorable direction. A comparable calculus prevails today and is likely to remain valid in the coming decade. The Chinese and Soviets, if ideologically united and coordinated militarily, could pose a significant threat to the United States as well as to our European and Asian friends and allies. Our policies must not serve to enhance the likelihood of such a development.

At the other extreme, actual warfare between the Chinese and Soviets cannot be in our interest. There would be a danger of being dragged into such a contest against our will. Such a war could quickly escalate to the nuclear level, with unforeseeable consequences from nuclear and political fallout around the globe. The devastation and disorder that would result from either a conventional or nuclear war and the possible dismemberment of China could not possibly be a desirable outcome. Even those who might hope that such a war would reduce the size of the Soviet threat to our own interests could not be sure of the outcome; an opposite result is equally conceivable.

To reduce the likelihood of either extreme coming to pass, there are a number of options for U.S. policymakers. Questions for the next decade will include the following:

1. Since it is likely that the Soviet Union, with its growing military might and its ability to project that power to all parts of the globe, will for the coming decade represent by far the greatest potential threat to U.S. security, how should we manage our security relationship with China so as to help preserve the world balance of power? Specifically, to what extent, if at all, should we encourage and contribute to building up China's military power?
2. Outside the military sphere, how much transfer of scientific and technological information and know-how is it in our interest to transmit to the Chinese?
3. What other kinds of economic aid, and in what degree, should be made available to the Chinese?

U.S.–China Economic Relations. As stated above, the major opportunity for the United States and its friends and allies in Europe and Asia is, for the coming decade, to broaden the emphasis from the strategic to the economic, scientific, and cultural dimensions of our relations with China and to do in concert what we can to facilitate China's economic development.

To do so, U.S. policy should stress private sector economic cooperation with China primarily through trade, export credits, and direct investment. To support the private sector, the U.S. government should continue to offer Export-Import Bank credits, to provide Trade and Development Program support for such activities as financing project planning services leading to the sale of U.S. technology (both goods and services) in support of China's economic development, and to offer limited government assistance for training.[1]

Trade: Normal trade that benefits both nations economically but does not jeopardize the U.S. lead in the development and application of technologies at the cutting edge is desirable, not only for its economic value but also for its value in strengthening political bonds and decreasing the Chinese need for economic ties with the Soviet Union.

Closer trade ties between the Chinese on one hand and our Western allies, Japan, and the nations of Southeast Asia all have the effect of bringing China into the international economy after years of isolation and are also desirable. On the other hand, an obstacle in our relationship may be the export of American culture—the development of consumer tastes along Western lines or advertising for life-styles that are unattainable—which could be a matter of concern to many Chinese leaders.

The PRC is already a significant trading partner of the United States and is likely to grow faster as a market than many of our traditional trading partners. In 1982, Sino–American trade was $5.2 billion. With U.S. exports of $2.9 billion, China ranked eighteenth as a U.S. export market. Although still far behind Japan ($21 billion), it is only slightly behind Taiwan ($4.4 billion) and South Korea ($5.5 billion) as a market. As China develops its natural resources (such as offshore oil, coal, renewable resources, agriculture, and strategic minerals), its importance to the American economy will grow, not only as a market, but also as a source of natural resources.

As a result of efforts to date, there is now a substantial, long-term Western commercial presence in China. Western companies have made direct investments in 48 China joint ventures (78–81 when ventures in the Special Economic Zones are included). More than 500 foreign commercial firms operate permanent offices in the country. The opportunities for continued growth of commercial cooperation between the United States and China is significant but also offers areas of future competition and contention.

A source of contention in bilateral trade relations is the issue of market protectionism in both countries. American industries, alarmed by the sudden appearance of Chinese products on the domestic market after the PRC was granted most favored nation (MFN) tariff status in 1980, have filed a number of petitions with the International Trade Commission. These petitions have sought to restrict Chinese imports of such items as ceramic ware, textile piece-goods, and canned mushrooms. It must be noted, however, that even under MFN tariff rates, China continues to buy more from us than it sells. The U.S. bilateral trade surplus totaled $2.7 billion in 1980, $1.70 billion in 1981, and $621 million in 1982. When combined with China's earnings from the United States via "invisibles" (tourism, etc.), in 1982 the PRC achieved a net bilateral surplus in the economic relationship.

China's nonmarket economy, low wages, and lack of cost accounting make it particularly vulnerable to charges of unfair trade practices, and these charges are likely to continue. Chinese planners, however, place a tremendous emphasis on a bilateral trade balance with China's major trading partners, and if the PRC is to continue buying large quantities of American products, there is a clear need for Chinese products to have fair access to the U.S. market.

There are, of course, impediments to the growth of U.S.–China trade that stem from policies and practices in the PRC. A notable example is China's lack of legal protection for foreign technology. The PRC has no patent law, and it has not yet joined the Paris convention. Concerning imports, there have been complaints that "exclusive" arrangements with U.S. distributors have been unreliable. Other problems include a reluctance on the part of China's financial institutions to extend loan and performance guarantees and China's failure to promulgate domestic laws that directly affect foreign investment in China.

Perhaps the best way to minimize serious confrontation over these issues in the future is to reinforce the mechanisms that have been established for regular bilateral consultation. Through these mechanisms, China could be alerted to industry concerns before they come to legal action and could be helped to diversify its exports to the United States.

The bilateral Joint Economic Committee (JEC) was established in 1979 to coordinate economic relations between the United States and China in order to strengthen and expand these relations. The U.S. Department of Treasury and the Chinese Ministry of Finance are the responsible agencies. The bilateral Joint Commission on Commerce and Trade (JCCT) was conceived by the Department of Commerce and proposed to the Chinese nearly two years ago. The first annual meeting of the commission was held May 24–26, 1983, in Beijing.

The committee feels that through the use by the JEC and JCCT of their respective working groups, which could meet between annual meetings to consider economic and trade problems and explore each side's applicable laws and regulatory processes, much could be done to defuse explosive issues arising from asymmetries in business practices. Trade problems concerning export controls, foreign investment, financing and legal issues, as well as protectionism, could be addressed by these forums.

None of these problems will be solved quickly or easily. What is necessary for the near future is attention to mechanisms for bilateral consultation. Commercial relations between the United States and China are still in their infancy, but they have grown beyond the point where they can be dealt with through "trip diplomacy."

Advanced Technology Transfers: One of the most vexing current problems between the United States and China revolves around the transfer of advanced technology to the PRC. Which items, of what degree of sophistication, at what risk of unagreed conversion to military use by the Chinese, under what laws and circumstances, should be transferred? These issues are not easily resolved and will continue to be troublesome. How decisions will be arrived at within the American government and under what guidelines have not been articulated as of this writing (July 1, 1983), though the problem was receiving attention at the highest levels.

The Chinese are seeking a vast range of advanced technology in areas such as computers, telecommunications, software, nuclear energy, oil exploration equipment, and the like. The United States has declared itself in favor of "a strong, secure, and friendly China." Common sense would indicate that the U.S. government should be willing to sell advanced technology to the Chinese except where such technology could be used either by the Chinese or by third parties to whom it could be disclosed, for purposes inimical to our national interest.

But the matter is not so simple. Ever since normalization, the U.S. government has struggled with these questions:

1. What criteria should govern decisions within the U.S. government on the transfer of the "dual-use" technology (i.e., technology with both civilian and military applications)? As a friendly nonaligned country China, in June 1983, was transferred by the president to a category that includes the NATO countries, India, Yugoslavia, and others, but it is not yet clear what operational effect will follow from this. Certainly China should not be treated as harshly as the Soviet Union (in which category China had originally been placed) but neither should it qualify for the same kind of treatment as our NATO allies and Japan.[2]
2. By what process should national security considerations condition or prohibit sales of equipment that are too sensitive for transfer?
3. How can proprietary interests in certain equipment and technology be protected once it has been transferred? The Chinese do not currently adhere to international conventions on trade (e.g., GATT), patents, copyrights, and so forth.

The committee proposes the following general concepts and recommendations as its approach to these difficult issues.

1. The transfer of a broad range of technologies can have desirable results not only for the Chinese economy but also for the U.S.–China relationship. The committee, however, recognizes that a strong Chinese industrial base could be used in the future for military purposes not consistent with our national interest. To allay

these fears, a broad study should be conducted to identify and quantify the probable impact of Western technology on China's industrial capability.

2. The U.S. government should be most responsive to Chinese requests for "dual-use" technology for use primarily in the civil sector (communications, transport, power supplies, renewable resources development, etc.). On the other hand, technologies that would make a direct and significant contribution to nuclear weapons and their delivery systems, electronic and antisubmarine warfare, and intelligence gathering should continue to be generally withheld, though each area should be carefully examined to ensure that only the most sensitive are automatically denied.

3. The committee also recognizes the importance in evaluating technology requests of the need to protect the U.S. lead in the development and application of critical military technologies. Other factors should include the degree of protection accorded U.S. interests, economic need, ability to absorb, intended use, and willingness to accept standard U.S. restrictions against the onward transfer of certain technologies to third countries or parties.

4. Since the issues have become so sensitive, the U.S. government must quickly come to an agreement within its own ranks as to how best to expedite decisions, so that promises and agreements can be kept. Having said this, it should be added that each request will raise specific and possibly unique questions having to do with complex scientific, military, and technological questions that are beyond the competence either of this committee or of many government decisionmakers to resolve in any orderly and predetermined fashion. What is important, though, is that these matters be handled with care and high-level attention and that they not be permitted to fester endlessly within the bureaucracy.

These problems will continue to trouble the relationship throughout the coming decade. The committee urges the U.S. government, however, to point out to the Chinese government that there is much it can do to ease the difficulties.

First, it must understand the difference between the private and public sectors in the United States—a difference that does not exist in the PRC, at least in theory. Commitments and promises made by U.S. firms to Beijing are not the same as official approval by the U.S. government.

Second, if it desires to be treated as a friendly, nonallied nation, it should take rapid steps to integrate itself into the existing international framework for trade and technology transfer, with appropriate domestic implementing legislation.

For its part, the U.S. government must keep in mind that the PRC can turn elsewhere for many types of technology, either to our allies or to the Soviet Union or Eastern Europe. In formulating our own guidelines, it makes little sense to create ill will on the part of the Chinese and economic hardship for American businesses by prohibiting the export of certain technology if the Chinese can just as easily obtain it elsewhere.

With respect to our allies, the U.S. government should associate with other Western nations in working with the PRC to identify, promote, and facilitate the transfer of those technologies that are consistent with China's economic development needs and abilities to absorb, as well as the common security interests of all nations concerned.

Finally, in the new world where the use of technology and management come together, it should be remembered that there are distinct national advantages for the United States in establishing close connections with the advanced sectors of the PRC through the transfer of management and organizational techniques, English language training, and other common programs that accompany the transfer of technology. Other things being equal, it is far better for the Chinese to develop a relationship in these areas with us or other Western countries than to become dependent on the Soviet Union.

Mutual Understanding. When Sino–American relations go through a period of some erosion, as they did from mid-1980 to August 1982, there is a tendency for Beijing to castigate the United States for being insensitive to China's needs, especially, of late, its sense of sovereignty. While the United States must show appreciation of Chinese needs, sensitivities, and domestic political context, the same is required of the PRC toward the United States. If the relationship is to move forward and continue to enjoy broad public support in the United States, the Chinese must demonstrate greater awareness of American sensitivities and appreciation of our domestic political system (including the separation of powers) and our pluralistic society. For example, the U.S. press, unlike that of the PRC, is not the official voice of government, and thus U.S. policy should not be inferred from the press. Continual hectoring of the United States or inflammatory public statements on specific issues can only irritate American officials and public alike. The tendency to lump together the United States and the USSR in terms of hegemonic policies or threats to peace and the sharp attacks on American policies in the Third World (even when they objectively serve Chinese interests by eroding Soviet influence) should also be held in check. U.S. officials should make clear that Chinese rhetorical excesses only serve to undermine support in the United States for strengthening

U.S.–Chinese relations and complicate U.S. diplomacy on international issues.

U.S.–PRC Security Relations. The United States' security interests and policies for the coming decade will rest on the fundamental assumption that our relationship with the Soviet Union will remain intensely competitive, that the Soviets will probably continue to sustain a steady increase in defense expenditures (4–5 percent annually in real terms), and that against the backdrop of their substantial and increasing military power, their policymakers will continue to look for external targets of opportunity that they can exploit, directly or by proxy, to expand Soviet influence and diminish that of the United States.

Apart from its strategic nuclear threat to the United States itself, the Soviet threat stretches across three major theaters: Western Europe, the Middle East, and East Asia. Nor is the western hemisphere itself immune. The Soviets have reduced the credibility of U.S. nuclear forces as a deterrent to conventional attack by building up their own strategic nuclear forces. The United States and its allies have not yet resolved the problem of spreading their conventional forces across the theaters mentioned above in sufficient strength.

The United States has vital political, economic, and security interests in an East Asia that is stable, peaceful, and much more closely associated with the United States than with the Soviet Union. It is especially important to us that the Japanese industrial powerhouse contribute to the strength and vitality of the market economies of the world. Sino–Soviet differences inhibit the Soviet Union from feeling free to transfer major forces from the Soviet Far East to service elsewhere. In East Asia, the United States relies on a strategy involving separate defense treaties with Japan, the Republic of Korea, Australia and New Zealand, Thailand, and the Philippines.

The committee believes that the Sino–Soviet adversary relationship has been beneficial in a number of ways: It has enabled the United States to drop China as a putative military adversary. Sino–Soviet antagonism has resulted in the creation or upgrading of Soviet forces such that at present roughly one-fourth of their ground forces are committed in East Asia. That antagonism has aroused historic Russian concerns about the dangers of a two-front war. It has removed any likelihood of Soviet naval or air bases along the Chinese coast or Soviet access to Chinese ports for repairs and refueling of naval vessels. This denial somewhat limits the mobility of the Soviet Pacific fleet, making its egress from the Seas of Japan and Okhotsk more critical. Finally, it appears evident that the Chinese have exercised a restraining influence on the North Koreans. (On the other hand, the presence of Soviet naval forces in Cam Ranh Bay is a source of deep concern to the ASEAN countries and threatens the sea lanes between the Pacific, the Indian Ocean, and the Middle East.)

It follows, therefore, that it is in the U.S. national interest to avoid pushing China into a new close relationship with the Soviet Union or into an adversarial relationship with ourselves and our allies.

A number of conclusions flow from that logic. It is important that the United States maintain its forces in East Asia and the Pacific. It is also important that the Chinese and our friends and allies in the area be reassured that we are committed to a forward military defense of our interests in the region. These forces are symbolic to an extraordinary degree; their draw-down in any substantial number is likely to have political consequences that would seriously undermine our defensive strategy.

Second, the United States would welcome a more reciprocal relationship with China in military support areas, such as intelligence and military education, although it is not in the interest of either party to seek a formal alliance or to take actions that would be seen by the Soviet Union or by our friends and allies in the region as provocative or aggressive.

Third, there are areas for further cooperation between the United States and PRC, such as Indochina and Afghanistan, where coordination of policies has been desirable. For example, Washington and Beijing should continue to consult on possible solutions to the Vietnamese occupation of Cambodia and on ways of achieving the withdrawal of Soviet troops from Afghanistan. The United States should seek consultation on regional refugee affairs. We should also pursue policies toward Korea that would encourage the Chinese to continue their parallel policy of reducing the danger of the outbreak of hostilities on the Korean peninsula. The United States should urge the PRC to develop contacts with South Korea that could point the way to eventual cross-recognition.

The handling of the relationship between the United States and the PRC must not be left to ad hoc trip-driven diplomacy by busy U.S. officials. Rather, it should be based on a sound appraisal of the long-term evolution of U.S. and Chinese interests and capabilities, as well as those of our friends and allies and handled through normal diplomatic channels.

With respect to the future bilateral U.S.–PRC military relationship, it is unlikely that during the decade either country will desire to enter into any large-scale U.S. program of military assistance. Chinese military technology is about a generation behind that of the United States and the Soviet Union. Chinese weapons are based largely on Soviet designs. Chinese hard currency is limited. Chinese industry cannot absorb quantum advances in technology. In addition, recent Chinese budgets have given a relatively low priority to spending for military purposes. Any massive assistance program would still fall short of significantly raising Chinese equipment to the levels of the Soviets. Such assistance could, however, result in raising perceptions of Chinese capabilities to a point where other nations in the area might feel threatened.

The United States must discipline itself to avoid any temptation to seek to have the PRC create a Chinese military force in America's own image. Neither geography, economics, nor culture support such a thrust. Rather, the United States should recognize that the PRC will develop a military force that builds on its unique national resources.

The United States should recognize that China is not willing to accept a tactical or strategic dependence on the United States and will follow an independent course, not necessarily always to our liking.

The United States must take the security interests of Japan, the Republic of Korea, the nations of ASEAN and ANZUS, and Taiwan into account. The United States should consult closely with Japan, the Republic of Korea, and the nations of ASEAN and ANZUS prior to any future military cooperation with China.

The United States should be responsive to PRC requests to purchase weapons designed primarily for protection, such as antitank or antiaircraft weapons. Other material sales might include command, control, and communications equipment, early warning radar, and land transportation equipment. Chinese-initiated negotiations for the commercial procurement of U.S. military equipment, as compared with U.S. Department of Defense initiated and/or negotiated foreign military sales, permit the United States to be responsive yet retain sufficient controls over what China can buy without creating an aura of Chinese dependency.

Finally, it behooves the United States to consult closely with its Western European allies on forms and methods of security cooperation with the PRC. Although their interests tend to be regional while ours are global, the lesson should have been learned that security for all is indivisible and that weaknesses offering temptations to an expansionist Soviet Union in any part of the globe can raise serious problems for all.

In sum, therefore, our bilateral defense relationship should be characterized by a modest amount of defense cooperation, when and if asked for by Beijing, rather than by large and rapid substantive contributions to a Chinese military buildup. The strategic contribution of Chinese forces (i.e., the degree to which they offset Soviet military power) is not likely to expand greatly in the near term whatever we do, and the risks of entering into a closer relationship or of assuming the trappings of an alliance outweigh any potential gains. It is our *potential* for acting together against the Soviet threat that will provide the best deterrent.

This relationship may include political and diplomatic signals, such as mutually supporting communiqués in response to Soviet challenges, occasional official defense consultations, intelligence exchanges on a limited basis, observation of military exercises, military education exchanges at the senior service college level, an occasional exchange of naval visits if conditions are right, and some degree of consultation on developments in third countries. Any further developments must await the evolution, if it happens, of a more sound political relationship, such as the clarification of Chinese purposes in the Third World, especially in those areas most important to U.S. interests. Additional military cooperation, while it cannot be ruled out for the future, will depend on the long-term development of both Sino–American and Soviet–American relations.

U.S.–China Cultural and Educational Relations

Education of Chinese in the United States. While the United States generally favors educational and cultural exchanges with almost all nations and cultures of the world, the case for educating China's future leaders requires special comment. It is an important fact that many of China's leaders in education, science, and technology in recent years have been trained in the United States. The United States has come to play a special role in offering training to future Chinese leaders; about 9,000–10,000 Chinese students are currently receiving college or graduate level training in various fields.

It is profoundly in our interest that this trend should continue and be strengthened. In doing so, we can open channels for communications and understanding with China's future leadership that will be very helpful in managing U.S.–Chinese relations in the future. The vast cultural and societal differences between China and America place a heavy burden on those who can bridge them, and this U.S.-educated elite can serve as an important bond from which other kinds of relationship can grow.

Education of Americans about China. The American understanding of China is also deficient. The number of freshly-minted Ph.D.'s, LL.B's, and M.A.'s trained at our leading China centers now roughly equals the available openings in government, business, journalism, law, education, and research centers. The deficiency therefore is not in the number being trained but in the adequacy of training, the escalating costs of graduate programs, the maintenance of the existing institutions, and the maintenance of knowledge of China through Chinese publications and sources. The following items are of specific concern:

1. Through funding by the United States Information Agency, National Science Foundation, Department of Education, and National Endowment for the Humanities, the various programs of the Committee on Scholarly Communications with the People's Republic of China funds eighty senior and junior scholars in the sciences, social sciences, and humanities to travel to China annually to engage in advanced research, thesis research, and language study. Our scientists require assured access to Chinese laboratories and to the field to collect geological, zoological, or botanical specimens. Our humanists require assured access to libraries, archives, and museums. Our social scientists, confronting severe problems of access, need nonetheless to increase their knowledge of the living society. China is largely unmapped from a scientific perspective, and the research that is going forward promises to integrate the Chinese experience into more general theories about man and nature. Another problem is that American funding for research in and on China is uncertain and, in certain areas, inadequate.

2. Over the past generation, an institutional infrastructure was developed to study China. This included six comprehensive centers for the study of China at universities within the United States, the Inter-University Chinese Language Training Center at Taiwan University (clearly recognized as a leading center for this purpose), the Universities Service Centre (USC) in Hong Kong (with its extraordinary library and research facilities) and the Joint Committee on Chinese Studies of the American Council of Learned Societies and the Social Science Research Council, which sponsors research conferences and awards research grants for non-PRC-based research. This institutional infrastructure has seen a steady deterioration in its funding, and several of the institutions—particularly the USC—face immediate severe (possibly terminal) funding problems. As this core apparatus weakens, the United States becomes more dependent on China for the illumination of its own condition. We think it is essential for the United States to retain an independent capacity to understand China.

3. The outpouring of Chinese language publications has left both the government and academic communities unable to handle the available materials. The translation services cover but a small

portion of the total, and significant portions of the Chinese press go essentially unscanned both within and outside the U.S. government. An aggressive acquisitions program and a clearinghouse and/or clipping service would be appropriate additions to the research apparatus now in place.

4. While the current number of students in Chinese studies is about adequate, certain aspects of their training—particularly language training—are not as high in quality as they could be. Opportunities for Americans to take part of their graduate training in China should be supported. Few Americans attain genuine bilingual proficiency. Within the U.S. government, proficiency in language and area expertise are not always adequately rewarded. The use of career incentives for language and area specialists, not just for China but for other countries, merits special study.

In short, China has changed in a decade from an inaccessible adversary to a somewhat accessible partner in world affairs, but this change has not diminished our need to understand the internal dynamics or foreign policy of China. Indeed, we believe the need for sound research on China has never been greater, but the funding has been decreasing at a rapid rate. The results are twofold: we are more dependent for many subjects on Chinese self-assessments than in the past; and, if current trends in our research capacity persist, we will not have the requisite understanding of China a decade hence. What happened in connection with the decline of Soviet studies in the United States in recent years is a warning. We believe this warrants considerable able attention both within and outside the government.

ROLE OF THE SOVIET UNION

The Sino–Soviet split, which began in the early 1960s, reached a new degree of intensity in the winter of 1978–1979 when, after the United States and China normalized relations, China launched a "punishing action" against the Vietnamese, and the Soviets remained passive in the face of this attack against their ally. Today the Soviets maintain some forty-five to fifty divisions (representing roughly one-fourth of their ground forces) on their Chinese border, backed by an increasing number of SS-20 intermediate range ballistic missiles, Backfire bombers, the construction of a new railroad link (the Baikal-Amur Line) across eastern Siberia, and a large and growing naval presence in the western Pacific. Some of this build-up is doubtlessly part of its goal of improving their strategic position vis-à-vis the United States and may not be directly aimed at China; even so, the Chinese are aware of the possible Soviet threat to their territory.

Sino–Soviet relations seem, nevertheless, to be improving somewhat. Since 1979 the Soviets have ostensibly sought a resolution of their conflict with the Chinese at the political level, but the Chinese have responded by calling, among other possible signs of Soviet good faith, for a preliminary disengagement along the border. The Soviets fear that they will face a difficult choice of either conceding a predominant Asian role to China (especially in Indochina and to a lesser extent to Japan) or accepting the long-term burden of increased military protection of the Soviet Far East, an area ripe for economic development.

It appears that in 1980–1981, the Soviets chose to seek some reconciliation rather than further confrontation, partly because of the deterioration in U.S.–Soviet relations since 1980 and the increased prospects for U.S.–Chinese military cooperation. While the Soviets still fear the long-term Chinese threat to their interests in East Asia, they have probably perceived that China's military modernization will be slower than they originally had anticipated. Soviet leaders in the post-Brezhnev era have inherited difficult—by U.S. standards—economic problems; it is conceivable that they will seek some slackening of massive military spending. A reduction of tensions along the Sino–Soviet border may therefore seem prudent. Given some encouragement from the Chinese, who are also likely to view a reduction in tension with relief, there could occur a modest reconciliation between the two Asian powers. This limited accommodation is unlikely to reach the stage of a fundamental political accord, however. A settlement of minor border issues will not resolve longer term Soviet anxieties about Chinese threats to their Siberian territories and resources nor cause them to withdraw a significant number of forces from the Sino–Soviet frontier. Nor is it likely that the Chinese would move so far toward accommodating the Soviets that they would jeopardize their relations with the United States.

A limited reconciliation between China and the Soviet Union is not necessarily inimical to American national interests. Put differently, high tension leading to hostilities between these two powers could not, in the end, be in our interest. In any event, the United States has only modest influence on this relationship. It is important, nevertheless, that Soviet planners be forced to keep in mind the ever-present possibility of U.S.–Chinese military cooperation in response to Soviet aggressive behavior around the world. And the United States should, in its relations with the PRC, attempt to establish a record of consistency, reliability, and credibility that will induce Chinese leaders to develop a degree of confidence in the long-term benefits of closer relations with the United States and will avoid the danger of driving the Chinese into dependence upon the Soviet Union.

On the other hand, it is not in the U.S. interest to enter into military agreements that could have the effect of causing the Soviets to increase further their military power in Asia and the Pacific, or to raise tensions with the Chinese to the point where a Sino–Soviet war would become likely.

The committee opposes any attempt to use our relations with China —particularly our strategic relations—as a short-term, tactical response to Soviet provocations in third areas. To do so would damage our relationship with Beijing in that it would be seen as an attempt to treat China as a pawn that we can manipulate in a broader strategic game. Nor has it been particularly effective in the past in convincing the Soviet Union to alter its behavior. It will be important, moreover, particularly during the post-Brezhnev period in the Soviet Union, to keep open the possibility of greater cooperation between the United States and USSR to relieve tension and minimize the risk of war.

TAIWAN

Since Chinese leaders have asserted that the future of Taiwan is so central to the entire Chinese world view, so central to the purpose of the Chinese revolution, and accordingly so emotional for this and possibly for future generations of Chinese leaders, one must try to project the evolution of events on the island itself. This is a formidable task.

In the coming decade, Taiwan's present leader, Chiang Ching-kuo, is likely but not certain to pass from the scene; his passage could produce either a smooth transition or the struggle of Mainlander hardliners with Mainlander pragmatists and moderate Taiwanese, perpetuation of the status quo, the evolution of passive understandings concerning the extent of interaction between the leaders in Taiwan and Beijing, an eventual willingness to negotiate some form of association with the PRC, or the emergence of an independent Taiwan regime.

From Beijing's perspective, several interrelated factors will bear on their posture toward Taiwan—namely, Taiwan's attitude toward the Mainland, the state of U.S.–China relations, the existing military balance across the strait, and the domestic political pressures within China. Japan may also come to have a powerful voice in the outcome during the coming decade. The Taiwan issue will also be a source of domestic political controversy within the Chinese leadership.

From Washington's perspective, Taiwan is today an island of remarkable prosperity and significant U.S. investment and trade, a member of the international economic system, and a former ally whose well-being is a matter not only of moral concern but of law under the Taiwan Relations Act of 1979. Any overt aggression by Beijing to take over the island forcibly would be met by a strong reaction by the United States. Taiwan is also a domestic political problem in Washington as a highly vocal and influential minority believes that Washington has already tilted too far in the direction of closer relations with Beijing. A majority of Americans would oppose any solution that would simply abandon Taiwan to a takeover by force, but it is also unlikely that a majority of Americans would want to go to war over Taiwan. We know relatively little about the political attitudes and future preferences of the 85 percent of the 18.1 million population of Taiwan who are indigenous to the island. It is fairly clear, however, that few of them desire to see unification of Taiwan with the Mainland that would subject them to complete control by the PRC regime. Correspondingly, relatively few would press for Taiwan independence unless this was perceived as the only alternative to such control.

It is possible to imagine a vast number of policy options in response to a vast number of developments affecting the future of Taiwan, but there are too many variables to make such an exercise worthwhile. The committee, therefore, proposes the following principles for guiding our conduct on this matter:

1. The ultimate solution to the problem of Taiwan must be a Chinese solution, arrived at by the Chinese on both sides of the Strait of Taiwan. Any American effort to coerce or mediate a final solution will be ineffective and possibly counterproductive.

2. The U.S. role should be limited to making as sure as possible that the solution, which will probably be a process rather than a single formal comprehensive agreement, will have been achieved without coercion or force of any kind.

3. The United States should neither stand in the way of a maximum amount of contacts and interaction between Taiwan and the Mainland (including trade, visits, exchanges, and the like) nor try to play a direct role in promoting any particular solution.

4. Assuming that Beijing sticks to peaceful methods, the United States should stick to the August 1982 joint communiqué, namely, its arms sales should "not exceed, either in qualitative or quantitative terms, the level of those supplied in recent years . . .," and it should "reduce gradually its sales of arms to Taiwan, leading over a period of time to a final resolution."[3]

5. The seeds of a possible Chinese solution could be present in the designation of Taiwan as a special administrative region under the new Chinese Constitution of 1982 (Article 30) and/or the concept of one nation with multiple systems of government. The ability of all Chinese on both sides of the Strait to live with ambiguity and uncertainty on this question has been amply demonstrated over more than three decades. The United States should avoid promoting or coercing either party into adopting any particular solution, insisting only that the use of force be avoided.

6. The committee is particularly concerned by the excessive emphasis placed up until now on the Taiwan issue—by both sides. The United States obviously cannot control Taiwan's future and should not claim to or try to. The gradual evolution of Mainland/ Taiwan relations neither requires nor benefits from excessive attentions, suspicions, or false claims of urgency. Precipitous actions by either side would most likely be both counterproductive and unsuccessful. Moreover, the group considers that the PRC's use of Taiwan as a "control rod" in Sino–American relations is far from constructive. While the Taiwan wounds can best heal at a natural pace, there are far more pressing issues of common national interest which deserve priority attention.

At least two possibilities could arise that could thwart a peaceful settlement. First, a strong, independent, well-organized Taiwan independence movement, with support from Japan or elsewhere, could arise, declare itself independent, and defy any attempt by Beijing to take it over. Second, Beijing could decide that, whatever the risks and difficulties, immediate reunification should be attempted, possibly to forestall the first possibility (above). Each of these would have serious implications for U.S. policymakers. Suffice it to say now that in all likelihood neither development could occur overnight, and there would be ample time available to consider different responses.[4]

OTHER ASIAN VIEWS

While the committee has focused mainly on relations between the United States and China and necessarily upon the triangular relationship of the United States, the Soviet Union, and China, it is important to keep in mind that the nations of Asia that lie on the periphery of the Chinese mainland are historically and culturally bound to be most immediately concerned with the course of events in the PRC. Since American interests in the nations from Japan and the Republic of

Korea southwest through ASEAN and ANZUS are substantial and growing, a rational China policy must take account of their interests and anxieties.

Attitudes, of course, vary from one country to another, and differences exist within some countries. In Southeast Asia, for example, Thailand tends to be more sympathetic to American military cooperation with China than Indonesia, since Thailand feels threatened by Vietnamese encroachments (with Soviet backing) in neighboring Laos and Cambodia, while Indonesia has an historical concern about the loyalties of its Chinese minority population.

In Japan, there is a range of views on China and its role in the security of the western Pacific. One prevailing opinion is that giving the Chinese substantial military assistance (or even appearing to join Beijing in a united front against the Soviet Union) would be unnecessarily provocative toward Moscow, would end any hope of Japan's accommodation with the USSR, and would disturb Tokyo's relations with Southeast Asia as well. Thus, the Japanese have not only reiterated that they will not sell arms to China, but they have also placed strict limits on exchanges of visits by Chinese and Japanese military personnel. In addition, the Japanese have consistently urged that the United States exercise caution in its own military cooperation with the PRC. When Secretary of Defense Harold Brown visited Beijing in early 1980, just after the Soviet invasion of Afghanistan, for example, some prominent Japanese newspapers warned that any moves toward military cooperation among Tokyo, Beijing, and Washington against the Soviet Union would irritate the Soviet Union, disrupt stability in Asia, and risk "increasing military tension between Japan and the Soviet Union." Similar views were expressed after Secretary Haig's offer to sell China defensive weapons in 1981, although there has been some relaxation of this concern since the 1982 elections.

Similar opinions have been expressed in the Republic of Korea. Stability and peace in Asia are critical to development and economic progress; excessive military cooperation with the PRC is not desirable.

Our Asian friends are concerned about what they believe to be emotionalism and idealization in American images of China. The continuing American commitment to Taiwan is regarded as reflecting, to a degree, a sentimental attachment to the Nationalists, rather than a rational assessment of the national interest. Conversely, many allies believe that we have, in our euphoria about our new relationship with China, overstated our common interests in China and disregarded the remaining differences in foreign policy objectives and socio-political structure.

Many Asians, both in Japan and in ASEAN, express reservations about the degree of exceptionalism that characterizes American attitudes about China. They acknowledge that China is unique in some ways, especially in its combination of size of population and extent of national territory. But they insist that, in other respects, China is not as exceptional as Americans often claim. As much as China, other Asian nations have also had to reconcile their pride in their own traditional cultural identities with the fact of Western technological and military superiority. Other nations, and not just China, have had to respond to the challenge of the West and find ways of ensuring national sovereignty and promoting socio-economic modernization. The notion, common in the United States, that these dilemmas are more intense for China than for other parts of the world is indignantly rejected by observers in both Japan and Southeast Asia. What is exceptional about China, according to one frequently heard rejoinder, is not that the problems have been greater but that the responses have been less effective.

The combination of emotionalism and exceptionalism in American attitudes toward China produce what many Asian (and for that matter many European) observers believe to be an overestimation by the United States of the role that China can play in the global strategic balance and in the international economy. The very concept of a "strategic triangle," they believe, vastly exaggerates China's military and economic significance, not only now but also for the foreseeable future. While some Americans tend to view China as a potential superpower— consider the Nixon-Kissinger concept that China was one of five major power centers in the contemporary world—Europeans and many Southeast Asians tend to view China as a regional power at most.

Many of our friends in Asia complain that, while Americans exaggerate China's effect of the global balance, Washington pays too little heed to China's long-term ambitions in the region. Washington and Beijing have common interests vis-à-vis the Soviet Union, and it is these similarities that have led to discussion of Sino–American military cooperation. But, as we have seen, many Asians believe that the United States ignores the remaining differences between China and other Asian states, especially in Southeast Asia.

It is important to acknowledge that some reservations expressed by our European and Asian partners strike some Americans as being rather hypocritical and others as realistic. Europeans caution the United States not to sell arms to China for fear of provoking the Soviet Union and simultaneously welcome window-shoppers from the Chinese People's Liberation Army who visit European arms exhibitions and military installations. And our friends in Europe and Japan clearly share with the United States an interest in a peaceful settlement of the Taiwan issue, but they want us to bear the responsibility for seeing that the interest is realized.

This does not mean, however, that American policymakers would be well-advised to ignore the remaining reservations expressed by our friends. The United Sates should listen seriously to the advice that our friends and allies are giving us. They are cautioning that close alignment with China may not be the best way to manage the West's relations with the Soviet Union; that American military assistance to China may, in the long term, have a destabilizing effect on Asia; and that emotional American commitments to Taiwan may risk forfeiting the strategic benefits of the new Sino–American relationship. These propositions may or may not be correct. But they are thoughtful arguments and deserve careful consideration.

Even more important, our partners look to see whether the United States takes these reservations into consideration in making its decisions about China. The choices Washington makes about China are seen, to some degree, as a measure of American priorities and also as a test of the procedures by which American policy is formulated. When forced to choose between China's position and that of our other friends and allies, which side does the United States take? And when making decisions on its policy toward China, does Washington consult its partners in advance, or does it announce its conclusions only after they have been reached?

Indeed, there is widespread resentment, especially in Asia, that the United States does not consult adequately with other interested parties before making important decisions with regard to China. Many Southeast Asians charge that the United States, especially during the latter half of the Carter administration, accepted all too readily the Chinese position on Vietnam—a policy of isolation and pressure—rather than accepting the somewhat more flexible ASEAN line. There is also concern as to the degree to which this policy has been identified with the morally abhorrent Pol Pot regime in Kampuchea.

Similar views are prevalent in Japan and South Korea. The United States informed Tokyo of the Kissinger visit to China in 1971 only minutes before the events were announced to the American public on television. Although the situation seems to be improving, the Japanese still complain of inadequate consultation between Tokyo and Washington over the normalization of Sino–American relations in 1978 and military relations between China and the United States.

On either substantive or procedural grounds, therefore, American China policy is too important to be left to Washington and Beijing alone. Four main conclusions are possible. First, and most fundamentally, our friends and allies are pleased with the dramatic improvements in Sino–American relations that have occurred over the past decade. Second, there are some reservations, especially in Southeast Asia, Japan, and South Korea, but to a significant degree in Western Europe as well, about the rapid development of a further military and security relationship between Washington and Beijing. Third, while there is substantial sympathy for Taiwan in many quarters and an understanding of American obligations toward the island, there is also the hope that Washington's residual military ties with Taipei will not do serious damage to its relationship with Beijing. And finally, as of now, there have been relatively few tensions between the United States and its friends over economic relations with the PRC.

RELATIONSHIP OF ATLANTIC AND PACIFIC SECURITY

The United States, its NATO and ANZUS allies, and Japan agree on one fundamental matter—that the Soviet Union poses the principal external threat to their security. The PRC takes the same view. Given agreement on this basic point, a substantial amount of cooperation in meeting the common threat might be expected. In fact, however, strategic cooperation is limited to that between the United States and its NATO allies in the Atlantic theater and the United States, Japan, Australia, and New Zealand in the Pacific. The tentative moves by the United States toward a strategic relationship with China have been viewed askance by its NATO allies and by Japan. None of the latter has given serious thought to forming its own strategic relationship with China.

Thus, "Atlantic" and "Pacific" security are linked on one hand by the presence of the Soviet Union in both oceans and on the other hand by the existence of U.S. security arrangements with allies in each region to defend against the Soviet threat. The military security concerns of U.S. allies are predominantly regional, although they share with the United States a global outlook on economic issues. The U.S. NATO allies do not contribute militarily to the defense of Japan, nor does Japan contribute to the defense of the NATO region, although intermediate nuclear force (INF) negotiations are making the linkage between European and Asian security increasingly more important to both.

Although the NATO allies and Japan agree with the United States that the Soviet Union is the principal threat, they disagree significantly on ways to deal with it. The European allies, in part because of the special situation of divided Germany, tend to place greater emphasis on détente, arms control, and economic relations with the Soviet bloc. Their rejection of U.S. efforts to block use of American technology to build the gas pipeline between the Soviet Union and Western Europe dramatically demonstrates the difference in viewpoint. Also, the Japanese place a higher priority than the United States government does on efforts to reduce tensions and expand economic relations with the Soviet Union. They are proceeding with the joint Soviet–Japanese project to drill for offshore oil and gas off Sakhalin. They disagree with the United States on what can be done about the level of Japanese forces required to counter the Soviet threat to Japan. Although there is not a great deal of interaction between Europeans and Japanese concerning security matters, to the extent that both hold a more moderate view of the Soviet threat than the U.S. government and would place greater emphasis on nonmilitary means of coping with it, they reinforce those in the United States who hold similar views.

The Middle East, geographically and economically, constitutes a link between the Atlantic and Pacific regions. As the world's principal oil exporting zone, it is more important economically to the European and Pacific allies, particularly Japan, than it is to the United States. Internal instability and war between Middle Eastern states is a greater immediate threat to the security of the region than Soviet forces. The European and Pacific allies, recognizing that upheaval in the Middle East and possible Soviet military intervention there would seriously threaten their own security, would reluctantly accept diversion of some U.S. forces from the Atlantic and Pacific to that area if the threat to their interests was clear and immediate.

Both the NATO and ANZUS allies and Japan approve in general the expanding U.S. relations with China. They view the ending of military confrontation between the United States and the PRC as releasing U.S. forces for other uses, including the strengthening of Atlantic and Pacific defenses against the Soviet threat. Moreover, even though the United States, its NATO and ANZUS allies, and Japan compete commercially in seeking trade with China, they agree that these economic connections with the West contribute to the modernization and political stability of China in which they have a common interest.

The European and Asian friends and allies are skeptical, however, about the desirability of an active U.S.–China military relationship. The Europeans believe that it would take many years for China to significantly narrow the gap between the capability of its forces and that of the Soviets. During this period, extensive U.S.–Chinese military cooperation would be a provocation to the Soviet Union without providing greater security. The reaction of the Japanese is more complex.

They share the Europeans' concern with unnecessarily provoking the Russians but are also concerned about Moscow's build-up of missile, bomber, and naval forces in the Far East. Many strongly oppose the concept of a U.S.–China–Japan strategic entente, which the Soviets charge is already in the making. They also worry that the United States may have a long-term intention of making China rather than Japan its principal ally in East Asia. And, as a regional power in the Pacific, Japan is more sensitive than European NATO nations to Korean and ASEAN concerns about the risks associated with China's becoming a strong military power.

The Asians and Europeans are somewhat ambivalent concerning the differences between Washington and Beijing on the Taiwan question. Their economic relations with Taiwan have expanded in recent years, and they would prefer a separate Taiwan to the island's unification with the Mainland. Most would be troubled, however, if the United States were to place its interests in Taiwan ahead of its interests in cultivating good relations with the PRC. Hence, they welcomed the August 1982 joint communiqué on U.S. arms sales to Taiwan, which enabled Washington and Beijing to set that issue to one side, at least temporarily. They would deplore serious deterioration in U.S.–China relations over the Taiwan issue, which would encourage those in the PRC interested in improving relations with the Soviet Union and might ultimately lead to a revival of military confrontation between the United States and China over Taiwan.

The absence of enthusiasm in Europe and Asia for an active U.S.–China military relationship and even the doubts expressed by some allied or friendly nations, such as South Korea and Indonesia, have not become major issues in the relations between the United States and those countries. Consequently, paying heed to the views of allies and friends on this matter does not necessarily require the United States to reverse itself and withdraw from the limited point so far reached in developing military relations with the PRC. These views do, however, add weight to other reasons for the United States to proceed slowly and cautiously with such a relationship. The unwillingness of the United States to provide a large amount of weapons to China, the reluctance of the Chinese to become dependent on a foreign power for arms, the Chinese desire to concentrate first on developing a modern industrial base for arms production, and the dispute between Beijing and Washington over arms sales to Taiwan all counsel caution, including avoiding the temptation to exaggerate the significance of the relationship in an effort to gain political points.

A military relationship between the United States and China that would significantly affect the balance of power in the Pacific region is a possibility for the 1990s and beyond, not the 1980s. It would require a much more extensive and solid network of economic and other relations between the two countries than exists today. It would also require a much wider range of carefully identified and defined common interests and policies than exists today. It presupposes a China that has put behind it the animosities and tensions created by the Cultural Revolution and that has demonstrated a capacity to maintain political stability and a growing economy over a prolonged period.

The 1980s, then, are likely to be a period of reciprocal probing and experimentation in the area of military relations between the United States and China, following, not leading, the development of stronger economic, geopolitical, and cultural relations. Progress in this area can ultimately improve both "Pacific" and "Atlantic" security. But if the process is not to create friction and misunderstanding between the United States and its Atlantic and Pacific allies, the United States must pay more attention to securing their understanding and cooperation.

POLICY RECOMMENDATIONS

General Recommendations

1. The United States government should develop a sound, long-term posture through the next decade that seeks enhanced cooperation with the People's Republic of China (PRC)—a very large and underdeveloped country—which, as an independent, nonaligned international and regional entity, shares some but not all of our global and regional objectives, particularly in Asia and the Pacific.

2. An economically healthy, stable, and secure China that contributes to the peace and stability of the region is in the national interest of the United States and is an interest shared by our Asian and European friends and allies. To this end, the United States should place priority on the continued development of a sound geopolitical relationship with China and on the enhancement of cooperation with China in developing its economic potential.

3. Relations with the PRC and other countries in the region require that the United States maintain a strong military presence in East Asia and the Pacific and that we make clear we are committed to a forward military defense of our interests in the region.

4. The United States, more than it has in the recent past, should consult with and take into account the views of its Asian friends and allies in dealing with the PRC and encourage reciprocal consultations. Specifically, the security and economic concerns of Japan, the Republic of Ko-

rea, and the nations of ASEAN and ANZUS, and the population of Taiwan should be taken into account.

5. Our Atlantic friends and allies should also be consulted with respect to our China policies and encouraged to consult with the United States with respect to their policies. It is important that our respective policies be compatible, particularly in the areas of technology transfer and international trade. The United States and its industrialized friends and allies in the coming decade should do in concert what we can to facilitate China's economic development. A process for continuing consultations among the allies should be established to facilitate cooperation in helping China in such areas as joint feasibility studies for projects to be financed by government funding.

Bilateral Relations

6. The United States and China share certain geopolitical objectives (such as opposing Soviet expansionism) that make cooperative efforts in various forms possible. Our policy objectives with respect to Afghanistan and Indochina are similar and call for further consultations. On the Korean Peninsula, despite the fact that the United States and China support different parties, our objectives in avoiding hostilities are parallel. The United States and the PRC should urge their respective Korean allies to adopt policies supportive of these objectives. The United States should also encourage the PRC to develop further contacts with South Korea that could point the way to eventual cross-recognition. In other areas, such as the Middle East and Southern Africa, we should seek out common interests; and wherever and whenever our interests converge, we should cooperate.[5]

7. The basis of our relations with China should not rest exclusively on our common opposition to the Soviet Union. We should seek to expand the basis of the relationship to rest on economic, scientific, and cultural ties, on shared efforts to maintain stability in Asia, and on Chinese involvement in the search for solutions to the problems that transcend national boundaries (such as arms limitations or international economic issues).

8. While the United States must show appreciation of Chinese needs, sensitivities, and domestic political environment, the same attitude is required of the PRC toward the United States. If the relationship is to move forward and continue to enjoy broad public support in the United States, the Chinese must demonstrate greater awareness of American sensitivities and appreciation of our domestic political system (including the separation of powers) and our pluralistic society. U.S. officials should make clear that Chinese rhetorical excesses only

serve to undermine support in the United States for strengthening U.S.–Chinese relations and complicate U.S. diplomacy on international issues.

9. Throughout the next decade, the United States should cooperate with the PRC primarily through trade, export credits, and direct investment in the Chinese economy. The United States should facilitate and promote U.S. private sector participation in Chinese economic growth and encourage China to establish a favorable climate for American enterprises, as, for example, in the areas of developing coal, renewable energy resources, potential of off-shore oil and gas reserves, and agriculture.

10. To facilitate commercial trade in line with U.S. export policies, the committee recommends that the Joint Economic Commission and the Joint Commission on Commerce and Trade and their working groups should explore each other's applicable laws and regulatory practices in order to defuse potentially disruptive trade issues stemming from asymmetries in business and government practices.

11. The United States should actively promote the transfer of technologies that are consistent with China's economic development needs and abilities to absorb. At the same time, the United States should continue to press the PRC to promulgate and enforce laws (patent, copyright, etc.) necessary to protect the interests of the industrialized nations in technology transferred. Correspondingly, the PRC should join such international agreements as General Agreement on Tariffs and Trade, the Paris Convention, and the Universal Copyright Conventions.

12. The committee asserts that it is in the U.S. national interest that the Chinese national economy move toward modernization. It recognizes, however, that this course involves a degree of risk, since a strong Chinese industrial base could be used in the future for military purposes not consistent with our national interest. To allay these fears, a broad study should be conducted to identify and quantify the probable impact of Western technology on China's industrial capability.

13. The United States should quickly agree as to how best to expedite decisions on applications for the transfer of "dual-use" technologies and should be most responsive to those requests that would best contribute to the civilian sector (communications, transportation, power supplies, renewable resources, etc.). Technologies that make a direct and significant contribution to nuclear weapons and their delivery systems, electronic and antisubmarine warfare, and intelligence gathering should continue to be withheld, though each area should be carefully examined to ensure that only the most sensitive technologies are routinely denied.

14. The U.S. government should not press weapons systems and technology on the Chinese but rather should wait for their initiatives. The United States should be responsive to requests from the Chinese armed forces, including arms sales, in developing China's ability to protect itself. This cooperation must be consistent with U.S. law, international agreements, and commitments to allies of the United States. The United States, however, should not encourage the Chinese to carry out a program to modernize and expand its armed forces to a degree that would significantly increase the Chinese capacity to project force beyond its current borders. Neither should the United States seek to enter into a military alliance with the PRC.

15. In negotiations with the USSR on strategic and intermediate range nuclear missiles, both the United States and the PRC should be sensitive to the possible interests and concerns of the other.

16. The United States should actively encourage and support the education and training of the Chinese in a variety of fields: scientific and technological, as well as in the social sciences, the arts, and the humanities. It is in our national interest that the coming generation of leaders in China have exposure to and benefit from the best that can be offered by our universities, businesses, and other training facilities.

17. The United States should ensure the future of sound research and education about China by assuring direct access in China for our scholars, scientists, and journalists, by ensuring the continued funding of our library and research facilities, by enhancing our ability to acquire and utilize the large volume of Chinese language publications available, and by encouraging our China specialists to develop their background knowledge and language proficiency.

18. The United States should not construe expected improvements in Sino–Soviet relations as necessarily adverse to our national interests but should judge such improvements with respect to their contribution, if any, to peace and stability in the region.

19. The Taiwan situation should be worked out peacefully by the Chinese on both sides of the Strait. The U.S. government should avoid promoting or coercing either party into adopting any particular solution, insisting only that the use of force be avoided.

NOTES

1. Jeffrey B. Gayner comments: "The report does not indicate the extreme caution with which the development of economic relations with China should be pursued, particularly given the experience in dealing with other Communist countries. Moreover, the United States should only encourage major economic investments

and more liberal trade terms with the Chinese if we have some greater assurance than at present that their economic system will change significantly away from their Soviet legacy. Much greater movement in the direction of decentralization and the use of incentives must be encouraged. It would be both futile and even counterproductive to assist a system that remains structurally unsound."

2. Christopher H. Phillips dissents from the advanced technology transfer section (pp. 00–00) and comments: "The administration has publicly explained that its decision to move China to Country Group V under the Export Administration regulations 'is intended to emphasize that sales to China should take place on a similar basis as to most other friendly countries' (Department of Commerce press release, June 21, 1983). This means that the export of most goods and technology will be routinely approved and not subject to a worse-case analysis of how they *could* be used.

"There are risks in selling dual-use goods and technology to any destination. In moving China to the V Group, however, the administration is saying, and I agree, that such exports to China should be restricted only when the risk to the national security is clearly and demonstrably greater than that involved in selling to other V Category Countries to which such items would be approvable for export."

3. Roy A. Werner comments: "The desire to create a process allowing for peaceful resolution is one I strongly support. However, a troubling precedent has been set by ignoring statutory law (PL 96–8, TRA) and the inherent contradictions contained in the August Communiqué concerning defensive arms. Furthermore, the posture taken by the administration erodes the character of our commitment to our allies.

4. Jeffrey B. Gayner comments: "The report does not contribute to the creation of an effective and realistic U.S. policy on Taiwan. Instead the report largely endorses the drift of policy in recent years which has increasingly disengaged the United States from Taiwan. In particular, the report undeservedly endorses the August 1982 Communiqué, which unreasonably restricted arms sales to Taiwan. The greatest danger to the peaceful settlement of the conflict between Taiwan and the PRC will emerge over the next decade if the political, economic, and military balance between them is further disrupted by the continued erosion of U.S. relations with Taiwan. Only by reaffirming the letter and spirit of the Taiwan Relations Act can U.S.–Chinese policy be placed on a firm realistic footing again that would restore U.S. credibility in Taipei. Only a secure and confident Taipei will be able to deal effectively and equitably with Beijing. Unfortunately the report would only exacerbate the present problems by further eroding the military capabilities of Taiwan while simultaneously augmenting the economic and military capabilities of the PRC."

5. Jeffrey B. Gayner comments: "Aside from their perceptions of Afghanistan, Indochina, and the general military build-up of the Soviet Union, the Chinese share few foreign policy positions with the United States and even oppose almost all U.S. actions in the Middle East, Africa, and Latin America. If the United States is going to cooperate with Beijing in pursuing policies dealing with the vital border areas of China, then Beijing should be willing to reciprocate this action by pursuing policies more supportive of U.S. vital interests, such as in Central America. Moreover, they should not back revolutionary movements that are primarily supported by the Soviet Union.

Chapter 2

U.S. China Policy From an Atlantic Perspective

Alfred D. Wilhelm, Jr.,* and George R. Packard**

For two years the China Policy Committee of the Atlantic Council of the United States studied future U.S. policy toward China from the perspective of the United States and its European and Asian allies. Within the committee the views of the allies were ably presented by several distinguished European and Asian foreign policy specialists, as well as by a number of American diplomatic, military, and scholarly observers of European and Asian affairs. Working papers, which analyzed the views of the allies, were prepared by some of these member-experts and then discussed and critiqued by the committee. This "in-house" expertise was supplemented by discussions with scholars, parliamentarians, government officials, and media representatives visiting Washington from Europe and Asia, and by discussions held in Europe and Asia by individual committee members and by delegations sent by the committee. The most recent delegation visited Brussels, 18–19 November 1983, to attend a roundtable discussion of U.S.–China policy organized by the North Atlantic Assembly and co-sponsored by the Atlantic Council of the United States. By meeting with more than thirty-five European parliamentarians, NATO and European community officials, and European scholars shortly after the public release of

*Senior Fellow, the Atlantic Council of the United States.
**Dean, School of Advanced International Studies, Johns Hopkins University.

the committee's policy paper, the U.S. delegation was able to sample European reactions.*

Most of the conferees agreed with the general findings of the policy paper, but there were spirited discussions that yielded suggestions of areas that need further exploration and ideas for implementing some of the recommendations. The following discussion summarizes European views, as expressed by the conferees, concerning China's problems and policies, the common interests of the U.S. and its European allies in "out-of-the-NATO area" issues, and means for implementing several of the China Policy Committee's recommendations, particularly through consultation with the West European governments, the Organization for Economic Cooperation and Development (OECD), and the Western European Union (WEU).

EUROPEAN PERCEPTIONS OF CHINA

Economic Policy

An "economically growing, secure, and modernizing China"[1] is important to Europe. However, there was little optimism among the conferees that the PRC will be able to develop a strong economy in the foreseeable future or that any external influence, including foreign investment, can make much difference. Optimism with respect to the long term was conditioned upon the continuation of reforms already undertaken. "Development depends on the economic transformation of China."[2] Should these reforms be a tactical expedient to energize the economy, as was Lenin's economic policy of 1921, the future is bleak.

Discussion of near term concerns focused first on China's birth rate, which was noted to be "soaring again" as an unintended result of new economic policies. Even if the rate was reduced to 1 percent, there would still be 1.3 billion Chinese by the year 2000. Yet the Chinese are encouraging consumption to the detriment of investment. "They are eating up their future."

Other conferees were concerned that, although China's leaders have studied development in Yugoslavia, Hungary, and Romania, they still do not have a development plan. Not only is the economy weak and without much direction, but it lacks integration. China's vertical organization with limited lateral integration is a hindrance to economic growth. Shanghai's leaders, for example, were said to have little knowledge of how their city's economy interacts with the nation's economy.

*A list of participants is found at Appendix A

More training in Western management techniques, such as that provided by Italy and the United States, is desperately needed.

Similar concern was expressed about China's ability to absorb technology. China has demonstrated that it has small quantities of the scientific and technical skills required to develop and produce in almost any field of high technology provided that the national security priority is sufficiently high to warrant the sacrifices that would have to be made in other areas. An obvious example is the PRC's nuclear weapons program. But across the breadth of China's society there is an acute shortage of technical skills at all levels, particularly among those whose education was interrupted by the Cultural Revolution—the mid-level managers, technicians, and scientists.

Increasingly Beijing faces the dilemma of maintaining its political system, avoiding the economic problems of the Comecon countries, and fostering economic development. Western education and training lie at the heart of this dilemma. Essential to China's long-term success, it is a form of imperialism, which not only transmits scientific knowledge, research and organizational methodologies, and equipment preferences, but also transmits values and an awareness that Western economic successes are closely linked to the Western political systems that support them. The "social contamination" that is creeping into China through the Special Economic Zones (SEZs) is visible proof of China's vulnerability to such "contagion." Yet the SEZs are deemed essential to China's development. Furthermore, failure would demonstrate China's inability to assimilate unlike systems and, in turn, would impact on China's hope for the peaceful reunification of Hong Kong and Taiwan.

Although there was no agreement among the conferees as to whether Sino–Soviet trade is complementary,[3] it was clear from the discussion that China has reached a ceiling in its textile exports to the West, where the West's textile industry faces a crisis. On the other hand the Soviet market could absorb a large amount of China's textiles, as well as many other products. Reciprocally, given the expense and the labor saving design of most Western machinery, China could benefit greatly from the adequate, less expensive, and more labor intensive machinery of the Soviet Union and Eastern Europe.

Chinese concern over the corrosive impact of "things Western," the emergence of a generation of leaders educated by Soviet bloc personnel and thus less distrusting of the Soviets, expanding trade with East Europe, and the need to balance Western education with socialist technology and management skills, may lead to a somewhat closer relationship with the Soviet bloc than now exists. This will not be a dependent relationship but a more independent and flexible economic and foreign policy position that will enable China to draw selectively from both the West and the Soviet bloc.

On a more positive note, it was pointed out that despite these problems the current Chinese administration has established its priorities and been reasonably successful in gaining a national consensus. Defense spending is fourth in priority, not so much because the Chinese feel militarily secure, but because they feel that the economic threat to national security is much greater ("a distinction to which the United States has not been sufficiently sensitive in the past" according to some conferees). A reasonably strong, albeit not robust, economy was viewed as possible in the long term, given this commitment and a modicum of political stability.

Defense Policy

In the European view, there is indeed a need to help the PRC secure itself, but not because a weak China is a tempting target, an invitation to invasion, as the Atlantic Council's policy paper indicates.[4] Rather there is a need to avoid the unrest in Southeast Asia that a weak China might foment in self defense. There is also need to help China with its defense capabilities vis-à-vis the Soviet Union.

This does not mean that the PRC will seek large numbers of NATO weapons. The PRC is less fearful now of the Soviet Union since China's strategic posture has improved. China's nuclear deterrence is adequate for the present vis-à-vis the USSR and has a record of steady improvement. Also, while avoiding alliances, China has established defense relations with the West that have created an uncertainty in the USSR that enhances China's deterrent posture. If deterrence fails, a more professional and increasingly better equipped PLA would "lure the enemy deep." Such a conventional defense will be supplemented in the future with tactical nuclear weapons the Chinese are preparing to develop.[5]

This strategy, in conjunction with economic considerations, governs not only what China will examine but also what it will buy. New systems require training and doctrinal changes, enhancements of logistic systems, and investments in equipment, not to mention changes in strategy, that the PRC is not able to adopt. Consequently, despite expectations raised in the West by China's many military delegations, China has not made any major purchases of NATO equipment. Not even the willingness of nations, like France, to make major governmental concessions has changed the Chinese perception that NATO equipment is too expensive. Nevertheless, China's military "window shopping" delegations have greatly enhanced Chinese knowledge of the capabilities of Western and Soviet military equipment and confirmed the need for the infusion of Western technology into China's efforts at "self-reliance." Of greater interest to some conferees was the fact that Chinese window shopping for weapons had a "high political content." Those delegations have made the European defense community more aware of China and even, more importantly, have shown a degree of cooperation by the PRC with the West that has worried the Soviets. One conferee noted that Brezhnev wrote West European leaders in late 1978 to discourage cooperation with the PRC.

The conferees thought that China is now focusing more of its efforts in Europe on the political dimension of defense. Chinese leaders have expressed an interest in annual consultations with European leaders concerning defense. They see a convergence of the interests of China and Europe in avoiding being dominated by a "continental hegemonist" or being defined in terms of Soviet–American relations. The Chinese continue to encourage NATO Europe to stay strong and united, because they see this as the key to deterring the Soviets as well as attracting Soviet attention to Europe and away from the PRC. But at the same time the Chinese are encouraging the Europeans to think in terms of a multipolar world. China would be more comfortable if the blocs were less tightly bound to the superpowers.

Domestic Political Policy

There was a general feeling among the conferees that the policy paper's assumption that the most likely domestic political scenario for the next decade is "a continuation of the present situation," with "maximum efforts to modernize through pragmatic policies" was somewhat optimistic.[6] They felt strongly that the Chinese could not experience the political turbulence of the Cultural Revolution even if their leaders wanted. To a degree "ideology is dead" among the masses; they remember too well the excesses of that "ideological binge." However, domestic challenges will arise from time to time that will create a cyclical pattern in politics characterized by shifts between cooperation and conflict, decentralization and centralization, and the encouragement of initiative and repression. These challenges will limit political stability to being the optimum situation, sought but seldom fully achieved.

There were a number of sources of domestic challenges discussed, but little consensus as to the imminent challenges. It was argued that the Party has already begun to turn to "repression, harsh discipline, and 'internal remedialism' in the bureaucracy, and recentralization in politics and economics,"[7] in order to counter the ideologues who are attempting to regain ascendancy in response to the "excesses" of the current administration. Others argued that, while ideology is and will remain dominant within the national leadership, the ideologue is not a serious threat to the managers and technicians. The critical base of opposition to Deng Xiaoping is in the People's Liberation Army (PLA). These conferees noted that Deng has imposed his will, for the time being, upon the military as witnessed by the loyalty oaths administered in the PLA; but, they argued, at some point in the next decade he would be vulnerable to more vigorous demands for military modernization and thus possibly to opposition from within the military. A third source of challenge is the next generation of leaders, a large percentage of whom are Soviet trained. Concern has been privately expressed about their pro-Soviet views. Whatever the source of challenge, however, it was generally felt that the PRC's future will not be externally driven, except ever so slightly at the margins.

Foreign Policy

Described as nonalignment, China's foreign policy also emphasizes flexibility and the benefits to be obtained through foreign relations for China's economic development and security. Alliances are shunned. Those entered into in the 19th and 20th centuries, including that with the Soviet Union, resulted from China's weaknesses and are viewed by the Chinese as having retarded China's development with minimum compensation in security. To clarify this point, the similarity between China's attitude toward alliances and that of France toward the NATO alliance was raised.

These foreign policy principles translate into the two near-term objectives of good relations with the United States necessary to keep the USSR off balance, and of improving relations with the USSR to ensure nonalignment. In terms of long-term objectives, these principles translate into good relations with Europe, both East and West, that are necessary to foster the development of a multipolar world. The Chinese see multipolarity as less dangerous and more suited to their needs. Thus China's diplomatic efforts in East Europe, largely through economic activity, seek to encourage a more independent role for East Europe as part of the effort to bring the "second world alive." A few conferees felt that China's initiatives in East Europe are actually an aggressive effort to split East Europe away from the Soviet bloc.

In discussing the PRC's encouragement of West European pacifists versus the PRC's support for NATO, the consensus was that the PRC is not trying to separate West Europe from the United States. Rather, it was argued that Chinese foreign policy is maturing, as discussed above, and is less inclined to such extreme policies as those that had prompted some politicians to refer to China as "the 16th member of NATO." While still supporting the solidarity and strength of NATO, the Chinese now point out the differences between West European countries and the United States. The emphasis is on flexibility by the second tier of nations when dealing with issues not directly related to security.

While most of the PRC's initiatives in Europe have been state-to-state, the Chinese Communist Party (CCP) has demonstrated in Europe a willingness to establish relations with any communist party irrespective of size, history, and whether or not it is in power. Asserting that all communist parties are equal, the CCP will not establish such relations if it means recognition of the Soviet Union-dominated Communist International (Comintern). Since establishing relations under these circumstances would effectively atomize the Comintern, the CCP has not yet enjoyed any significant expansion of its Party contacts in East or West Europe. However, some conferees felt that the PRC has begun to chip away at the acceptance by the European communist parties of the Soviets' exclusive right to the leadership of the international communist movement.

The conferees felt that the policy paper underplayed the importance of the relationship between China and Japan. Japan is critical to China's economic development and the Chinese know that they must cultivate Japanese cooperation. So important is this relationship that it was considered a brake on any movement to improve China's relations with the Soviet Union.

COMMON INTERESTS OF EUROPE AND THE UNITED STATES IN CHINA

Economic Policy:

"An economically growing, secure, and modernizing China" was agreed by the conferees to be a shared interest of Europe and the United States, but the discussion soon made clear the need for multilateral consultations on policy. First, the conferees felt that the financial needs of the PRC could place a greater strain on the capabilities of the industrialized nations than they can bear. The West is already experiencing considerable difficulty in supporting the efforts of the IMF and the World Bank to deal with the financial needs of the Latin American and other third world nations, without even addressing the desires of the PRC to receive assistance from the World Bank at least equal to that of India. Will this competition for foreign aid generate fights with and between the Western nations?

China's needs are so great that a strong economy is generations away. Some felt that the West should focus on developing relations with the

PRC and on encouraging economic stability, rather than encouraging rapid economic growth. There is very little that the West can do to improve the military capabilities of the PRC and even less to help economic development. Unlike Taiwan, where a few billion dollars were crucial, China is like a "bottomless pit."

If China's development is encouraged, can the United States really conduct trade for trade's sake? Will there be political objectives that go beyond the short term expectations of stable leadership to attempting to influence the long-term transformation of China's social order? Similarly, is the West ready for China as in independent trade partner? The West expects the PRC to participate in the institutions of its "free trade system," but China's socialist system may not be willing or able to accommodate these expectations. Furthermore, Leninist principles are designed to interject tension between the capitalist nations. The West may not be prepared to deal with these tensions.

Another big problem for the industrialized nations, in addition to readjusting their aid programs to make room for the PRC, will be determining how to balance their trade quotas to accommodate the PRC. Of great importance to West Europe and, hopefully, to the United States is the impact on the ASEAN countries of increased quotas for the PRC. There is also the question of Sino–Japanese economic relations, which the conferees felt are the key to China's development. How this relationship develops will have a major impact on how U.S. and European relations develop with the PRC.

A special plea was made by several conferees for multi-government consultations to devise an approach. The Organization for Economic Cooperation and Development (OECD) was cited as a possible forum, since it reviews China's economic policies on a regular basis. Also, Japan has been very active in encouraging the OECD to accept the PRC as a "developing country."

Technology Transfer Policy

Insofar as technology transfer policy was discussed in the policy paper, the conferees found it acceptable; however, they pointed out that only U.S. policy was presented. There was no discussion of China's policy, of the limitations on China's ability to absorb technology, of how to deal with these limitations, or of the importance of the 1949 Coordinating Committee (COCOM) agreement to multi-national policy concerning technology transfers.

It was pointed out that the PRC is wary of the Japanese approach to technology transfers because of the long-term commitments that the Japanese insist upon. West European technology tends to be too expensive, and to avoid dependence on any one supplier or group of suppliers, the Chinese are increasing their interaction with East Europe.

China's ability to absorb technology, some felt, is overrated. While China has demonstrated the ability to effectively develop and utilize some of the most advanced technologies, such efforts consume a major portion of China's scientific capability. The technological base is small and the organizational structure is vertical and relatively inflexible. Both must change if technology is to assist effectively in China's development.

In Europe it is felt that China's first priority ought to be education management training and the acquisition of technology for agriculture and resource development. Correspondingly there is a need for the West to determine what kind of capability China should have and how it should be transferred. For example, will the relationship be between Western companies and Chinese government corporations or will the West be represented by corporations backed by governments able to provide incentives beyond the sale proposed by the individual corporations? Should the West sell equipment containing the components relevant to strategic defense systems in "black boxes," such as the intertial navigation system sold in the Boeing 707 relevant to ballistic missile programs? Such "black box" sales require an act of faith and may be too tempting for the Chinese. It was pointed out that there is the argument that if China has demonstrated a particular capability, such as its ICBM, then the West should pull down trade restrictions compatible with that level. Other conferees responded that a limited development and production capability does not equal a mass production capability. One conferee noted that the French government is prepared to sell any technology except strategic weapons. Others responded that a "Sell it to them and let them break their teeth" approach increases waste and inefficiency and in the long run is detrimental to good relations.

The conferees generally agreed that the issue of technology transfers required cooperation and coordination irrespective of any country's perspective, but that such coordination is possible only if the heads of state are involved, and can agree. The conferees agreed that it was on this subject that the policy paper's tendency to be too unilateral—insufficiently alliance-oriented—was strongest. While calling for greater cooperation, the policy paper fails to mention the COCOM. COCOM was praised repeatedly as a crucial Western organization for the multilateral coordination by OECD countries of limits on the transfer of high technology for national security reasons. On the other hand, it was pointed out that in the future there will be resistance in both Europe and Japan to adding new items to the COCOM list. Memories are still vivid of how some countries are perceived to have manipulated the list to their trade advantage. To strengthen and complement the efforts of COCOM, the conferees felt there is a need for a broader forum in which to discuss technology issues beyond the purview of COCOM. Some suggested that an independent technology commission be formed to advance technology transfers to China, while others stressed that this was an appropriate role for the OECD.

Security

The conferees agreed that the policy paper correctly reflects European concerns that "U.S.–China rapprochement could lead toward a military relationship that the Soviet Union would view as excessively hostile or threatening. [They fear that] this trend, if it continued, would prove destructive to the process of detente with the Soviet Union."[8] From a European perspective, the U.S.–PRC relationship has already contributed to the Soviets' rationale for the SS-20 deployments east of the Urals. If Europe is to achieve arms control (or disarmament, as preferred by some conferees) then the United States and China cannot push strategic cooperation or play the other as a "card." Furthermore, the policy paper's assumption that the Soviet Union will oppose the West throughout the decade may not be valid. Nor is it likely, it was argued, that China can be "lured into the West's camp. China could develop into a threat to the United States, Europe, and the USSR alike."

Europeans appreciate the importance of the Sino–Soviet split for it tends to direct Soviet energies away from West Europe. Soviet resources are limited and any committed to the Pacific cannot be committed against Europe. On the other hand, many Europeans recognize that this relief is to a degree illusory, since a war in Asia involving the Soviets would affect Europe. Thus while tensions are normal and cannot be entirely eliminated worldwide, a high level of tensions in the Pacific must be avoided. Europeans are sensitive to the high tensions in Asia and, although they see virtually no chance of a Sino–Soviet war, they are concerned that the U.S.–USSR conflict will be replicated in the Pacific. They also are worried about the growing arms race in Asia, where arms balance is not an accepted principle, as it is in Europe. China has a lot to learn about arms control, yet does not appear to be very interested, despite membership on the U.N. Committee on Disarmament.

The conferees disagreed with the policy paper's assertion that the "security concerns of the [European] allies are predominantly regional." The European nations and especially the Western European Union support the concept of "indivisible global security issues" and where resources have permitted they have supported "out-of-area" activities.

The conferees did note that the "one-front" nature of European security, and its limited resource base versus the "two fronts" of the United States and its bigger resource base requires the European governments to be far more selective in their "out-of-area" activities than the United States. Several conferees noted that there is a greater understanding—though not necessarily agreement—of the possible need for the United States to reallocate forces outside the NATO area and a greater awareness that West Europe may have to take up the resulting slack.

The conferees agreed that "the NATO allies and Japan agree with the United States that the Soviet Union is the principal threat" but they felt that since the Williamsburg Conference, no longer do "they disagree significantly on ways to deal with it [the USSR]."[9] The European "emphasis on détente, disarmament, and economic relations with the Soviet bloc" has been given equal importance with military posture within the security framework agreed upon at Williamsburg.

Foreign Policy

Europeans would like to see relations between the United States and the PRC improve so that Europe can have a more fruitful relationship with the PRC. According to the Western European Union (WEU) there is a need for "a European policy which is more concerted and more alive than hitherto to the realities of the People's Republic of China."[10] As the conferees stressed, European interests in China are more than economics and security. The foreign policy element of a Sino–European relationship could strengthen Europe's sovereignty and independence.

> Europe wishes to be neither dominated by a continental hegemony nor defined solely in terms of present bipolarity, i.e. the state of American–Soviet relations. The development of an independent power in Asia can but help to give weight to Europe provided the latter manages to combine forces sufficiently to define a policy.[11]

The conferees affirmed the assessment of the policy paper that the "Soviet Union poses the principal external threat to their [Europe's] security" but that they "would place greater emphasis on non-military means of coping with it,"[12] than the United States. Similarly the greatest emphasis in dealing with the PRC should be on non-military means. Since both Europe and China would be devastated by a Soviet–U.S. war, there is considerable basis for cooperation in pursuing world peace. As was pointed out, for such an approach to be successful, it would be necessary to adhere to the WEU conclusion "that systematic criticism of China for the ideology it pursues is not in Europe's interest . . . particularly since China seems to have given up ideological expansionism."[13] Another reason for having a strong political relationship with the PRC was stressed by the observation that as the PRC develops economically, its foreign policy influence will also grow. A web of political relationships could help "keep China from running amuck" over an issue like the islands of the South China Sea.

Of possibly even greater foreign policy significance is the potential of the Sino–Japanese relationship. The policy paper gives very little attention to the future of this relationship, yet the Sino–Japanese relationship is one of China's most important economically and portends foreign policy and security interests yet to be explored.

The great need for consultations between Europe and the United States over their respective policies toward China was repeatedly stressed. Difficulties between U.S. and European interests in China tend to become salient, when there are not adequate consultations to ensure the development of common interests and the mitigation of differences.

Other Asian Views

"China is not unique in Asia, so why does the United States treat it as such? It is only a bigger version of the other Asian nations and it has not handled the West's intrusion as well." For Europeans and Asians there are a number of economic and security issues involving China that are more important than Taiwan. Among these not mentioned in the paper are China's relations with India, Pakistan, and, to a lesser extent, Timor (referred to by some in a jesting comparison with Macao as "a Portuguese territory with an Indonesian administration"). The French have possessions in the Pacific that make China's position on the Law of the Sea of strong interest. The ASEAN nations are concerned about competition from an economically strong China and some of them are concerned about a militarily strong China. While there is no common position in Europe concerning formal relations with Vietnam, not enough attention has been given to Vietnamese fear of the Soviet Union. France with a guilty conscience over colonialism is more sympathetic to Vietnam than the others, which has created an element of distrust between Beijing and Paris. However, the rest of Europe has aligned itself with the United States behind ASEAN, though apparently, none of these efforts have reduced the perception of the threat to ASEAN from Vietnam.

TAIWAN

The conferees felt that too much attention was given to Taiwan in the policy paper. The nations of Europe and the Western European Union have dropped their diplomatic relations with Taiwan, preferring to "maintain contact with the authorities on Taiwan through lobbies." However, conferees felt that the approach outlined in the policy paper was balanced. The one exception involves the discussion of arms sales to Taiwan. In Europe these arms sales are viewed as unnecessary challenges to the U.S.–PRC agreement. Further arms sales will only aggravate relations between China and the West. "Why continue arms sales at all? Since there are no tensions in the Straits, there is no military justification." Nor, since Europeans don't believe that the termination of sales would be perceived to mean that the United States is abandoning Taiwan, is there any political justification.

Most Europeans believe that Taiwan will probably reunite with China in the far distant future, if the PRC deals with Hong Kong wisely. Hong Kong is increasingly spoken of in Europe as a model for Taiwan, although at best it is only a technical comparison. The Chinese of Hong Kong are far more prosperous than the Mainlanders and have seen the effect of the PRC's broken promises in Shanghai (1950s) and Tibet upon political-economic systems different from communism. The Chinese of Hong Kong and Taiwan have to be convinced that their systems will not be destroyed also. Thus the nine point proposal advanced by the PRC as a formula for Taiwan's reunification is a beginning, but it is unrealistic if the PRC expects the people of Taiwan to accept it in the foreseeable future.

Among the conferees, there was considerable interest in Hong Kong as a model, but because the British feel that this is a private bilateral issue between them and the Chinese, there were not very many strong opinions as to the likely solution. The Portuguese solution to Macao also was viewed as a possible model. Following the Portuguese revolution, the new government attempted to rid Portugal of its colonies. When the Chinese were approached concerning Macao, they rejected the offer. The Portuguese government then unilaterally acted in its 1976 Constitution by declaring Macao Chinese territory with a Portuguese administration without any termination date. It was asserted that the Chinese have accepted this practical approach, which solves the Chinese concern about sovereignty and retains Macao under a NATO country's administration in the event of a crisis.

The policy paper's statement that "Japan may also come to have a powerful voice in the outcome"[14] of the Taiwan question was challenged as being too strong. Although Japan has strong economic and security interests in Taiwan—particularly with respect to sea lines of communication—it was felt that Japan would support the basic position of the other major powers and not be a major actor in the matter. Most Japanese would not be supportive of U.S. arms sales to Taiwan or of the Taiwan Independence Movement, since such actions would be seen as supporting intervention in Chinese internal affairs. It was also noted that similar attitudes prevail in the ASEAN nations and that even the Republic of Korea is moving in the directions of establishing relations with the PRC.

The problem was recognized to be a deeply based emotional issue that time, and possibly Western assistance in narrowing the economic gap, may heal.

IMPLEMENTING THE POLICY PAPER'S RECOMMENDATIONS

Recommendation 5:

This recommendation encourages members of the Atlantic Community to establish continuing consultations with each other in order to insure compatible China policies and to facilitate cooperation in helping China's economic development. In response, two ideas were advanced by the conferees: (a) The conferees strongly agreed with the need for consultations over how to facilitate China's economic development. The Organization for Economic Cooperation and Development (OECD) was recommended as the potentially most useful forum for aligning the political and economic interests of the industrialized West with China's economic needs. The OECD Consortium on Turkey was cited as a possible precedent for such cooperation. The Consortium acts to some degree as a clearinghouse for all OECD member countries concerning the various types of aid given to Turkey. The arrangement is considered very successful. Although China is not a member of the OECD, there are no apparent insurmountable obstacles to the formation of such a consortium on China, as long as it is perceived to be in the interest of the member countries. Another OECD practice that was considered a relevant precedent, is the agreement signed on 30 September 1961 between the OECD and Yugoslavia. According to this agreement, Yugoslavia takes part as a non-member in the work of the OECD. (b) Some conferees felt that the Assembly of the Western European Union (WEU)[15] might be a useful forum for discussions of China policy, since the WEU considers security in a world context, with greater emphasis on "out-of-area" issues than NATO. The PRC ignored an approach by the WEU six years ago. Then, in 1982 the PRC took the initiative to invite the WEU to send a delegation to China. The WEU–PRC consultations that took place in May 1983 are the first of a series of regular consultations. Following the May visit the Assembly of the WEU adopted the following recommendations on China and European security:

> Assembly recommends that the Council:
> 1. Ensure that the Western European countries start regular consultations with the Government of the People's Republic of China in the most appropriate frameworks on matters relating to the maintenance of peace in the world;
> 2. Carefully examine in the appropriate frameworks the possibility of increasing Western Europe's trade and economic co-operation with China;
> 3. Remove all current obstacles to the development of trade and co-operation;
> 4. Impress this point of view on the United States and on its partners in the OECD;
> 5. Insist that the negotiations on intermediate-range nuclear weapons do not allow the Soviet Union to deploy in Asia weapons withdrawn from Eastern Europe;
> 6. Urge its members to pursue a concerted policy in order to lay the foundations for lasting peace in Eastern Asia and, inter alia, to endeavour to re-establish an independent state in Cambodia and to facilitate the search for a negotiated settlement for Hong Kong.[16]

Key to this discussion was the conference conclusion that consultations among the allies are of high priority. The consequences of failing to consult concerning China policy are likely to be the unwise investment of billions of dollars, bitter competition between allies, and unwise security policies.

Recommendation 6

In discussing the merits of this recommendation's emphasis on cooperation between the United States and China "wherever and whenever . . . interests converge," it was pointed out that the WEU also has encouraged cooperation between Europe and China, including security. "In security and defence matters, the search for methods of disarmament which do not increase the threat to peace or the overwhelming influence of the two great powers seems to be in the interests of both China and Europe."[17]

Although the policy paper states that U.S. and PRC "policy objectives with respect to . . . Indochina are similar" some conferees argued that this should be recognized as a superficial similarity. It is not at all clear that the PRC fundamentally agrees with the ASEAN position on Indochina, or that Pol Pot is the lesser of two evils, when compared to the Vietnamese government.

Recommendation 7

This recommendation's caution that "relations with China should not rest exclusively on our common opposition to the Soviet Union" suggested to some conferees that there was a need for common opposition to the USSR in order for a relationship between China and the United States to exist and that the USSR would be a threat throughout the decade. They argued that it is not clear that the USSR will remain a threat throughout the decade, which would then cast the future of U.S.–PRC relations in doubt, based on the policy paper's assumptions. Others felt that there may not be a need for common opposition; the economic relationship might be sufficient.

Recommendation 9:

The conferees protested that to "encourage China to establish a favorable climate for American enterprises" is too U.S.-oriented and too condescending. The conferees felt that this is an issue of considerable interest to West European governments. There is definitely a need for consultations over a set of standards acceptable to all Western nations.

Recommendation 13:

If, as recommended, the United States is to "expedite decisions on applications for the transfer of dual-use technologies," the rules of COCOM must be followed. Recommendation 13 does not refer to COCOM, yet the transfer of "dual-use" technologies is clearly an area where the allies must consult with each other within the existing framework of COCOM.

Recommendations 16 and 17:

It was noted that the WEU also has underscored the need for reciprocal educational exchanges between China and the West.[18]

NOTES

1. Atlantic Council Policy Paper, "China Policy for the Next Decade," p. 6. Hereafter referred to as Policy Paper.
2. Assembly of Western European Union. General Affairs Committee. *China and European Security,* by Mr. Caro, Rapporteur. Document 945. (Paris, France: May 18, 1983, pp. 26). Hereafter referred to as WEU Report.
3. WEU Report (Paragraph 61, page 14) states that "the Soviet Union, whose economy is not complementary to that of China, cannot be a leading economic partner for China for any length of time." Other experts at the conference argued that while some of the major exports of the Soviet Union and China are the same, the areas of greatest potential are complementary.
4. Policy Paper, p. 6.
5. WEU Report, p. 12.
6. Policy Paper, p. 16.
7. Policy Paper, p. 17.
8. Policy Paper, p. 5–6.
9. Policy Paper, p. 39.
10. WEU Report, Para. 143, p. 25.
11. WEU Report, Para. 144, p. 26.
12. Policy Paper, p. 40.
13. WEU Report, Para. 145, p. 26.
14. Policy Paper, p. 33.
15. A defense alliance that was organized in May 1955 and consists of Great Britain, France, Italy, Belgium, the Netherlands, Luxembourg, and West Germany.
16. WEU Report, p. 4.
17. WEU Report, Para. 148, p. 26.
18. WEU Report, Para. 149, p. 26.

Appendix A: List of Participants

Prof. Paolo B. Brocchieri, Professor of History, University of Pavia, Milan, Italy.

Dr. Henri Burgelin, Conseiller, Commission des Affaires Générales, Union de l'Europe Occidentale, Paris, France.

Mr. Fernando Condesso, Member of Parliament (Portugal); Vice Chairman, Parliamentary Group of the SDP; Chairman, Labour Committee of the Assembly; Vice-Chairman, ad hoc Committee on the Revision of the Constitution; Member, North Atlantic Assembly.

Mr. Philippe Deshormes, Secretary General, North Atlantic Assembly, Brussels, Belgium.

Mr. Job L. Dittberner, Director, Institutional and Political Affairs, North Atlantic Assembly, Brussels, Belgium.

Dr. Reinhardt Drifte, Senior Fellow, China Division, Programme for Strategic and International Security Studies, Graduate Institute for International Studies, Geneva, Switzerland.

Prof. Joachim Glaubitz, Senior Research Fellow for East-Asian Studies, The Ebenhausen Foundation, Ebenhausen, Federal Republic of Germany.

Minister Robert Grey, Political Advisor to SACEUR, SHAPE, Mons, Belgium.

Ambassador U. Alexis Johnson, Chairman, Atlantic Council Committee on China Policy, Washington, DC, United States of America.

Mr. Alfred Kennedy, Deputy Public Affairs Counselor, US Mission to the European Communities, Brussels, Belgium.

Mr. Franz Klein, Director, Economic Committee, North Atlantic Assembly, Brussels, Belgium.

Mr. Bo Kristensen, Member of Parliament (Denmark), former Head of Air Force Department for Programmed Instructions; 1969–1972; Member, Conservative Party Executive Committee; Member, North Atlantic Assembly.

Mr. David Law, North Atlantic Assembly, Brussels, Belgium.

Mr. Jose Manuel Lello Ribeiro De Almeida, Member of Parliament (Portugal); Member, Committee on National Defence; Member, Socialist Party National Committee; First Secretary, Porto Socialist Party; Member, North Atlantic Assembly.

Mr. Eric Melby, Special Assistant to the Executive Director, International Energy Agency, Paris, France.

Mr. Georges Mundeleer, Member of Parliament (Belgium), former Chairman of the Liberal Party (Brussels); Deputy-Mayor of Ixelles for Arts, Literature, and Small Business; Leader of the Belgian Delegation, North Atlantic Assembly; Chairman, Scientific and Cultural Committee, North Atlantic Assembly.

Mr. Antonio Maria de Ornelas Ourique Mendes, Member of Parliament (Portugal), Social Democratic Party Member; Member, Committee on National Defence of the Assembly of the Republic; Director of the newspaper *Diario Insular*; Member, North Atlantic Assembly.

Dr. George R. Packard, Dean, School of Advanced International Studies, Johns Hopkins University; Rapporteur, Atlantic Council Committee on China Policy, Washington, DC, United States of America.

Mr. Jean Rémion, Assistant Secretary General for Administration and Finance, North Atlantic Assembly, Brussels, Belgium.

Col. Thomas Roberts, Policy and Plans Division, NATO International Military Staff, Brussels, Belgium.

Mr. Rainer W. Rupp, NATO Economic Directorate, Brussels, Belgium.

Mr. Jefferson Seabright, Director, Military Committee, North Atlantic Assembly, Brussels, Belgium.

Col. Richard R. Sexton, Deputy Chief, Policy Branch, SHAPE, Mons, Belgium.

Mr. Jean-Marie Simonet, Directeur Scientifique de l'Institut Belge des Hautes Etudes Chinoises, Musées Royaux des Arts et d'Histoire, Brussels, Belgium.

Dr. Cornelius Sommer, Counselor, Policy Planning Staff, German Ministry of Foreign Affairs, Bonn, Federal Republic of Germany.

Mr. Abraham Stemerdink, Member of Parliament (Netherlands), Labour Party (P.v.d.A.); 1973–76 Minister of Defence; 1981–82 Secretary of State for Defence; Member, Second Chamber Committees on Defence and Foreign Affairs; Member, North Atlantic Assembly.

Dr. Douglas T. Stuart, Associate Professor of International Relations, Johns Hopkins Bologna Center, Bologna, Italy.

The Honorable Leonard Sullivan, Jr., Defence Policy Consultant, System Planning Corporation; Member, Atlantic Council Committee on China Policy, Arlington, Virginia, United States of America.

Mr. Georges Tan Eng Bok, Resident Fellow, Atlantic Institute for International Affairs, Paris, France.

Dr. William T. Tow, Professor, University of Southern California School of International Relations, Munich, Federal Republic of Germany.

Mr. Frans Uijen, Member of Parliament (Netherlands), Member, Labour Party (P.v.d.A.) Committee of Defence and Labour Party Committee on Foreign Affairs; First Chamber Defence Committee; 1981–82, General Rapporteur, Economic Committee, North Atlantic Assembly; Member, North Atlantic Assembly.

Mr. Marc Verdon, Member of Parliament (France), Socialist Party; Mayor of Mouterre-Silly; Member, National Assembly Committee on National Defence and Armed Forces; Member, North Atlantic Assembly.

Col. Alfred D. Wilhelm, Jr., Project Director, Atlantic Council Committee on China Policy, Washington, DC, United States of America.

Mr. Mike Witunski, Corporate Staff Vice-President, McDonnell Douglas Corporation; Member, Atlantic Council Committee on China Policy, St. Louis, Missouri, United States of America.

PART II

Current U.S./PRC Bilateral Relations

Chapter 3

Reflections on the Making of American China Policy

*Michel Oksenberg**

Much has been written in recent years about the making of China policy in the United States. One thinks, for example, of the illuminating passages in the memoirs of Richard Nixon, Henry Kissinger, Jimmy Carter, Cyrus Vance, and Zbigniew Brzezinski. Earlier, Roger Hilsman and James C. Thompson, Jr. provided their perspectives, derived from their years in the Kennedy and Johnson administrations. In a more scholarly vein, Robert Sutter of the Congressional Research Service in his 1978 *China Watch: Toward Sino–American Reconciliation* and Richard Morstein and Morton Abramowitz in their brilliant 1971 RAND study, *Remaking China Policy,* dealt effectively with the subject in an earlier era. Because of the extraordinary growth in our relations with China, these earlier monographs are now somewhat dated, although they still offer relevant insight.

Based on my own exposure to the American foreign policy process, I find the memoirs, for all their strengths, not totally satisfying. While revealing, each memoir inevitably is a partial account, since it reconstructs events from the vantage point of only one, albeit important participant. The author perforce is cast as a more central actor than in fact he was. Naturally, what the participant did not know or did not influence is not recalled; as a result, the total decisional process is distorted.

*Professor of Political Science, University of Michigan.

People from the White House or the seventh floor of the State Department, for instance, frequently neglect the importance of the Congress, private organizations, or lower level implementing agencies around Washington, not just in State and Defense but in such departments as Treasury, Agriculture, Commerce, and Transportation. Caught up in the rush of events, officials at the height of power and even later in their memoirs focus on what they themselves perceive to be the issues. From a more detached and scholarly perspective, however, the historically significant problems and issues may never have fallen fully or even primarily in their domain.

In my opinion, for example, one of the major, long-term developments of Carter administration China policy was the initiation of a broad-based program of American and Chinese government-sponsored exchanges in sciences and technology. To be sure, both President Carter and Dr. Brzezinski were very supportive of this program, each for his own reasons. But from my vantage point, much of the credit on the American side for this development should go to the President's advisor on science policy, Dr. Frank Press. He and two of his key aides in the White House Office of Science and Technology Policy (OSTP), Benjamin Huberman and Anne Keatley, early in the Carter administration mapped plans for scientific exchanges with the People's Republic. Indeed, even before entering office, Press and his crew envisioned broadened exchanges, not just with China but with scientific communities around the world. Press felt that the vibrancy of America's intellectual community is maintained through exchanges and that to transcend certain problems confronting all mankind requires cooperation among all scientific communities. Granted, Press' program would have gone nowhere without a propitious foreign policy setting and without Carter's and Brzezinski's support, but the initiative and vision belonged to Press. The role of Press and OSTP, however, receives little mention in Carter, Vance, or Brzezinski's memoirs; his issue had not gripped those at the "commanding heights," who had to devote themselves to more immediate and pressing concerns.

Another example is the crucial role played by the China specialists in the foreign service. Neither Kissinger nor Brzezinski give the attention and credit due to such as William Gleysteen, Paul Kreisberg, Roger Sullivan, and their junior associates. Their conceptualizations proved absolutely crucial throughout the 1970s. Their roles and their influence will become evident when diplomatic historians have access to the full record.

These examples illustrate that "instant memoirs," though deepening our understanding of the making of American foreign policy in general and China policy in specific, often distort the process. Muckraking books such as Seymour Hirsch's *The Price of Power* and William Shaw-cross' *Sideshow* further distort understanding of the foreign policy process by making it appear more driven by personal rivalries, a lust for power, and petty vengefulness than is the case. As I see it, policy results instead from the interplay of concerns for national security, bureaucratic interests and perspectives, and individual concerns. China policy results from clashes of opinion over what course might best advance the national interest and conform to Congressionally mandated bureaucratic missions. There is no simple way to portray the making of American China policy, however, because the process occurs in many arenas, each characterized by its own process, because the process changes over time, and because American processes are linked to Chinese processes in complicated fashion. Far from being solely the product of strong individuals imposing their wills—as portrayed in memoirs—the shape of China policy arises from the interplay of personalities and the governmental structures in which they are embedded. This notion, familiar to students of American foreign policy, inspires this essay on the structures and processes of American China policy.

THE STRUCTURE AND PROCESS

The president, whose most precious commodity is time, depends upon a select handful of foreign policy advisors—his national security advisor, the secretary of state, the secretary of defense, director of Central Intelligence, the chairman of the Joint Chiefs of Staff, and others he may select, such as the vice president, White House chief of staff, press secretary, and so on—to alert him to the issues he must confront, to inform him of the range of choices he enjoys, and to screen him from the issues he need not confront. His advisors may seek a consensus on such issues and act essentially on their own, they may postpone choice, or they may place the issues elsewhere for resolution.

Each of the president's advisors has a personal staff of foreign policy specialists, including one or more China specialists. The national security advisor draws on the staff of the National Security Council (NSC) to draft material on instructions from him that he then edits and sends to the president. The NSC staff member also represents the national security advisor in various interagency deliberations and draws problems to the attention of the national security advisor. The NSC China specialist further is charged with monitoring the implementation of presidential directives on China policy, a task that can bring him in conflict with recalcitrant bureaucracies. To perform his multi-faceted tasks well, an NSC staffer depends upon assistance, often silently rendered, from middle and lower ranking officials throughout the government bureaucracy.

The secretary of state draws principally upon the East Asian Bureau (EA) for his papers and briefings on China, which in turn he may submit to the president. The chief positions here are the assistant secretary of state for East Asian and Pacific Affairs (the head of EA), the deputy assistant secretary with responsibility for China, and the head of the China desk, a large office that seeks to give coherence to China policy within the government and that tracks the communications with the American Embassy in Beijing and the consulates in Guangzhou and Shanghai. In addition to his China specialists in the East Asian Bureau, the secretary of state draws on officials with special responsibility for Chinese affairs within the Bureau of Planning (S/P) and the Bureau of Political and Military Affairs (PM). The latter monitors the military-security dimension of foreign relations, focusing on such matters as arms sales, while S/P tries to bring long-term coherence to policy. Finally, the secretary is not exclusively dependent on the Central Intelligence Agency for his briefings on developments in China. The Bureau of Intelligence and Research (INR) provides its own assessments of Chinese intentions and strategies in world affairs.

The secretary of defense has a similar bevy of assistants who have special China responsibilities, located in the offices of the assistant secretaries of defense for International Security Affairs (ISA) and International Security Policy (ISP), the Defense Intelligence Agency (DIA), and such bureaus as those that must approve export of sensitive technology and equipment to China. The director of Central Intelligence also has staff personnel at roughly the assistant secretary-deputy assistant secretary level, while the joint chiefs of staff are served by military officers of equivalent rank.

Thus, an interagency community exists of senior staff from each of the departments and agencies with special responsibilities for China. Similar groups of advisors exist for other geographic and functional areas: Soviet Union, Western Europe, arms control, international economic affairs, and so on. These groups of staff specialists are mostly political appointments who link the president and his chief foreign policy advisors to the bureaucracy. Since time is almost as precious a commodity for the president's chief foreign policy advisors as it is for the president, the advisors must rely on their staffs to alert them to the issues they must address, to screen them from issues of lesser priority, and to present them with the policy options they enjoy. To facilitate coordination of policy, the China specialists at NSC, State, Defense, and CIA meet regularly and, to the extent their bosses permit, share information. If they can reach a consensus on a contentious issue among themselves, they present their consensus to their bosses for approval. When no agreement can be achieved, or when a staffer believes—with an informed sense of his superior's inclinations—that his superior would disagree with the consensus, the issue is forwarded to the president's advisors for discussion and resolution. If no agreement is reached at that level and the issue is deemed sufficiently important, the issue then goes to the president for resolution.

While the president and his few foreign policy advisors are obviously at the apex of the structure, in fact almost every cabinet secretary can lay claim to a piece of the action, for almost every cabinet-level department has Congressionally mandated responsibilities that deal with China. The Department of Justice, for example, plays a role in the granting of political asylum, which resulted in the attorney general being an important actor in handling the celebrated defection of the Chinese tennis star Hu Na. The Department of Agriculture has a definite mission to sell agricultural products abroad. The Department of Commerce is charged with supervising the interagency review process for granting export licenses; Congress has also mandated this Department to promote U.S. exports and to aid U.S. businessmen abroad. The United States Information Agency (USIA) obviously has a major responsibility to promote cultural exchanges with China and to enhance Chinese understanding of the United States. The president's special trade representative negotiates trade agreements with the Chinese, in consultation with pertinent agencies. The Department of Energy and the Arms Control and Disarmament Agency, concerned about nuclear proliferation, monitor Chinese assistance to other countries in the nuclear field and encourage the Chinese to join the International Atomic Energy Agency. Even the regulatory agencies get in the act. For example, the Civil Aviation Board helps award U.S. airlines routes to China, while the Food and Drug Administration inspects Chinese factories that process and export agricultural products to the United States.

Two bodies attempt to coordinate and bring coherence to this welter of activity. Foremost are the EA Bureau at State and its Office of Chinese Affairs. They are at the hub of China activity, where the institutional memory is best retained and the commitment to continuity, the strongest. Due to inadequate manpower, access, and clout, however, EA is unable by itself to impose priorities and order upon a sprawling operation. Indeed, even within State, EA does not always reign supreme, and on occasion the views of one of the functional bureaus—Human

Rights or Political-Military, for example—may prevail in a specific issue. For instance, on the Hu Na case, EA advocated a different approach than the granting of political asylum, but the views of other Bureaus prevailed.

EA does not dominate the policy process for another reason. Even if the assistant secretary for East Asian Affairs enjoys the total confidence of the secretary of state, the secretary of state does not instruct other departmental secretaries. The secretaries of Treasury, Commerce, Agriculture, and so on may defer out of respect to the secretary of state, but they are not subordinate to him. If these other secretaries disagree with State on a China matter under their jurisdiction, they may seek a hearing in the White House. The national security advisor plays a role in adjudicating such disputes, or the President may step in personally. If the secretary of state enjoys the confidence of the president, State will win the issue; indeed, the issue may not arise. But if the Washington community senses that the secretary of state is not preeminent and the national security advisor enjoys greater confidence on the issue, then the other departments are emboldened to take their cases to the White House. For example, in the Reagan administration during the spring of 1983, the State Department was advocating relaxation of export controls to China, but elements within the Defense Department were opposed. Secretary of Defense Weinberger was torn between conflicting advice from his China people. The issue was not settled until Secretary of Commerce Baldridge, preparing for a China trip, stressed its importance to National Security Advisor Clark. Baldridge advocated the State position, Clark sensed the time was ripe for a presidential decision, and Reagan decided in favor of Shultz, Baldridge, and a portion of Weinberger's aides. State's EA Bureau alone lacked the capacity to move policy in the direction it desired.

Thus, we have a multitiered, segmented governmental structure handling China policy: the president, his inner core of principle foreign policy advisors, cabinet members with responsibilities for China programs, the group of China specialists in the White House, State, Defense, and CIA who serve as staff to the president's advisors and who link these advisors to the bureaucracy and the implementing agencies. Three other institutions remain to be added to complete the picture: the Congress, private agencies, and the press.

Congress plays a major role in the making of China policy. It establishes the legal framework within which policy must be conducted. Such legislation as the Taiwan Relations Act, the Jackson-Vanik amendment, and the laws governing export controls or arms sales establish the parameters for how the executive branch can and cannot deal with China. The appropriations process and the role of Congress in ratifying treaties and approving appointments also involve the Congress in the execution of China policy. In addition, congressional hearings can significantly affect the climate within which the executive branch considers China policy, and the call for formal testimony from administration spokesmen to Congress may induce decisions or clarifications that the administration prefers to avoid. Visits to Beijing by either congressmen or staff at a minimum affect Chinese perceptions of American policy. The comments the visitors make to their hosts can affect Chinese policy, and this channel offers the Chinese an independent avenue to try to affect American policy. Less measurable but no less important are the speeches, quiet interventions, and consultations by which congressmen influence executive branch deliberations. The assistant secretary for East Asian Affairs tries to keep the Senate and House foreign affairs committees and their East Asian subcommittees well informed of his activities and are sensitive to the policy preferences of the chairman, his committee members, and staff. A similar, close relationship is struck between each department and the relevant members of Congress. For example, when Secretary of Treasury Michael Blumenthal entered into negotiations with the Chinese over the settlement of blocked claims, he first elicited the views of Russell Long and Jacob Javits, the leaders of the Senate Finance Committee, which would have to approve the terms of the settlement. Walter Mondale personally briefed the Congressional leadership before his trip. And Harold Brown raised the ire of House Asian Affairs Subcommittee Chairman Lester Wolf because Wolf felt he had not been adequately consulted on the January 1980 decision to sell China military equipment. Prior to Nixon's opening to China and Carter's normalization decision, the administration carefully calculated the congressional mood, but in neither instance were the congressmen openly and extensively consulted. The resulting resentment probably cost the executive branch some support in its subsequent dealings with China.

Major aspects of the Sino–American relationship are now dealt with outside the government's domain. Such private bodies as the National Committee on U.S.–China Relations (a cultural exchange organization), the National Council for U.S.–China Trade (an organization that facilitates commercial relations), and the Committee on Scholarly Communication with the People's Republic of China (an organization sponsoring exchanges in the natural sciences, engineering, social sciences, and humanities) help shape bilateral relations. Each has its own counterpart Chinese organizations with which it maintains extensive contacts. In the last few years, hundreds of other private organizations—foundations, universities, corporations, tourist agencies, professional associations, and so on—have developed their own contacts and exchanges with Chinese organizations. The fabric is still fragile and vulnerable to changes in government policies, but at present the relationship has expanded to a point beyond the easy control of the U.S. government.

Finally, the American press is part of the foreign policy structure and process to an extent often unappreciated. Journalists are used by government officials to assist in advancing their policy preferences; and the stories by journalists help shape the agenda of issues that officials confront. Further, the Chinese are not without some sophistication in handling American journalists for their purposes. For instance, Zhou Enlai performed brilliantly throughout 1971–1972, reaching out to such journalists as James Reston and Joseph Alsop, to alter American perceptions of China. Deng Xiaoping also probably was not unaware of the consequences when he communicated through Robert Novak to the Chinese writing posters on Democracy Wall in November 1978. There is still room for an extensive and careful study of the precise role the press plays in the making of American China policy. No doubt it is considerable.

OBSERVATIONS

Bundles, Sticks, and Fibers

"China policy" or any other policy is an analytical construct, an abstract concept. To the extent "China policy" exists in any meaningful sense, it is a bundle of more specific issues, such as military relations, trade and commercial policy, science policy, and so on. The sticks in the bundle further are composed of sub-issues. For example, military relations with China consist of such sub-issues as our China arms sales policy, Taiwan arms sales policy (which can be further subdivided into the specific weapons systems under consideration), the exchanges of military delegations, the sharing of estimates concerning Soviet military strength, and keeping each other informed of our policies in Thailand and Indochina to counter Vietnamese aggression in Kampuchea.

The analytical point is that the sticks and fibers that constitute the bundle of issues we label "China policy" are simultaneously part of other policy bundles as well. Policy on arms sales to Taiwan constitutes not only part of our China policy but also is part of the "global arms sales" bundle and, from the president's vantage, is one of the issues involved in placating the Republican right wing. Sharing of nuclear technology with China or licensing of sale of nuclear-energy plants is part of nuclear non-proliferation concerns, and our posture toward the Chinese legal system is also part of our human rights policy.

Seven Policy Arenas

No single decisionmaking process characterizes the making of China policy. The search for an overarching model is misplaced. Process varies according to where an issue is located within the structure. China policy is formulated in at least seven distinctive arenas: (1) the presidential arena, where issues receive the president's protracted attention (e.g., negotiations with the Chinese for normalization), (2) the crisis arena, where issues command the immediate attention of the president and his advisors in a crisis atmosphere (e.g., the Chinese incursion into Vietnam), (3) the arena of the foreign policy advisors, where issues are handled by attaining a consensus among the president's chief foreign policy advisors and informing the president of their consensus (e.g., the American posture on sale of arms to China by our European allies), or when consensus cannot be achieved, seeking guidance from the president by securing his brief attention (e.g., the timing of a visit to China by Secretary of Defense Brown or the American posture on normalization of relations with Vietnam), (4) the trip arena, where issues are evaluated and decided immediately before or during a high-level visit (e.g., the numerous decisions reached prior to Vice President Mondale's August 1979 trip to expand economic relations with China or the decisions that Vice Premier Deng Xiaoping's January 1979 visit crystallized concerning the desirability of expanding bilateral relations), (5) the bureaucratic arena, where issues are resolved at lower levels within government agencies (e.g., the administration of export controls, the implementation of accords on official exchange agreements in the sciences, or the early negotiations on such matters as textiles or civil aviation), (6) the executive-legislative branch arena, where issues are shared between the executive and legislative branches (e.g., the Taiwan Relations Act or the need to inform and consult Congress on foreign military sales), and (7) the private arena, where issues are decided within the private domain (e.g., student and cultural exchanges, American investment in China, or tourism). Each of these arenas has its own processes, and the policy considerations brought to bear in each arena differ as well.

A Changing Configuration

Another point follows logically from the first two. At any moment in time, the different "sticks" and "fibers" of the China policy bundle are scattered among and decided within the seven different arenas, and, over time, the specific issues move from one arena to another. That is, there is continual change in the overall configuration of the individuals and agencies that are determining China policy. At one time, China policy may be largely determined with one or two arenas, and a few months later, other arenas may have the action. For analytical purposes, the key question therefore becomes not, "How is China policy made?" but "What determines the changing locus of issues within the structure?" Here, a combination of factors are at work: the capacity of a particular individual to bring an issue under his wing; the objective importance of an issue, with an issue of growing importance propelled to higher levels; the displacement of an issue from the agenda of, say, the president's advisors by more pressing matters and then either its passage to another arena or neglect; the successful effort by people outside the system (such as the press, the Chinese, and/or interest groups) to transfer the issue to an arena that is deemed more suitable, and so on.

The Political Calendar

The distribution of issues and the whole tenor of government is also affected by the political calendar. Indeed, I find this a significant omission in the existing literature on American foreign policy. Since 1960, the United States has had six presidents. One might say a cycle has begun to characterize the making of policy. The first year of a newly elected administration involves rejecting the policies of the predecessor, searching for new alternatives, fulfilling often ill-conceived campaign pledges, and capturing issues for presidential decision that had gravitated toward the bureaucracies in the previous administration. The first year also involves newcomers learning how to run the machinery of government. The second year and especially the few months after the mid-term congressional elections provide maximum opportunity for initiative and innovation. This is the time to plan Kissinger's secret mission to China or to recognize China. The new policies are in place, the innocence remains, the energy is still great, the commitment to the president and his policies among those he brought to office remains high. In the next phase, sometime in the third year, the new boys become old boys. They have learned their limitations. Some of the new policies succeed, but many encounter difficulties, and the administration is driven back to the policies of its predecessor. The policymakers have learned how issues in different policy bundles are inter-related. Further, the process of socialization to the norms or ideology of one's agency begins to have its effect, and the president's appointees take on the coloration of the agencies in which they are situated. White House-bureaucracy tensions grow. Then comes the fourth stage—presidential election year. Beginning in the late fall before the election year, the president's domestic advisors begin to view foreign policy issues with an additional consideration in mind—how they affect re-election chances. Issues that affect chances for re-election, such as a Nixon or Reagan trip to China, come under exacting White House control, but peripheral issues must be settled with minimum presidential involvement. Presidential appointees in the bureaucracy begin to wonder about how they will earn a living one year hence. As White House attention rivets on the election, particularly if the president's standing ebbs in the polls, the bureaucrats are emboldened to recapture issues that they may have lost in the preceeding two years. The rival presidential candidate pledges new steps affecting China policy (for Carter in 1976, Korean troop withdrawal; for Reagan in 1980, upgrading relations with Taiwan) without fully understanding the issue. The stage is set for a renewal of the cycle.

Bilateral Linkages

It is inadequate to discuss the making of China policy strictly within the American context. To a considerable extent, our policy process is penetrable; Chinese become actors on our stage, just as we become actors on theirs. The authorities on Taiwan have long been participants in the making of U.S. China policy in both visible and invisible ways. Now, the mainland Chinese are beginning to be similarly involved. The Chinese try to play upon rivalries within our government, assisting those whose views they perceive to be more compatible. In both the Nixon–Ford and Carter years, Mao, Zhou, and Deng sensed a greater affinity with the world views of national security advisors Kissinger and Brzezinski than of Secretaries of State Rogers and Vance; and the Chinese helped to maneuver the American management of China policy into the hands of Kissinger and Brzezinski.

Linkages are established at lower levels as well. Indeed, each governmental agency that has a China issue on its agenda interacts with its Chinese counterpart. Over time, the American side acquires an interest in the welfare of its Chinese partner. For example, the American specialists in Beijing's Ministry of Foreign Affairs and the China specialists in the Department of State have forged bonds of trust and understanding. Each side to some extent hopes the other side can fend off those internal rivals who may be more nationalistic and less sensitive to the needs of the foreign partner. As tacit alliances arise across boundaries, between, say, Senator Jackson and China's Deng Xiaoping or between Senator Goldwater and Taiwan's Chiang Ching-kuo, Sino–American relations become embedded in the domestic politics in the two countries. America's China policy and China's America policy reflect the ebb and flow in the domestic standing of those who link the two societies. If the linkage becomes a political liability, the individual or agency may seek to rid himself of the burden; likewise, a politically beneficial linkage encourages the political figure or agency to cling to the issue. For example, Zhou Enlai's and Richard Nixon's domestic political difficulties from mid-1973 on caused the Sino–American relationship to atrophy, since at that time these two individuals held the relationship in their hands. To both Henry Kissinger in 1975–1976 and Deng Xiaoping in 1979–1980, management of the Sino–American relationship was a source of their domestic strength. Each resisted efforts by the other side to reduce its dependency at the time on the fortunes of one man. In 1974–1975, the Chinese sought to establish links with Kissinger's rival, Secretary of Defense Schlesinger, while in 1979–1980, the Carter administration wished to broaden its contacts among the Politburo. In both instances, Kissinger and Deng thwarted the design of their partner.

This phenomenon is not limited to the apex and to government bureaucracies, however. Alliances are established between American corporations and different agencies in China. For example, one U.S. corporation may successfully cultivate a manufacturing ministry—say, the Ministry of Electronics, or Agricultural Machinery—in its effort to sell a product (computers, tractors, engines) while a competing U.S. corporation may persuade an end-user ministry—for instance, the Ministry of Transportation, Agriculture, or Education—that its product is the superior one. The decision on which computer or jet engine to purchase will be a product of bureaucratic politics waged within China between the producing and consuming agencies.

The Global Context

I return to the notion of bundle and sticks for a final observation about the making of China policy. Some of the most significant issues in the China bundle are not evaluated primarily on their own merits, or in terms of their impact upon and relationship to other issues in the China bundle. Rather, several China issues have been repeatedly considered in light of other strategic issues and decided in terms of their impact on the global balance-of-power and on the Sino–Soviet–American strategic triangle. Such issues as the forging of a military relationship with China, the relaxation of controls on exports of technology to China, or the timing and purpose of presidential visits have often been considered primarily in terms of their consequences on the strategic triangle. For example, Kissinger's memoirs illuminate how the timing of Nixon's 1972 visit was integrated with American policy toward the Soviet Union, while Brzezinski's memoirs reveal how Brzezinski desired that Deng's January 1979 trip should precede the anticipated Carter-Brezhnev summit. (The inability of the United States and the Soviet Union to reach a SALT agreement in the weeks following Sino–American normalization dashed these hopes.) The January 1980 decision to sell military equipment to China was part of the American response to the Soviet invasion of Afghanistan.

Equally important, Chinese reactions to an administration decision are frequently considered on issues that could also easily be evaluated without reference to their impact on Sino–American relations. A case in point is the American position in arms reduction talks with the Soviet Union that SS-20s now in Europe cannot be redeployed east of the Urals. This stance was adopted partially in response to American concerns for Japanese and Chinese security interests. American opposition toward the Vietnamese domination of Kampuchea similarly acknowledges the views of the ASEAN states and of China. When the web of security issues is disregarded and issues are treated on their own merits, as sometimes occurs, the consequences are unfortunate. In a particularly egregious case, the two earliest moves of the Carter administration in East Asia were to pursue the remains of those missing-in-action (MIAs) in Indochina and to reduce U.S. forces in Korea. Both actions grew out of campaign rhetoric; neither were carefully considered in terms of their impact on the other issues in the Indochina or Korea bundle or on China policy. Yet, in retrospect, these actions baffled the Chinese, South Koreans, and Vietnamese, all of whom derived erroneous conclusions from these two actions concerning the priorities of the new administration. The South Koreans feared abandonment, the Vietnamese falsely perceived themselves to be central to the new administration's concerns, and the Chinese tentatively concluded the Carter administration lacked strategic sense.

China policy is shaped successfully, in short, not when the entire bundle of issues pertaining to China is coherently considered as an isolated whole, but rather when the key issues in the China bundle and the key issues in other policy bundles are integrated into a coherent and sustainable strategy. This can only be done by the president and his chief foreign policy advisors; only they can bring all the strategically significant issues together.

IMPLICATIONS

In a volume assessing American policy toward China in the coming decade, this question naturally arises: What are the implications of this policymaking process for the policy recommendations one might make? It is idle to advocate policies that are so complex or subtle that the government could not adopt or implement them. Several implications seem to flow from the structure and process already described.

Pleas for total coherence and a perfect degree of coordination in the making of China policy are unrealistic. Some inconsistencies are inevitable. For reasons already noted, neither the East Asian Bureau at State for lack of clout nor the president's foreign policy advisors for lack of time are able to bring within their arena all the issues in the China bundle and impose coherence upon them.

As a corollary, the Chinese are going to have to learn to cope with such vexing anomalies in American China policy as the decision of a U.S. District Court in Alabama that the People's Republic must appear in his court to defend itself against a suit claiming Beijing is liable for railroad bonds issued in 1910. (This is the so called Hu Guang railway case, in which a judge held China in default for not appearing in his court.) Nor can the Chinese fault the president and his advisors for decisions made in arenas genuinely beyond their reach. The American system openly invites the Chinese to seek to influence our decisions; it does not enable the top American policymakers to control the process in each arena so that Chinese sensitivities are taken into account without Chinese representation.

In light of our analysis, another unrealistic recommendation is for the development of a widespread consensus on a particular issue before a decision is taken. This plea has been frequently made concerning technology transfer or U.S. arms sales to China or to Taiwan. The fact is that consensus is probably impossible to attain when so many interested parties are involved. At the same time, given the multiplicity of arenas and access points, it is easy to block, delay, or sabotage policy initiatives. On several occasions in the past decade, decisions to relax export controls have been made in the presidential or foreign policy advisor arenas, only to see the decision eroded when it was returned to the administrative agencies for implementation. Policy recommendations must identify those arenas of resistance that have the capacity to reverse the policy and suggest ways for handling the opposition.

Heightened sensitivity to the execution of policy also entails attaching budgetary figures to the recommendations. What precisely will be the Congressional appropriations required to implement a particular policy, and can the appropriation be secured? Or, if the cost is to be borne by the private sector, will it shoulder the burden? Again, because of the multiplicity of arenas and segmented structure of government, all too often the president and his foreign policy advisors have endorsed programs and informed the Chinese before the budgetary implications were carefully examined. So far little reference has been made to the Office of Management and Budget (OMB) as an essential partner in the shaping of policy. The national security advisor has been reluctant to draw OMB fully into the policy process for fear that few initiatives will pass its stern scrutiny. The idea has been to enunciate policies and then force the budgetary and administrative agencies to devise ways to implement policy. The problem with this strategy is that expectations may be aroused that cannot be met. Perhaps now in an era of financial stringency, strategic planners must learn to attach fiscal and implemental plans to their proposals at an early stage.

Sino–American relations, in short, have become an integral part of American foreign policy. China policy does not stand alone, enjoying a special or distinctive status. Today, the making of China policy is similar to the way we make policy toward other major countries with global influence. Given the pluralistic and open nature of our processes, China policy can no longer be formulated secretively by the president and his advisors. The China breakthrough of Nixon and the normalization agreement of Carter probably could not have been decided in any other way. At that time, the relationship was weak and susceptible to rapid change. But in the coming decade, dramatic breakthroughs are unlikely, just as rapid change in American relations with any country are rare. Policy recommendations that do not take this setting into account are unrealistic.

Logic brings a surprising conclusion, especially given my previous inclinations. China policy is not necessarily well served when the bulk of the policy bundle is firmly managed in a single arena. To be sure, this promotes maximum coherence, but it risks maximum opposition. Perhaps in the coming decade, while retaining strong coordinating capacity in the EA Bureau and the NSC staff, it is equally important to ensure that the separate sticks in the China policy bundle are well integrated into the other bundles of which these same sticks are a part. Our technology transfer policy to China cannot depart greatly from our overall technology transfer policy, or it will not endure long. Our policy on arms sales to Taiwan must be supportive of our overall strategic posture in East Asia, and not be based on domestic political considerations or the desire to placate old friends. Arranging the sticks in the China bundle to produce a closer fit with the sticks in other bundles will mean the sticks in the China bundle will not fit as neatly with one another.

But the policies are likely to endure and to elicit the cooperation of those who implement them.

The remaining papers in this book are written in this spirit. Hence, the repeated call for steady progress, not rapid advance; for meshing China policy with other pertinent policies, and not treating China in isolation; for ensuring that rhetoric and performance are in proximity; and, for setting goals that are attainable. To those with high aspirations, the recommendations may be modest, but they have the virtue of being credible and sustainable.

Chapter 4

Viewpoints of America's Friends And Allies

Harry Harding*

When Americans think about China policy, we usually think first of our bilateral relationship with the People's Republic. We consider the mutually beneficial opportunities for trade and investment, cultural and artistic exchange, and scientific and educational cooperation, and try to find channels for developing them. We examine the issues that have complicated relations between the two countries—including the sale of American arms to Taiwan, the controls on the transfer of advanced American technology to China, the restrictions of Chinese imports on textile producers in the United States—and try to devise ways of resolving or managing them.

We have also become accustomed to the concept of a "strategic triangle," linking our policy toward China to our relationship with the Soviet Union. Parallel interests in opposing Soviet expansion enabled China

*Senior Fellow, Foreign Policy Studies Program, The Brookings Institution; formerly Associate Professor of Political Science, Stanford University.

I wish to express my appreciation to Lillian Lee of Stanford University for her research assistance. Many of the ideas contained here were drawn from conferences I have attended in Europe, Asia, and the United States over the last several years. Particularly valuable were those held in Tokyo, Singapore, and Bellagio in the summer of 1981 as part of the project on China's foreign policy sponsored by the China Council of the Asia Society. While I have quoted some of the participants of these meetings in this essay, I have not felt it appropriate to identify them by name.

and the United States to achieve a rapprochement in the early 1970s. Within only a few years, however, latent differences in the two countries' policies toward the Soviet Union—Washington intending Sino–American accommodation as a way of furthering détente with Moscow, Beijing meaning it as a way of containing Soviet hegemonism—caused the first serious strain in the new relationship. By the end of the decade, the Soviet invasion of Afghanistan led both Americans and Chinese to explore the possibility of further strategic and military cooperation as a counterweight against Soviet aggression in Asia. And, more recently, we have attempted to gauge the impact of the resumption of the Sino–Soviet dialogue on our relationship with both China and the Soviet Union.

As important as these two perspectives are, we need to place our China policy in a broader context. China is not merely a bilateral issue, or even a triangular problem, for American policy. The posture that the United States adopts toward China is of intense concern to our friends and allies in Asia and Europe. What is more, many of our partners abroad have come to believe that we do not fully recognize the ways in which our relationship with China affects their national interests, and that, when forced to choose, the United States tends to assign greater priority to its connection with China than to older friendships and alliances.

An overview of the attitudes of American friends and allies—particularly Japan, South Korea, the five members of the Association of Southeast Asian Nations (ASEAN), and Western Europe—toward our relationship with China does not lend itself to ready generalization. There are not only striking differences of opinion between Europeans and Asians, but also significantly divergent attitudes within each region. For example, Thailand tends to be more sympathetic toward American military cooperation with China than is Indonesia, just as, in Europe, Great Britain is more sympathetic than Germany. What is more, as is to be expected with vigorous pluralistic societies, there are often wide differences of opinion within individual states.

Despite these divergent perspectives, it is still possible to reach some general conclusions about our partners' attitudes toward the major themes in American China policy over the last decade. First, and most fundamentally, our friends and allies are pleased with the dramatic improvements in Sino–American relations that culminated in formal diplomatic relations in January 1979. Nonetheless, there have been significant reservations, especially in Southeast Asia, about the rapid development of a military and security relationship between Washington and Beijing. Third, while our friends have substantial sympathy for Taiwan and understand U.S. obligations toward the island, most of them have also hoped that Washington's residual commitments to Taiwan would not do serious damage to the American relationship with Beijing. And finally, as of now, there have been relatively few tensions between the United States and its friends over the prospect of close American economic relations with the PRC.

The differences between the United States and its friends over our China policy—particularly those involving Sino–American strategic cooperation—stem from the fact that American perceptions of China are often more emotional, idealized, and optimistic than those of our counterparts in Europe and Asia. Our friends' assessments of China and their reservations about our China policy may not necessarily be correct, but they deserve careful and sympathetic attention as we plan our relations with Beijing over the rest of the decade.

SUPPORT FOR THE SINO–AMERICAN RAPPROCHEMENT

With the exception of Taiwan, our friends and allies in Europe and Asia universally support the improvement of Sino–American relations that has occurred since the late 1960s. They appear convinced that the improvements in Sino–American relations have not only enhanced the chances for peace and stability in East Asia, but also removed some irritants in their own relations with Washington.

Through most of the 1950s and early 1960s, many Western Europeans and Japanese believed that American policy toward China was misguided.[1] For much of that period, American policy was to promote the internal collapse of the PRC by isolating it from any contact with non-Communist countries. In so doing, our allies in Europe and Japan believed, the United States had tied itself too closely to Taiwan, overlooked opportunities for a *modus vivendi* with Beijing, overestimated the PRC's subservience to Moscow, and overstated the danger that China posed to the rest of Asia.

In the rest of Asia, the attitude toward American policy toward China was somewhat different. By the early 1960s at the latest, virtually all the non-Communist states of Southeast and Northeast Asia considered themselves to be under threat, directly or indirectly, from Beijing. The non-Communist parts of the divided countries in Asia—Taiwan, South Korea, and South Vietnam—feared attack from their Communist rivals in Beijing, Pyongyang, and Hanoi. Many of the other non-Communist nations of the region, including Thailand, Malaysia, the Philippines, and Indonesia, suspected Beijing of supporting, both morally and materially, local insurgencies and guerrilla movements. Most of these

Asian nations were initially concerned that any softening of American policy toward Beijing would jeopardize their national security. But by the height of the Vietnam conflict, some of them began to wonder whether American power was sufficient to isolate China indefinitely. Increasingly, they suspected that a policy of dialogue with Beijing might ultimately be more productive than a policy of containment alone.

The rapprochement between Beijing and Washington was therefore welcomed in both Europe and Asia. For the Japanese and the Europeans, the improvement in Sino–American relations meant that the United States would no longer obstruct normal trade, exchanges, and diplomatic contacts with Beijing, and that relations with China would cease to be an issue in their ties with the United States. For the smaller countries of Southeast and Northeast Asia, the new Sino–American relationship substantially increased the prospects for peace and stability in the region. China was now less likely to place diplomatic or subversive pressure on countries allied or aligned with the United States, as it had done at various times in the 1950s and 1960s, or to use military force against Taiwan. And the rapprochement between China and the United States also raised the possibility that China would help restrain Vietnam and North Korea from using force to gain control over Indochina and the Korean peninsula.

Many of our allies also recognized that the new Sino–American relationship helped create a stronger counterweight against Soviet expansion. During the decade of direct American military involvement in the Vietnam conflict, the balance of forces between the Soviet Union and the United States had steadily shifted in Moscow's favor, as the USSR launched a massive buildup of its military forces, and as Americans seemed to tire of sustaining their other military commitments overseas. But the rapprochement between China and the United States helped, at least to a degree, to redress this imbalance. From the European perspective, the improvement in Sino–American relations greatly reduced the chances that the United States would find itself in a war in Asia. The United States might, therefore, be able to devote a larger proportion of its military resources to deterring conflict in the Middle East and Western Europe. For Asians, the growing cooperation between China and the United States likewise provided a greater counterweight against a growing Soviet military presence in Siberia and the Western Pacific.

To be sure, the improvement of Sino–American relations was a mixed blessing for our friends and allies, especially in Asia. The alignment of China and the United States signalled the Soviet Union that it could expect little immediate improvement in its relations with Beijing, and may have encouraged Moscow to extend its diplomatic and military position in Southeast and Southwest Asia as a means of retaliation. What is more, the Sino–American rapprochement, occurring as it did before the end of hostilities in Vietnam, also contributed to the deterioration of relations between Beijing and Hanoi and, ultimately, to Hanoi's decision to align itself more closely with the Soviet Union.

While Washington's alignment with Beijing may have introduced new complications into Sino–Soviet relations, it also helped reduce the prospects that the dispute between Moscow and Beijing would explode into all-out war. And though the new Sino–American relationship may have exacerbated tensions between Beijing and Hanoi, it also created the opportunity for China, the United States, and ASEAN to design parallel or coordinated actions against the Vietnamese and Soviet expansion in Southeast Asia.

RESERVATIONS ABOUT SINO-AMERICAN MILITARY COOPERATION

Despite their generally favorable reaction to U.S. policy toward China, our partners in Europe and Asia have expressed some strong reservations about the strategic and military relationship that has developed between Beijing and Washington since the early 1970s.

The strategic connection between Beijing and Washington was forged at the same time as the diplomatic rapprochement between the two countries. In late 1968 and 1969, when Zhou Enlai and Mao Zedong first explored the possibilities of improving their relations with the United States, their principal motive was to find a strategic counterweight against growing Soviet pressure along the Sino–Soviet frontier. By 1971, at the time of the war between India and Pakistan, the United States had concluded, according to Henry Kissinger's memoirs, that it would not be in the American interest to see China "crushed" by a Soviet attack,[2] and that it would be willing to join Beijing in an alignment against the Soviet Union.

For the next decade, from the Indo-Pakistani War of 1971 to the inauguration of the Reagan administration in 1981, when American arms sales to Taiwan began to complicate Sino–American relations, strategic cooperation between Washington and Beijing developed rapidly and extensively along four parallel tracks. First, there were repeated expressions, especially during the Carter administration, of an American interest in seeing that China was militarily strong and secure against Soviet attack. U.S. defense officials reportedly also drew up contingency plans for American assistance to China in the event of a conventional Sino–Soviet war.[3] Together, these developments amounted to a partial American commitment, albeit tacit and informal, to the security of China.

Second, there were increasingly detailed, candid, and frequent consultations between Beijing and Washington on a wide range of military and political issues, including the Soviet invasion of Afghanistan and Vietnamese expansion in Indochina. These consultations, which developed especially rapidly after the normalization of Sino–American relations during the latter half of the Carter administration, were aimed in large part at identifying common or similar interests in pursuit of which the two sides could take parallel or coordinated actions.

Third, there was a gradual relaxation of American export controls to China. In the 1970s, during the Nixon and Ford administrations, the United States permitted the sale of advanced civilian technology to Beijing on a case-by-case basis, including such items as Boeing 707s, advanced computers, and satellite ground stations. In the Carter administration, Washington ceased its opposition to the sale of European weapons to China, made China eligible to purchase sophisticated civilian technology on a regular basis, and expressed willingness to sell Beijing certain kinds of non-lethal military support equipment. Then, during his visit to Beijing in June 1981, Secretary of State Alexander Haig told the Chinese that the Reagan administration would consider their requests to purchase American defensive weapons. In this connection, the United States proved willing to share with the Chinese information about Soviet capabilities and deployments with the Chinese, including that gleaned from satellite reconnaisance.

And finally, there was growing consideration of the ways in which China might provide assistance to the United States in its strategic competition with the Soviet Union. In June 1981, just after Secretary Haig's visit to Beijing, it was revealed that in 1980 the Chinese and the United States had placed, on Chinese territory, electronic surveillance stations to monitor Soviet missile tests, replacing similar stations closed after the Iranian Revolution in 1979.[4] In 1982, the Reagan administration reportedly envisioned using military assistance to China to ensure that Soviet forces would be tied down along the Chinese frontier during a war between the United States and the Soviet Union.[5] And American defense analysts identified a wide range of other helpful actions that the Chinese might be persuaded to undertake, including the sale of strategic minerals to the West and the provision of air corridors linking American bases in the Far East with areas of crisis in the Middle East.[6]

Not all of these developments were unwelcome to America's friends and allies in Europe and East Asia. Most understood that, by symbolizing the American interest in China's security and building support for the American connection within the Chinese armed forces, strategic cooperation between Washington and Beijing was helping to consolidate the new American relationship with China. Some Europeans who saw weapons and other military technology as a potentially important and profitable part of their sales to China were pleased that the United States had agreed to relax allied controls on the export of strategic goods to the PRC. And some Europeans and Asians shared the view that strategic cooperation between China and the West would build a stronger barrier against Soviet expansion by enabling China, Japan, and NATO to work together to counter Soviet actions in the Third World, and by forcing the Soviet Union to prepare for the possibility of major war on two widely separated fronts.

Nonetheless, most of our partners have expressed reservations about some aspects of the growing strategic relationship between the United States and China, especially the sale of American arms and military equipment to Beijing. The degree of concern varies within and among Japan, Western Europe, Korea, and Southeast Asia. But the grounds for our allies' unease can be grouped in three categories.

First, there has been apprehension in the countries of both Western Europe and Northeast Asia that joining China in an anti-Soviet united front might complicate, rather than improve, their relations with Moscow. Many Europeans remain committed to détente as the best long-term strategy for dealing with the Soviet Union, and see a strategic relationship between China and the West—and particularly between the United States and China—as incompatible with such a policy. When then Chinese Premier Hua Guofeng visited Europe in 1979, for example, most of his hosts sought to disassociate themselves from his anti-Soviet position and to emphasize the commercial aspects of his tour.[7] And in June 1981, when Secretary of State Haig offered to sell defensive American weapons to China, Japanese commentators urged the United States to exercise great caution lest such a step disrupt American and Japanese relations with the Soviet Union. Some even suggested that Japan disavow the American action by undertaking "peace diplomacy, independent of the U.S. and Chinese moves, to foster dialogue instead of confrontation" with Moscow.[8]

Indeed, many of our partners fear that an American alignment with China might provoke Moscow into some kind of retaliatory action against the West and its friends in Asia. The Soviet invasion of Afghanistan in late 1979, and growing Soviet ties with Vietnam, are occasionally described in both Europe and Japan as Moscow's response to its perceived encirclement by China and the United States. Some analysts suspect that further strategic cooperation between Beijing and Washington would produce more reactions of this kind, perhaps including Soviet attempts to destabilize the Middle East or the Korean peninsula.

Second, like some analysts in the United States, some Europeans and Japanese ask whether China can provide a counterweight to the Soviet Union that is substantial or effective enough to warrant taking these risks. Japanese analysts, for example, tend to see the Soviet challenge primarily in naval terms. Not only do they wonder whether providing military assistance to Chinese ground forces will do that much to strengthen Japanese security, but they also worry that helping modernize the Chinese navy might over the longer run increase Beijing's abilities to take military action against island territories where Japanese interests are directly at stake, including both the disrupted Senkakus and Taiwan.

Europeans, in contrast, see the Soviet challenge largely, although of course not exclusively, in terms of the confrontation of two armies on continental Europe. But they, too, question whether cooperation with China would make much of a contribution to their security. In response to the argument, frequently heard in Beijing, that China ties down substantial Soviet forces that might otherwise be deployed on the western front, Europeans reply that the Soviet Union, through its military buildup in the 1970s, was able to increase its forces in Asia without reducing those stationed in Europe. As a result, many Europeans remain convinced that China would not significantly influence the outcome of a military confrontation in Europe. In William Griffith's phrase, many Europeans see China as "weak and far away"—as an Asian regional power that "remains essentially irrelevant to their principal problems."[9]

The third set of considerations involves China's long-term intentions in Asia. Many of our partners worry that China retains hegemonic ambitions in the region, and that American military and strategic cooperation with Beijing would only increase China's capability to pursue those goals. China's recent attempts to build greater confidence in Southeast Asia—the visits by highranking Chinese officials, the attenuation of Beijing's ties with regional Communist parties, and a clarification of China's attitude toward Overseas Chinese—have not been completely effective in alleviating these misgivings.

This is not to say that China is seen as an immediate military threat to Southeast Asia, for it is still relatively backward economically and weak militarily, as illustrated by its inability to administer a decisive punishment to Hanoi in the Sino–Vietnamese war of early 1979. Instead, there is apprehension that, over the coming decade, the ethnic and political problems in Southeast Asia might become so serious that China could easily become a destabilizing factor in the region should it decide to abandon the moderate foreign policy it has been pursuing in recent years. Subversion, through the reactivation of China's links with local Communist parties, rather than direct military force, would be Beijing's most effective mechanism for placing pressure on unfriendly governments.

Over the longer run, moreover, many Asians suspect that American assistance to the Chinese armed forces would give Beijing greater ability to exercise military and diplomatic coercion against its neighbors to the south. From their perspective, China's unremitting military pressure against Vietnam is an alarming harbinger of its future policy toward other Southeast Asian states which might dare to defy Chinese wishes. Since many Southeast Asians foresee an ultimate reconciliation—or at least a significant reduction of tensions—between China and the Soviet Union, they also worry that the military equipment originally given to China as a counterweight against Moscow might eventually be transferred from China's northern boundary to its southern frontiers.[10]

In consequence, many ASEAN countries have ambivalent attitudes about Sino–Vietnamese relations. On the one hand, uneasy about Hanoi's own intentions, they welcome Beijing's assistance in containing Vietnamese expansion. On the other hand, they also realize that, if successful, Beijing's policy of humiliating Vietnam would remove a potentially important barrier to China's later political and military expansion in Southeast Asia. ASEAN does not share China's view that Vietnam be "bled white" as punishment for its invasion of Cambodia. Instead, ASEAN prefers that, once Vietnam has been forced to give up its goal of hegemony in Southeast Asia, Hanoi should serve as a substantial regional counterweight to China.[11] Accordingly, ASEAN has feared that American arms sales to China, or other forms of military cooperation with Beijing, might represent Washington's tacit approval of the Chinese approach to the Vietnam question.

The question of China's intentions toward Southeast Asia is, of course, of greatest import to the members of ASEAN. But the issue is understood in Europe and Japan as well. Even though few Europeans or Japanese see China as a direct threat to their own security, they do recognize that Southeast Asians feel differently, and often recommend that the United States take ASEAN's concerns more fully into account. Japanese newspapers, in urging the United States to move cautiously in its development of military ties with Beijing, have often noted that "many Asian countries do not want China to become a military power."[12] Europeans who retain a global perspective also understand the wariness in Asia about military cooperation with China. As a member of NATO's Economic Directorate has put it, "We should not be under any illusion that long-term Chinese interests in Asia are in any way similar to our own. . . . [L]ong before the Chinese military could effectively oppose the Soviets, it would have to have reached an intermediate plateau where its military power by far exceeded that of any other nation in the region."[13]

These assessments of risk and reward have produced a broad spectrum of opinion among America's friends and allies abroad about the desirability of American strategic cooperation with the PRC. This spectrum ranges from substantial sympathy and support in much of Western Europe to skepticism and apprehension in most of Asia.

Perhaps the most supportive are conservatives in Western Europe, Australia, and New Zealand who see China as a potential partner of the West in an emerging global alignment against the Soviet Union. In discussing the "deck of China cards" available to the United States and Western Europe, for example, *The Economist* urged that the West should "play them warily, but play them."[14] Similarly, the London *Daily Telegraph,* commenting on Secretary Haig's announcement that the United States would consider selling defensive weapons to China, described the decision as "another refreshing sign that Mr. Haig, clearly with President Reagan's support, believes that power—within the rules—is there to be used, not merely talked about."[15] Both the Australian and New Zealand governments supported the Reagan administration's decision on arms sales to China, on the grounds that the Soviet Union, and not China, is the major threat to the security of the Western Pacific. As New Zealand's prime minister, Robert Muldoon, explained his country's position: "From where we sit, out in the South Pacific, we're perfectly happy with the [American] decision. We don't see any such arms [sold to China] being pointed in our direction."[16]

Liberal and socialist circles in Europe and Australia, in contrast, have expressed somewhat greater concern about the risks attendant upon Sino–American military relations. In Europe, the principal consideration is the effect of Sino–American military cooperation on détente with the Soviet Union. The German newspaper *Badische Zeitung,* for instance, noted that "an alliance between the billions [sic] of people in the country of the yellow dragon and the world's strongest industrial and trade nation cannot leave the Kremlin unconcerned," and cautioned that such an alliance might simply increase Moscow's "fear of encirclement."[17] In the words of a report of the North Atlantic Assembly in 1979, cooperation with China should not be allowed to become an "alternative to cooperation with the Soviet Union," for "there is no such alternative."[18]

In Australia, in contrast, the issue is less the fate of U.S.–Soviet détente than the sensitivity of many ASEAN countries to the strengthening of China's military capability. Some Australian officials are concerned that, by moving rapidly toward a strategic partnership with

Beijing, the United States might seriously damage its relationship with ASEAN for the sake of limited and temporary gains in its relationship with China. What is more, some Australian Asian specialists have charged that, by endorsing the strategic relationship between the United States and China, the Australian government and ASEAN "are going in different directions vis-à-vis China," and that Australia has therefore violated its pledge to develop foreign policies in close consultation with its neighbors in Southeast Asia.[19]

The unease about Sino–American military relations is even greater in Japan than in Europe or Australia. While views on this issue differ among knowledgeable Japanese, the prevailing opinion is that giving the Chinese substantial military assistance (or even appearing to join Beijing in a united front against the Soviet Union) would be unnecessarily provocative toward Moscow, would end any hope of an accommodation with the USSR, and would disturb Tokyo's relations with Southeast Asia as well. Thus, the Japanese have not only reiterated that they will not sell arms to China but have also placed strict limits on exchanges of visits by Chinese and Japanese military personnel. In addition, the Japanese have consistently urged the United States to exercise caution in its own military cooperation with the PRC. When Secretary of Defense Harold Brown visited Beijing in early 1980, just after the Soviet invasion of Afghanistan, some prominent Japanese warned that any steps toward military cooperation among Tokyo, Beijing, and Washington would irritate Moscow, disrupt stability in Asia, and risk "increasing military tensions between Japan and the Soviet Union."[20] Similar views, as we have seen, were expressed after Secretary Haig's offer to sell China defensive weapons in 1981.

Elsewhere in Asia, as one Singaporean diplomat has summarized the situation, opinions on military cooperation between the United States and China range from "disquiet to dismay." In four countries—South Korea, Thailand, Singapore, and the Philippines—the prevailing view is that the present strategic relationship between Washington and Beijing is acceptable, at least for the moment. To Thailand, for example, a strategic partnership between China and the United States helps Beijing to counterbalance an assertive Vietnam. To South Korea, a sound Sino–American relationship plays a significant role in restraining an attack by its Communist rival in Pyongyang.[21] In Singapore and the Philippines, Chinese military power presently seems more distant and less threatening than that of the Soviet Union.

But even in these four countries, Sino–American military cooperation is viewed as potentially dangerous over the longer run. Some in ASEAN are concerned that, since the United States has no overall strategy for its relationship with China, Washington will not be able to set reasonable limits on its strategic partnership with Beijing. The *Bangkok Post,* commenting on the "lack of a discernible American foreign policy" in the Reagan administration, charged that "Washington has embraced China with a fervour which has made its friends nervous and its potential foes enraged."[22] And in Korea, there is apprehension that excessive military cooperation between Beijing and Washington might lead the Soviet Union into trying to play a "Korean card" against the United States. At a minimum, this might involve wooing North Korea away from Beijing, with the argument that China was sacrificing North Korean interests in its new alignment with the United States. Or, in more extreme form, it might even entail support for Kim Il-Sung in placing more military pressure against the South. In addition, there is also the worry in Seoul that, over the longer run, the present moderate leadership in Beijing might be replaced by a more radical regime, which might use its increased military power in support of the North Koreans.

The two remaining members of ASEAN, Malaysia and Indonesia, appear adamantly opposed even to the present moderate levels of American military cooperation with China. In large part, their opposition stems from concern about the loyalty of their large Chinese minority populations, the residual links between the Chinese Communist Party and their own local Communist insurgencies, and Beijing's long-term intentions in Southeast Asia. Indonesian Foreign Minister Mokhtar Kusumaatmaja has been particularly outspoken on the issue, noting on several occasions that the growing strategic relationship between Washington and Beijing poses a potentially serious threat to the peace and stability of Southeast Asia.[23] And Malaysian Foreign Minister Ghazali Shafie has argued that, since China maintains connections with insurgencies in his own country and in Thailand, American arms sales to Beijing "might be negative to us."[24]

Despite these differences between Indonesia and Malaysia, on the one hand, and Thailand, Singapore, and the Philippines, on the other, ASEAN has tried to find a consensus position on the issue. And that consensus can best be described as skeptical. The members of ASEAN appear to agree that, over the long run, it is China and not the Soviet Union that will be the more dangerous threat to regional security. Although China is presently weak, and may never prove to be as expansionist as some fear, the non-Communist states of Southeast Asia still are concerned about the long-term implications of a strong China. Accordingly, while they may well be persuaded that the benefits of a cautious program of American military cooperation with China outweigh the risks, they will have to be convinced that their own uneasiness about Chinese designs for Southeast Asia has been given full consideration in Washington.

The spectrum of opinion on American military cooperation with China, then, runs from substantial sympathy and support in Western Europe to skepticism and apprehension in most of Asia. To be sure, none of our friends and allies, except Taiwan, appears to be unconditionally opposed to any kind of military connection between the United States and China. In fact, some forms of strategic cooperation—particularly measures, such as consultations between Washington and Beijing on issues of common concern, that would not involve American assistance to the modernization of China's armed forces—are relatively uncontroversial; but where the sale of military equipment is concerned, virtually all our partners in Asia, and influential groups and individuals in Europe and Australia as well, have expressed some unease about American intentions and their likely consequences.

CONCERN ABOUT TAIWAN

While American security cooperation with China has been the aspect of Sino–American relations that is of the greatest direct consequence to our partners in Europe and Asia, it lost much of its immediacy after the inauguration of Ronald Reagan in 1981, when Beijing began to express serious objections to American foreign policy toward Taiwan. Not only did Beijing threaten to downgrade its relations with the United States unless its demands were met, but it also halted further progress toward Sino–American military ties until American policy toward Taiwan had been clarified. With Beijing's change in policy, the issue of American military assistance to China became moot, at least for the time being. But China's new position produced a second area of concern for America's friends and allies: American policy toward Taiwan, and its potential impact on Sino–American relations.

The immediate cause for Chinese concern was the possibility that the United States might agree to sell to Taiwan a more advanced generation of fighter aircraft, the so-called F-X, to supplement the less sophisticated F-5Es already in the island's arsenal. But there were two broader factors behind Beijing's actions. First, there were the statements by Mr. Reagan, both before and after his election, expressing his disapproval of the Carter administration's treatment of Taiwan and his intention to upgrade, in some way, American relations with the Nationalist government. Second, there was China's disappointment that neither the end of American diplomatic relations with Taiwan, the termination of the Mutual Security Treaty, nor Beijing's own diplomatic overtures toward the island had produced any progress toward the reunification of Taiwan and the Mainland. Significantly, too, Beijing's analysis saw an inextricable connection between the two develop-ments: it was the Reagan administration's expressions of support for Taiwan that enabled the Nationalists to refuse negotiations with the PRC.

In late 1981, therefore, the PRC began demanding a major change in American policy toward Taiwan. China requested a more explicit American acknowledgment of Chinese sovereignty over the island, a schedule for ending American arms sales to the Nationalist govern-ment, and a modification of the Taiwan Relations Act. If the United States did not comply with these demands, Beijing warned, Sino–American relations would be seriously and adversely affected. While Beijing never made a full public declaration of what it planned to do, it is likely that the Chinese intended to withdraw their ambassador from Washington, cut back on imports of American goods, and reduce the level of cultural and scientific exchanges with the United States.

Our partners in Europe and Asia watched these developments with some concern. They agreed with Washington's overall goals: to main-tain friendly relations with Taiwan and ensure a peaceful solution of the Taiwan question, while preserving the Sino–American relationship to the greatest extent possible. But they appear to have been worried that the Reagan administration might choose to overemphasize the for-mer objective at the expense of the latter.

Few of our friends abroad were uninterested in the future of Taiwan. For one thing, a large number of them have significant and beneficial relations with the island that they would like to maintain. Japan's eco-nomic stake in Taiwan remains substantial: even after the normaliza-tion of Sino–Japanese relations in 1972, Taiwan has remained a host for large amounts of Japanese foreign investment, an attractive desti-nation for Japanese tourists, and one of Tokyo's most important trading partners. Europeans, too, have discovered the advantages of doing business with Taiwan. In the past several years, after it became clear that the termination of American diplomatic relations was not going to cause the island's economy to collapse, there has been a substantial in-crease in the number of European banks and firms doing business on Taiwan, and in the number of European countries establishing trade offices and cultural centers in Taipei.

Indeed, there even remain a number of military connections between Taiwan and America's friends. The Dutch government agreed to sell submarines to Taiwan in 1980, even at the cost of reducing their diplo-matic representation in Beijing to the level of chargé d'affairs. The Singaporean armed forces quietly conduct military training on Taiwan. And Paris reportedly offered to provide Mirage fighters to Taiwan if the Nationalist authorities agreed to purchase nuclear power generators from France.

As another consideration, Taiwan is still seen, especially in Asia, as a test of America's willingness to maintain inconvenient commitments to its smaller allies. This point should not be overstated, for many of our friends—even the South Koreans—understand the special circumstances of the Taiwan problem that distinguish it from their own situations. Nonetheless, few would be indifferent if the United States were suddenly to abandon its interest in a peaceful resolution of the Taiwan question. Just after normalization of Sino–American relations, for example, the Bangkok *Nation Review* noted that the American decision to terminate its mutual defense pact with Taiwan "raises an important question for other countries which have defense treaties with the United States."[25] And at the height of the controversy over U.S. arms sales to Taiwan, the *Korea Herald* pointed out that the one consideration in the American decision should be "to keep its word and commitments made to its allies and friends."[26] Our allies see the Taiwan issue as an index of America's ability to deal firmly and effectively with the PRC, and to use its leverage to gain concessions from Beijing instead of capitulating completely to the Chinese position.

But there was also a concern that the United States might go too far in its support of the Nationalists. Our partners asked whether the United States fully understood the symbolic importance of the Taiwan issue to the Chinese. They worried that Washington might incorrectly assume that Beijing is motivated solely by an interest in maintaining the United States as a counterweight to the Soviet Union, and mistakenly conclude that Beijing would accept whatever policy toward Taiwan the United States might choose to adopt. Our partners also saw the vacillation in the United States over policy toward Taiwan as an example of a lingering romantic attachment—what the London *Times* called an "alluvium of emotion"—to the Nationalists,[27] and of the power of the remnants of the China lobby of the 1950s. The inability of the United States to develop and sustain a coherent policy toward China was regarded as a symptom of a chronic tendency in the United States to view China emotionally rather than rationally.

Thus, during the crisis over American arms sales to Taiwan, some of our partners expressed their apprehension that U.S. insensitivity to China's interests might have far-reaching consequences for Beijing's foreign policy. French officials said privately that they feared that the dispute might lead to a Sino–Soviet reconciliation.[28] The Japanese government reportedly worried that a deterioration in Sino–American relations might damage their own relations with Beijing. They also feared that deterioration in Sino–American relations over the Taiwan issue would serve only to weaken, rather than to enhance, the island's security. Most of our partners believe that a peaceful future for Taiwan can best be ensured not by American security guarantees to the island, or even by American arms supplies, but rather by maintaining a friendly relationship between Beijing and Washington. If preserving the American commitment to the island caused tensions in Sino–American relations, the result might prove in the long run to be more harmful than helpful to a peaceful solution of the Taiwan question.

Despite our allies' concern that Washington was heading toward a confrontation with Beijing, the Reagan administration responded to the crisis over Taiwan in a conciliatory fashion. In January 1982, it announced that it would not provide the F-X to Taiwan's air force, and agreed to open discussions with Beijing about American arms sales to the Nationalists. The result of these discussions—a joint communiqué issued in mid-August 1982—reflected significant concessions by both sides. The United States agreed to reduce its arms sales to Taiwan, and promised that its future sales would not exceed, in either qualitative or quantitative terms, the level reached since normalization. Washington also stated that it had no intention of infringing on Chinese sovereignty or pursuing a "two China" or a "one China, one Taiwan" policy. China, for its part, declared that a peaceful solution to the Taiwan question was its "fundamental policy."

At the same time, the communiqué was also worded in such a way that both governments could claim that they had remained faithful to their basic principles. The PRC could deny that it had renounced the use of force against Taiwan. The United States, in turn, could point out that it had refused either to agree to a fixed schedule for terminating arms sales to Taiwan, or to engage in prior consultations with Beijing before making any future sales. What is more, Washington could also claim that its commitment to reduce arms sales to Taiwan was predicated on Beijing's continued willingness to seek a peaceful solution for Taiwan's future.

The compromise between China and the United States reflected in the August communiqué was widely welcomed by our friends and allies abroad. The Japanese government hailed it as promoting "peace and stability" in Asia; the *Asahi Shimbun* described the communiqué as a "wise" and "practical" agreement; and the *Dong-a Il-bo* commented that the two sides had "defused a diplomatic crisis in a way which still saves their faces."[29] But there was also widespread recognition that the agreement did not provide a final resolution to the issue. *The Economist,* for example, described the communiqué simply as a "break between rounds" in an ongoing dispute between China and the United States, and noted that the agreement had not eliminated the "new scepticism which has affected both sides of the once uncritical Chinese–American embrace."[30]

THE PRESENT CONSENSUS
ON ECONOMICS

As *The Economist* predicted, the August 1982 communiqué, unlike the earlier Sino–American agreements of 1972 and 1978, did not produce a renewed spirit of good will between Beijing and Washington. China continued to describe the United States as a hegemonic power, and to state openly its differences with Washington on a wide range of foreign policy issues. For its part, the Reagan administration was undergoing what some officials described as a "demythologizing of China"—a realization that strategic cooperation with Beijing was not going to occur rapidly, nor greatly improve the American position vis-à-vis the Soviet Union.[31]

As the likelihood of a close mililtary relationship between China and the United States declined, economic matters began to assume a relatively greater role in Sino–American relations. Writing in the *New York Times* in October 1982, for example, Richard Nixon implied that the strategic interests that had "dominated our dialogue" with China in the first decade of the relationship would now be supplemented, if not supplanted, by an economic partnership between the two countries.[32]

If economics are now a somewhat larger part of relations between Beijing and Washington than in the past, it is important to consider the effect of U.S.–China economic ties on our friends and allies abroad. What attitudes do America's partners in Europe and Asia hold toward economic cooperation between China and the United States?

Immediately after the normalization of Sino–American relations, there was some concern in the United States that growing economic connections between Beijing and Washington would produce tensions with some of our other friends and allies. It was feared that Beijing would compete with other developing countries for access to American markets, capital, and technology; and that Americans would vie with businessmen from other developed nations for sales to China. Both these areas of economic competition, it was believed, might ultimately produce political problems between the United States and its partners abroad.

And yet, so far, the development of economic relations between China and the United States has occurred without creating the strains in American relations with third countries that some had predicted. There has, to be sure, been some tension between the United States and other developed countries as they compete for access to the China market. Both the Canadians and the Australians have reportedly resented the Sino–American grain agreement, charging that this constitutes an

American invasion of their traditional export markets.[33] The Japanese have complained that the United States has vetoed, through COCOM,* the sale of Japanese computers to China, while approving the sale of even more powerful American computers to Beijing. Washington, in turn, has accused Tokyo of providing China with export credits at rates below those of the international market. But these tensions have been minimal.

Indeed there appears to be a widespread agreement among the United States, Japan, and Western Europe that they have a shared interest in furthering, to the greatest degree feasible, the civilian modernization of China. Some stress the need to prevent China from becoming a major claimant on the rest of the world's scarce food and energy resources. Others argue that support for China's modernization efforts will bolster the legitimacy of the current regime, and encourage it to maintain a foreign policy course favorable to the West. The British journal *The Economist,* for example, in an editorial entitled "Better Zhao than Mao," concluded that "the rewards for the West of consolidating economic ties with China could one day be great. China is looking forward to the time when it will be a force to be reckoned with. So should everybody. . . . If China is to be a megapower one day, the right sort of encouragement now may help it to be the right sort of megapower."[34]

Japanese leaders have additionally argued that economic assistance to China might earn enough good will to cushion the West against any disruptive change in China's foreign policy. If, for example, China were to decide to repair its relations with the Soviet Union, a record of mutually beneficial economic relations between China and the West might enable Japanese, European, and American relations with Beijing to proceed relatively unaffected. In the words of Heishiro Ogawa, former Japanese ambassador to China,

> . . . [I]t would be better to take into consideration that a Sino–Soviet rapprochement might come eventually. I, therefore, consider it all the more necessary that we consolidate our economic ties and expand cultural and scientific exchanges with China. We should also support Chinese students who come to study here [in Japan] and will become future leaders in their country so that our good relationship will become cohesive and long-enduring through them.[35]

---

*COCOM is the Coordinating Committee, composed of most NATO countries plus Japan, that regulates the flow of advanced Western technology to all Communist countries, including China.

Indeed, Tokyo has even proposed that Japan and the United States begin consultations so as to coordinate their economic and scientific assistance to China.

The growth of Sino–American economic ties has had a somewhat greater effect on American relations with the developing world, including some of the smaller states of East Asia. There has been apprehension that China has been given a disproportionately large share of the American textile market, that China will draw away American foreign assistance from other developing countries, and that loans to the PRC would mean that less concessionary capital would be available to other developing countries from international lending institutions.

But here, too, the impact to date has been less than was originally expected. For most developing countries in East Asia—not only such newly industrialized countries as South Korea and Singapore, but also such "second tier" countries as Malaysia and Thailand—China is not, at present at least, a powerful economic rival. Foreigners have encountered such difficulties in setting up joint ventures and co-production arrangements in China that the PRC has not yet proven to be a major competitor for overseas investment capital. Moreover, it is likely that most other East Asian countries can simply begin producing more sophisticated exports, leaving more labor-intensive technologies to the Chinese, and that China itself may prove to be a significant export market for the rest of Asia. As one Southeast Asian economist put it,

> The opening up of China to the outside world may affect adversely the trade prospects, especially for labour-intensive manufactured exports, in the 1980s. It is unlikely, however, that China will be able to organize its outward-looking manufacturing sector quickly and smoothly enough to pose a formidable threat to the Southeast Asian exporters in the early 1980s. At the same time, the possibility of a *complementary* relationship between China and Southeast Asian countries cannot be ruled out.[36]

It is the larger and poorer developing countries, such as Indonesia, for whom the Sino–American economic connection may pose the greatest potential problem. In particular, they will be looking to see what attitude the United States takes toward low-cost loans to China from the International Development Association (IDA), the "soft window" of the World Bank. Under present circumstances, such loans would probably come at the expense of loans to other developing countries, unless the United States and other developed countries were to increase their contributions to IDA or permit the World Bank to make loans beyond the total of its capital and reserves. Even here, however, unless China becomes eligible for large amounts of direct U.S. foreign economic assistance—an unlikely prospect at present—the tensions are likely to be moderate.

In short, our economic relations with China have not yet produced major problems in our relationships with other friends and allies. Indeed, there appears to be a consensus on the desirability of promoting a close economic association between China and the West. In large part this is because China's own economic retrenchment has reduced its demand for foreign capital and technology, and because potential competitors have been able to find room for China in international export markets. Should China's demand for capital and markets increase dramatically in the 1980s, however, this issue may yet take on greater prominence for American policymakers in the coming decade.

CONCLUSION

In late 1978, officials of the Carter administration claimed that they had finally resolved America's historic dilemma in Asia. In the past, it had been impossible for the United States to have friendly relations with both Beijing and Tokyo at the same time. After World War I, we had accepted Japanese claims in Shantung over those of China; in the 1920s and 1930s, we supported China, at least in our rhetoric, against Japanese pressures for concessions and territory; in World War II, we fought side by side with Chinese against Japan; and in the era of containment in Asia we had forged an alliance with Japan that was directed, in part, against the PRC. But with normalization of Sino–American relations, the United States, for the first time in a century, had good relations with both China and Japan.

At the same time, with Sino–American rapprochement, a similar pattern emerged on a broader scale. The United States no longer has to choose between China and the non-Communist states of Southeast Asia. Nor do Japanese and Europeans have to choose between trade with China and their alliance with the United States. Instead, in the great realignment that has occurred since the 1960s, China, Japan, Southeast Asia, Western Europe, and the United States are linked together on the same side of the global balance. Even with the resumption of Sino–Soviet negotiations in 1982, China remains tied much more closely to the West than to the Soviet bloc, and Beijing's foreign policy interests remain much more similar to Washington's than to Moscow's. Now the Soviet Union, and not the United States, must worry about a two-front war. Generally speaking, too, the population and resources of China are added to the industrial strength of Japan and the West in forging a counterweight to Soviet ambitions.

But, to borrow an image from a Chinese proverb, while we are all now in the same bed, we are still dreaming different dreams. China's recent reassertion of its foreign policy differences with the United States illustrates its view of the remaining limits to the Sino–American relationship. And, as we have seen, although our friends and allies in Europe and Asia support the normalization of Sino–American relations and the strategic realignment that it reflects, they retain reservations about some of the particulars of the new relationship between Beijing and Washington, especially the pace of military cooperation.

Those reservations, in turn, stem from the fact that American perceptions about China differ, in some ways fundamentally, from those that are commonly held by our friends in Western Europe, Japan, and Southeast Asia. First of all, our friends are concerned about what they believe to be emotionalism and idealization in American images of China. As we have already noted, the continuing American commitment to Taiwan is regarded as reflecting, to a degree, a sentimental attachment to the Nationalists, rather than a rational assessment of the national interest. Conversely, many allies believe that we have, in our euphoria about our new relationship with China, overstated our common interests with China and disregarded the remaining differences in foreign policy objectives and sociopolitical structure. Americans often describe China as a "friend, but not an ally." In the eyes of other nations, we might be better served if we saw China as an ally, but not yet a friend. Commenting on the joint communiqué on arms sales to Taiwan, the *Dong-a Il-bo* of Seoul noted that the Sino–American relationship "lacks a solid bedrock. This sharply [contrasts] with the ties the United States maintains with West European countries—a relationship tied by racial, spiritual, and cultural kinship against the backdrop of . . . the common political ideology of Western democracy."[37]

Secondly, many Asians, both in Japan and in ASEAN, have expressed reservations about the degree of exceptionalism that is embodied in American images of China. They acknowledge that China is unique in some ways, especially in its combination of size of population and extent of national territory. But they insist that, in other respects, China is not as exceptional as Americans often claim. As much as China, other Asian nations have also had to reconcile their pride in their own traditional cultural identities with the fact of Western technological and military superiority. Other nations, and not just China, have had to respond to the challenge of the West, and find ways to ensuring national sovereignty and promoting socioeconomic modernization. The notion, common in the United States, that these dilemmas were more intense for China than for other parts of the developing world is indignantly rejected by observers in both Japan and Southeast Asia. What is exceptional about China, according to one frequently heard rejoinder, is not that the problems have been greater, but that the responses have been less effective. As one Japanese China specialist once put it, "China is, in fact, an ordinary country—just underdeveloped and extraordinarily big."

Third, the combination of emotionalism and exceptionalism in American attitudes toward China have produced what many European and Asian observers believe to be an overestimation by the United States of the role that China can play in the global strategic balance and in the international economy. The very concept of a "strategic triangle," they believe, vastly exaggerates China's military and economic significance, not only now, but also for the foreseeable future. One British China specialist has suggested that Americans and Europeans have still not resolved the issue that divided Roosevelt and Churchill during World War II: whether or not China should be considered a major power, on a par with the USSR, the United States, Britain, and France. As he sees it, Americans believe that China is a superpower—recall the Nixon–Kissinger concept that China was one of five major power centers in the contemporary world—while Europeans tend to view China as a regional power at best. Many in ASEAN hold similar views. As one Southeast Asian specialist on international affairs put it, "China is our neighbor; we have to take her seriously. But China does not border the United States. Why, then, do you think China is so important?"

In like manner, a major difference between American and Japanese perceptions of China involves the future of the Chinese economy. While there are optimists and pessimists on both sides of the Pacific, Japanese tend to be more guarded in their forecasts of China than are Americans, and more worried about the possibility that China's economic modernization program may fail. As the report of the 1981 Shimoda Conference put it, "On the whole, the Japanese participants were more skeptical than the Americans on the impact of outside economic assistance and more pessimistic about China's ability to promote its economy as long as it maintained a state-controlled, centrally managed economic system."[38]

Fourth, many of our friends in Asia complain that Washington pays too little heed to China's long-term ambitions in the region. Washington and Beijing do have common interests vis-à-vis the Soviet Union, they acknowledge, and it is these similarities that have led to Sino–American military cooperation. But many Asians believe that the United States ignores the remaining differences between China and other Asian states, especially in Southeast Asia. As Malaysia's Foreign Minister Ghazali has put it, "If the United States wishes to support China in terms of global strategy, by all means do so. But if the Americans do not take into account Chinese designs in Asia, their assistance toward China may be negative towards us."[39] In the words of a Japanese international relations specialist, "In a global context, the merits and demerits of a strategic alignment with China may be balanced, but in a regional context it is clearly undesirable."

What are the implications of these differences for American policy? To begin with, it is important to acknowledge that some reservations expressed by our European and Asian partners may reasonably strike Americans as being rather hypocritical. Europeans caution the United States not to sell arms to China for fear of provoking the Soviet Union, but simultaneously welcome windowshoppers from the Chinese PLA to European arms exhibitions and military installations. And though our friends in Europe and Japan clearly share with the United States an interest in a peaceful settlement of the Taiwan issue, they want us to bear nearly all the responsibility for seeing that that interest is realized.

Even at their most extreme, moreover, the arguments put forward by our European and Asian partners hardly represent a scathing repudiation of American policy toward China. In general, to repeat one of the principal conclusions of this chapter, our friends in Europe and Asia support the broad outlines of the Sino–American relationship that has developed since the early 1970s.

This does not mean, however, that American policymakers would be well-advised to ignore the remaining reservations expressed by our friends. For one thing, we might benefit from listening seriously to the substantive advice of our friends and allies. They are cautioning that close alignment with China may not be the best way to manage the West's relations with the USSR; that American military assistance to China may, in the long term, have a destabilizing effect on Asia; and that emotional American commitments to Taiwan may risk forfeiting the strategic benefits of the new Sino–American relationship. These propositions may or may not be correct. But they are thoughtful arguments, and deserve careful consideration.

Even more important, our partners are waiting to see whether the United States takes their reservations into consideration in making its policy toward China. The choices Washington makes regarding China are seen, to some degree, as a measure of American priorities, and a test of the procedures by which American policy is formulated. When forced to choose between China's position and that of our other friends and allies, which side does the United States take? And when making decisions on its policy toward China, does Washington consult its partners in advance, or does it announce its conclusions only after they have been reached?

Indeed, there is widespread resentment, especially in Asia, that the United States does not consult adequately with other interested parties before making its China policy. Many Southeast Asians charge that the United States, especially during the latter half of the Carter administration, accepted all too readily the Chinese position on Vietnam—a policy of isolation and pressure—rather than accepting the somewhat flexible ASEAN line. As one Indonesian official put it with regard to Cambodia, "Rhetorically [the Americans] said they were going to support ASEAN. But in fact they are going to tie up with China."⁴⁰ They also accuse the United States of telling them about its willingness to sell arms to China only after Secretary Haig had visited Beijing, and not before. Indonesian Foreign Minister Mokhtar has said that prior notification that Washington's intended to sell arms to China would have been "a sign of [America's] regard for us."⁴¹

Similar views are prevalent in Japan. The United States informed Tokyo of the Kissinger visit to China in 1971 only minutes before the events were announced to the American public on television. Although the situation seems to be improving, the Japanese still complain of inadequate consultation between Tokyo and Washington over the normalization of Sino–American relations in 1978 and the development of strategic relations between China and the United States. Some Japanese, according to *The Economist,* have resented the fact that the United States seems to be even less concerned about Japanese desire not to provoke the Soviet Union than about European desires for East-West détente: "The Japanese suspect that American politicians reckon they can afford to be gruffer in Asia than they would ever dare to be in Europe."⁴²

On either substantive or procedural grounds, therefore, American China policy is too important to be left to Washington and Beijing alone. Our other friends and allies in Europe and Asia need to be consulted, and our policy coordinated, to the greatest degree possible, with theirs. In general, the United States will find them supportive and sympathetic. But they deserve to have their remaining reservations and advice taken into full account.

NOTES

1. For a review of European and Asian policies toward China in the 1950s and early 1960s, see A.M. Halpern, ed., *Policies Toward China* (New York: McGraw-Hill, 1965).

2. Henry A. Kissinger, *White House Years* (Boston: Little, Brown, 1979), ch. XXI.

3. In the spring of 1980, it was reported that Secretary of Defense Harold Brown had requested his staff and the heads of the military services to examine the possible

use of American technology, including non-nuclear cruise missiles, to assist China in the event of a conventional Sino–Soviet war. See *Armed Forces Journal International*, May 1983, pp. 23, 69.

4. *New York Times*, June 18, 1981, pp. A1, A14.
5. *New York Times*, May 30, 1982, pp. A1, A6.
6. *New York Times*, December 27, 1981, p. 12; *China Business Review*, September-October 1981, pp. 55–69.
7. Douglas T. Stuart, "Sino–Soviet Competition: The View from Western Europe," in Douglas T. Stuart and William T. Tow, eds., *China, the Soviet Union, and the West: Strategic and Political Dimensions in the 1980s* (Boulder: Westview, 1982), pp. 213–22.
8. *Tokyo Shimbun*, June 18, 1981, p. 4. See also *Senkei Shimbun* (Tokyo), June 18, 1981, p. 10.
9. William Griffith, "China and Europe: 'Weak and Far Away' " in Richard H. Solomon, ed., *The China Factor: Sino–American Relations and the Global Scene* (Englewood Cliffs: Prentice Hall, 1981), pp. 159–177, especially p. 176.
10. See, for instance, the speech given by Singapore's prime minister, Lee Kuan Yew, at the Commonwealth Heads of Government Meeting, October 1, 1981, excerpted in *The Mirror* (Singapore), October 15, 1981. According to Lee, "In several countries in Southeast Asia . . . there are apprehensions at the long-term implications of a strong modernised China." (p. 8).
11. On differences of approach between China and ASEAN on the Indochina question, see *Far Eastern Economic Review (FEER)*, October 31, 1980, pp. 22–24, and *FEER*, November 13, 1981, pp. 40–42.
12. *Senkei Shimbun*, June 18, 1981, p. 10.
13. Rainer Rupp, "China's Strategic Aims and Problems of Military Modernisation," *NATO Review*, February 1981 pp. 14–20.
14. *The Economist* (London), August 1, 1981, p. 11.
15. The *Daily Telegraph* (London), June 17, 1981, p. 18.
16. *New York Times*, June 23, 1981, p. A8; and *FEER*, June 26, 1981, p. 12.
17. *Badische Zeitung*, cited in *Foreign Broadcast Information Service (FBIS): Europe*, June 19, 1981, p. J2.
18. North Atlantic Assembly, Political Committee, "General Report on Alliance Political Developments" (Brussels: International Secretariat, North Atlantic Assembly, October 1979), p. 12; quoted in Douglas P. Stuart, "Prospects for Sino–European Security Cooperation" (unpublished manuscript), p. 35.
19. Nancy Viviani, "Political and Strategic Aspects [of the Senate Committee Report on Australia and ASEAN]," *Asian Studies Association of Australia Review*, 4 (April 1981):3, 15–20.
20. *Mainichi Shimbun* (Tokyo), January 10, 1980, p. 2. See also *Yomiuri Shimbun* (Tokyo), January 11, 1980, p. 4.
21. One Korean newspaper described Secretary Haig's June 1981 visit to China as a "good start" in "enrolling China as a mighty partner in a global strategy aimed at checking Soviet expansionism." The *Korea Times* (Seoul), June 18, 1981, p. 2.
22. *Bangkok Post*, June 28, 1982, p. 4.
23. Jakarta domestic radio, June 21, 1982, in *FBIS: Asia and the Pacific*, June 24, 1892, pp. N1–N2, and OANA (Jakarta) in *ibid.*, November 16, 1982, pp. N2–N3.
24. *FEER*, October 23, 1981, pp. 42–43. For further descriptions of the views of Malaysia and Indonesia, see *New Straits Times* (Kuala Lumpur), June 18, 1981, p. 18; *The Nation* (Bangkok), August 24, 1981, p. 4; and *The Economist*, March 22, 1980, p. 42.

25. *Nation Review* (Bangkok), December 18, 1978, quoted in Bernard K. Gordon, "Normalization and Southeast Asia," in John Bryan Starr, ed., *The Future of U.S.–China Relations* (New York: New York University Press, 1981), p. 128.
26. *Korea Herald* (Seoul), January 7, 1982, p. 4.
27. *The Times* (London), January 14, 1982, p. 11. See also *The Economist,* August 1, 1981, p. 11; and *ibid.,* January 9, 1982, p. 13.

PART III

China's Policy Evolution, 1983–1993

Chapter 5

Domestic Politics Of The People's Republic Of China

Thomas W. Robinson*

THE ESSENCE OF CHINESE POLITICS

The interaction among China's political, cultural, and economic spheres largely determines domestic developments and is the most important element in the formulation of Chinese foreign policy. While there is an absolute need to modernize the country as fast as possible, it is the political-cultural framework that determines the degree to which the Party's modernization goals and, to a large degree, its foreign policy objectives will be achieved.

The political-cultural framework consists of an uneasy amalgam of three factors: Leninism, factionalism, and bureaucratism. Since 1949, these three forces have combined in varying degrees with the demands of the internal and external environments to determine the course of Chinese history. Most of the 1950s appear to have been a period dominated by Leninism, the early and late Cultural Revolution and the Great Leap Forward to have been times when factionalism (i.e., domination by the Maoist group) was most important, and the early–middle 1960s and the early post-Maoist eras to have been times of bureaucratic

*Sun Yat-sen Professor, Georgetown University School of Foreign Service and former Professor, the National War College.

primacy. A degree of balance among all three was achieved in the late 1950s and since 1978, while at the height of the Cultural Revolution, 1967–1971, the "system" was swept away by the course of domestic disorders.

If we can essay convincingly the probable relationship between these three forces during the 1983–1993 decade, we will be in a good position to render useful judgments on Chinese futures. To do that, the essential qualities of each factor must be explicated, if only briefly. Leninism is perhaps the easiest to describe.

Leninism is organizational Machiavellianism attached to a Marxist *Weltanschauung*. It centers on the dominance of society by the polity, of the polity by a single party, and the party by one group (sometimes one person). It represents history's most extreme attempt at concentrating power for social ends, and is often summed up by Lenin's well-known pronouncement on democratic centralism, since 1919 written into the fundamental document of practically every communist party across the globe, including its guiding light.[2] It is highly unlikely that, during the 1983–1993 period, the Chinese Communist Party will deviate much from the "four principles" of socialist ownership of the means of production, party leadership, proletarian dictatorship, and Mao's interpretation of Marxism. Leninism is still the most important element of Chinese politics.

Factionalism is the admixture of Chinese political culture and Leninism.[3] It is a natural concomitant of Leninism as well as the normal manner in which Chinese political life is conducted, even in pre-1949 times. Factions are historical networks led by a single leader that tend to be independent of institutions, geographic areas, or generations in Chinese politics. Usually tacit and latent, factions can be mobilized through political rhetoric and ideology. Chinese politicians pretend factions do not exist because of the cultural need for consensus, but the reality persists, occasionally threatening political stability and influencing the general direction of Chinese foreign policy. Factional differences have only tenuous connections with the commonly agreed goal of modernization, but they will probably determine much of the character and relative success of modernization efforts over the decade.

Bureaucratism is the device that, to a degree, tames and rationalizes the excesses of Leninism and factionalism in China. But it is also a constant problem. As the country proceeds with modernization, modern methods of management will increasingly challenge Leninism's demands for extreme centralization and total politicization and factionalism's substitution of personalism for rationalism and efficiency in administration. These tensions tend to produce lowered ideological commitment, poor cadre morale, inadequate skill levels, inadequate and inaccurate information about China's society and economy, rank inefficiency, alienation of the bureaucracy from the masses and the Party, and widespread corruption.

The Party's answer to these problems will probably be to stress again one or another form of what Harding terms "internal remedialism:" indoctrination, rectification, and political campaigns directed against the bureaucracy to reform itself from within, organizationally and personally, and be more responsive to Party directives and goals. The campaign style characteristic of internal remedialism seems to imply a more "leftist," "inward," and ideological stance toward modernization of the economy and, perhaps, in foreign affairs as well.

During the 1983–1993 decade, it appears likely that the administrative controls and repressive features of Leninism must strengthen as ideology weakens, as has happened in the Soviet Union. Second, factionalism probably will persist within the framework of collective leadership. A Chinese Stalin seems unlikely, although the intensity of factional differences will probably increase with modernization. The more highly educated managers, scientists, and technicians will rise to do battle with the remnants of old groups—Cultural Revolution cadres, senior Army leaders, and ideologues, resulting in a weakening of the rough consensus that existed in the half decade since Mao's demise. Administrative Leninism[5] will seek to counter the disunity attendant upon more open competition for power. Third, the problem of bureaucracy will probably rise, as the Party again stresses internal remedialism. This is particularly likely if, as seems probable, the promotion of a mixed economy on the basis of market-based rationality together with Party-based administrative control progressively fails.

There is the likelihood of growing instability in Chinese politics, as bureaucratism and factionalism combine in an atmosphere of economic crisis to force the Party to adopt more stern, repressive measures. The imperatives of modernization stand for the most part directly opposite the tripartite nature of Chinese politics.[6] Thus, by 1993, China could well have entered a period of economic and political crisis. Once modernization is begun in earnest, it cannot be turned back or halted;[7] but it can be delayed by the weight of the past and by the configuration of the polity to deal with modernization. That weight is enormous, as Chinese history for over a century and a half has shown, and that configuration—as described here—is not designed to be efficiently responsive to the enormous demands and changes imposed by a modernizing process begun, paradoxically, by the Party's policy of the Four Modernizations.

DOMESTIC POLITICAL GOALS, OBSTACLES, AND ISSUES

In addition to the configuration of politics, how the domestic political situation evolves depends on the relationship between political goals, obstacles to those goals, and the specific issues they produce. The Party's goals for the next decade include, first and foremost, support for economic modernization as redefined by Zhou Enlai in the mid-1970s from one of the Party's major programs since 1949. The Party essentially has a compact with the Chinese populace to lead the country into full economic modernization by the early twenty-first century. If it fails, theoretically, it will have lost the right to rule. The demands of modernization, the losses of the Cultural Revolution, doubts among the population, and the general decline in revolutionary–ideological ardor[8] make the next decade the critical period. The new politico–economic edifice will be finished and decisive evidence will be coming in as to its efficacy.

Two other equally important goals of the Party are, one, preserving and re-energizing Party rule, and, two, restructuring the Party in terms of leadership, qualifications, and composition. The first is dependent on the success of economic modernization and how the Party comports itself internally. Party restructuring will require the following: installing a new and forward-looking leadership without losing the experience and commitment of the revolutionary generations; revising Party norms, consistent with Leninism, in the direction of democracy; encouraging the best of the newly educated youth to join the Party and accept Marxism-Leninism-Maoism; retraining cadres to compete with non-Party managers; and preserving overall Party unity in the face of persistent factionalism.

If the Party is able to reform itself and demonstrate reasonable short-term success with the Four Modernizations, it will be able to preserve its right to rule for some time. However, the prospects for economic success are not very good. There is a possibility that the Party will have to retreat to maintaining itself in power against popular will as it appears dangerously close to losing its mandate.[9]

OBSTACLES

Given the difficulty of fulfilling basic goals, the problem is even more fearsome when the traditional difficulty of keeping China unified is considered. The natural unity provided by the dominant Han culture and population is counteracted by the size of the country, the large percentage of land occupied by non-Han minorities, and the many regional differences, including spoken languages, even in the Han areas themselves. While there is little likelihood that such differences alone would cause insuperable difficulties—indeed modernization should tend to smooth out these differences—problems could arise if the central government were to insist on eliminating regional differences. Because the stakes get bigger as modernization proceeds, some regions may stand to gain more than others,[10] thus magnifying historical variations. While the problems should be put under the category of "problems of success," they often can be even more severe than "problems of failure." Just as an industrial enterprise can go bankrupt from too rapid expansion, so countries can break down into civil war from too rapid modernization.[11]

Another obstacle is the three-sided relationship between Party, Army, and government. Because of their shared experiences during the Chinese civil war, the same group of leaders have dominated all three institutions. Consequently, when serious differences occurred during the 1949–1976 era (as in local rebellions during the Cultural Revolution and the Lin Biao conspiracy), the Leninist norms of Party discipline prevailed. That will gradually change through the decade as the inter-institutional unity disappears as old leaders retire and pass on.[12] Second, the Party has consciously moved to remove the PLA from too great a role in politics by cutting its budget, stretching out military modernization, and moving the military back to the barracks and out into the field.[13] During this transition, resistance to being removed from politics, dissatisfaction with the priority of military modernization, and fears that it could not successfully cope with external security threats, could lead to conflict between the Party and the Army.

On the other hand, the military has still to live down completely the Lin Biao affair.[14] More importantly, it appears to understand the necessity of putting military modernization last among the Four Modernizations. Further, it has tolerated diminishing defense budgets since the early 1970s, even in the face of the Soviet military challenge, and has also gone along (albeit sometimes reluctantly) with the political-strategic opening to the United States. So long as military budgets are sufficiently high to allow reasonable progress in modernization and the acquisition of modern military technology, and the military continues to be respected by the Party and the populace, the military will not be a major domestic political problem during the decade.

As for the government, there are signs that suggest it will be a more independent actor than it has been in the past. The Party appears to want to withdraw to become, like the Yugoslav League of Communists, mostly a policysetting and appraisal organization, leaving the question of how best to carry out policies, as well as most matters of administration and organization, in the hands of various governmental bodies.[15] Moreover, with the installation of several new legal codes, the promulgation of a new state constitution, renewed activity of the courts, more frequent meetings of a more lively National People's Congress, and even the holding of contested elections at various local levels, it would seem that an increasing portion of the total political life of the country is shifting to the governmental sector,[16] a process that economic modernization should enhance during the decade. But it is unlikely that these trends mean "the government" will become an autonomous and equal third member of the Party-Army-government triad. The Party will still retain ultimate control of policy and will continue to dominate the government, probably from the inside through interlocking directorates and personal ties.

The third potential obstacle is generational differences. The "political" generations during the coming decade include (a) the pre-1949 political and military revolutionaries and the Party administrators of the early 1950s; (b) the large number who joined between the mid-1950s and Mao's death in 1976—especially the ideologues of the Cultural Revolution; and (c) the post-Maoist groups of younger, more highly trained technicians and managers. The politics of generations roughly revolves around the alliance of the old revolutionaries led by Deng Xiaoping with their chosen successors, the young manager-technicians, against the Cultural Revolution-era ideologues symbolized by Hua Guofeng. The old revolutionaries are fighting against time, since the "Grim Reaper" steadily gathers them in and since it takes time to train the youngsters and put them into positions of responsibility. The Cultural Revolution ideologues, on the other hand, also find time and circumstance not entirely in their favor, since the number of young successors will eventually increase to flood proportions and since the ideologues will never possess the proper qualifications to run a complex and modern China.

Over the decade, the generational issue could be submerged in other conflicts. On the other hand, the evidence of the early 1980s and of the Cultural Revolution indicate that the generation question must be taken seriously. Moreover, the contest soon will be conducted directly between the ideologues and the technicians, since the revolutionaries will largely have left the scene through death or enforced retirement. Chinese history indicates that young technicians, trained and returning from abroad, may arrogantly feel it their "right" to take over the country from their "unqualified" predecessors. In most every previous case,[18] such people were purged directly out of the system or assigned lower level positions of no important political power. This could happen again, despite the damage such a conflict would impart to modernization.

Intra-generational conflict, however, probably will not be severe. First, Leninism is an important force for unity, even among those younger Party members whose Marxism may be nominal. Second, the conflict will take place over the decade and thus not break out into the open. Third, the charismatic leadership necessary for overt confrontation is unlikely to develop since the coming era is one of increased emphasis on collectivism and rationality in decisionmaking. Finally, although there may be a generational overlay to factional conflict, factionalism will continue to dominate Chinese political life.

ISSUES

Together with economic questions, there are three specific political issues that should determine the direction of Chinese politics in the decade ahead. The first is the problem of personal leadership succession. Will the bias in Chinese politics toward personalist leadership, so consistently evident in the past, persist throughout the coming decade or will that tendency be replaced by one favoring collective leadership and the ever greater conversion of politics into administration? Both Leninism and factionalism point toward personalist leadership, as was plainly evident under Mao Zedong, Deng Xiaoping, and even Hua Guofeng; and the general direction of Chinese politics—and therefore economics and society—tended to reflect the personalities of these leaders. Bureaucratism leads to the replacement of one-man leadership with collective leadership and of personalism with process. Over the decade, two factors not previously present in China militate against the emergence of a new strong man. One is the reaction against the personalism of Mao Zedong. This is a vaccine that should hold its potency for most of the coming decade. The other is the probability that Deng can hold onto his power for much of the decade, which, combined with the two or more years it takes for political succession and the tendency of factions to counter each other's attempts to dominate the other, should result in a propensity toward collective leadership even more than is evident at present. Hence, the succession issue may not be as important as problems of political economy stemming from difficulties with the Four Modernizations policy.

The second issue is how to renew ideological enthusiasm among the populace and how to arrive at an agreed-on ideological synthesis within the Party. The Chinese have admitted to three crises: a lack of popular faith in Marxism-Leninism, a declining confidence that the Four Modernizations will be carried through, and a shortfall of trust in the Party's ability to run the country according to popular desires and in response to rational requirements. The consequences have been privatization and consumerism as a substitute for participation in politics and enthusiasm for economic construction; an increase in factionalism, loss of ideological verve, and higher levels of corruption within the Party; and the rise of the "philosophy of concrete benefits" in place of the altruism preached by Mao. If such trends were to continue, the Party would have to substitute raw coercion for lack of faith. Cynicism would be so rampant that the Party would eventually find it difficult to rule even in the minimum sense much less push the population into heroic efforts in the name of progress.

What is to be done? The Party must do the best possible job in modernization, namely, acting in a reasonably liberal, rational, and open manner and thus slowly gain back popular trust, confidence, and faith. However, China's economic and environmental limitations and the Party's problems with implementing needed economic reforms, irrespective of ideology, may not provide the necessary policy room and time for maneuver. The Dernberger analysis suggests the possibility of failure; the Party will have to reimpose direct Stalin-like discipline on the population, recentralize, and tighten Party rule. There are many indications—in culture, social policy, and education—that such a tightening process is already underway.[19]

How long can the Party go in two directions at once; one policy of liberalization-decentralization-rationalization in the economy and the supporting sectors and another of strict control-recentralization-discipline everywhere else? There is no good answer. One possibility for the coming decade may be for the Party to steer a middle course, deviating sometimes to the left and at other times to the right. The Party probably still has enough reserves of popular support and authority to get away with not addressing the issue frontally for a considerable time. Thus, what in analysis seems an intolerable contradiction may in reality be a serious but not insoluble difficulty. The experience of other states confirms that ruling classes can sometimes have it both ways. Taiwan and South Korea are two Asian countries that have followed successfully a policy of political and social conservatism along with economic liberalism. The older communist states—principally the Soviet Union—have long since discovered that one can have reasonable economic success (at least quantitatively) while practicing severe repression at home. The penalties are severe, as the Soviet case clearly shows, but extreme choices do not have to be made. This may be China's fate also.

The third issue is foreign policy. No state is immune to the influence on its domestic political system from foreign policy issues, the actions of important foreign states, and the general trends in regional and international systems. Most minor issues are dealt with at the foreign ministry level without influencing Chinese society directly. Our concern is with those issues that affect the overall orientation of Chinese policy, which will continue to be a subject of intense Party debate.

Since 1949, the major issue for China has been what its policy should be toward the two superpowers, the United States and the Soviet Union. During the 1950s, the decision was to lean far to the Soviet side in response to a perceived security threat from the United States, to ideological attraction to Stalin's Russia, and to offers of economic assistance from Moscow. In the 1960s, when the American security threat was perceived to have lessened somewhat, when the Russians were thought to have committed serious ideological errors, and when China wished to emancipate itself economically from Moscow, the policy was, roughly, to seek a path independent from both the superpowers. In the 1970s, the situation was roughly the reverse of the 1950s and policy was changed accordingly: now the Russians were the security threat, it was the Americans who could render important economic and technological assistance, and it was the more appealing ideologically. A lean to the United States policy was thus put into effect. The issue for the 1980s is whether, how far, and at what pace China should move away from too close an embrace by the United States and into a posture of relative equidistance from both Washington and Moscow in order to gain true independence from both. One implication is that China would have to adjust its Soviet policy, which means coming to terms with the Russians on at least some of their mutual differences in state and ideological matters. Already, movement away from the United States and toward the Soviet Union is perceived,[20] although not at the same pace or with regard to the same issues.

The issue for the 1983–1993 decade is how far to move away from America and how much to restore ties with Russia. Such a move would carry obvious security and economic implications for China, and these in turn could hold major risks for success of the Four Modernizations and for keeping China at peace. In the past, foreign policy differences have been issues between the various Party factions, but at no point were they decisive in redirecting domestic policy as a whole. It could be different in the 1980s were a proposed sharp movement away from the United States (over Taiwan) to come at the same time as an economic crisis. As modernization proceeds along presently envisaged lines, the degree of integration with the world economy and the supply of technology and capital from abroad will increase. If the proposed change in China's position between Washington and Moscow were coupled with major Soviet concessions on the border question and offers of Soviet capital infusion, factional confrontations could peak and a political crisis ensue. The outcome is unpredictable. The point, however, is that foreign policy could become one of the central political issues of the decade, along with the economy, succession, and ideology.

POLITICAL SCENARIOS FOR THE NEXT DECADE

From a myriad of possible paths of development for China during the 1983–1993 era, two or three reasonably distinct possible outcomes come to mind. First is the continuation of the present *laissez faire* pragmatism, directing all efforts to fulfilling the modified Four Modernizations program with a minimum of intra-Party strife. In this scenario, the Party would successfully postpone conflict between generations, regions, factions, and new claimants to power. The ideological crisis would be postponed and the residual loyalty of the populace would be retained by pointing to the near-term benefits of economic progress. Internal remedialism as a solution to the bureaucratic problem would be avoided. A liberalization-decentralization-rationalization policy would be continued, in spite of problems from continuing to open China to the infusion of international influence. There would be no decisive move away from the United States and no more than a marginal move toward the Soviet Union. This alternative presumes above all that the fruits of the present policies will ripen comparatively rapidly, that the economic and political adjustments and reforms adopted in the 1977–1982 period were basically "correct," and that the international environment would permit China to develop in relative peace and security (that is, the Soviets would not attack and the international economy would not fall further into the crisis of depression).

The second outcome would not be kind to China. The various conflicts previously noted would come to a head faster than anticipated and would feed upon each other. The environment, domestically and internationally, would not stand still but would actively upset the Party's programs and calculations. The policy of addressing each issue as it came up would lead to a series of disasters, as obstacles and issues crowded onto the agenda with such ferocity that decisionmaking fell into a style of reaction, which would soon turn into the lethargy of political paralysis. Stymied by disunity, carried along by events instead of seizing hold of its fate, and unable to solve economic problems, the Party would be unable to carry out a strong foreign policy and would thus become the ever more docile creature of the Russians and the Americans and of the rapid sweep of international events. The danger of having to fight a war for which China was unprepared would rise, as would the eventual emergence of a revolutionary situation at home. The Party would be unable to fulfill its promises in the economic sphere, as the fruits of its previous decisions would indeed ripen but turn out to be sour. Realizing that popular repression, discipline, and the substitution of ideological rectitude for pragmatism and rationalism would only exacerbate the problem, but not knowing what else to do, the Party leadership would lurch from crisis to crisis until finally confronted with the weakening of central control and the emergence of varying degrees of regional independence.

The third is, in some ways, a combination of the first two. Seeing that trends in the economy, in domestic politics and society, and in the international system were all inimical to carrying out a program of successful modernization at home and a strong policy abroad, the Party would change direction more or less abruptly in favor of repression, discipline, ideological primacy, internal remedialism in the bureaucracy, and recentralization in economic and political administration. The conflict between ideologues and technician-managers would be brought to a head through the unexpectedly early departure of the old revolutionaries, and would be won hands-down by the ideologues. With a probable charismatic strongman having suddenly arisen from their ranks and with support from disgruntled sectors of the military, the ideologues would impose modified bureaucratic Stalinism on the country. Renewed leftism at home and abroad would thus be the order of the day. A combination of ideological incentives and force would replace remuneration as the means to persuade citizens to do the Party's bidding;[21] the campaign style[22] would return with a vengeance, the latter-day emphasis on legality, small democratic freedoms, constitutionalism, and relatively wide scope of artistic creativity would gradually be whittled back down to its Maoist form; and the order of the Four Modernizations would possibly be revised in favor of heavy industry and weapons production instead of agriculture and light industry. Abroad, a deliberate decision would be taken to separate China from the United States, with all the implications that would follow for Sino–Western relations; and the Soviet Union would again stand as a "friend of China" (albeit hardly in the same sense as in the 1950s). A revolution in world politics would probably thus take place, and security and stability in Asia would be threatened as the Party would come to thrive on the putative existence of the American-led, capitalist threat.

To be sure, these three different futures are more starkly drawn, for expository purposes, than might be the case in reality. Nonetheless, for analytic purposes, the range of realistic options for China in the next decade will probably not fall outside these possibilities.[23] If the environment is not totally unfavorable, the first course, successful pragmatic muddling through, is more likely to be China's future than its unsuccessful opposite or the sharp reaction eventuating in Chinese-style, bureaucratic Stalinism. Finally, it should be noted that there is a certain progression among the various courses. Successful pragmatism may be succeeded by its opposite, which in turn may be replaced by Stalinism. But that would probably take place, if at all, in a time period longer than the decade 1983–1993.

NOTES

1. Still the best study of Leninism is Alfred J. Meyer, *Leninism* (New York; Praeger, 1957). Other good works are listed in the bibliography of Wolfgang Leonhard, *Three Faces of Marxism*, (New York: Holt, Rinehart, & Winston, 1970). The best study of Maoism as an adjunct of Leninism is John Bryan Starr, *Continuing the Revolution* (Princeton: Princeton University Press, 1978). It contains an authoritative bibliography.

2. *Beijing Ribao,* March 31, 1979, quoting speeches by Deng Xiaoping on March 16 and 30. These were constantly reiterated thereafter and inscribed in the documents of the Twelfth CCP Congress, September 1982.

3. The most authoritative work is Lucien W. Pye, *The Dynamics of Chinese Politics* (Cambridge, Mass.: Oelgeschlager, Gunn, & Hain, 1981). It has an extensive bibliography on the subject. See also, Andrew J. Nathan, "A Factional Model of CCP Politics," *The China Quarterly,* January–March 1973, pp. 34–66; William L. Parrish, "Factions in Chinese Military Politics," *The China Quarterly,* October 1973, pp. 667–679; and Tang Tsou, "Prolegomenon to the Study of Informal Groups in CCP Politics," *The China Quarterly,* January 1976, pp. 98–114.

4. Harry Harding, Jr., *Organizing China: The Problem of Bureaucracy, 1974–1976* (Stanford: Stanford University Press, 1981). The analysis and categories of these two paragraphs depend on this fine work.

5. The term arose first to describe the Soviet system after Stalin's terror had subsided. The question was whether a Leninist polity could survive without the irrational use of violence. See Alan Kassof, "The Administered Society: Totalitarianism without Terror," *World Politics,* July 1964, pp. 558–575.

6. The literature on modernization is legion. But there seems to be general agreement that it promotes the gradual emergence of a complex phenomenon, including rapid social and economic change—urbanization, spread of education and literacy, industrialization, increase in health standards, decline in death and birth rates and thus rapid population increase, etc.—spread of science and technology, gen-

eral rationalization of daily life, resurgence of nationalism, and mass-based democracy. See, in general, S. N. Eisenstadt, *Modernization: Protest and Change*
(Englewood Cliffs, N.J.: Prentice-Hall, 1966); Daniel Lerner, *The Passing of Traditional Society* (New York: Free Press, 1958); Marion Levy, *Modernization: Late-
comers and Survivors* (New York: Basic Books, 1972): Myron Weiner, ed., *Modernization: The Dynamics of Growth* (New York: Basic Books, 1966); and Cyril Black,
The Dynamics of Modernization (New York: Harper & Row, 1966).

7. This is the general conclusion of the author's survey of modernization in Asia from
1860 to 1980, as reported in his "Prolegomena to the Study of Modernization and
Asian International Relations," 35 pp., presented to Asian Studies Symposium,
Georgetown University, May 24, 1982.

8. See three papers presented to a conference, "The Limits of Reform in China,"
Woodrow Wilson International Center for Scholars, May 3, 1982: Hong Yung Lee,
"Deng Xiaoping's Reform of the Chinese Bureaucracy," David Zweig, "National
Elites, Rural Bureaucrats, and Peasants: Limits on Commune Reform," and Vera
Schwarz, "Reflections on the Intellectual Climate in China." See also Dorothy J.
Solinger, "The Fifth National People's Congress and the Process of Policymaking:
Reform, Readjustment, and the Opposition," paper presented to the 11th Sino–
American Conference on Mainland China, Taipei, June 7–11, 1982.

9. Michael B. Frolic, *Mao's People* (Cambridge: Harvard University Press, 1980); Fox
Butterfield, *Alive in the Bitter Sea* (New York: Times Books, 1982); Thomas Gold,
"China's Youth: Problems and Programs", paper presented at 11th Sino–American
Conference on Mainland China, June 7–12, 1980, 24 pp.

10. The Chinese Communist Party pledged in its early years in power to eliminate
regional differences, especially those allegedly the product of Western imperialist-
induced coastal development. Yet the regime found in subsequent years that such
inequities were very difficult to eliminate and were in fact the product of national—population, ecological, climatic, and resource—differences. After Mao,
Beijing came full circle, not only capitalizing on such differences, but even went
so far as to invite the same Western countries back in to invest in special export
processing zones that bore some resemblance to the semi-colonialism of yore. A
reaction against coastal dominance (Shanghai produces some 40 percent of China's industrial output) and Western investment seems inevitable.

11. That is what happened in Iran. It could happen in the Philippines. And—given
the Chinese leadership's past propensity to fight among itself—it could happen in
China too.

12. The Twelfth Party Congress in September 1982 created a new institution—advisory councils for old but venerated leaders to retire to. An increased proportion of
the old leadership should join these bodies in the middle 1980s. In any case, the
geriatric tables indicate that by late in the decade the "Grim Reaper" will have
taken most of them.

13. For a survey of these matters and a forecast of likely developments in the decade
under consideration, see the Thomas Robinson, "Chinese Military Modernization
in the 1980s," *The China Quarterly*, June 1980, pp. 231–252.

14. The trial of several of Lin's alleged accomplices and the linkage of them, through
the trial and in Party propaganda, with the "Gang of Four" served as a warning to
the military to keep out of politics. The military cannot do that, of course, so long
as the Chinese Communist Party and the state structure it runs are so closely tied
and so long as the Party leadership and the Army leadership are essentially one.
Nonetheless, the long-term trend is toward separation of the two institutions.

15. For these developments, see Frank Ching, "The Current Political Scene in China," *The China Quarterly,* December 1979, pp. 691–775; and Parris H. Chang, "Chinese Politics: Deng's Turbulent Quest," *Problems of Communism,* January–February 1981, pp. 1–21. If the results of the 12th Party Congress in late 1982 are any indication, however, the Party appears to have put aside such thoughts in favor of reassertion of totalistic leadership of every aspect of Chinese society or Leninism.

16. Jurgen Domes, "1976–1982: Evolution of a New CCP Line?", paper presented to the 11th Sino–American Conference on Mainland China, Taipei, June 7–12, 1982, 26 pp.

17. Michael Yahuda, "Political Generations in China," *The China Quarterly,* No. 80, December 1979, pp. 793–805; William W. Whitson, "The Concept of Military Generation," *Asian Survey,* November 1968; Robert A. Scalapino, ed., *Elites in the People's Republic of China* (Seattle: University of Washington Press, 1972).

18. Chinese who returned from the West in the late 19th and early 20th centuries, from the Soviet Union in the 1920s and early 1930s, and again from the Soviet Union in the 1950s, all suffered these fates.

19. See Lowell Dittmer, "China in 1981: Reform, Readjustment, Rectification," *Asian Survey,* January 1982, pp. 33–46; Stephen W. Mosher, "Birth Control: A View from a Chinese Village," *Asian Survey,* April 1982, pp. 356–368; William Parish, "Egalitarianism in Chinese Society," *Problems of Communism,* January–February 1981, pp. 37–53; Suzanne Pepper, "Chinese Education After Mao: Two Steps Forward, Two Steps Back, and Begin Again?," *The China Quarterly,* March 1980, pp. 1–56.

20. Thomas W. Robinson, "Why China Must Play its Soviet Card," *Far Eastern Economic Review,* March 4, 1982, p. xxx.

21. The Party has three incentives to persuade the citizenry to do its bidding: persuasion by ideological conviction and propaganda; increased monetary remuneration and perquisites; and force. Chinese politics have often been seen as a cynical variation among these. See Andrew Nathan, "Policy Oscillations in the PRC: A Critique," *The China Quarterly,* "Compliance Cycles in Rural Communist China: A Cyclical Theory," in Amitai Etzione, ed., *A Sociological Reader in Complex Organizations* (New York: Holt, Rinehart, & Winston, 1969), pp. 420–426.

22. The "campaign style" is the product of a number of influences, including the 3-part incentive structure noted just above, the legacy after 1949 of the Yenan-learned military orientation of the Party, and Mao Tse-tung's own personality. See, *inter alia* Michel Oksenberg, "The Political Leader," in Dick Wilson, ed., *Mao Tse-tung in the Scales of History* (New York, Cambridge University Press, 1977), pp. 70–116, especially pp. 88–94; Oksenberg, "Policy-Making Under Mao, 1949–68: An Overview," in John M. H. Lindbeck, ed., *China: Management of a Revolutionary Society* (Seattle: University of Washington Press, 1971); and Richard Solomon, *Mao's Revolution and the Chinese Political Culture* (Berkeley: University of California Press, 1971).

23. See the various examples in Nazli Choucri and Thomas W. Robinson, eds., *Forecasting in International Relations,* (San Francisco: W.H. Freeman, 1978).

Chapter 6

National Interests And Objectives Of The People's Republic Of China

*Thomas W. Robinson**

Three words express Chinese national interests in the 1983–1993 decade: development, security, and independence. Of these, the most important is development. Policy independence, while currently third in priority, is a major factor in decisions concerning the first two.

Since the foreign policy of economic modernization must attempt to foster optimum conditions for growth at home, it follows that China's most important positive goal will be to obtain the technology, capital, and management know-how from the best supplier, the capitalist West and in particular the United States. The most important negative goal is to avoid war or severe threat of war, and the accompanying destruction or economic crisis. The foreign policy of the Four Modernizations is thus one of peace and of balance of power. Because the American-led capitalist West is the only external means of deterring Soviet attack, some form of security cooperation, however attenuated, seems likely to continue until the Soviet threat has definitively subsided.

Security cooperation and the need for the West's economic assistance put severe limits on China's foreign policy freedom of action. If independence is to be satisfied in an era of relative Chinese weakness and superpower domination of world and Asian affairs, China must move,

*Sun Yat-sen Professor, Georgetown University School of Foreign Service and former Professor, the National War College.

delicately but deliberately, from exclusive dependence on the West and the U.S. and toward the middle ground between Washington and Moscow. That means, in turn, that China must constantly diversify and possibly slowly loosen economic ties with the West, looking wherever possible to internal resources as a step toward eventual economic self-reliance. China must re-emphasize its own military prowess, and (most importantly) must restore a measure of good relations with the Soviet Union.[1] China can then move on to secure some of her longer-term national interests and focus on the Third World. In Beijing's eyes, a China-led coalition of Third World states and political movements (Marxist or not) would offer the best hope for eventually replacing the superpowers' iron grip on global affairs with a "truly moral and progressive" process of revolution and development.

Difficult obstacles will severely impede the Party's rapid attainment of these foreign policy goals, the most important of which lies within China itself. Irrespective of domestic developments, China will remain in a relatively weak international position for most of the coming decade, if not beyond. That does not mean, however, that Beijing will not move as far and as fast as domestic circumstances permit. China most likely will deliberately loosen its security ties with the United States, emphasize economic relations with Japan and West Europe at the expense of America, and move slowly and carefully to normalize relations with the Soviet Union. But until China possesses a disposable surplus of readily projected power (particularly military),[2] there are severe limits as to how far the country can proceed.

International circumstances will act as additional impediments. Most of the 1980s in all likelihood will be dominated by the increasingly severe, and militaristic, competition between Washington and Moscow for influence and advantage. There is even a high probability of direct Soviet–American clashes as the Soviets strive to expand their influence, mostly through military means. The United States will counter with alliances, assistance to states threatened by the Soviets, its own rearmament program, and readiness to confront the opposition where necessary. China can do little during the period to change this basic fact, particularly because the Soviet Union seems likely to continue to threaten Chinese territorial integrity in the most severe and direct manner and to spread its influence along the Chinese periphery. China will therefore have restricted room for maneuver and must remain at least partially on the American side of the great divide.

Regionally, China is surrounded on practically all sides by strong, defensible, united, and rapidly growing states. Ten of the world's fifteen largest armies are Asian, and the world's most rapidly growing and modernizing nations are located around China's borders. Only Burma is weak. The rest are allied or aligned with the Soviet Union (India, Afghanistan, Mongolia, Vietnam), the United States (Japan, South Korea, Taiwan, the ASEAN states, Pakistan), or carefully balance between Moscow and Beijing (North Korea). Accordingly, China has little room for gain in Asia. And geography plus lack of available power prevents projection of Chinese influence much farther. It is doubtful that this situation will change greatly in China's favor during the next decade.

China will continue to be deficient in instruments of power. Its military will gain strength significantly during 1983–1993, but then will continue to fall behind in its efforts to catch up with the levels of technology and quality of equipment of the superpowers.[3] It is possible that by the 1990s Beijing will find its security even more compromised than in the early 1980s. This would be especially true were Japan to rearm and seek to play a major role in Asian security affairs.

As another instrument of power, China's trade, will grow vastly and thus have a greater influence on the international economy, so too will the trade of other nations. China will remain largely the object of other states' trade policies rather than a country operating independently on a world scale. It is doubtful China would be able to invest directly in distant lands or participate in international consortia. Direct foreign aid will probably remain low for lack of capital and because it buys comparatively little influence.[4] China could become a more significant arms supplier, albeit at the low end of the technology spectrum. Military assistance is an important instrument of policy, though the greatest degree of supplier influence is found at the high end of the spectrum.

China will thus be left with prestige and diplomacy as residual policy instruments. *If* the country moves ahead successfully in the Four Modernizations, it could reclaim the title of model for Third World development that it once held. The probabilities of that occurring depend, of course, on its domestic political and economic performance. China's cultural diplomacy is yet another potential major asset, especially in Sinic areas of Asia. China, however, has a recent past to live down, one that essentially neutralizes this instrument during the coming period.

Diplomacy—the art of maneuver and the efficient use of available power for national purposes in conditions of threat and uncertainty—is thus China's only hope for matching accomplishments with goals. States can often substitute a crafty diplomacy for lack of power,[5] as was done by the extraordinary personalities of Zhou Enlai and Mao Zedong. China's potential for maneuver in the middle ground between the superpowers is reasonably large, which enables it to attempt to use the Americans and the Russians against each other. There are enough issues on both sides (Taiwan, trade and capital infusion, the Korean question, the Chinese role in Southeast Asia, relations with India, competition for Japan's favor, rivalry with both Russians and Americans in the Third World and in international institutions, etc.) to provide China with the means to maneuver.

SECURITY

Given these goals, obstacles, and instruments of policies, what is China's security policy likely to be? Toward the United States and the Soviet Union, China is likely to move cautiously and gradually out of the American embrace and, equally carefully, to address on their merits the range of outstanding disputes with the Soviet Union. Given the innately insoluble nature of the Soviet military threat and the continuous lead of the United States and its allies in technology and capital infusion, it is doubtful whether China by the beginning of the next decade would go as far as a 50–50 tilt decisively toward the Soviet Union. Still, a 60–40 tilt toward the U.S. should provide most of the freedom of maneuver that the Chinese desire.

Policy toward the U.S. will involve the following: some, but not much, continued security cooperation against Moscow, depending on Soviet expansionist propensities; as much economic and technological assistance from America as can be obtained without fatally compromising economic independence; diplomatic attacks on the United States and siding with American opponents in the Third World and at the United Nations; and constantly goading Washington on the Taiwan issue. Policy toward the USSR will address, for the first time in two decades, the border question on its merits and engage in negotiations with Moscow over boundary location and troop disposition; progressively rising levels of trade with the Soviet Union, including restoration of a flow of Russian technology and capital into China in exchange for Chinese consumer goods and primary produce; improved cultural exchange, including training of an increasing number of Chinese in the Soviet Union; discussing a broad range of ideological questions; and a mixture of cooperation and competition in Southeast Asia—even in Vietnam—and on the Korean peninsula.

As for Japan and India, it is in China's best interest to befriend these countries, to encourage them to assist in China's economic modernization, to claim a portion of the middle ground surely to emerge as Japan progressively separates itself from the U.S. and India moves away from the USSR, and to prevent the possible outbreak of regional rivalry among the three. To these ends, China should seek, to the extent domestic conditions permit, Japanese investment, paying for Tokyo's capital and technology with Chinese oil and other commodities. China should further promote official visits and tourism, thus maximizing China's cultural and political influence in Japan. Toward India, China should forget twenty years of enmity and concentrate on solving the two border questions through viable compromise. Beijing and New Delhi could then proceed to establish an informal protectorate over Pakistan against Soviet penetration and to increase trade ties.

Yet Japan and India are bound to clash with China by virtue of their large size, location, and expanding economies. To the extent that Japan rearms beyond minimal defense needs, for instance, China could not help but feel threatened. India would no doubt wish to retain some Soviet military ties for insurance purposes, thus limiting Sino–Indian friendship. To the extent that China expands its range of interests and its projected power, Japan and India would suspect China of a desire to dominate Asia, and act accordingly to defend themselves and to rival China in sub-regional influence.

Vietnam and Korea are two representative problems for Chinese policy in the 1983–1993 era. Both seem intractible. China wants to extricate the Soviet military presence from Vietnam, separate Hanoi diplomatically and economically from Moscow, and compel the Vietnamese to retreat from Kampuchea and perhaps even from Laos. In general, China would break up the Indochinese federation, isolate Hanoi, and retain the potential to dominate all of Southeast Asia. While the probabilities are small, the more China does to threaten Vietnam, the more deeply Hanoi will be driven into the Russian embrace. Chinese efforts to separate the Vietnamese question from other Sino–Soviet issues would be resisted by both the Russians and the Vietnamese.

The Korean problem is even more difficult, and the potential for disaster, greater. The North Koreans are not overly susceptible to Russian or Chinese influence and could plunge the Peninsula into war at any moment, leading to another American–Chinese confrontation. The problem is exacerbated by the question of leadership succession in Pyongyang and by the diminishing time the North has before the South achieves rough military parity. American military involvement outside of Asia, for example, in the Middle East or the Carribbean, coupled with political disorder in the South (exaggerated though they may be by the North) could lead to conflict over which Beijing has little control, ideologically, militarily, or economically. Thus, under some circumstances, China's diplomatic future—and perhaps also the fate of the Four Modernizations—may be decided in Pyongyang and Jerusalem.

DEVELOPMENT

The "Four Modernizations" has been the Chinese Communist Party's principal domestic program since before Mao's demise, and economic development in general has been a central component of the Party's basic program since before 1949. Chinese foreign policy, therefore, has always contained an economic development component, which in the 1983–1993 decade will be focused on three specific goals. The first is to maximize importation of capital, technology, and management skills, all at minimum financial and political cost. The second is to generate trade levels and trade surpluses to pay for these imports without seriously overtaxing the domestic economy. And the third, within the framework of the first two goals, is to enhance China's economic independence and to separate imports from their social side effects.

To carry out these three goals, China must establish and maintain good economic relations with a wide range of foreign suppliers. Because of the West's limited ability to supply imports to meet China's essentially insatiable demands, and because of the emphasis on modernizing existing plant capacity, China must improve economic relations with the Soviet Union and East Europe. A second policy is to continue to send students abroad at early 1980s levels (about 20,000 worldwide). A reasonably high percentage of these students, perhaps 40 percent, are expected to return, although specific policies are needed to mitigate the undesirable social side effects of their changed attitudes.

A third policy is to increase exports to pay for the augmented level of imports for modernization. Because China will continue to be oriented largely to its own internal markets, severe limits will be set on the amount and kinds of imports. A fourth policy is not to become unduly dependent on foreign aid or the international capital market. The historic policy of maintaining rough equilibrium in bilateral trade relations will probably continue, although China will continually be confronted with the "threat" of deficits with capital suppliers.

A specific policy will undoubtedly be to develop offshore oil resources to help pay for imports, and the like. This means long-term contracts with multinational corporations, which must be as specific as possible to minimize their influence within China. Another policy would be to not import large numbers of whole plants or machines, but rather to seek single copies for experimentation, reverse engineering, and replication. In general, the acquisition of technology and management skills will take priority over capital importations.

As analyzed by Robert Dernberger (Chapter 7), many domestic obstacles exist to the attainment of these goals. These include excess fear of foreign influence, reluctance to go into debt, reluctance to allow foreign trade to become an important component of the economy, and a Soviet-style economic system. As long as self-reliance is a central principle, trade will not be accompanied by such benefits as rapid rates of growth, accelerated technological transformation, and the spread of modern practices throughout China as they were in such countries as Japan and Korea.

External obstacles include the reluctance of Western countries, in particular the United States, to significantly assist in the development of a country that is fundamentally anti-Western. The closer China's relationship is with the USSR, the less willing the United States will be to spend its own scarce resources on China and the more likely the United States will be to discourage its allies and clients also from supporting China. The Soviet Union and its clients cannot make up for all of this shortfall because of the general shortage of exportable capital and the relatively backward state of Soviet technology and management skills.

A large number of other developing countries also need the infusion of economic resources from the developed West. Since their demand is likely to increase over the next decade, and some will be more willing to accept short-term limits on their sovereignty for the sake of development, their competitive advantage will be greater than that of China.

From these goals, means, and obstacles five conclusions stand out concerning the next decade. First, foreign trade will probably be a slowly rising component of China's gross national product. Nonetheless, even a decade hence it will probably not be a very large percentage of the total, never going much over ten. China will continue to be more or less independent from the vagaries of international trade, finance, and the political-strategic relations behind them.

Second, the value of China's foreign trade volume is likely to be quite large in comparison not only with the past but also with trade volumes of its neighbors. China's trade would thus be very important. Among the Asian states, only Japan's trade would be greater. One implication is that China could use its newly-found trade muscle as an increasingly important tool of foreign policy, particularly with regard to Southeast Asia.

Third, diversification of trade partners will continue, principally by reincluding the Soviet Union and the East European countries. China's motivation is to trade according to its comparative advantages and to support its overall political policy of equidistance between, on the one hand, the United States and its allies and, on the other hand, the Soviet Union and its clients. Large increases in trade will occur with Third World countries, particularly those in Southeast Asia and Africa, for both economic (earning hard currency) and political (emphasizing

China as a Third World country and diversifying trade away from over-dependence on the West) reasons.

Fourth, China's desire for economic independence will complicate the use of foreign trade to speed up domestic economic modernization. Many leaders will argue that trade should never be allowed to become a large (above 15 percent) component of China's overall economy. They will be willing to sacrifice the general advantages of international trade—international specialization of labor and the comparative advantages of production—as well as to forego fully utilizing China's potential for obtaining development loans from foreign states and banks and the international banks. They would, finally, argue against allowing certain sectors of China's industry and agriculture and such geographic regions as the former coastal treaty ports from more or less exclusively orienting themselves toward the international market. Others will maintain that the expected gains are worth these risks, that they are controllable, and that China's overall modernization program will likely fail without them. For political-ideological reasons this debate will favor those for continued near-total economic independence. China's economic modernization, therefore, will proceed at a slower pace than might otherwise be possible. Unless other economic factors compensate, the overall success of the Four Modernizations might be jeopardized.

Lastly, China will continue efforts to balance its trade bilaterally as well as globally, which tends to cause trade to be highly politicized and economic rationality to take a back seat. Moreover, China will probably maintain its policy of punishing countries that trade with or diplomatically recognize Taiwan. Thus, China will probably forego the many advantages of trade with South Korea and others. There may be a relative de-emphasis on trade with the U.S. as the PRC distances itself politically from Washington and restores a measure of harmony with Moscow. There will be more debate about whether trade should serve only economic modernization or other foreign policy goals as well. The probable conclusion is that trade will continue to be an instrument of policy and never an economic end in itself.

POLICY INDEPENDENCE

China's global and ideological objectives in the Third World are fourfold. First, by uniting Third World countries around Chinese leadership, China would have an independent power base to counteract and ultimately shrink the influence of the two superpowers—a modern version of a strategy enunciated by Lenin in 1916. Second, if successful,

China could relatively quickly and easily spread its influence into regions and over distances otherwise impossible, given limits of its power. Third, it would help rekindle ideological enthusiasm in China, reinforcing the Party's continued monopoly of power and the sacrifices imposed on the populace in the name of modernization. Finally, Beijing would feel that it is part of the mainstream of future global affairs, which it and many others believe lies in the Third World.[6]

This policy means rendering support to most any state, movement, or issue that has a high anti-superpower content, regardless of specific political or ideological character. Thus, China supported Argentina against Britain, a U.S. ally, over the Falkland Islands, maintains reasonably close ties with the Palestine Liberation Organization because it is anti-Israeli and hence anti-American, and votes with Third World countries on such litmus paper tests as seabed mining rights at the Law of the Sea Conferences. Never mind that Argentina is governed by a strongly anti-communist military dictatorship, that the PLO is a terrorist group, or that China's own interests in redefining the Law of the Sea are closer to those of the United States and the Soviet Union than to the Third World states. Third World states too closely associated with the United States (South Korea) or the Soviet Union (Vietnam), pariah states (South Africa), or regional rivals (India) are not considered to be *bona fide* members of the "movement." In these cases, China will continue to distinguish between the "people" and their "rulers" in a traditional united front from below to attempt to separate the two and stand in good stead with the former.[7]

Another policy characteristic is China's attempts to join such Third World organizations as the Group of 77 at the U.N. and the Non-Aligned Nations Movement, even though these organizations are sometimes led by states and leaders (e.g., Cuba and Fidel Castro) who are strongly opposed to China. The idea is to overcome such opposition, especially when it is Soviet-sponsored, to become a full-fledged member, and finally to succeed to its leadership.

The many obstacles to China's Third World policy are principally of Beijing's own making. Chinese leaders assume some mythical unity of the Third World in accord with the Maoist Three Worlds thesis,[8] but the world does not divide into such neat categories, nor is the Third World a single entity. There are "genuine" Third World states (Tanzania), solidly capitalist strongly anti-Communist Third World states (Saudi Arabia), solidly communist but strongly anti-Chinese Third World states (Cuba), Newly Industrializing Countries at the borderline of the Third World (Singapore), "fourth world" countries whose GNPs are and will continue to be exceedingly low (Bangladesh), and many other categories. The Third World is partially a myth and is destined to become even more so during the 1980s, which flies in the face of the Chinese theory.

Another obstacle is the suspicion by many third country leaders of Chinese motives. The competition for leadership of the "movement" is severe and few want to see the Chinese claiming the prior right of leadership. With the Soviet Union so influential in many Third World organizations, there is great reluctance to allow the Chinese through the door. Internal disunity would be the only consequence.

The major problem is that most of Beijing's foreign policy energies during the coming decade must go into security and development, with little left over for investment in the Third World. One cannot conduct a foreign policy cheaply, or at least not for very long.

Another obstacle is that a successful development policy must emphasize good ties with the West and eventually with the Soviet Union and East Europe. A successful third world policy would negate that same emphasis. Since China cannot for long have it both ways and since development policy is much more central to China's future, third world policy will have to take a distinct back seat. China will still be interested in a policy of independence, but it will have to pursue that goal through some means other than unity with and leadership of the Third World.

These obstacles will take their toll on China's interest in policy independence in the decade ahead. China will have to fall back on security and development or else find some other way to claim global ideological leadership. It is likely that by the early 1990s the goals of Chinese foreign policies will be recognized, inside and outside the country, for what they are: security, development, and influence, motives little different from those of every other state. At that point, a new era in Chinese foreign policy will have begun.

NOTES

1. Thomas Fingar, ed., *China's Quest for Independence* (Stanford: Stanford University Press, 1979), Chapters by Fingan, Harding, and Fenwick; Thomas Gottlieb, *China's Foreign Policy Factionalism and the Origins of the Strategic Triangle* (Santa Monica, Calif.: The Rand Corporation, 1976); Thomas W. Robinson, "Political and Strategic Aspects of Chinese Foreign Policy," in Donald C. Hellman, ed., *China and Japan: A New Balance of Power* (Lexington, Mass.: D. C. Heath, 1976); H. Lyman Miller, "Chinese Foreign Policy Factionalism and Soviet Options in China," ms., 1980.
2. Thomas W. Robinson, "American Policy Toward the Soviet Union and China in Asia," *Asian Pacific Community,* (Winter, 1981), pp. 1–14, and "American Policy in the Strategic Triangle," in Richard A. Melanson, ed., *Neither War Nor Detente?:*

Soviet–American Relations in the 1980s (Charlottesville, Va.: University of Virginia Press, 1982), pp. 112–134.

3. Seymour J. Deitchman, *New Technology and Military Power: General Purpose Military Forces for the 1980s and Beyond* (Boulder, Colo.: Westview Press, 1981).
4. John F. Cooper, *China's Foreign Aid* (Lexington, Mass.: D. C. Heath, 1976).
5. Many examples come to mind: Tallyrand and Castlereigh at the Congress of Vienna; Metternich in the 1830s; Trotsky in the early 1920s; Hitler before 1939; Chou En-lai at the 1974 Geneva Talks; and Kissinger during Watergate.
6. Roger Hansen, *Beyond the North–South Stalemate* (New York: McGraw-Hill, 1979), and Robert W. Tucker, *The Inequality of Nations* (New York: Basic Books, 1977) are two major works, taking contrary approaches.
7. J. D. Armstrong, *Chinese Foreign Policy and the United Front Doctrine* (Berkeley: University of California Press, 1980).
8. King C. Chen, ed., *China and the Three Worlds* (White Plains, N.Y.: M. E. Sharpe, 1979).

/

Chapter 7

The Domestic Economy And The Four Modernizations Program

Robert F. Dernberger*

Domestic economic policies and the success they achieve in the modernization of China's economy will be a major determinant of that country's foreign policy and international relations over the next decade, according to China's leaders. Mao's hand-picked successor, Hua Guofeng, emphasized in 1978 that economics—not politics—must be in command. "In order to make China a modern, powerful socialist country by the end of the century, we must work and fight hard in the political, economic, cultural, military, and diplomatic spheres, but in the final analysis what is of decisive importance is the rapid development of our socialist economy."[1] In January 1980, Deng Xiaoping listed the three major tasks facing the leadership: to oppose hegemonism, bring about the return of Taiwan, and step up the economic modernization of the economy, but then pointed out that, "The crux of these three major endeavors lies in economic construction, the main prerequisite for the settlement of our international problems."[2]

A forecast of the economic policies China's leaders will adopt and implement over the coming decade and their possible success is at best a knowledgable guess. However, there are three known determinants of China's future economic policies. First, the general characteristics of the economy—the resource base, the economic system, and China's

*Professor of Economics, University of Michigan.

level of economic development—are unlikely to undergo any dramatic changes. Second, the principal short-run and fundamental long-run economic problems which China's policymakers must attempt to solve are unlikely to change dramatically. Third, the historical record of attempts to solve these economic problems over the last five years provides informative indicators of the policies the post-Mao leadership are likely to implement.

RESOURCE BASE[3]

China's energy resources are largely its coal reserves and the hydroelectric power potential of its rivers, despite the publicity given its offshore oil deposits. Although the world's third largest consumer and fourth largest producer of energy, the Chinese could go on exploiting their coal reserves at the present rate of growth in production for another century and their current hydroelectric power capacity is less than six percent of China's "economically exploitable" potential.[4] With few exceptions, China is richly endowed in ferrous and non-ferrous metals and in non-metallic raw materials. There are locational and quality problems, as well as technological and capital cost problems associated with the exploitation of these resources; nonetheless, in terms of its resource base China "can be considered an industrial giant."[5]

ECONOMIC SYSTEM

During the past three decades, China's leaders have been engaged in a major program of economic development using the economic system they transplanted from the Soviet Union in the mid-1950s, as modified to meet China's special economic and political conditions. Within this system, the means of production in the industrial sector are nationalized and run by public managers who are assigned production targets determined by the state's bureaucratic planning administration; agricultural production is collectivized and the collectives are assigned plans for cropping, yield, delivery quotas sales and tax payments to the state; trade—the purchase and distribution of key commodities including all producers' goods, most major agricultural products, and all foreign trade—is monopolized by the state's trading agencies under a unified state supply plan; public finance is unified in the state budget, with the profits of state enterprises collected as budget revenue and allocated as unilateral grants for investment projects or as subsidies to cover losses incurred by state enterprises; prices are set by the state and workers are hired by the state's labor bureaus and assigned to factories where they are paid wages set by the state. Some interpret the economic reforms introduced in recent years as an indication that this economic system will be different soon. In fact, the reforms which have been *implemented* only supplement the system with incentives systems, market forces, and private sector activities; they do not abandon the basic system of central control and the planned allocation of resources.[6] This policy was stated by Premier Zhao Ziyang at a conference on Industrial and Transportation Work (March 1982):

> We have domestically implemented the policy of activating our economy, delegating some power to the local authorities and enlarging the enterprise's decision-making powers for the purposes of whipping up the enthusiasm of the local authorities. . . . Efforts to expand decision-making powers and activate the economy are also apt to . . . weaken and depart from the state's unified plan, to interfere with and break up the unified market of socialism and to affect our efforts to take the whole country and the overall situation into consideration. . . . Ours is a unified socialist nation. We must have a unified plan and a unified domestic market. . . . In order to strengthen centralization and unification in economic work, we must adhere to the overall plan on major issues while allowing freedom on minor issues. . . . The products to be transferred according to state plans, including farm and sideline products, must be transferred strictly according to such plans. . . . The commodity price and revenue system must be centralized and unified. . . . No matter what reform is to be carried out, the general guideline is to combine the strengthening of centralization and unification with the activation of the economy and to bring into full play the initiative of the localities, departments, enterprises, and people under the guidance of state planning and the principle of taking the whole country into account.[7]

Experimentation with economic reform of China's basic Soviet-type economic system is being conducted in order to improve its results, not to replace it with a different economic system.

LEVEL OF ECONOMIC DEVELOPMENT

China was an underdeveloped country in 1949, remains an underdeveloped economy today, and is unlikely to change significantly in the coming decade.[8] As Table 5.1 illustrates, considerable economic

Table 5.1 Selected Macro-Economic Indicators

	1952	1957	1965	1970	1975	1981
Gross Value of Output[a] in constant 1952 prices[c]	82.7	124.1	198.4	311.6[b]	450.4	691.9
	82.7	114.6	183.2	263.6	381.0	585.4
National Income[d] in constant 1952 prices[c]	58.9	90.8	138.7	199.2[b]	250.5	388.0
	58.9	83.8	117.5	168.5	218.7	305.5
Ratio: Gross Value Output to National Income	0.71	0.73	0.70	0.64	0.56	0.56
Rate of Consumption[e]	.786	.751	.729	n.a.	.661	.700
Consumption[f]	46.3	62.9	85.7	—	144.6	213.9
Population[g]	574.8	646.5	725.4	825.3	919.7	996.2
Labor Force[g]	207.3	237.7	286.7	344.2	381.7	405.8[h]
in Agriculture	173.2	293.1	234.0	278.1	294.6	294.3[h]
Labor force as share of population	0.36	0.37	0.40	0.42	0.42	0.42[h]
Labor force in Agriculture as share of the labor force	0.84	0.81	0.82	0.81	0.77	0.73
Per capita national income[i]	102.5	129.6	162.0	204.2	237.8	306.7
Per capita consumption[j]	80.5	97.3	118.1	—	157.2	214.7

Table 5.2 Average Annual Rates of Growth

	1952/ 1957	1957/ 1965	1965/ 1970	1970/ 1975	1975/ 1981	1957/ 1975	1952/ 1981
Gross Value of Output	6.7	6.0	7.5	7.6	7.4	6.9	7.0
National Income	7.3	4.3	7.5	5.4	5.7	5.5	5.8
Consumption	6.3	3.9	5.4^k		6.7	4.7	5.4
Population	2.4	1.5	2.6	2.2	1.3	2.0	1.9
Per capita national income	4.8	2.8	4.6	4.7	4.3	3.4	3.9
Per capita consumption	3.9	2.5	2.9^k		5.3	2.7	3.4

Table 5.3 Total Factor Productivity in Industry

(Indices with 1952 = 100)

	1957	1965	1975	1979
Gross Value of Industrial Output (constant prices)	189.5	344.4	819.3	1146.2
Net Value of Fixed Asset in Industry (constant prices)	220.4	651.4	1482.1	2014.8
Labor Employed in Industry	246.7	242.7	527.6	609.6
Total Factors^l	171.2	324.9	845.4	1077.5
Total Factor Productivity	110.7	106.0	96.9	106.4

Table 5.4 Annual Rates of Growth in Total Factor Productivity

1952/1957	1957/1965	1975/1979	1957/1975	1952/1979
+2.5%	−0.5%	+2.4%	−0.7%	+0.2%

Sources for Tables 5.1–5.4: State Statistical Bureau, "Communique on Fulfillment of China's 1981 National Economic Plan," *Beijing Review,* Vol. 25, No. 20, May 17, 1982.

Annual Economic Report on China (1981), Chinese edition, Hong Kong, 1981.

China Yearbook, 1981, Chinese edition, Shanghai, 1981.

Notes for Tables 5.1–5.4: ªGross value of output in agriculture and industry, in billion yuan. 1952 in 1952 prices; 1957 and 1965 in 1957 prices; 1970, 1975, and 1981 in 1970 prices. ªAuthor's estimate. Average annual rates of growth for the gross value of agricultural and industrial output and national income for 1966–1970 and 1971–1975 are given in "Ups and Downs of Some Major Economic Targets (1953–1979)," a table presented in *Beijing Review,* No. 12 (23 March 1981), p. 25. Using the rate of growth in 1966–1970 and the absolute level in 1965 and the rate of growth in 1971–1975 and the absolute level in 1975, the gross value of agricultural and industrial output in 1970 is estimated as 313.8 and 309.4 billion yuan, respectively. The estimate presented here is the mid-point between these two estimates. The same procedure is followed to estimate national income in 1970, resulting in the mid-point between an estimate of 207.6 and one of 190.8 billion yuan. ᶜMy estimates. Conversion of values in other than 1952 prices in this table into 1952 price equivalents based on following price index (*Annual Economic Report of China* (1981), VI-23): 1952 = 112.1; 1957 = 121.4; 1965 = 132.3; 1975 = 128.4; and 1979 = 130.9. Index for 1981 obtained by multiplying above index for 1979 by 1.06 and that product by 1.024; price growth has occurred in the past three decades. For a quarter of a century, the average annual growth rate of the gross value of output (in constant prices) was 7.0 percent, or almost 6.0 percent when the effect of double counting and the decline in the ratio of net output to gross output is considered. Total consumption also increased at an average annual rate of more than 5.0 percent, despite a 5.0 percent increase in the accumulation rate. Converting these aggregates to a per capita basis to account for population growth, per capita national income increased by about 4.0 percent a year and consumption by 3.0 percent.

These results mean the Chinese used Stalin's model to achieve high rates of accumulation, the rapid accumulation of fixed capital, and, thus, rapid rates of growth. Benjamin Ward and Hollis Chenery argue that these results are the same as those achieved wherever the Soviet model has been adopted and are largely due to the one-time shift from a low to a high rate of accumulation. These high rates are not sustainable and thus dissipate after a few decades.[9] Moreover, these relatively high growth rates are largely due to an increase in factor inputs, especially fixed capital. A better indicator of sustained economic development is sustained growth in factor productivity, the complement of increasing efficiency *and* technological change. In industry, factor inputs increased more rapidly than did outputs, while total factor productivity declined by approximately 0.7 percent a year in 1957–1975.

Thus, even if the Chinese were able to maintain the growth rates achieved over the past three decades over the next decade, China would

---

increases for 1980 and 1981, respectively, reported in State Statistical Bureau's annual reports on results of the economic plan in 1981 and 1981. The resulting index for 1981 with 1952 = 100 is 127. 1970 price index with 1952 = 100 calculated on basis of table in *China Yearbook*, 1981 (p. 222) showing 1980 price index with 1970 = 100 was 111.7 and with 1952 = 100 was 131.4; resulting 1970 price index with 1952 = 100 is 118.2.
[d]Net material product in industry, agriculture, construction, transportation and communications, and commerce. Billion yuan in current prices. 1981 figure is a preliminary estimate.
[e]One minus rate of accumulation. Source for rate of accumulation in 1981: Zhao Ziyang, "The Present Economic Situation and the Principles for Future Economic Construction, *Beijing Review*, No. 51 (21 December 1981), p. 11.
[f]Billion yuan. In 1952 prices, rate of consumption times national income in constant prices.
[g]Million people.
[h]1979 instead of 1981.
[i]Yuan, in 1952 prices. National income in constant prices divided by population.
[j]Yuan, in 1952 prices. Total consumption divided by population.
[k]Average annual rate of growth in 1965–1975.
[l]Capital and labor combined in total factor index at weights of 0.333 and 0.667, respectively. These are the relative factor shares in national income that Kuznets found for the underdeveloped countries included in his statistical sample. Simon Kuznets, *Modern Economic Growth* (New Haven, Conn.: Yale University Press, 1966), p. 405.

still be an underdeveloped country in 1993. After three decades of annual growth in per capital national income and consumption of 3.9 and 3.4 percent, respectively, per capita national income in 1981 was still only U.S.$175 (official exchange rate), while consumption per capita was $123.[10] By 1993, at these rates, per capital national income and consumption would be (1981 dollars) $277 and $184, respectively, and it would take until the year 2015 to reach a per capita income of $1000.[11] Economic development is a long-run cumulative phenomenon that China's leaders must deal with for *several* decades to come.

DOMESTIC CONSIDERATIONS: ECONOMIC POLICY QUESTIONS

In the coming decade, economic policies in China must attempt to sustain the growth trends of the past three decades, as well as cope with the many serious economic problems created or exacerbated by the development strategies and policies the Chinese have pursued throughout these decades.

Short-run Economic Problems

Most of China's short-run economic problems result from economic waste and inefficiencies, which are due to the inappropriate allocation of resources (allocative inefficiencies) and to the inappropriate management, use, and coordination of resources once they are allocated (*X*-inefficiencies).

Allocative inefficiencies, when compared with the maximum possible results, are due to errors made (1) in the division of national income into accumulation and consumption, (2) in the allocation of investment, (3) in the allocation of inputs to the units of production, and (4) in the mix of goods and services produced. The Soviet-type economy has no automatic system to correct for the allocative errors of the central planners. Once these allocative inefficiencies accumulate to the extent they must be corrected or further growth will be impossible, the planners do not have a set of rational or scarcity prices to use in making the necessary calculations for achieving "rationality" in their decisions. The attempt to correct for these accumulated allocative inefficiencies by decentralization, or giving those who directly manage the units of production more authority to make allocative decisions, does not solve the problem, as long as their decisions also are based on the system of irrational or non-scarcity prices.

Chinese press reports and the speeches of China's leaders over the last few years make it clear that allocative inefficiencies had accumulated to serious levels by the end of the 1970s and had become even more serious than was true in other Socialist countries. Chief among these problems is the excessive rate of accumulation maintained by the Chinese planners. Despite the 2.7 percent annual increase in per capita consumption for 1957–1975, much of this increase was due to an increase in employment in the modern sector as a share of the total labor force. More meaningful to the population are the statistics concerning their basic necessities:

> For nearly all of the twenty years from the Second Five-Year Plan period (1958–62) to the downfall of the Gang of Four in 1976 there was little or no rise in living standards. Each peasant's annual grain ration remained for a long time at around 400 *jin* or 200 kilograms of unprocessed grain . . . and the consumption of vegetable oils, eggs, and aquatic products, according to our estimates, has not returned to the 1957 level.[12]

Industrial workers fared no better than the peasants:

> In the 21 years from 1957 to 1978, the average per capita grain supply in urban areas dropped 3.2%; the supply of vegetable oil decreased 33.3%; the supply of cotton cloth decreased 2%. And this level of supply was maintained only by reducing supply to the countryside and importing grain, edible oils, and cotton.[13]

In the next decade, China's policymakers must achieve *an increase* in the standard of living to make up for their past neglect and *sustain this increase*—critical to China's modernization—over the long run.

The traditional Stalinist strategy of high rates of accumulation requires the present generation to sacrifice increases in the standard of living for the sake of accumulation, in order to bring about eventual increases in consumption that will exceed levels obtainable in the long run by means of a more balanced growth strategy. After 1949, China's planners allocated such an excess in investment to the productive sectors that they not only failed to build a fixed capital base that would yield rapid and self-sustained growth, but they created a structure of production that threatened to preclude future growth. Because of low agricultural investments, the provision of foodstuffs for the population failed to provide a per capita increase in consumption, and industrial facilities utilizing agricultural products as inputs had relatively low capacity utilization rates. Inadequate transportation investment meant that goods in short supply in one location sat in warehouses in another location, causing production facilities to shut down. Industrial facilities had to close down during periods of energy short supply, and the shortage of building materials led to a considerable lengthening of project completion time, which tied up sizable investment funds. Their allocation of investment resulted in a structure of production in the late 1970s that was out-of-balance, creating serious problems in equating supply and demand throughout the economy.

In any Soviet-type economy these sectoral imbalances are compounded by the difficulty of getting supply to equal demand for particular commodities—the need to make commodities available to those who need them at the right time and place. China's level of development, size of the economy, excessive bureaucratic structure, and style of administration (let alone decisionmaking), poor statistical network, and lack of qualified personnel make these problems even more growth-inhibiting. Since the Chinese are likely to retain the basic elements of a Soviet-type economy, they need to pursue investment priorities that will achieve greater balance in the productive capacity among sectors at the micro-economic level.

Most planners in Soviet-type economies attempt to restrict dependence on foreign trade. Under the Maoist principle of self-dependence, foreign trade was a necessary evil; imports were limited to essentials not available domestically and exports to those necessary to pay for the imports.[14] Since 1949 and in the mid-1970s in particular, China has exhibited one of the lowest foreign trade dependency ratios in the world, and thus has forgone the significant economic benefits of international specialization in production. Although unlikely to pursue an open economy strategy, China's leaders face the problem of better integrating China into the world economy to reduce the real resource costs and the time required to achieve China's modernization.

Of even greater consequence was China's policy of self-sufficiency that restricted the borrowing of foreign technology. As Kuznets has argued, the acquisition, implementation, and generation of new technology is a major cause of significant and sustained increases in total factor productivity, a necessary condition for economic modernization. An essential step in the process is to determine how borrowed, foreign technology is adapted by means of innovation to meet indigenous circumstances and needs.[15] Yet the Maoist principle of self-sufficiency significantly restricted the borrowing of modern technology, especially after the break in 1960 with the USSR.

Thus increased growth in the agricultural sector came largely from a more intensive use of traditional technology. In industry, the Chinese

relied upon a combination of large-scale, modern, single product industries selectively imported; medium-scale, multiproduct enterprises inherited in 1949 that utilize old fixed capital and outdated technology;
and small-scale, rural industries that were claimed to utilize indigenous technology.[16] However, Soviet-type economic systems are weak in
incentives that would lead enterprises using outdated and inefficient
technology to innovate and catch up with those enterprises in the same
industry using more advanced and efficient technology. The poor record
to date of transferring technologies has left present Chinese leaders to
face the difficult problem of modernizing China's existing production
capacity, keeping pace with technological developments abroad, and establishing an indigenous research and development sector for providing new technology. The solution will not be easy to find; but it lies at
the heart of economic modernization in China.

The Maoist principle of self-sufficiency also made a virtue of limiting
specialization and trade both within and among provinces and economic regions. For example, truck factories built throughout China attempted to produce as many of their major inputs as possible. Agricultural areas better suited for non-grain crops were forced to raise
sufficient grain to meet their own needs. Thus, significant increases in
efficiency or output can be obtained by promoting greater specialization
in production and creating the necessary transportation and trading
system to make this specialization in production and trade possible.

Another problem is that Socialist planners—like businessmen in
market economies—have periods of optimism and pessimism caused by
poor agricultural years, politics, balance of payments problems, and so
on, which result in significant swings in the level of central investment
by these planners. These swings are amplified by the pendulum nature
of the political struggle between the two wings of the Party. These
swings over the three decades after 1949 led to alternating periods
of "great leaps" followed by retrenchment accompanied not only by
changes in the level of investment in a single year of more than 50 percent, but by major institutional and economic policy changes as well.[17]
Thus, the present leadership must create a somewhat stable pattern
of organizational and economic policies and a set of decisionmaking
guidelines based on economic criteria so as to insulate—as much as
possible—the economy from the waste and inefficiencies of such sudden
shifts in objectives.

Given the allocation of capital, inputs, and labor to the individual
unit of production, as well as the technology it has to work with, why
does China fail to achieve its potential output? Obvious in any visit to a
Chinese factory are the problems of X-inefficiency. Inexperienced managers and inexperienced and unskilled workers, who must acquire the

necessary experience and skills by "learning-by-doing," did not reduce the problem of X-inefficiency in the Chinese economy, they only made it worse over time.

Due to interference in the day-to-day operations of the unit by either the Party or the Revolutionary Committee, able managers were forced to "stand aside" and not impose measures which would have improved productivity and the quality of output. Once hired, the workers received their fixed wage in a guaranteed job for life. Promotions and monetary bonuses for outstanding work were "vestiges of capitalism." Work was organized not with individual workers assigned specialized tasks according to their skills and engaged in continuous serial production, but with work gangs of interchangable workers. Production lines were run only to move work from one position to another and work done on machines was done periodically in batches. Industrial enterprises involving specialized work assignments and serial production had exceptionally high rejection rates of the output that was produced and were frequently shut down due to lack of maintenance and repairs.[18]

While not attributing the waste and inefficiencies in China's economy solely to problems of X-inefficiency alone, the following indicators suggest these problems are, nevertheless, serious.[19] In 1976–1979, every 100 yuan of investment in fixed assets increased national income by 34 yuan, down from 52 yuan in 1953–1957. Raw material consumption per yuan of output was 56 percent in 1979 compared to 44.3 percent in 1953–1957. In terms of energy consumption per 100 million yuan of output value, 95,000 tons of standard coal were required in 1979, compared to 62,000 tons in 1953–1957. Finally, 31 yuan of circulating capital was required for every 100 yuan worth of output in 1979, compared to only 17 yuan in 1956. Table 5.1 shows total factor productivity in industry declined by 0.7 percent a year between 1956 and 1975. At the end of 1978, 24 percent of the state enterprises were operating at a loss. According to the State Statistical Bureau's Communiqué on the Fulfillment of the 1981 Economic Plan, labor productivity in industry declined by almost 2 percent in 1981. The number of state enterprises suffering losses increased to 27 percent of the total, and approximately 50 percent of the indices for material consumption per unit of output rose. The above indicators support the argument that waste and inefficiencies due to allocative and X-inefficiencies were becoming worse over time.

Long-run, Fundamental Economic Problems:

Solving the short-run problems will not assure the successful modernization of China's economy. Modernization also requires the solution of several fundamental long-run economic problems. Yet these long-run fundamental economic problems will impose constraints on China's policy options in trying to solve those short-run economic problems. For example, since 1949, agricultural production has been increased by the intensive expansion of traditional technology—considerably more labor and organic fertilizer inputs per unit of output and a considerable increase in multiple cropping. While this achieved the yield potential of traditional technology, it did not achieve the potential of modern scientific technology. The Chinese are now tackling this problem, but it is more difficult. The population is twice as large as in the 1950s, over 70 percent of the labor force is still engaged in agriculture, and yet the cultivated area is slightly smaller. Solutions must be found to short-run problems that do not exacerbate the long-run problems.

Population and agriculture were long-run economic problems in 1949 and their ultimate solution still remains uncertain. The Chinese have reduced the annual population growth rate from 2.4 percent in 1952–1957 to 1.3 percent in 1975–1981 (see Table 5.1) and set a zero rate of increase as their goal by the end of the century. Yet further decreases will be difficult to achieve due to the age and sex structure and to agricultural reforms. Even if the present rate of growth were to decline steadily over the decade by 0.5 percent, the problems would not be much affected.[20]

At the same time, China's large population will mean serious employment problems and a considerable increase in the demand for basic necessities. Even though non-agricultural employment increased by 53 million in 1952–1975, the agricultural labor force increased by 121.4 million. This increase in the agricultural labor force means that the cultivated area per worker declined from 0.6 hectare in 1952 to 0.3 hectare in 1975. While the average productivity (in constant prices and gross value of output) of the agricultural labor force declined by 17 percent over this same period,[21] when converted to the net value of output and when the tremendous increase in work days per year is taken into account, the marginal product of labor effort declined. "According to preliminary [Chinese] estimates, there will be more than 100 million surplus laborers in the countryside by the end of the present century."[22]

The post-Mao leadership relaxed control over migration to the urban areas, largely to allow the urban youths that had been "sent down" to the countryside to return to their families in the cities. To cope with the large scale urban unemployment that resulted, the central authorities allowed and even encouraged the unemployed to form their own cooperatives or individual businesses and, thus, abandoned the traditional Socialist principle of guaranteeing every school graduate a job. Whether continuing this policy or resuming the allocation of surplus labor force to the rural sector as disguised or semi-disguised unemployment, the present leadership must achieve increases in labor productivity, while avoiding large-scale open unemployment.

As for the consumption problem, China can supply the basic necessities to match population growth over the next decade. The real problems are: how to limit, even reduce, the level of imports required to maintain the present level of per capita consumption; how to meet expectations for a significant increase in per capita income and consumption; how to provide a material incentive system for obtaining increased productivity without inflation, and how to catch up in areas neglected in the past, such as housing.

To meet these consumption needs, per capita consumption was allowed to increase at an annual rate of 4.6 percent in 1975–1981, but resulted in large increases in agricultural imports, inflationary price rises, and a significant decline in the rate of accumulation. China's problem for the decade is to allow for a significant and sustained increase in per capita consumption, while avoiding growing imports of foodstuffs, inflationary pressures, and financing consumption from accumulation.

The solution to China's second long-run problem, agriculture, lies in the continued adaptation of modern scientific technology to realize the significantly higher and more stable yields that technology can provide. Unfortunately, this transformation cannot be made in a decade, for the Chinese face the problem of transforming an agricultural sector in which all the arable land is under cultivation and being farmed by labor-intensive means. Non-agricultural employment will not grow fast enough to allow for a decrease in labor intensity in agriculture as this modern technology is introduced. Instead, the labor-to-land ratio is likely to increase in the future. Thus, to avoid large-scale rural unemployment, the Chinese must adopt modern, scientific technology in agriculture that is labor-using, not labor-saving; a problem that no other country has solved before.[23]

Great regional diversity in rainfall, growing seasons, urbanization, transportation, and other conditions produce significant differences in production and income earning possibilities throughout rural China. The more fortunate regions have progressed considerably in modernizing agricultural production and have achieved high and stable yields and incomes;[24] yet large areas of rural China have not and will not achieve such yields and incomes until the benefits of modernization in the urban and richer rural areas trickle down and spread to them.

Regional diversity is especially serious because of, first, the inability to migrate from the poorer areas to the richer areas and the lack of a mechanism for transferring resources and income *on a large scale* from richer to poorer communes,[25] and, second, the political unacceptability, under China's revolutionary ideology, of this traditional pattern of regional inequity. Thus, during the coming decade, policies adopted must benefit the poorer, as well as the richer rural areas; or there must be sizable welfare schemes for transferring either resources or income from the richer to the poorer areas.

ECONOMIC POLICY EVOLUTION: THE PAST FIVE YEARS

The situation of China's present leadership is far from hopeless. First of all, successful policymakers rarely completely solve problems. They bring them under control, reduce them to manageable proportions, and—hopefully—eliminate or greatly reduce their worst consequences. Second, the present leadership has emerged from decades of political struggles to introduce and implement those policies they believe will achieve the economic modernization of China. They enjoy unprecedented success in eliminating the most serious opposition to their leadership, and have acted to implement the economic policies they advocate. In the past year or so, the major speeches of Zhao Ziyang have focused on these economic problems and the economic policy solutions advocated. Thus, an analysis of those policies and their success so far will be informative in forecasting China's economic policies during the coming decade.

Economic Ideology

Deng Xiaoping's argument that "truth" must come from practice, that is, be tested on the basis of proven results, prevailed over Hua's defense of Mao's economic principles at the Third Plenum in December of 1978. This explicit rejection of Mao's intuitive interpretation of the economic laws of socialism led some Western observers to interpret the slogan of "learning truth from practice" as a rejection of ideology, meaning economic policies would be based on empirical tests to reveal which policy worked best. Developments over the past few years clearly indicate this slogan merely argues for the empirical tests of policies to determine if they work. The policies to be tested must still be consistent with the economic laws of socialism. Testing will continue throughout the decade. At this point, only a few major, but very important, principles have been agreed upon and adopted as guidelines for future economic policies.

Most important are the "four fundamental principles" incorporated in the constitution adopted in 1982.[26] These principles specify that China will be a socialist state, organized according to the people's democratic dictatorship, guided by Marxism-Leninism and Mao Zedong thought, and under the leadership of the Communist Party of China (CCP). Based on the economic laws of socialism, a socialist economy consists of public, collective, and private ownership and production; but the public sector must dominate the economy. While national, local, and individual interests will exist, conflicts among these various interests are to be resolved in favor of the national interests, which will be ensured by the organization of the state according to the principle of the people's democratic dictatorship under the leadership of the CCP. The dominance of the planned and public sector, as well as the national interest, will be achieved by the system of unified planning.

This new economic ideology represents a much more orthodox interpretation of Marxism and represents an even greater rejection of Maoist economic principles. Reliance on material incentives is justified under the principle of "from each according to his ability, to each according to his work." Reliance on a greater specialization and division of labor with the resultant increase in domestic and foreign trade is accepted as a necessary means for achieving the development of the means of production during the socialist stage. In fact, the revised constitution even goes so far as to permit foreign investment and loans, as long as the foreigners abide by the laws of the PRC. China's leaders now argue that commodity production continues under socialism, that capital goods produced by public enterprises are commodities, and that the law of value and economic accounting must guide the planners in determining the allocation of resources and outputs.[27] The planned and public sectors dominate the economy. The economy is still regulated or controlled by an extensive, economic administrative bureaucracy, whose decisions are to be based on economic accounting (costs and benefits, profits, etc.) and "economic levers" (interest rates, prices, taxes, etc.), rather than on the intuitive judgments or preferences of the individual or group making the decision, as in the past. Finally, the objective of socialist production has been redefined (or rediscovered) as serving the needs of the people.

These economic principles indicate what is meant by saying economics, not politics, is now in command. However, these principles raise many questions of application, such as: How dominant must the planned and public sector be before it is dominant enough? How do you determine what are the constraints on the rewards for work done? How are the planners to reach a compromise between abiding by the law of value and giving priority to national interests?

China's leaders respect the need to justify their economic policies as being consistent with and furthering the economic principles and objectives of socialism. The economic policies they adopt and implement over the next decade will be for problem solving, but will be adopted and implemented within the context of the leadership's economic ideology and objectives. The evolution of that economic ideology and its success in filling the vacuum left after the rejection of the Maoist interpretation of the economic principles of socialism will be one of the most exciting and critical developments in China over the coming decade.

Development Strategy

Hua Guofeng presented to the First session of the Fifth National People's Congress (NPC) the Ten-Year Plan for 1975–1982, referred to as the "Four Modernizations," that is, the modernization of agriculture, industry, science and technology, and defense. Yet there was little new since achievement of the Four Modernizations by the end of the century meant using the same slogan, objectives, and timetable set forth by Mao in the 1950s and Zhou Enlai in the 1970s. The key to achieving that objective and timetable was still more accumulation and investment. Investment in industry over the next 7 years was to be greater than that of the entire past 28 years. Industry was to grow by more than 10 percent a year, with the construction of 120 major projects. The traditional priorities, steel and machine building, would take the lead. As in the past, agricultural growth of 4.5 percent would be achieved "or exceeded" through the peasants' own efforts. The Four Modernizations were a reaffirmation of the strategies and policies of the past. But the Ten-Year Plan was unfeasible. According to Xue Muqiao,

> at this juncture the imbalances in the internal relationships of our national economy [were] becoming very serious. . . . In 1978, the errors of the "Great Leap Forward" were once again committed. . . . The insufficiency of materials for construction caused a squeeze on production, while insufficient supplies for heavy industrial production caused a squeeze on light industry and all joined together to cause a squeeze on agriculture.

> The growth in industrial production in 1977 and 1978 not only was of the nature of a recovery (there was no industrial growth in 1976) but it also comprised certain false elements. Many of the plants, anxious to fulfill their production plans, allowed the kinds of products not needed in the market or by the consumers and these had to be stockpiled in the warehouses. Production of machinery and iron and steel claimed to have the

highest speed but the stockpiling of products of these two categories was the highest and most serious. What kind of economic result was actually achieved from this high production speed?[28]

The Third Plenary session of the Eleventh Central Committee moved to correct this "sad state of imbalance in the economy." The Third Plenum concluded that "the country should devote three years beginning from 1979 to readjusting, restructuring, consolidation, and improving the national economy [the 'eight-character program' of economic reform] in order to bring it, step by step, onto the path of sustained, proportionate, and high-speed development."[29] The Ten-Year Plan was shelved and the new economic policies of the "eight-character program," many experimental, were introduced throughout the remainder of 1979 and 1980.[30]

Impressive recovery and growth in aggregate output and money incomes continued through 1979, but many old economic problems continued to plague the new leadership and many new ones were created by the readjustments and reforms of the eight-character program. China's import surplus was almost U.S.$2 billion in 1979 and over U.S.$1 billion in 1980. Open unemployment appeared in the cities, with some Chinese estimates placing the 1980 level at about 20 million. The budget incurred a deficit of U.S.$10 billion in 1979 and exceeded the planned deficit in 1980 by 50 percent. The resulting inflationary pressures led to price increases, both official and illicit. The "official" 1980 rate of inflation is 6 percent (13.8 percent for foodstuffs), but most observers believe it was well above 10 percent. Even the macro-economic indicators of growth began to decline.

At the Third session of the Fifth NPC (September 1980), Hua reported that "practice has proved the ['eight-character'] policy . . . is correct and has revitalized our economy and led it on to the path of sound development." Other speakers, however, noted budget deficits, inflation, import surpluses, declining growth rates, large pockets of poverty in the rural areas, and urban unemployment. They noted that reforms caused a considerable loss of control over capital construction, as well as budget expenditures, imports, prices, and wage and bonus payments. The time period for putting the economy back on the track of self-sustained economic growth was increased from three to five years and a new five-year plan for the period 1981–1985 was to be drawn up.

By early 1981, it had become known that economic performance in 1980 was worse than had been anticipated at the Fourth session of the Fifth NPC. The one-year plan for 1981 was scrapped and replaced. Further experimentation with reform of the economic system was stopped and a "consolidation" of experiences was required. The eight-character economic program was endorsed until the economy is restored to the path of self-sustained growth, which will probably require "more than five years." Control over the economy by the central authorities was to be enforced, that is, readjustment was to take precedence over reform.

The recentralization of control over the economy throughout the remainder of 1981 was effective. The budget deficit was reduced to less than U.S.$2 billion, although 4.6 percent of the revenues came from domestic bond sales, and 7.6 percent from foreign loans,[31] and the import surplus was reduced to less than U.S.$10 million. Although open urban unemployment continues to exist, almost 9 million urban workers found jobs in 1981; 56 percent of these found employment in public enterprises, 40 percent in urban collectives, and 4 percent in private trades.[32] Demand still exceeded the supply of many consumer goods, but the inflationary gaps and pressures were greatly reduced in 1981 and the cost-of-living index increased by only 2.5 percent. Capital construction expenditures by the central government were reduced by 26 percent in 1981, but unfortunately, the inability to control lower level government investment expenditures means that the investment expenditures of the central government now account for less than half of the total investment in capital construction in state-owned units. Thus, the attempts of the leadership to reassert central control over the economy have not been completely successful at the present time.

As economic policy evolved in 1978–1981, several developments occurred which are meaningful indicators of economic policy in the coming decade. First is the very important change in the attitude of China's leaders as to the objective of modernization. In general, much less emphasis is placed on specific targets, objectives, timetables, or the quantitative dimensions of economic development, while much greater emphasis is placed on the achievement of a sustained and regularized process of behavior, decisionmaking, and performance, or the qualitative indicators of successful modernization. Thus, economic policies are now adopted to improve management procedures, productivity, the quality of the work force, the quality of products, the process of innovation, and education and research. Investments are made in "non-productive" social overhead capital, the development of the infrastructure, and the modernization of existing plants, rather than in building new ones. Economic policies for the decade will focus on creating behavior patterns and norms that will facilitate economic growth and modernization in lieu of issuing administrative orders and targets. To the extent this change guides economic policymaking in the future, it is an important step toward the achievement of China's economic modernization sought by Deng Xiaoping and his followers.[33]

Second, China's leaders recognize that they must achieve the objectives of the eight-character program, a decade-long process, as a *precondition* to rapid and sustained economic growth. Premier Zhao Ziyang makes this development clear in his "Report on the Work of the Government" to the Fourth session of the Fifth NPC at the end of 1981.[34] This very lengthy (presented on two days) and important speech is almost exclusively devoted to the presentation of ten principles for economic policies in the eight-character program for the future. These ten principles were "proposed" by the State Council and "sum up our experience in the past thirty-two years, and particularly in the past three years." These principles will guide China's economic policies within the context of the eight-character program through the decade as Zhao expects the economy will "probably enter a new period of economic renewal in the last decade of the century," but that it will be twenty years before "our economy should be in a position to take off from a new starting point, from which it will be able to advance more swiftly and catch up with the more developed countries."

CHINA'S ECONOMIC POLICY EVOLUTION OVER THE COMING DECADE

The eight-character program refers to the four pairs of Chinese characters that are rendered in English as "readjusting, restructuring, consolidating, and improving." The policies related to readjusting have the purpose of rebalancing the economy to achieve a better equation of supply and demand throughout the economy and an equilibrium rate of growth. Restructuring deals with the reform of the economic system and enterprise management to create greater incentives and freedom of action for the units of production within the planned, centrally controlled sector to achieve greater efficiency in production, higher total factor productivity, and a better matching of supply and demand. Restructuring also refers to those reforms that increase the role in the economy of markets and market forces as a supplement to the planned and centrally controlled sector. Consolidating includes the elimination of those units of production that have low productivity, waste resources, and continually suffer losses, and the reorganization of enterprises to achieve greater specialization in production. Improving calls for the increase in the level of technology effectively utilized in production throughout the economy, by increasing the borrowing of modern technology from abroad, and more importantly, by spreading the more advanced technology already being utilized in some units of production more widely throughout the economy.

I. Readjustment

Readjustment must be given the greatest priority within the eight-character program. It requires priority be given: to the development of the agricultural sector, the consumer goods sector, the energy and transport sectors; to limiting the rate of accumulation and investment, while increasing the effectiveness of these investment funds in obtaining more goods and services needed by the economy; and to the better integration of China's economy into the world market, that is, increasing the foreign trade dependency ratio. Six of the ten principles in the eight-character program are directly related to achieving these objectives.

Principle One: Accelerate the development of agricultural output by relying on correct policies and on science. To increase agricultural output and the peasant's income, the leadership increased the prices paid for quota deliveries of most agricultural products to the state in 1979 and 1980, and paid even higher prices for deliveries above the quota. Unwilling to raise the urban retail price for basic necessities for fear of the political consequences, the state increased the price of only non-staple foodstuffs and awarded workers a monthly subsidy to cover the increase in the urban cost of living. This method of stimulating increases in agricultural production achieved a one-time increase in output, but the resulting burden on the state budget and losses suffered by the state procurement and supply network accounted for a major share of the budget deficits in 1979 and 1980. As a result, China's leaders have rejected this means for achieving sustained and accelerated growth of agricultural production. Significant direct investment by the state in the agricultural sector also was rejected because of the state's efforts to reduce the overall rate and level of accumulation and investment and the competing needs of other neglected sectors for the available investment funds.

With the "immense labor power in the countryside," the major problem is "how to get them to do these things [developing the rural economy] willingly and actively" and "to work efficiently and achieve good results." Institutional reform (or "correct policies") will give the peasant the incentive through a greater role in production decisionmaking and a greater share in the results of their efforts. "Good results" will be achieved by the proper application of science and technology. Already judged effective, these "correct policies" are the revised 60 Articles (Regulations on the Work of the People's Communes) that were adopted by the Third Plenum in late 1978 and the "contract responsibility system" approved by the Central Committee of the Party at a work conference at the end of 1981. The 60 Articles set a framework for determining the obligations to the state of the production team and its members, then leave them free to allocate their resources, meet those obligations, and maximize their income in both kind and money, in other words, to get the state and lower level cadres off the peasant's back. The state and its lower level cadres still interfere with and issue administrative orders to the production teams, but the effective implementation of the 60 Articles is the major means for stimulating peasant initiative and effort.

Encouraged by the thrust of the revised 60 Articles, however, cadres and peasants in some areas in 1980 and 1981 went even further by reinstating or adopting another policy that had been experimented with in the early 1960s: the contract responsibility system. A wide variety of forms and labels for these systems have been adopted throughout rural China. At the end of 1981, 90 percent of the production teams had adopted one of these,[35] the most dominant of which are the payment of "remuneration according to a short-term contract, paying seasonal remuneration for specialized farm work done, or fixing output quotas based on production groups." Each of these forms leaves the team as the basic accounting unit for resource allocation, production, and income distribution purposes. About 10 percent of the teams are reported to have adopted contract responsibility systems which involve "alloting [*sic*] work to individual households"—basically a transition to household farming.

According to the Summary of the National Conference on Rural Work, approved by the Central Committee at the end of 1981, under the first three forms:

> Peasants contract with the production team to produce a particular quality of a crop or product. This amount must be delivered to the collective, with the remainder going partly or wholly to the peasants themselves as reward. As members of the collective they also receive an allotment which is apportioned from the collective produce. The specialization contracts divide labor according to specialized jobs while the production group contracts do not specify a division of labor.[36]

These systems merely change how the team allocates work assignments and distributes income, tying more closely income earned with work performed. It does not, however, change the team as the basic accounting level unit in agriculture.

The system allotting work to the individual households, however, introduces a dramatic change. According to the Summary,

the contractors [i.e., households] deliver to the production teams the part retained by the collective, with the remaining part belonging to the peasants themselves. They do not receive an allotment from collective distribution.[37]

Thus, the team becomes an administrative unit, allocating its resources (including land) to the individual households, assigning them their share of the team's taxes, sales quota, welfare fund, and so on, and collecting those assignments in return; other than these fixed responsibilities, the households are on their own to maximize their output and income. That increase in output can be consumed, sold to the state, or sold on the market. The positive effect on incentives and effort has already resulted in some peasants increasing their output and incomes significantly.

Confident in the ability of the peasants to increase output and incomes under these "correct policies," China's leaders also recognize the importance of science and technology to achieving the high-yield threshold of modern, scientific agriculture. Premier Zhao hopes that

the departments concerned will concentrate greater efforts, and, within a relatively short period of time, achieve further notable success in breeding and popularizing fine seed strains, improving farming methods and crop patterns, changing the composition of chemical fertilizers, applying fertilizers rationally, producing highly efficient farm chemicals low in poisonous residue, and popularizing selected and suitable farm machinery. (p. 16)

A review of seven areas in which "strong and well-coordinated" farm support services are needed (agricultural research and extension and provision of seeds, fertilizer, agrochemicals, irrigation, credit, machinery and repair) concludes that "the required long term effort" in this area will pose a much greater challenge to the Chinese leadership than their attempts to restructure farm management by implementing "correct policies."[38]

Principle Two: Give prominence to the development of consumer goods industries and further adjust the service orientation of heavy industry. According to Premier Zhao, such prominence will be "for a long time yet," as these industries must be assured of energy and raw materials, loans and investments, scientific and technical personnel, and imports of foreign technology and equipment. Heavy industry must alter its structure of production to serve the needs of agriculture and light industry better, as well as to supply consumer durables. The expansion of light industry is not just consumer oriented for it will enhance China's export trade, as well as lower import and investment requirements and raise employment per unit of output. Two important conditions have been placed on the future development of the consumer goods industries, however. Increases in output must not come at the expense of quality. In addition, local authorities are prohibited from using the increased retained earnings and revenue placed at their disposal to create consumer goods industries that compete with established state enterprises in the major industrial urban centers for raw materials. Thus, local areas "must ensure the fulfillment of their quotas in purchasing raw materials for the consumer goods industries and sending them to other areas" in order to meet "the needs of the old industrial bases."

Principle Three: Raise the energy utilization ratio and promote the building of the energy industry and transport. These sectors "are now the weak links in the chain of [China's] economic development (p. 17)." However, no quick fix is offered for the coming decade, outside of a few specific guidelines. "The building of the energy industry and transport should go hand in hand." Development of transportation should start "a bit earlier" and be given "top priority" by the central authorities in the allocation of investment for construction "in the next few years," while trying to "muster funds for opening new oilfields." Foreign firms will be relied upon to cooperate to "step up exploration [of offshore oil] and open and build up new oil fields as soon as possible." Thermal power plants and hydroelectric power stations are to be built, but the former depend on coal, the latter on large investments. Construction is not stressed, instead, expanded coal production is viewed as the key to increasing energy supplies in the near term. Expanded production will come primarily from the transformation and expansion of existing coal mines, with opening of expensive new large coal sources to be "staggered" in the future.

Over the next decade the solution to China's energy problem lies in the consumption, not the supply side. According to Zhao Ziyang, "China's waste of energy is shocking," and he is right. Improvements in the past few years were largely due to changes in the structure of production in favor of less energy intensive sectors, while "little has been achieved through improved management and technical transformation (p. 17)." Factories that fail to meet strict quotas or targets are to be shut down. Coal consumption is to replace oil consumption where possible.

In Premier Zhao's speech he is realistic about China's energy and transportation problems, which will be constraints on China's economic development for some time to come.

Principle Six: Raise more construction funds and use them thriftily through improved methods of acquisition, accumulation, and spending. Readjustment involves lowering the *rate* of accumulation and investment. Here Premier Zhao is concerned with the *level* of accumulation and investment, especially its sources and allocation. The solution to increasing the level of investment lies in increasing the income and wealth of society. Funds will be raised for investment by the usual appeals to cut costs and eliminate wastes in production, to reduce the amount of circulating capital required per unit of output, to shorten the completion time required in construction, and to practice economy. Policy decisions will be made concerning: the imposition of commodity taxes; maintenance of the state monopoly on tobacco and alcoholic drinks; the use of a "determinant part" of the bank deposits of local authorities; enterprises; and individuals for state planned construction versus unilateral grants from the state budget. In short, investment expenditures are to remain controlled and planned by the central government, while funds for those expenditures provided by the central government are to be gradually diminished in scope and concentrated on the energy, transportation, and "new" industrial sectors. Projects "involving shorter investment cycles and yielding fairly large profits, as well as urban construction projects" are to be financed as far as possible by local authorities or enterprises.[39]

Principle Seven: Persist in an open-door policy and enhance our capacity for self reliant action. For the near future this means that China should expand its foreign trade, import advanced technology, utilize foreign loans and credits, and enter into different forms of international economic and technological cooperation. Export earnings, not loans and credits, are the necessary means to accomplish these tasks. Thus, the rate of increase in exports should be higher than the rate of growth of the Chinese economy, meaning China's foreign trade dependency ratio will increase. Long term foreign loans at low interest rates "should be used chiefly in such infrastructure projects as the development of energy and transport." Foreign exchange earnings should not be utilized to import complete or duplicate sets of equipment. In order to assimilate foreign know-how and technology emphasis should be placed on the "imports of technology and single machines or key equipment" that cannot be produced domestically. Assimilation by means of joint ventures and special economic zones should be continued, but Premier Zhao warned that the objective of China's socialist modernization, socialist system, and socialist morality should be ensured and China's experience in "this sphere should be summed up in good time (p. 24)."

This is not an open economy policy. As a principle, "persist in an open-door policy" is understood when compared with the closed door of the past. Increased imports are necessary to make the Chinese economy more self-reliant, but they are to be kept to the minimum level necessary for that purpose.

Principle Ten: Proceed from the concept of everything for the people and make overall arrangements for production, construction, and the people's livelihood. While Zhao claims China's leaders "have done [their] best to improve the people's standard of living [since the Third Plenum], significantly raising the income and level of consumption of the overwhelming majority of the people" (p. 208); his emphasis is on the constraints they face in achieving further gains in this regard. Increases in the standard of living must be "based" on increases in production, and, as the latter "can only grow gradually," increases in the standard of living must be gradual. A necessary condition for this gradual increase is the strict and effective control of population growth. Unfortunately, as Zhao reports, due to the agricultural contract responsibility system, "an upturn in the birth rate has been reported in some places." The State Statistical Bureau reported the birth rate as 1.1 percent in 1980 and 1.4 percent in 1981.

II. Restructuring

Only one of the ten policy principles deals directly with the economic system reforms of the past few years.

Principle Eight: Actively and steadily reform our economic system and realize the initiative of all concerned to the full. In his discussion of Principle Eight, Premier Zhao reiterated the importance of readjustment and the decision (Spring 1981) that unified state control over specific areas of the economic system. He repeated these points again in his speech to the National Conference on Industry and Communications in March 1982.[40] However, Zhao makes it clear that reforms of the economic system have not been abandoned, but are to be actively and steadily promoted and pursued *in the long run*, especially after the economy is restored to the path of equilibrium and sustained growth. Yet the experiments in economic reform are intended to supplement the unified and centrally controlled sector, with national interests having dominance over local and individual interests. To discuss future economic reform, Zhao gives his own opinion, which he makes clear is not based on decisions of the State Council. Planners must utilize the law of value (i.e., prices) when drawing up state plans (i.e., the targets to be assigned to enterprises). The state should have complete control over all commodities of importance to the economy and to the people's living standards, but enterprises should be given different degrees of decisionmaking powers, presumably based on the commodities they produce and their scale of operations. Workers should be given democratic rights in the management of their enterprises. Rules, regulations, and economic levers (i.e., prices, taxes, interest rates, etc.) should replace administrative decrees in running the economy. Since change requires further study in "both theory and practice," economic reform needs "to be preceded by sober investigation and study, feasibility analysis and well-conceived planning, and should be popularized step by step through experiment (p. 26)."

III. Consolidation

Only one Principle is directly related to consolidation, but Zhao clearly indicates that closing down or reorganizing enterprises that are suffering serious financial losses year after year or that are wasteful of scarce resources in production is to be given a much higher priority than in the past. Through experience, China's leaders have learned that depending on the initiative of local authorities to consolidate will not work. Since local administrations that controlled enterprises wasting resources were able to make profits merely due to the state's administered price system—relatively low input prices and relatively high prices for certain end products—they did not want to close these enterprises; nor did those who operated inefficient plants suffering losses because they were subsidized by the state for these losses. Finally, the local units within the bureaucratic administrative network were so segmented and isolated that each locality wanted to keep its own industrial facilities for producing a whole range of products that the locality needed, rather than surrender them to a larger association of enterprises organized along similar product lines. Thus, the merger of 19,300 enterprises into 1,900 specialized companies or associations by the end of 1980[41] had been accomplished only by promising that the local authorities controlling participating enterprises would be guaranteed no loss in profits, assets, or employment in those enterprises. In any event, despite the statistics cited for the success of consolidation, the number of enterprises suffering losses had increased, profits submitted to the state declined, and the waste of scarce inputs continued to be shocking in 1981.

Principle Five: Carry out the all-round consolidation and necessary reorganization of enterprises by groups. Here, Zhao repeats several past policy guidelines that seek to combine central control with local initiative: assign workers responsibility for a fixed production task or output quota; enforce worker discipline; assure the full responsibility of the factory director; allow congresses of workers to participate in major discussions affecting their interests; grant enterprises "a measure of economic authority;" and reward enterprises and workers with a share of the surplus revenue generated as a result of successful operations. That share is not to exceed the rate of growth in output or of total profits, however, and greater supervision should be exercised over the enterprises' accounts, wage and salary distribution, and bonus and welfare payments.

Zhao also presents a specific program for dealing with those enterprises experiencing serious losses or excessive waste. Each enterprise will undergo a critical evaluation and the first group selected for this purpose will be "about 300" enterprises of special importance to the national economy. Those enterprises producing products in excess or of very poor quality, utilizing energy or raw and semi-finished materials at too high a rate, incurring losses "over the years," or causing serious pollution are to be closed down, amalgamated with other enterprises, or required to change their product line—depending on the merits of each case. The State Council "has already" issued instructions for establishing—by industry—"minimum requirements for batch production, quality, and material consumption." Those enterprises "that fail to meet these requirements within a certain time limit must either suspend production pending consolidation, or close down." To avoid the problems in their earlier attempts at consolidation, not only will the local level Party organizations be in charge of the consolidation, they are to be assisted in their efforts by Party cadres from higher levels.

IV. Improvement

Sustained technological change is one of the most important characteristics of modernization, but the package of knowledge, values, and behavior required to generate sustained technological change is achieved by means of cumulative long-run social and economic changes. China's leaders acknowledge the need to elevate the level of technology effectively utilized throughout their economy, not only to close the wide gap between their average level of technology and that utilized in the industrialized countries, but also to eliminate the wide gaps between the levels of technology utilized within the Chinese economy. They also recognize that these problems will not be solved quickly. Thus, the two principles that are directly related to the improvement of the economy are principles for overcoming the most immediate problems in this area while introducing general proposals aimed at the long-run technological transformation of China's economy.

Principle Four: Carry out the technical transformation step by step in key units and make maximum use of existing enterprises. Zhao explicitly argues that the technological transformation of China's economy will not be achieved by importing new complete plants from abroad. China cannot afford the number required nor does this approach increase the level of technology in existing units of production. Thus, the fundamental approach will be the technical transformation of existing units of production, relying on imports only for key pieces of equipment and technology. Yet the most that can be accomplished over the next decade is to replace outdated equipment by updating a few key installations that requires a greater share of the investments' funds and to increase the depreciation rate. These depreciation funds and retained earnings should be devoted to updating existing equipment—not to the construction of new projects.

While the import of key pieces of equipment will be allowed, the bulk of the "sophisticated machines and equipment" are to be provided by the domestic machine-building industry that is to be transformed for that purpose. Priority is to be given to new equipment that will reduce the consumption of raw materials and energy, improve the quality and mix of output, and increase allocative efficiency that is, make greater use of relatively abundant resources, while conserving the use of scarce resources.

Principle Nine: Raise the scientific and cultural level of all working people, and organize strong forces to tackle key scientific research projects. Raising the scientific level of the people calls for policies that will expand the quantity and quality of higher education and cause an increase in secondary vocational schools, rather than secondary general education.[42] Enrollment will emphasize quality, not quantity. Spare-time, television, and correspondence universities are to be developed "so as to encourage people to become educated by teaching themselves." China's indigenous scientific and technological research capabilities are to be reorganized and developed so as to create those conditions for the long-run improvement of the Chinese economy. The development of science and technology should be directly related to the solution of the key problems in the economy that promise major economic benefits without weakening efforts at basic research. No specific policies are offered as to how this can be done. Zhao can only give a rather lengthy list of specific areas where technical innovations are "important and necessary for the accelerated development of our national economy (p. 28)."

This discussion of the Ten Principles of the eight-character program indicates the framework of China's economic policies over the coming decade. However, these policy statements mean little, no matter how appropriate, unless they are successfully implemented.

Several factors will determine their fate. The most important are: how likely are Deng Xiaoping and his chosen successors to remain in power over the decade; will they modify these Ten Principles; how likely are the Ten Principles to be adopted and implemented by the bureaucratic and political cadre at lower levels; and finally, how likely are the Ten Principles to solve China's short-run economic problems.

A FORECAST OF CHINA'S ECONOMIC EVOLUTION IN THE NEXT DECADE

Merely listing the four major questions above and the history of the past three decades tends to lead one to a rather pessimistic conclusion about China's economic future. The PRC has not had long periods of stable political leadership, pursued a fixed economic policy framework for a decade, or exhibited uniform and successful implementation of economic policies that conflicted with local or group interests or economic policies that did not promise quick-fix solutions. Finally, if we were to assume a 50–50 chance of success in each of the four areas of the eight-character program, then the possibility of the Ten Principles leading to an effective solution of China's short-run economic problems would only be one out of sixteen, or less than 10 percent.

Problems of Policy Implementation

Of the four factors that will determine whether or not the economic policy program is successful, I am most optimistic about the current leadership's ability to remain in power over the coming decade. Maoist ideas will continue to serve as a constraint on the current leadership in its attempt to achieve economic modernization. It is doubtful, however, during the coming decade, that these ideas will generate a leadership group able to challenge successfully the current leadership. I agree with Tom Robinson's analysis that the continuation of the status quo is the most likely scenario.

The current leadership is sufficiently experienced in the art of political accomodation to ensure that it remains in power over the coming decade. Zhao's presentation of the Ten Principles is undoubtedly an extreme expression of those principles. As the derivative economic policies are successful, special interests will be harmed, which will lead to pressures against these policies. Compromises will result. Nonetheless, inasmuch as these Ten Principles are based upon the leadership's experiences over the past several years and the result of considerable deliberations and decisions involving a large element of the leadership, these future compromises and concessions will not negate or alter the basic thrust and purpose of the Ten Principles.

The Ten Principles are basic approaches to China's economic problems. They do not specify any particular allocations or rates of investment, any timetable for accomplishing particular tasks, or any target rates of growth for particular sectors or for the economy as a whole. Thus, unlike previous policy frameworks, they are a realistic and feasible statement of principles for solving China's economic problems. An attempt will be made in the coming decade to accelerate the rate of growth, to elevate the rate of accumulation, to devote more of that investment to heavy industry and defense, and to reduce the emphasis given to light industry. The compromise between current and past priorities in China's development strategy will not be a rejection of the Ten Principles as the basic framework for China's economic policy over the coming decade.

As for the second factor, the prospects are not particularly good for the successful implementation of the particular economic policies derived within the framework of the Ten Principles. The effective implementation of any economic policy depends upon the administrative decisions and activities of the millions of lower level cadres spread throughout the lowest level of the extensive political and economic administrative network. These decisions and activities are informed by, as well as constrained by, the tremendous influence of personal ties and relationships, established patterns of behavior, and self-interest of those many local centers of power. Thus, as Deng Xiaoping and his followers readily admit, the experiments with economic policy reform over the past few years have encountered considerable resistance from these local cadres who are said to be influenced by the remnants of "feudalistic" attitudes and behavior.

To remedy this situation, the Chinese leadership has launched a campaign to weed out the incompetent and those who fail to support and implement the new economic policies, and to recruit a new generation of capable cadres dedicated to the implementation of the new economic policies. This need to transform the existing administrative bureaucracy, especially at the lower levels, may be the most important obstacle to China's sustained and rapid long-term growth.[43] Given the nature of the problem, and the history of bureaucracy in China, progress is bound to be slow and depends heavily on the ability to recruit and train a new class of professional and dedicated cadres. Moreover, the very nature of China's political and economic system—a highly bureaucratic system on both counts—means that many or most of these problems in the successful implementation of the new leadership's economic policies will not be solved by a mere change in personnel. Thus, these inefficiencies in policy implementation by the administrative bureaucracy will continue to serve as constraints on the ability of these policies to restore sustained and rapid growth to the Chinese economy.

The Economic Policies to be Implemented

From this analysis of the major determinants of China's economic policies during the coming decade, we conclude that the current leadership coalition will continue its efforts to solve China's current economic problems within the framework of the eight-character program along the lines of the specific policies spelled out in Zhao's speech to the Fourth session of the Fifth NPC at the end of 1981. More specifically, those economic policies will call for a somewhat lower rate of accumulation (higher rate of consumption) than in the past, but those rates will remain at the extreme limits allowed for by the need to pursue a more balanced growth policy. In other words, the Chinese will not adopt a consumer-oriented balanced growth policy. Investments in heavy industry and transportation will continue to make up a dominant share of total investment but during the coming decade, will be concentrated on the major sectors that now present severe bottlenecks to sustained growth (i.e., energy, transport, construction materials, infrastructure, etc.). As for agriculture, rapid growth in this sector will be sought not by large increases in its share of total investment, but by policy reforms already adopted, along with the hoped-for provision of technological innovations to the producer by those working in the science and technology sector. These attempts to readjust, or rebalance, the economy will remain the major concern of China's leaders over the coming decade.

To facilitate these readjustments, China's involvement in foreign trade will increase somewhat. Although definitely higher than in the past, China's foreign trade dependency rates will not exceed those normally exhibited by large, continental countries. In other words, China will not pursue an open economy strategy, nor engage in large-scale, long-run foreign borrowing to finance a large share of the domestic investment program. Thus, in their attempts to "improve" the economy, China's leaders will slowly attempt to elevate the adoption and spread of "more" modern technology throughout the economy. They will not attempt to "catch up" with the industrialized countries in modernizing their economy. To achieve the desired "improvement" of the economy, it will be necessary to "consolidate" the many terribly inefficient and wasteful units of production. To achieve much greater success than in the past, the central authorities will play a greater role in forcing the desired changes on the "targeted" units of production.

Finally, the need for the central authorities to reassert their control in order to reflect the "national interests" so as to achieve the above policy objectives means that reform of the economic system, or "restructuring," will proceed slowly, at best, until those objectives are achieved. In other words, reforms which would significantly alter the basic features of China's centrally administered Soviet-type economic system, as well as a major price reform, are to be indefinitely postponed until the objectives of readjustment, improvement, and consolidation are achieved. The economic policies for achieving these objectives, however, will suffer from their improper implementation by local authorities due to the inefficiencies, opposition, and private interests within the local level bureaucracy.

Results of the Policies Implemented

With the effective controls available to the central government in the public finance, banking, and investment sectors, the rate of accumulation will possibly decline to 25 percent, or even less, of national income in the immediate future and drift slowly upward to between 25 and 30 percent as the readjustment of the economy begins to reduce the many financial and real constraints on the level of investment. Consumption as a share of national income, therefore, may continue to increase over the next few years, but begin a slow process of decline to a level of 70 to 75 percent throughout most of the coming decade. By concentrating their efforts in the development of the "bottleneck" sectors within heavy industry, especially energy and transportation, they will restore greater balance to the economy; such progress will be painfully slow. China's rapid economic growth will continue to be seriously constrained by energy shortages over the next ten years. Progress in the other sectors will also be slow but may be more significant, alleviating these sectors as "bottlenecks" before the end of the coming decade.

Industry and consumer goods will continue to receive more favored treatment than in the past, but the very rapid rates of growth in this sector over the past few years should decline noticeably in the near future for several reasons. The available investment funds will be mobilized by the central government to concentrate on the development of such sectors as energy and transportation, which act as constraints on growth of the whole economy; funds will also be mobilized for those sectors such as defense and education that are high priority sectors whose needs and demands far exceed their present allocations of funds. The expansion of light industry will depend more on self-provided funds. Furthermore, continued increases in the light industrial sector will force it to encounter both raw material input constraints and the need to improve quality in order to meet the test of market demand, develop new products, and absorb new technology. The rapid development of light industry is a temporary phenomenon, and the restoration of balance to the economy will serve to place greater constraints on growth in the light industrial sector, unlike most other sectors. This future growth in light industry assumes that per capita income and consumption will resume a lower, but steady, rate of growth of about 3 percent a year, or approximately the rate of increase in labor productivity. Labor productivity should resume a slow, steady rate of increase as a result of the many reforms, especially incentives, and the policies which will lead to greater efficiency in production.

These crude projections indicate, within ten years, a rate of accumulation of between 25 and 30 percent, a rate of increase in both heavy and light industry of between 7 and 10 percent, and a rate of growth in per capita consumption and labor productivity of approximately 3 percent. An inequality of income typical of a country at China's level of per capita income will be experienced among regions and individuals. While this phenomenon will generate considerable pressure for the adoption of large-scale income redistribution programs, it is unlikely that egalitarianism will be allowed to thwart the progress in solving China's economic development problems. In summary, the Chinese should make slow and steady progress in restoring their economy to the path of rapid and self-sustained growth during the next decade, but they have no guarantees that rapid and self-sustained growth will be achieved in "the last decade of this century."

Forecasting that China's economy will be able to resume a path of rapid and self-sustained growth by the end of the coming decade assumes the adoption and absorption of modern technology and the creation of an indigenous science for the continuous generation and implementation of technological innovation. Thus, the opening of the economy and reliance on imported technology, the restoration of educational and research institutions and associations, and the high priority given to improving China's economy and fostering growth by means of technological innovations are very promising signs for the future.

Yet, China is a developing economy with a Soviet model economic system, and most Soviet model economic systems continue to have difficulty in absorbing modern technology, even those considerably more developed than China.

The generation and implementation of technological innovations in the agricultural sector, in particular, have already been singled out by China's leaders as a major source for the long-run solution of their agricultural problems. The major policy changes to obtain rapid growth in that sector have already been introduced with significant one-time increases in productivity. In early 1982, the Central Committee decided policy changes should end, "our work" should be to "stabilize the situation."[44] Thus, rapid and sustained growth of China's agricultural production depends on the generation of technological innovations. While the Chinese leaders speak rather optimistically about the future in this regard, now that they recognize the importance of "science" to their problem, the conclusions of Robert Haveman's econometric analysis of the impact of science and technology on agricultural production in the developing countries lead to a more guarded or even pessimistic forecast.[45]

China's strong point is in its well-developed agricultural extension system, but Haveman finds the quality of these extension systems are not that important, it is the innovation being introduced that makes the difference. Furthermore, the innovations that work are those that are developed under the condition of the given environment or site, not developed abroad or at high level research institutes. Also, the time-lags involved are considerable; it takes approximately eight or nine years after an innovation is developed before it leads to a significant contribution to increased output. Finally, unless basic *and* applied research are continuously carried out, not only in the directly related areas, but in sister-sciences as well, the gains obtained from a single innovation will soon be lost. The process of innovation must be continuous. The above considerations merely indicate why the road to modernization of China's agriculture will be difficult; they do not foreclose the possibility of the successful modernization of China's agriculture.

By the inclusion of non-crop growing agricultural activities the Chinese will achieve a rate of growth in agricultural production over the decade of between 3 and 4 percent a year. Thus the maintenance of a 3 percent annual average increase in the standard of living will require continued dependence on large-scale imports of foodstuffs from abroad and a continuation of the existing systems for distributing those necessities, that is, rationing and a unified supply system under central control.

Maintenance of this 3 to 4 percent rate of increase would be an impressive achievement, but how impressive depends upon whether or not this growth is accompanied by increasing, stable, or declining labor productivity in agriculture. In the rural sector, the contract responsibility system has already weakened the communes' ability to find employment for and assure an adequate standard of living to all households and individuals. Thus, while the unemployed workers are urged to find work in the private and collective sector and the urban sector, the rural sector will find it increasingly difficult to absorb the increase in population, while also maintaining increases in the productivity of labor and average per capita consumption. The hope for a rapid expansion of non-crop agricultural activities would help reduce the problem to manageable proportions in the short run, while achievement of zero population growth would provide the solution in the long run. Neither solution, however, is likely to eliminate the problem in either the short or long run. Rather, developments during the next ten years are most likely to represent a continuation of an ineffective compromise of labor intensive methods of production for the sake of labor absorption, at the expense of more rapid gains in labor productivity and efficiency, meaning continued large scale imports of foodstuffs to maintain the standard of living.

During the next ten years, there will be approximately 175 million new entrants to the labor force. If we assume a 5 percent annual rate of increase in employment in state-run enterprises over the next ten years (the rate from 1957 to 1979), a 5.5 percent increase in employment in urban collectives (averaged 5.8 percent in 1957–1979), and the restoration of the urban private sector, though still very small, to its level in 1952 by the end of the coming decade, an annual rate of increase over the next decade of 23 percent (it was 40 percent in 1981), would allow the urban sector to absorb 75 million of the new entrants. The remainder of the new entrants, or 100 million, would represent a one-third increase in the agricultural labor force. If collective enterprises, forestry, and fishing (which together employed 12 percent of the agricultural labor force in 1979) were to increase their employment by 11 percent over the coming decade, full employment with no increase in the labor force engaged in crop growing would be achieved. These hypothetical calculations show that during the next decade the employment problem faced by the Chinese leadership is at least manageable, under optimistic assumptions, and that they may even be able to make some progress in coping with that problem. While the actual developments are unlikely to be as favorable as pictured, by the end of the decade the rising growth rate in production and, possibly, declines in the rate of population growth could begin to help alleviate the employment problem.

The major conclusion of this paper, therefore, is that China's leaders and the economic policies we believe they will pursue over the coming decade should restore the Chinese economy to the path of rapid and sustained growth by the end of the decade. No major breakthroughs are in sight and their success in restoring the economy to the path of a rapid and sustained growth is threatened with many pitfalls. As far as the long-run agricultural and employment problems are concerned, we are less optimistic, but believe they should be able to at least hold their own and be in a better position to cope with those problems ten years hence than they are now.

Foreign Policy Implications

This analysis leads to a very clear and important conclusion. Access to foreign supplies of foodstuffs and technology will be of vital importance to China's leaders in their attempt to cope with their economic problems. Thus, while subject to the political and economic constraints indicated, Chinese leaders will continue to maintain the increased level of foreign trade participation that followed their coming to power. This larger dependence on foreign trade participation, in turn, will reinforce the more moderate foreign policy, especially its reorientation toward the West. Given China's short-run economic problems, the policy options of China's new leadership are not very great. On the other hand, as progress is made in coping with these problems, their policy options with regard to foreign policy should become considerably less constrained.

The constraints placed on China's foreign policy options by domestic economic problems and policies, however, should not be interpreted as applicable in all cases or as the single most important determinants. Two important examples of difficult, policy choices for China's leaders are: the search for long-term, low-interest rate loans in competition with other members of the Third World, and the role of Hong Kong as an important source of foreign exchange, investment, entrepreneurial talent, and technology for China's economy.

China seeks to affirm its position as a member and spokesman for the block of Third World countries. The Chinese also have made very explicit demands on their "rightful" share of the soft loans or grants of the International Monetary Fund, World Bank, and other such international institutions. Given China's population and standard of living, China's "rightful" share is relatively large. Since most nations want to encourage China's increased participation in the world economy, China's requests are likely to be granted. Yet the other developing nations view these increased loans and grants to China as directly reducing the amounts of loans and grants available to them, especially in a period when the total amount of loans and grants available to the Third World is being reduced. Loans and grants to China are bound to generate tension and thus obstacles to China's attempt to maintain peaceful relations with these countries, much less China's attempt to assume a leadership role within the Third World. In this case, domestic economic needs may generate problems and conflicts in China's international relations rather than foster more moderate and harmonious relations as our general conclusion predicts.

The case of Hong Kong illustrates a different kind of exception. As Richard Nations points out in Chapter 20, Hong Kong is a valuable asset to China's economy, in terms of trade, investments, overseas Chinese remittances, and modernization expertise. Hong Kong is important to China's economic modernization, and China may thus adopt a moderate policy with respect to Hong Kong's future after the lease runs out in 1997; however, Hong Kong's importance to China should not be overemphasized. China's leaders have justified giving top priority to economic modernization on the grounds that it is a prior necessity for achieving their domestic and foreign political objectives. Despite the record of the past few years, there is little evidence they have sacrificed domestic and foreign political objectives for the sake of economic modernization.

NOTES

1. Hua Guofeng, "Unite and Strive to Build a Modern, Powerful Socialist Country!," Report on the Work of the Government to the 1st Session of the 5th NPC, *Beijing Review*, No. 10 (10 March 1978), p. 18.
2. "The 1980s: A Promising Decade," *Beijing Review*, No. 9 (3 March 1980), p. 23. This is the English version of a *Renmin Ribao* article (5 February 1980) by "Commentator," recognized both inside and outside of China as the officially published version of Deng's major speech on January 16, 1980.
3. K. P. Wang, "Natural Resources and Their Utilization," in Yuan-li Wu, *China: A Handbook* (New York: Praeger, 1973).
4. Based on installed capacity of 12.8 gigawatts and an estimate of 220 gigawatts "economically exploitable" hydropower resources. See CIA, *Electric Power for China's Modernization: The Hydroelectric Option* (ER 80–10089 U, May, 1980).
5. K. P. Wang, "The Mineral Resource Base of Communist China," in Joint Economic Committee, U.S. Congress, *An Economic Profile of Mainland China* (Washington, DC: U.S. Government Printing Office, 1967), p. 169.

6. For a detailed argument, see Robert F. Dernberger, "The Chinese Search for the Path of Self-Sustained Growth in the 1980's: An Assessment," in Joint Economic Committee, U.S. Congress, *China Under the Four Modernizations* (Washington, DC: U.S. Government Printing Office, 1982).

7. "Zhao Ziyang's Speech at Industry Conference," *Foreign Broadcast Information Service* (FBIS), April 1, 1982, quotations selected from pp. K6–8.

8. Simon Kuznet's extensive study of the quantitative and qualitative measures of the process of economic development defines an underdeveloped country as one in which per capita standards of living are low, the productivity of labor is low, a large share of the labor force is engaged in agricultural production, and the process of capital accumulation and technological innovation fails to produce significant and sustained increases in the productivity of labor and declines in the share of the labor force engaged in agricultural production.

9. The Chinese press over the past five years has provided us an almost infinite variety of detailed arguments to support this point of view.

10. The use of the official exchange rate undervalues the real purchasing power of our U.S. dollar estimate for Chinese per capita consumption in 1981. Irving B. Kravis utilized commodity price and expenditure share data in the United States and China to estimate the real relative per capita consumption of China in 1975. His estimates indicate that while the official exchange rate indicates per capita consumption in China is only 2.4 percent that in the United States in 1975, a purchasing power parity comparison shows it to be 9 percent that in the United States. Irving Kravis, "Real Relative Per Capita GDP of China," *Journal of Comparative Economics,* 5 (1981) 1: 69–70.

11. A few years ago, China's leaders proclaimed the Ten-Year Plan released at the First session of the Fifth National People's Congress was the first stage in the achievement of China's modernization by the year 2000, when per capita national income would be U.S.$1,000. As a result of their sobering experiences over the past few years, that plan and slogan have been abandoned.

12. Liu Guoguang and Wang Xianming, "A Study of the Speech and Balance of China's Economic Development," *Social Sciences in China,* No. 4 (1980), p. 19.

13. Liang Wensen and Tian Jianghu, "Final Products: A New Point of Departure," *Social Sciences in China,* No. 4 (1980), p. 61.

14. There were, of course, periods that represent a major exception to this principle—the 1950s when the Soviet Union and East European countries were major suppliers of China's fixed capital stock, the early 1960s when the Western countries were called upon to supply foodstuff imports and complete plants on a smaller scale, and in the first half of the 1970s, when there was a steady and growing level of foodstuff imports and complete plant purchases abroad. Although each of these periods was associated with a better record in the macro-economic indicators for economic growth, they also generated a successful radical backlash by the Maoists that reaffirmed China's principle of self-sufficiency.

15. This is the major theme of the paper by Larry E. Westphal and Carl J. Dahlman on "The Acquisition of Technological Mastery in Industry," presented to the Sino–American Conference on the Design of Development Strategies. An interesting and important point they make is that the seemingly undramatic, but continuous, minor indigenous adaptations made in the borrowed technology contribute far more to a country's economic development or growth than the basic technology when it is originally borrowed.

16. While the folklore of this indigenous, small-scale sector has created a blacksmith, carpenter, housewife, etc., working with a crude homemade adaptation of an out-

dated machine as the originator of the enterprises, the existing enterprises in this sector do not use indigenous technology. Rather they are equipped with used machinery from the modern sector, equipment based on technology used widely in the West at an earlier stage of economic development, or machinery produced locally according to plans supplied by provincial design bureaus.

17. It is very hard to identify any three-year period between 1949 and 1975 as remotely being typical or representative of the period as a whole. For example, while Table 5.1 shows the average annual rate of growth in the gross value of output in 1952–1981 was 7.0 percent (in constant prices), the actual annual growth rates of GNP (in constant prices) in 1952–1979 were as follows: two were greater than 15 percent, seven between 10 and 15 percent, five were between 0 and 6 percent, while five were negative. In the total of 26 years included in the sample, only four years yielded growth rates between 6 and 8 percent. Thus, in any particular year the Chinese economy was either growing considerably faster or considerably slower than 7 percent; the distribution of growth rates is bimodal and the mean (average) has little meaning.

18. The discussion of X-inefficiency here has been restricted to the industrial sector, where these problems are most serious. The Chinese peasant is very skilled and hard-working and many of the wastes and inefficiencies in the agricultural sector can be attributed to the constraints and administrative decisions imposed upon the production team by higher level authorities. Nonetheless, poor farm management practices, income distribution schemes which weakly relate income with the quantity and quality of work done, and improper work assignments also lead to problems of X-inefficiencies in the agricultural sector.

19. The statistics that follow are from He Jianghang and Zhang Zhouyuan, "Exert Efforts to Raise the Economic Results," *Renmin Ribao,* (30 March 1981) p. 5.

20. For a more lengthy and detailed discussion of China's population problem, see Robert F. Dernberger, *Economic Consequences and Future Implications of Population Growth in China,* papers of the East–West Population Institute, No. 76, East–West Center, Honolulu, Hawaii, October 1981.

21. Commentator, "Increase Economic Results and Broaden the Sources of Revenue," *FBIS,* 17 March 1981, L17.

22. *FBIS,* 11 February 1981, L21.

23. Advocates of the Fei–Ranis dual sector model would argue other countries, i.e., Taiwan, etc., have solved this problem with the modern high productivity and wage sector ultimately providing new technology for the low productivity and wage sector and absorbing the "excess" labor force in that sector. They would have argued China should follow this same path. They fail to appreciate the sheer magnitude of China's traditional sector; the past record that shows rapid growth of employment in the modern sector failed to absorb excess population from the traditional sector, and population increased significantly. Nor do they appreciate how long it would take before the modern sector was able to absorb that population and how large the agricultural labor force would become in the meantime.

24. It should be noted, however, that the richest communes in China are not engaged in grain production, but are communes that specialize in fishing and commercial crops, and are near large urban concentrations of population. Furthermore, richer communes have a large share of their income coming from industrial and sideline activities.

25. This argument obviously contradicts the basic conclusion of Nicholas Lardy in his study of the Chinese budget system, but his argument was restricted to budget transfers among provincial levels of government. See Nicholas Lardy, *Economic*

Growth and Distribution in China (Cambridge, England: Cambridge University Press, 1978). Except for such subsidies as the illicit funds provided Dazhai to try and make that Maoist model work, to the best of my knowledge there was no line item on the Chinese budget for unilateral grants to communes until the 1980 budget, when less than 1 percent of total expenditures was devoted to this purpose.

26. See "Draft of Revised Constitution Made Public" and "Brief Summary of the Draft of the Revised Constitution," in *Beijing Review*, No. 18 (3 May 1982).

27. Unfortunately, the Chinese Marxist theorists are still debating on what the law of value means in practice, i.e., what costs are included in determining prices and how they are to be calculated.

28. Xue Mauqiao, "Adjust the National Economy and Promote Overall Balance," *Jingji Yanjiu*, No. 2 (20 February 1981), p. 27.

29. Hua Guofeng, "Report on the Work of the Government," FBIS, 2 July 1979, Supplement.

30. For a detailed description and analysis of these many reform policies, see Dernberger, footnote 6.

31. Wang Bingqian, "Report on the Final State Accounts for 1980 and Implementation of the Financial Estimates for 1981," *Beijing Review*, Vol. 25, No. 2 (22 January 1982).

32. State Statistical Bureau, "Communique on Fulfillment of China's 1981 National Economic Plan," *Beijing Review*, Vol. 25, No. 20 (17 May 1982).

33. The phrase "to the extent this change guides economic policymaking in the future" should be emphasized. While this paper was being written, Hu Yaobang gave a major speech to the 12th Party Congress (September 1, 1982), "Create a New Situation in All Fields of Socialist Modernization," that relied heavily on quantitative targets and timetables very similar to Hua Guofeng's speech on the "Four Modernizations" in 1978. Hu's speech, obviously a political speech for rallying the Party cadres and people behind the new Party leadership, contrasts sharply with Zhao's Report on the Work of the Government, presented at the 4th Session of the 5th National People's Congress in 1981. The new slogan in Hu's speech is "the general objective of China's economic construction for the two decades between 1981 and the end of the century . . . is to quadruple the gross value of industrial and agricultural production [placing] China in the front ranks of the countries of the world in income." This slogan has resulted in a flood of articles, again reminiscent of 1978, which repeat the slogan and argue how developments in this or that sector will lead to the achievement of this target. When asked to explain this shift in emphasis from the principal themes of the Eight Character Program to a slogan and policy arguments more in keeping with periods of the past, Xu Dixin (former Director, Institute of Economics, Chinese Academy of Social Sciences) argued that the people (and Party cadre?) had difficulty in understanding and appreciating the more sophisticated and less quantitatively specific policies and objectives of the Eight Character Program and *needed* a simple slogan with quantitative targets and timetables for mobilizing their efforts. *Deja vu.*

   On the other hand, several important speeches and analyses still can be found that address China's near term economic problems in the spirit of the more realistic and rational, as far as economic policy is concerned, speech by Zhao Ziyang to the 4th Session of the 5th NPC. See Ma Hong, "On Steps to Achieve the Strategic Objective," *Renmin Ribao* (28 October 1981), p. 5, and (29 October 1982), p. 5. Also Zhao Ziyang, "A Strategic Question on Invigorating the Economy," *Beijing Review* (15 November 1982), pp. 13–20.

34. Zhao Ziyang, "The Present Economic Situation and the Principles for Future Economic Construction," *Beijing Review*, Vol. 24, No. 51, (21 December 1981), p. 29.

35. "A Program for Current Agricultural Work," *Beijing Review*, Vol. 25, No. 24 (14 June 1982).

36. *Ibid.*, p. 22.

37. *Ibid.*, p. 22.

38. Thomas B. Wiens, "Poverty and Programs in the Huang and Huai River Basins," in William Parish, ed., *Bureaucracy and Rural Development* (forthcoming). According to Wiens, "Very little meaningful or novel research has been done since the 1950's at any level, and understanding of scientific research techniques is concentrated at the top . . . Forms of research which are particularly lacking are those which would make it possible to distinguish which of any set of alternative techniques are more or less effective and economic."

39. For example, in her visit to Sichuan, Audrey Donethorne learned that one reason that province's retained share of budget revenue was increased significantly as a result of the post-Mao economic reforms was that the state simultaneously assigned Sichuan the responsibility of funding investment in a large number of planned construction projects.

40. See Zhao Ziyang, "Several Questions on the Current Economic Work," *FBIS* (1 April 1982), K1–13.

41. "Restructuring of Industry," *Beijing Review*, No. 17 (April 1981), p. 5.

42. In deciding to choose investments in vocational schools over general primary and secondary education the Chinese leaders may be making an unwise choice. Research by Professor Irma Adelman and others show that in the low income countries at least, investments in general education make a greater contribution to increases in per capita incomes than does an equivalent amount of investment in technical or vocational education.

43. Richard Baum argues that the current economic reform program will meet the same fate as most reform programs in China over the past century for much the same reasons; their tradition of bureaucratic behavior and their concept of knowledge (the latter stressing formalist normative typologies as against the scientific method of analyzing cause and effect). See Richard Baum, *Scientist and Bureaucratism in Chinese Thought: Cultural Limits of the "Four Modernizations,"* Research Policy Institute, University of Lund, Sweden, Discussion Paper Series, No. 145.

44. "A Programme for Current Agricultural Work," *Beijing Review*, No. 24 (14 June 1982), pp. 21–27. This is a "slightly abridged" translation of the 25 point "Summary of the National Conference on Rural Work," a conference held by the Party General Committee "towards the end of 1981."

45. For a pessimistic conclusion based specifically on a study of China's prospects for agricultural development, see footnote 39, above. The conclusions of Haveman's research were presented in a paper given to a seminar of the Resource Systems Institute, East–West Center, Honolulu, on August 9, 1982.

Chapter 8

National Security—The Chinese Perspective

*Alfred D. Wilhelm, Jr.**

The Chinese approach to national security places a different emphasis from that of the West on the nature of the strategic environment and how to respond to it. Many Western observers of the PRC's approach to national security focus on China's defense doctrine and strategies, which they regard as outdated and inadequate for the modern, technology-dominated battlefield envisioned in the West. Those Westerners who prefer to compare contending forces in terms of equivalency in armament and associated modern logistic systems generally consider Chinese discussions of strategy to be either naive or disingenuous.[1] Chinese assertions that China would absorb the blows of an enemy like the USSR until that enemy is exhausted and then defeat it, are often discounted as the braggadocio of those with no other recourse. Western analyses of the PRC's defense requirements based on quantity, quality, and power projection comparisons between the People's Liberation Army (PLA) and its potential opponents describe a need for expensive quantity and quality improvements.[2] Although similar opinions continue to be expressed within the PRC's leadership, defense policy changes since 1979 have not been as dramatic as many Westerners expected. The Chinese have neither sought nor accepted initiatives

*Senior Fellow, the Atlantic Council of the United States, Colonel, U.S. Army.

from the West involving extensive defense cooperation and arms sales and do not appear likely to do so within the decade.

Yet clearly the PRC's leaders are concerned about improving China's national security position. As they have commented, "China considers its security threatened by the large number of Soviet troops along the Sino–Soviet and Sino–Mongolian boundaries" as well as by the Soviet invasion of Afghanistan and Soviet support for Vietnam and India. It feels threatened by the "U.S. policy of discrimination against China in economic and trade affairs," and the U.S. policy toward Taiwan, technology transfers, Law of the Sea, and arms control.[3] China is concerned about the hostility it perceives in the international economic order, and the threat of "things foreign." And of course internally the current leadership is still very concerned about the question of succession and establishing an orderly transition.

These concerns reflect the heavier emphasis the Chinese place on political and economic challenges to their national security and the relatively lighter emphasis placed on Western-type evaluations of opposing military forces. The military threat is important—but not as overriding as in the West—when considered along with all the forces and trends that the Chinese believe must be correlated in the national security decision process.

The PRC's national security response also differs in emphasis. The most common reaction in the West is to develop an equal or greater capability—a counterforce—whether political, economic, or military. To a greater extent than most, however, the Chinese emphasize strategem as an ideal solution. They would prefer to surprise or deceive an opponent, to avoid the use of force, to deal with an opponent's weakness while neutralizing his strengths, to deal with images and perceptions. While they sometimes appear to fail (e.g., the Cultural Revolution and Vietnam), they have an historical awareness that gives them a long-term view on policy and less of a sense of urgency in finding a solution. Consequently, since 1949, national security decisions have been influenced more by long-term interests than short-term "quick fixes" and by the views of China's leadership of the more enduring threats to China's security.

Projecting the PRC's national security policy through the next decade, then, requires more than an evaluation of the PLA's capabilities. It requires an assessment of the Chinese perspective of the strategic environment and their preferred methods for dealing with the environment. This chapter first describes a Chinese perspective of the strategic environment in terms of the superpowers, regional issues, and their own domestic considerations. Then, in order of preference, the Chinese use of negotiations, alliances, and warfare are discussed as responses to the strategic environment.

STRATEGIC ENVIRONMENT— THE CHINESE VIEW

To the PRC's leadership, most of the years since 1949 have been rife with domestic economic or political turmoil as different Chinese Communist Party (CCP) factions have struggled for power, often advancing their own distinct views on national security as justification for the struggle. The purges that each administration since 1966 has used to lessen opposition to its policy line have also decreased initiative and support for official policy. Consequently concerns about possible future succession crises complicate the tasks of developing sufficient internal unity to protect China and the revolution from outside interference and of restoring the country's role as a major power—of creating the world's third center of power.

The Superpowers

Throughout most of the period since 1949, "U.S. imperialism" has been seen by the CCP as the principal threat to the long-term survival of communism in China. The intellectual challenge in 1949 to China's incomplete Communist revolution from the "subversive popularity" of U.S. democracy undoubtedly was one of the reasons the PRC's leaders rejected the hand of recognition that the United States appeared ready to extend.[4] The Party's fear, however, was soon overshadowed by the nation's growing fear of military conflict with the United States, a fear heightened by China's experience with a hundred years of nearly continuous warfare caused by Western imperialism.[5] The Chinese were directly affected first in North China by the Korean War of 1950 and MacArthur's march to the Yalu, then in Central China by the Taiwan crises of 1955 and 1958, and finally in South China by the "U.S. imperialist's" Vietnam War. The growing threat from the United States tended to unify the nation—until in the 1960s, when the Soviet Union became a major threat, especially in the northern parts of the nation. The two-front threat exacerbated the contending factional views of national security. A less-visible threat was the longstanding concern of the Party's ideologues about the gradual erosion of socialism by "things foreign," which the decade of Russian assistance significantly reinforced.

By 1969 Moscow's efforts to dominate communism worldwide (or "social imperialism") and age-old Chinese-Russian distrust combined to destroy the Sino–Soviet Communist fraternity of the 1950s. The USSR replaced the United States as the PRC's principal ideological threat. Soviet military forces in the Far East increased. By the time the United States withdrew from Vietnam, the military threat from the USSR dominated the PRC's thinking about security, particularly in the North. The USSR was becoming a "hegemonistic threat" not only to China but to the world, while the United States—now in second place—appeared to be lowering its profile, especially in the Pacific. Particularly worrisome was the continued increase and modernization of Soviet Far East conventional and nuclear forces, as well as a significant expansion of the Pacific Fleet's resources and missions. This threat further increased when Moscow enhanced its ability to direct and coordinate these Far East forces by consolidating the theater's command and control structure at Ulan-ude in 1978.[6] Although Brezhnev's 1969 "Asian Collective Security" concept never fully materialized, Soviet force improvements and the events leading to the Soviet–Vietnamese Treaty of Friendship and Cooperation (November 3, 1978) and a similar treaty with Afghanistan (December 4, 1978) constituted, from China's viewpoint, nearly complete encirclement. Just as America's containment policy was finally removed, the PRC found itself facing a vigorous containment effort by the USSR. The inauguration of a new relationship with the West, evidenced by the Sino–Japanese Treaty of Peace and Friendship (August 12, 1978) and the Sino–U.S. announcement in December that diplomatic relations would be established on January 1, 1979, resulted in large part from the PRC's fixation on this Soviet threat.

Possibly by as early as 1972, when the PLA budget was decreased, some of China's leaders had perceived a downward trend in the imminence of the Soviet threat. Certainly by 1979 the international correlation of forces, though still favorable to the USSR, had begun to improve for the Chinese. As evidence they pointed to the PRC's strategic success—despite tactical losses—in punishing Vietnam (February 17-March 16, 1979), the continued inability of the USSR to complete the pacification of Afghanistan begun in December 1979, unrest in Poland, the Carter administration's *volte-face* on national defense, and later the Reagan administration's added stress on countering the Soviet Union.

From the Chinese vantage point the Sino–Vietnamese War drove a wedge between the USSR and Vietnam by proving that the USSR cannot be relied upon to lend its full support in a crisis, just as it never fully backed the PRC during the Eisenhower threat to use nuclear weapons in Korea (1953), nor publicly supported the PRC over the Taiwan Crisis of 1958 until after the fact. Despite providing significant logistical support to both the PRC and Vietnam, the Soviets were unwilling to place direct pressure on either ally's adversary when the ally's actions threatened to involve Soviet forces in conflict with another nuclear power. Thus, it appears to the Chinese that the potential utility of the alliance with Vietnam to Moscow's "encirclement policy" has been eroded by Vietnam's concerns over the probable limits to Soviet support in a crisis, the very heavy economic costs of the war, the staggering expense of both post-war mobilization and the purchase of Soviet military equipment to reinforce its northern borders, and Vietnam's displeasure with its growing dependency on the USSR. Furthermore the financial cost of the alliance for the USSR increased significantly at a time when other foreign expenses, such as Afghanistan and Poland, were mounting.

From the Chinese perspective, the Afghan War proves once again that People's War is still an effective, albeit limited defense strategy. Technology has not proven to be the decisive factor that so many predicted. Vietnam, Afghanistan, and Poland, coupled with the enhancement of U.S. defense capabilities, have increased pressure on the USSR and have reduced the likelihood of an attack on China, thereby making it possible for China to be less committed to countering the USSR.

Besides the direct threat to the PRC from the USSR and United States, there also is the danger of war between the two superpowers, ultimately a worldwide conflict involving China. Until the early 1960s the Chinese were concerned about being dragged into such a conflict by their alliance with the USSR. Since the late 1970s there has been a growing concern that the PRC was becoming too closely aligned with the United States. As the world situation changed, including U.S. efforts to begin restoring the strategic balance between the USSR and the West, those Chinese concerned about relying too heavily on the United States felt it was time to lessen some of the tensions in Sino–Soviet relations. Some in Beijing suggested a course in which the PRC would lean 70 percent toward the United States and 30 percent toward the USSR.[7] As negotiations with the USSR stalled in 1983 and the United States appeared to de-emphasize its strategic relationship with the PRC, this formula was tactically adjusted a little in mid–1983 to pressure the Soviets by encouraging the United States. By adopting this course, China is courted strategically by both the United States and the USSR but not wholly dependent on either. Consequently China's concern about being automatically involved in such a world war is reduced though not eliminated, its political maneuverability and image as a third major power is enhanced, and pressure for short-term military expenditures decreased, all at a time when the internal and external efforts of the PRC must be focused on modernization goals. China is then in the optimum position to "sit on top of the mountain and watch the tigers fight."

Largely because of the PRC's geopolitical position between the two superpowers, the current Chinese administration forecasts that China will not have to defend itself against the USSR in the decade ahead. There will continue to be border problems of varying degrees of seriousness, all with the potential of accidentally becoming a major conflict, but no major conflict is anticipated. Nor is the United States viewed as a major conventional military threat since it is unlikely to significantly enhance its physical presence in Japan, Korea, or elsewhere on the Asian mainland by much more than the upgrading of existing capabilities. Even U.S. efforts to enhance military coordination with Japan will be viewed by the PRC as an anti-Soviet improvement, although this effort has generated concern among some Chinese strategic analysts about future implications for China.[8]

In the 1982 Constitution of the PRC, the threat is described as "those forces and elements . . . abroad which are hostile to China's socialist system and try to undermine it."[9] The mildness of this statement underscores the preeminence of economic modernization, a reduced concern over the Soviet threat, and increased concern over the socially destructive influence foreign things and ideas can have, particularly those from the United States. Further emphasized is the conflict between the goals of U.S. imperialism and Soviet social imperialism for global hegemony, especially in the Middle East. This conflict may increase the probability of war between the United States and the USSR toward the end of the decade and thereby increase the threat to the PRC and the rest of the Third World. According to the constitution's preamble, however, the future of the world is brightened by China's independence to strengthen its unity with the people of oppressed nations and developing countries to safeguard world peace.

If Deng Xiaoping's policy line fails or if he dies during the decade without ensuring the continuation of his designated heirs, a succeeding administration that polarized to the left probably would increase the emphasis on ideological concerns about U.S. imperialism, USSR social imperialism, the threat to world peace of their competitive, hegemonic policies in the Third World, and the exploitive nature of the international economic order. The tendency would be toward a more Sinocentric, isolationist viewpoint. A more rightist leadership (a more likely scenario if Deng were to die suddenly) might focus more on the Soviet forces on China's borders and the growing technological gap between China and the developed nations.

Regional Issues

From Beijing's perspective, regional issues are derivatives of strategic issues. Regional issues tend to be more tangible, however, and have a more immediate programmatic impact, especially for regional political and military leaders who, on a daily basis, are confronted with their opponent's strengths, and with their own weaknesses.

For those leaders concerned with China's northern borders, the presence of 25 percent of the forces of the USSR near their borders is the most dangerous threat. These leaders recognize that the creation of these forces by the Soviet Union was a defensive move aimed at containing the PRC, but it also produced a permanent ability to punitively attack China if necessary. These Soviet forces were not withdrawn from the European front, but were created and permanently added to the existing force structure so that the Soviets now have the capability to fight, at least defensively, on three fronts simultaneously. This capability was probably achieved in the early 1970s and demonstrated in the USSR's first global military exercise in 1971. Since then, improvements, aimed in part at the U.S. Pacific presence, have been made steadily in readiness, modernization, force structure, and command and control.

The Chinese acknowledge that these Soviet forces probably could occupy Northeast China down to the Yellow River, if Moscow is willing to pay a very heavy price. (In private some Soviets have suggested that the Great Wall is a more likely limit.) The Soviets could also sever the autonomous region of Xinjiang from China. On the other hand, China's leaders point out that 51 to 55 Soviet divisions spread out over a 10,000 kilometer border is a very low force density for anything more than defense. Chinese were taught by the Russians that a force ratio (considering troops and materiel) as high as 8:1 is needed for offensive actions with the 3:1 ratio cited in U.S. doctrine being too low.[11] The Soviets could certainly obtain an 8:1 tactical advantage for a short time in a limited area, especially when their materiel advantage is considered, but the overall ratio for troops in the general vicinity of the border is a very unfavorable 1:3. Even with major additions of materiel it would be difficult to correct this ratio.

Terrain, standard Soviet force structures, and Soviet concepts of war dictate that this force have a significant albeit limited offensive capability in addition to its defensive capability. This offensive capability is severely limited by the extent of the prepositioned logistics as well as the limited capacity of the trans-Siberian railroad, airlift, and the long sea lines of communication. It would be particularly difficult to move large numbers of military forces with their equipment from the European front to the Chinese front or vice versa. Not even the addition of the Baikal-Amur Main Line (BAM) will completely overcome this problem.

The main Chinese concern over the BAM line is not the enhancement of military logistics, but the degree to which its opening of the Soviet Far East to further Russian immigration and development will require more frequent attention by senior Soviet leaders and in so doing highlight the region's vulnerability to Chinese pressures. An increased Soviet feeling of vulnerability could generate even greater problems between the two societies.[12]

To the south, Vietnam is both a victim of Soviet hegemonism and a hegemonistic power whose ambitions run counter to China's own desires for influence in the region. Sino–Vietnamese conflict over Kampuchea will likely continue as long as Vietnam demands sole influence in that country. To the extent that any improvements in Sino–Soviet relations will influence Vietnam, a Sino–Vietnamese modus vivendi could develop. Nevertheless the potential for conflict will remain high as a result of Vietnam's continued aggressive role in Kampuchea as sustained by the Vietnam–Soviet alliance. Vietnam's claims in the South China Sea, a potentially oil rich area, also will make any improvements in Sino–Vietnamese relations difficult.

Militarily, Vietnam—"the Cuba of Asia"—has created significant problems for the PLA both on the battlefield and in the granting of access to ports to the USSR, which enhances the Soviet navy's ability to interdict sea lines of communication in the Pacific. Despite both its painful losses and smaller size, Vietnam's relatively more modern equipment and more experienced soldiers were able to punish China. Unlike the modernization gap between the Soviet and Chinese forces, the equipment gap between the PLA and the People's Army of Vietnam (PAVN) will begin to close over the decade as China pursues modernization and Vietnam wrestles with its stagnant economy. Still, PAVN forces will continue to represent a potential second front in the event of conflict with the USSR. More significantly, Vietnam's strength also will enable it to challenge China's territorial claims in the South China Sea and its desires for influence in Southeast Asia.

A more ideological and inwardly oriented Chinese leadership would be more vitriolic in attacking Vietnam for aligning with the Soviet hegemonists and more prone to direct conflict over Kampuchea and PRC claims in the South China Sea. A more rightist and possibly decentralized leadership might be more flexible and thus better equipped to find an accommodation with Vietnam, especially if relations with the USSR improve.

To the east, Taiwan is as much an issue of emotion as of reason. The origin of this emotion can be traced back to the early years of the still unresolved civil war, the protection by a foreign power of those who fled to Taiwan and the subsequent denial of the rewards due the battlefield's victors, the establishment on Taiwan as a "puppet" government reminiscent of China's past "humiliation at the hands of colonialists and imperialists," and the image of the PRC as a weak central government unable to control the outer provinces. Even as time has tended to soften these poignant bitter memories, Taiwan's economic success has tended to revive them and generate interest among many on the Mainland concerning the applicability to the PRC of specific trade and financial ideas and techniques used on Taiwan. Its success has raised questions concerning the PRC's failure to at least equal Taiwan's rate of development, and increased the threat from Taiwan as an alternative non-Communist model. Again, we see their fear of the influence of things foreign—with origins in the United States.

In contrast, the military threat from Taiwan is considered minimal. The island's ability to invade the PRC is severely limited by manpower and logistics and would be dependent on such improbable activities as mass uprisings, obtaining manpower and logistics on the battlefield, and the support of a major power. As long as the PLA is responsive to Beijing, the PRC will not fear an independent attack from Taiwan. On the other hand the PLA's contingency planners must keep in mind Taiwan's potential for such uses as the control of sea lanes, of which they are frequently reminded by Taiwan's leaders who speak of the comparison General MacArthur made between Taiwan and an "unsinkable aircraft carrier."

As a political threat, Taiwan is a problem for the current administration in Beijing. Because of the emphasis they have placed on Taiwan in the negotiations with the United States, Taiwan has become a symbol, a measure of China's weakness vis-à-vis the West, as well as a means to control the pace and intensity of relations with the United States. Because of the wide range of intense feelings within the different leadership factions over relations with the West, the Taiwan issue appears to have developed divisive potential within the senior leadership circles. This issue will continue to require very careful handling by the current leaders to insure a working consensus throughout the decade.

If a more ideologically oriented leadership style were to emerge, the emphasis would be on the threat of Western ideas, boding ill for a peaceful resolution of the Taiwan issue. A more decentralized or regionally oriented administration would likely place greater emphasis on the potential for regional economic development that could result from a more patient and cooperative approach to the Taiwan issue. An indication of this approach was seen in 1981, at the height of the current PRC administration's experiment with greater decentralized economic and political authority, when there was speculation in South China concerning the benefits of a political union for economic purposes between Taiwan, Guangdong, and Fujian.[13] Decentralization temporarily resulted in the expansion of informal bilateral trade between Taiwan and the Mainland, until curtailed by Beijing.

Currently Japan is a benign threat. In spite of the bitter memories of Japan's aggression during World War II and the fact that Japan is a Western-style democracy, Japan is now considered by the PRC to be nonaggressive, because of the bilateral peace and friendship treaty. The furor raised by the PRC, however, over the efforts of Japan's Education Ministry in 1982 to recast in the nation's textbooks Japan's war (1931–1945) against China—particularly the Nanjing Massacre—in less negative terms indicates how close to the surface and enduring the memories and emotions of Japanese WWII aggression are among the older Chinese, despite several years of friendly relations and frequent gestures of obeisance by the Japanese. China's leaders reacted to the textbook issue by inundating the public with stories and pictures of the horrors of that era. They revived cruel memories among the elder generation and educated those too young (the majority of the population) to know of that era. As a result, the influence of those years will be felt in Sino–Japanese relations beyond the end of the century.

Chinese concerns over future Japanese defense efforts also reflect China's wartime experiences with Japan. So long as Japan focuses its force modernization on its ground and air defense forces, Chinese leaders will have little to say. However, a major naval or air buildup by Japan, such as that demanded from some U.S. quarters, would generate considerable concern.[14]

Some Chinese analysts believe that leadership succession in North Korea (DPRK) will be the most troublesome issue on the peninsula during the decade. Despite the PRC's de facto acceptance of dynastic Communism, Kim Il-Song's son is unproven. If he were to "lean toward the USSR," and negate China's hard won influence in the DPRK, the Soviet Union's attempt to encircle China would be strengthened and the possibility of regional instability increased. As long as this threat exists, the presence of the United States on the peninsula and the strengthening of the ROK's military will be a source of concern but not an area of controversy. Because of the PRC's concern for stability, it also may use the unofficial trade that has developed between the ROK and the PRC to influence relations between the DPRK and the PRC and USSR.

Domestic Considerations

The government's focus during the next decade will be on economic development. The current PRC administration has permitted a degree of decentralization of economic authority in an effort to stimulate the revival of personal initiative (see Chapter 7 by Professor Dernberger). The potential benefits are enormous, but there is concern that these efforts might result in the revival of regionalism or the spinning apart of the state into many nearly autonomous states. These concerns will also influence the extent to which the national leadership continues to support efforts to make the PLA a more professional military force with strong national loyalties.[15]

Becoming more professional means the PLA becomes more oriented to the external threat. It means a greater emphasis on modern weapons, technology, and military training in addition to more discipline, improvements in command and control and a decrease in political training and non-military duties. Yet political leaders are at least as concerned about the role of the PLA as the final arbiter in civil affairs that threaten the security of the State. These different roles conflict and create stress. As was often demonstrated during the Cultural Revolution, too close an association by the PLA with the local populace and local government seriously erodes the authority of the State. Yet a political role for the military is expected, if not popular, for such a role has historical antecedents that are not only Marxist, but pre-Marxist. Furthermore, over the next decade potential domestic unrest could severely tax the abilities of the government, limiting the extent to which the PLA will be permitted to cast off its political responsibilities.[16]

Economic development creates intense competition for resources, including the military's manpower and production capability. Recruited from an agricultural society, the PLA will be expected to remain generally self-sufficient in agricultural and livestock requirements in order to reduce demands on the national budget. The use, however, of the military in economic production-oriented organizations is being reevaluated. The Production and Construction Corps, for example, has been abolished. Yet the PLA is the most directly responsive organization that the central government can call upon that has the necessary organization and resources to plan and execute in many parts of the country such major economic infrastructure projects as water control, highway and railroad transportation, and communications. Here too the pressure will be on demilitarizing as many of these functions as possible, as part of the continuing effort to decrease the number of military personnel, reduce the defense budget, and seek the most effective incentives and efficient means in Chinese society to accomplish these tasks. But the politics of modernization will require the central government to step in where local government is unable. This means the PLA will continue to have a development role.

Other military resources that can be tapped to support economic development are the research, development and production capabilities of the defense industries. Here too the current requirement for these ministries to devote capacity in excess of the PLA's needs to the economy at large has produced resistance and opposition. The opponents include those who resent the elevation of those who "work with their brains" to the status of workers and the replacement of the loyal but less competent cadre with modern managers. Others are opposed to the diversion of resources away from PLA and the trend toward the integration of civilian and military industries. Opposition to these efforts will slowly dissolve over the decade as the new system develops permanence, but in the meantime the modern managers must wrestle with such problems as inefficiency, redundancy, inadequate standardization, poor quality control, a lack of upward mobility, and if insufficient progress is made, another reorganization—the perennial panacea to bureaucratic inertia.

The flexibility and resilience of the PLA in responding to these and a complex array of domestic demands for modernization and professionalism make the PLA a critical institution in the modernization process. The internal allocation of the reduced defense budget among the many competing demands of education, training, equipment and technology purchases, research and development, production, and manpower often will predetermine the PLA's reaction to other demands from political leaders to assist in social modernization and social stability.

RESPONDING TO THE STRATEGIC ENVIRONMENT—NATIONAL SECURITY POLICY

A great deal changed in China as a result of the Communist revolution, but because of Mao it ultimately was an indigenous revolution based on China's unique circumstances. Mao was a great synthesizer who drew freely from Western thought, but he learned many of his greatest lessons about national security from China's classics. He frequently quoted from the works of Sun Tzu, the Spring and Autumn *Annals,* and the histories of the Three Kingdoms and Warring States periods. Just as Mao found great value in lessons from history, Chinese culture significantly influences all Chinese in terms of classical Chinese thinking. A teacher by training and instinct, Mao reinforced this influence by ensuring that the top leadership of the Party also studied China's military history for its application to the experiences of the Party.

China's leaders thus know, as Sun Tzu points out, that war is not the final arbiter of conflicts between nations, that there are no wars to end all wars. War is but one of many tools by which a nation's leaders attempt to secure their goals. It is an instrument to be used with great care since it generally creates bigger problems than it resolves, "for there has never been a protracted war from which a country has benefited."[17] Inherent in a decision to fight is an implicit admission of one's own failure, not the enemy's, "for to win one hundred victories in one hundred battles is not the acme of skill. To subdue the enemy without fighting is the acme of skill."[18] War should be limited. Conclude it as fast as possible, so that the nation's leaders may return to the use of more profitable and less destructive national security tools, such as negotiations. "Thus those skilled in war subdue the enemy's army without battle. They capture his cities without assaulting them and overthrow his state without protracted operations. Your aim must be to take All-under-Heaven intact."[19] The physical capture of an opponent is of far less value than his conversion to your viewpoint.

The result is that China's leaders devote a large part of their response to the strategic environment to influencing the perceptions of other nations about China's just claims, and to establishing a moral correctness for China's objectives. While physical strength is important, it is not the sole determinant of the outcome of a conflict. Thus national security is pursued with a primary emphasis on the diplomacy of negotiations. With infinite patience and determination, negotiations (backed by a Chinese approach to alliances and warfare) are used to turn a position of weakness in the strategic environment into a more favorable one.

Negotiations

For the Chinese, negotiations start long before negotiators sit down to the conference table. Negotiations are more than the formal finite process that concludes with a joint communiqué and a signed document. Going to the negotiations table is a tactic, not a strategy. It is but one phase of a dynamic process that is continually at work. Bilateral relations are continuous negotiations, with a dynamic agenda in which all elements are subordinated to the achievement of the PRC's national objectives. Diplomacy is a tactical means of influencing the milieu in which the negotiators must operate and which shape their perceptions of the process. War, or more precisely the fear of war, is but one tool of the negotiator. National objectives are not achieved by war; rather war is a means to lower opposition to cooperation. Formal negotiations are a period of time in a negotiations process in which the intensity of exchange between nations is of such volume and potential value that a conference atmosphere is practical. The conclusion of formal negotiations marks not the end of the negotiations, but recognizes that nothing more can be achieved at that time. Since the national objectives are enduring in nature, from the Chinese perspective, negotiations take on an indefinite character, a process that should not be hurried strategically, though there are occasions when tactics may dictate speed. The conclusions of today establish a plateau from which future negotiators can step to reopen the argument, a springboard to further discussions on issues opponents may have thought were settled.

Panmunjom (1952–1953) was the first twentieth century negotiating experience of the Chinese in which they dealt with the West from a position of relative equality. Although not everyone was ready to accept them as equals, the Chinese perceived that in Korea they had fought a powerful allied army representing the most modern and best of the West and had not lost. The stage was set for formal negotiations to begin. Clearly, survival or security had been primary reasons for entry into the war. The formal negotiations revealed another primary Chinese objective—acceptance by the international community as a legitimate major actor. Legitimacy was an important goal on the path to becoming accepted as a major power. Even though the United States successfully avoided any formal actions that might have legitimized the government of the People's Republic of China, the participation of the PRC's volunteers in Korea further nurtured the international community's perception of China as a major power.

The talks that began in Geneva in 1955 were important to the Chinese as another forum for furthering their objective of gaining acceptance in the international community as a major power. De facto recognition by the United States or acceptance by other countries of China's equality with the United States was necessary if China was to gain acceptance as a major power. Thus even the beginning of the talks represented another step forward, however small.

Geneva revealed a great deal about how the Chinese would negotiate with the United States. While the United States assiduously avoided topics that might lead to broad general agreements, preferring to deal with very specific issues, the Chinese continually strove to obtain agreement on broad principles or deal with issues that could lead to such agreements. The PRC delegate, Ambassador Wang Bingnan, pressed for progress on a wide range of issues from the U.S. trade embargo and bilateral high level conferences to cultural exchanges. The United States remained steadfastly focused on achieving an agreement on the release of Americans imprisoned in China and an agreement by the PRC not to use force in resolving the Taiwan issue.

For the United States, the talks were particularly frustrating. The only agreement signed was that dealing with the exchange of prisoners. Since the PRC did not release all the U.S. prisoners expeditiously, the United States increasingly felt betrayed and angry. On the other hand, since the Chinese had had no success in getting the United States to deal with items on their agenda, they were concerned that if they released all the prisoners immediately the United States would break off the talks.[20] To the PRC the talks were essential for creating an image of equality with the United States. This was especially true as the prospects for the PRC's entry into the United Nations faded. After the initial flurry of activity over the prisoner exchange, the talks became largely a communications vehicle, a mailbox, for the United States. For the Chinese, the talks were useful in helping to shape the world's perception of China. The enduring nature of the talks continued to erode the moral correctness of the United States' position of not recognizing the PRC.

By the time Henry Kissinger went to China in July 1971, the international stage was set. World opinion had moved to a de facto acceptance of China as a major power. Though U.S. domestic opinion was trailing, it moved sharply with President Nixon's 1972 visit in favor of good relations with China, a nation too important to ignore. Again, during the process, the United States focused narrowly on the specifics of normalizing relations while making concessions in areas of general principle. The Chinese focused on principles, fastidiously dealing with the moral (ideological) correctness of their position, while ensuring that with each important compromise a door was left ajar to permit renegotiation of the issue in the future.

The greatest common ground emphasized by both sides was security from the common threat, the Soviet Union. For the Chinese, however, the concern for security never became so dominant that other national objectives were not also advanced. Continually from the beginning of the Geneva talks in 1955 through the negotiations leading to the Shanghai Communiqué (February 28, 1972), the Joint Communiqué on the Establishment of Diplomatic Relations . . . (January 1, 1979), and the Joint Communiqué (August 17, 1982) concerning U.S. arms sales to Taiwan, the Chinese have used the issue of Taiwan as a control rod by which to regulate the PRC–US relationship. By withdrawing Taiwan from the center of attention they accelerate developments and then retard events by reinserting Taiwan as the central issue. Whether a conscious policy or not, the net effect has been favorable to the PRC. In 1955, as they advanced their interests at Geneva, the Chinese did not make Taiwan an issue. It was not until it became apparent that the United States would not be helpful that Taiwan was raised, the talks bogged down, and the fault was laid at the doorstep of the "U.S. imperialists." Similarly in 1972, the difficulties over Taiwan were few as the Chinese pressed to deal with the Soviet threat. However, as the 1980s opened and China's security needs dictated a foreign policy course correction, Taiwan was once again a major issue between the two countries.

From the perspective of China's leaders, the moral correctness of their position vis-à-vis the United States has been corroborated by and has contributed to the lack of unity among the Western allies on policy toward the PRC and Taiwan. Whereas there was a large degree of Western unity in 1955, by 1972 the Allies were each pursuing their own separate policies. Recognition of the PRC and relations with Taiwan were handled bilaterally, outside of a common framework. Even in 1972, as the British moved to resolve their differences with the PRC over the future of Hong Kong, there was very little coordination or even apparent interest among the Western allies. How the Hong Kong question is resolved probably will establish a clear precedent for Taiwan. Yet, to the satisfaction of the PRC's leaders, there has been little interest expressed in the United States, even in the Congress, in exploring Britain's policies concerning what may be one of the most significant problems in East Asia in the next decade. From the Chinese viewpoint, this is a bilateral issue between the PRC and Britain in which the Chinese position is based on universal truths. Deviations from these truths have been and may continue to be accepted temporarily to accommodate the objective reality of the other state's political conditions, but in the long run these truths will be fulfilled. For instance, Hong Kong is Chinese, was obtained as a result of an "unequal" treaty, and must be returned. The resulting pattern is that when a number of countries have to deal with the PRC on the same foreign policy issue, such as the normalization of relations with the PRC and the "de-recognition" of the ROC, a variety of unique and unrelated solutions will develop. Many of these solutions will be subject to future renegotiation because of some deviation in the compromise from the universal truth.

As previously mentioned, Taiwan is not viewed the same way by all of China's leaders. Although the United States has recognized the PRC, for some Chinese leaders it is still not a relationship based on equality.

China still is not in full control of its destiny. Taiwan remains an uncontrolled outer province, a puppet government under foreign control. For them this represents the same kind of problem that the Ching dynasty had when the Ming rebels fled to Taiwan and established a countergovernment. The authority of the central government must be affirmed. For others Taiwan represents a political issue that can be used as a domestic bargaining tool either for or against the current administration's policies. For yet others Taiwan is a hindrance to the establishment of a strong relationship with the United States that is badly needed to support modernization and, according to others, to counter the Soviet threat. Internally for China's leadership, Taiwan is a many-headed Hydra, a problem that must be solved in keeping with China's official position that Taiwan is a province of China, one that all must recognize and accept. This is reinforced as well as complicated by the fact that the Kuomintang government of Taiwan makes the same claim. Taiwan is an important issue for the PRC, domestically and internationally, but not one that is immutable. The PRC can compromise; U.S.–China relations attest to that. The question is whether a more permanent compromise can be achieved rather than "agreeing to disagree" for the moment with the expectation that the issue will be reopened repeatedly.

Based on these limited observations on Chinese negotiations between the PRC and the United States, a general style can be postulated. First the PRC attempts to influence the milieu in which the negotiations are conducted to achieve the most favorable situation. Generally this means that the United States is seen as anxiously pressing to open a dialogue, whether the impetus is in the administration or is rising from the American citizenry. This image has been enhanced in recent years by the U.S. fetish for "trip-book diplomacy," where most senior U.S. representatives visit Beijing bearing gifts in the form of a concession on the part of the United States, whether asked for or not. Conversely, the Chinese trips, such as Deng Xiaoping's, have not produced gifts; policy is made and announced in Beijing, seldom out of a suitcase. If gifts are used by the PRC, the intent is often to create in the United States a sense of obligation, which is how Ambassador U. Alexis Johnson evaluates Ambassador Wang's unexpected announcement—the day before their first meeting—of the release of eleven American flyers who had been shot down over the PRC in the 1950s. Designed to create a sense of obligation, the announcement placed the U.S. delegation on the defensive.[21]

The proposed agenda items of each side are likely to be very different. Whereas the United States may nominate practical matters for the discussion agenda, the Chinese will focus on issues that contribute to the establishment of broad general agreements, leaving the specifics of many sub-issues ambiguous. The focus may be a general agreement on a basic principle such as sovereignty, the legitimacy of the PRC, or a lesser issue, such as arms sales, upon which arguments concerning a larger principle can be built. The accumulation of a series of these lesser agreements can ultimately create a de facto accomplishment of a major objective. Senator John Glenn has argued that with each succeeding exchange with the PRC the issue of PRC sovereignty over Taiwan has gradually been conceded to the PRC so that there is confusion even in the minds of senior politicians as to the policy of the United States. In the Shanghai Communiqué of 1972, the United States did not challenge the position maintained by all Chinese on both sides of the Taiwan Straits "that there is but one China and that Taiwan is a part of China." In July 1982, Assistant Secretary John Holdridge told the Senate Foreign Relations Committee that "we [the United States] acknowledge that there is only one China and that Taiwan is part of China. This is our position, and it has not changed since it was originally enunciated in the Shanghai Communiqué of 1972." Yet Senator Glenn's presentation clearly shows that there has been a change, however subtle.[22]

Having achieved a general agreement, the Chinese then began the process of specific application from their viewpoint. Because different values and data lead to different conclusions, there is considerable room for disagreement between signatories. The Chinese system is based more on a commitment to a value system than is the West's system, which is based more on a set of laws with specific interpretations. The Chinese are then in the position of using their interpretation and claiming that the other party is violating the "spirit" of the agreement. The most frequent effect is to generate guilt in the other party, and the unquestioned adoption of the Chinese interpretation.

Time is on the side of the PRC if the national style of their opponent is to seek a quick solution to a problem. The Chinese, as well as other oriental societies, have a far more patient style that they use to great advantage, for instance, such time-honored techniques as arguing over the agenda, who can be present at the discussions, and many other administrative details. All of these details have the potential to influence the outcome of negotiations, but generally would not require a lot of time to resolve unless deliberately made an issue. However, if the idea is to wear down the patience of an impatient opponent, then such efforts may be fruitful. Henry Kissinger points out that the Paris peace talks were held up for three months in late 1968 over the shape of the conference table. When the Soviets proposed a round table at Hanoi's request, the deadlock was quickly broken by the American response. It was too hasty a response according to Dr. Kissinger, who now sees this as the principal foreign policy mistake of the Nixon transition team. The timing worked to Hanoi's benefit.[23]

There is always the fear in any negotiations that if you come to an agreement on the most important issue of your opponent before you have achieved your most important objectives, your opponent will use this advantage by threatening to terminate the talks or by walking out and blaming the failure to reach any further agreement on your own intransigence. In order to create an atmosphere of progress and cooperation, yet avoid giving their opponent such an advantage, the Chinese have developed the tactic of reaching an agreement and then adroitly managing the implementation in a number of phases. For example, the Chinese were afraid after they had reached an agreement with the United States on American prisoners in China, that if they released all of the prisoners at once, the United States would not be willing to continue the talks. It was important to the PRC at that time that the talks continue, so the prisoners were released gradually. First the talks added to their legitimacy and secondly they provided a vehicle for enhancing that position.

In every negotiation, the negotiator would like to have an issue with which to control the pace of the negotiations and to use as a lever to move even the most stubborn of the opponent's positions. Obviously this is not possible in all cases for all negotiators. Nations without the wealth and power of the United States have often decried the seeming onesided nature of negotiations with the United States. However, the Chinese early in their history found that great military or economic power is neither absolute nor always usable. Even the strong have weaknesses. The PRC's leaders discovered early the vulnerability of the United States over the issue of Taiwan. A spirit of cooperation is easily maintained by playing down the issue. Conversely if the relationship is moving too fast or other factors dictate less cooperation, the PRC needs only to raise the issue of Taiwan and make noises about the imperialistic nature of the United States. The result is not only to lessen cooperation but to shift the blame for the decreased cooperation onto the United States.

Beijing would prefer the United States keep out of the issue altogether, as Beijing's direct leverage over Taipei is limited as long as the United States appears to guarantee the security of Taiwan. Despite the stated policy of the United States that the Taiwan issue should be resolved by the Chinese themselves, the United States insistence that it be resolved peacefully in accordance with the Taiwan Relations Act (TRA) is an indirect guarantee of Taiwan's security. Peaceful resolution is a very imprecise requirement. It gives the United States license to enter the issue at any time that PRC pressure (whatever the form) on Taiwan to reach an accommodation exceeds what the American public will tolerate or that it violates the TRA. Unless the United States is willing to accept the absorption of Taiwan by the PRC over the objections of the people of Taiwan or is able to remove itself as the de facto arbiter of the issue, Taiwan will remain an issue between the United States and the PRC for the decade. The PRC will continue to use this issue to maximize its negotiating position with the United States by threatening to weaken the relationship, thereby raising fears and thus objections from U.S. business and others. The psychological pressures of such a threat may be more serious than the execution of the threat.

Americans tend to ascribe their own characteristics to the Chinese, imagining results to which Chinese threats will lead. Such results may or may not be intended, a characteristic China's leaders have often found helpful. Following the announcement of the Dutch sale of submarines to Taiwan, the PRC downgraded government-to-government relations with Holland, but contrary to U.S. expectations, in the area of people-to-people (particularly economic) relations, the Dutch have not suffered.[24] In April 1982, during the period when the PRC was threatening to downgrade its relations with the United States over arms sales to Taiwan, the PRC reassured those segments of the U.S. economy in which it has critical interests, particularly the oil industry. Senior PRC government officials reportedly told a group of U.S. oil representatives that they need not fear for there would not be any change in their business relationship with the PRC, irrespective of the outcome of the Taiwan issue.[25] China's leaders are able to make eminently practical distinctions between party-to-party, government-to-government, and people-to-people relations, thereby preserving a principle without seriously damaging other interests.

If a more ideological orientation were to reappear in the PRC government, the Taiwan issue would likely take on a more truculent and ideological nature greatly reducing China's flexibility over the issue during negotiations. If a more decentralized administration were to appear, Taiwan might disappear as an issue of negotiations entirely. A more decentralized administration would find the idea of one nation with multiple systems of government more compatible with its style than either the current administration or a more ideological left administration.

Even if the PRC and Taiwan were to reach an accommodation on Taiwan, there are several other potential issues between the PRC and the United States. There is the question of Cambodia. The United States finds itself in the philosophically uncomfortable position of appearing to support Pol Pot in tandem with the PRC in spite of the genocide that took place under the Pol Pot regime. Before there is any resolution of the Cambodian situation, there will certainly have to be a review of U.S. policy, which would generate opposition from Beijing.

Similarly in Korea, if at any point the PRC finds it useful to put pressure on the United States, Beijing need only to express its support for Pyongyang in more concrete terms. The present tacit understanding between the United States and the PRC is that U.S. troops in South Korea are useful but fragile. The understanding is almost completely dependent on the PRC's view of its own security relationship with the USSR and the U.S. perception of the nature of that relationship.

An even more potentially significant and enduring issue is China's claim to vast areas of the South China Sea. This could take the form of a conflict over the leasing of areas for oil exploration that other countries, like Vietnam, Indonesia and the Philippines, claim. Finally, there is the possibility of conflict over the application of the Law of the Sea Treaty to that area with one or more international corporations seeking to develop the area's potential mineral wealth.

Alliances:

As a part of each nation's national security policy, alliances are an essential force multiplier both on the battlefield and in support of the negotiator. Alliances range from the very legalistic, formal treaty or agreement between states to more amorphous relationships to promote common interests.[26] China's experiences with this spectrum cover several thousand years of history and range widely between the extremes of formal treaty systems and implied associations, from highly dependable to undependable alliances, from the flexible to the inflexible, and from alliances between equals to those between unequals. Within this abundance, there have been some experiences that appear to be more relevant than others to the PRC's efforts to shape its strategic environment today.

Though the history of the PRC is short, alliances have already played a significant role in the regime's national security. The PRC's termination of the Treaty of Friendship, Alliance, and Mutual Assistance with the Soviet Union (April 11, 1950-April 11, 1980) ended the only formal treaty alliance the PRC is known to have entered.[27] It was a necessary relationship of mixed blessings. China's military and industry today are largely the creations, including organization and management styles, of the massive assistance programs that the Soviets provided throughout the 1950s. Yet the degree of dependency was too stifling, a factor that has heavily influenced Beijing's decisions over the last decade concerning China's relationship with the West. Furthermore, in the minds of many there still lingers the feeling that China's dependency resulted in the PRC carrying the burden in Korea for a war of Soviet making. Also there is memory of the failure of the Soviet Union, in spite of the treaty, to back the PRC adequately against the United States in 1958 and against India in 1959 and 1962. In neither case was the USSR willing to confront the United States directly and in neither case did the PRC have the leverage of mutual interests to obtain full military cooperation from the Soviet Union.

The wartime experiences of the PRC in support of North Korea and North Vietnam suggest another type of alliance relationship, one in which China is more depended upon than dependent. In the North Korean case, China subsequently entered into a Treaty of Friendship, Cooperation, and Mutual Assistance (July 11, 1961). Although not formally called an alliance, it is the only Friendship treaty of both cooperation and mutual assistance and appears to rank just ahead of the PRC's Treaties of Friendship and Cooperation with countries of the East European bloc.[28] There was no comparable public treaty with North Vietnam; however, some evidence suggests there was a secret agreement, if not a treaty.[29] The PRC's alliance experience with these two nations has not been wholly satisfactory. Both nations have vacillated in their loyalties despite significant ideological and cultural commonalities, shared wartime experiences, and the PRC's proximity and support, because of the attraction of a more powerful patron—the USSR— and a reluctance to make the necessary concessions to ensure alliance solidarity.

These treaties were the product of China's relative weakness and the need to counter the threatening activities of the United States plus those of the USSR in North Korea. Despite the United States and USSR having the preponderance of physical power, from the Chinese view China's diplomatic efforts and the psychological impact of China's alliances significantly reduced the effectiveness of "superpower hegemonism."

The PRC's senior leaders also had experience with alliances during the Warlord era (1912–1949), a period of weak central government and strong local governments. Alliances between competing warlord governments were common, though tenuous. Even the Kuomintang (KMT) and Chinese Communist Party (CCP) joined in a "united front." These alliances often were the Trojan Horse that resulted in the absorption of the weaker by the stronger, developing unity but ending the alliance. Because of the nature of these alliances, individual members often found themselves with a war not of their own making, and with no alternative but to choose sides. It was clear that although survivability depended on alliances, alliances did not result in security nor were they effective for any sustained period of time. For the weak, alliances were based on fear and not mutual trust. The result was that alliance unity and reliability were never achieved.

During this same period, the experiences of China's weak central governments with international alliances were no better. World War I brought the disastrous Treaty of Versailles, and China's alliances with the Western powers during World War II resulted in the humiliation of Yalta. Despite being on the winning team in both wars, China's weakness resulted in it being the object of the victors' demands rather than the recipient of the fruits of war.

The historical knowledge of most Chinese about alliances is derived from their knowledge of the "Middle Kingdom," when for nearly 2,000 years China was the dominant imperial power of Asia. China's alliances with others were as master is to tributary minions, and teacher to pupils. The outer states or tribes provided a security buffer between China and the barbarians, either checking the threat or delaying it till China's forces were deployed. However, alliances meant more than physical security. In varying degrees, they also meant dependency on China for trade, economy, culture, and political system. Though the relationship with China was mutually supportive, China was the dominant element, if not physically at least psychologically. The Chinese thus were able to create an image of strength, even when weak, thereby altering their opponents' perception of reality. The ultimate defense, during those periods of internal weakness, was assimilation of the invader by China's stronger culture.

For a Chinese student of history, such as Mao, another of China's significant experiences with alliances was the Warring States period (453–221 B.C.) and the Spring and Autumn period (722–481 B.C.). Mao was knowledgeable of these periods and fond of citing from the chronicles and popular literature concerning lessons to be learned.

These were balance-of-power systems in which no one state was dominant, neutrality was not possible, and weak states could not survive without protection. Alliances were necessary. The power of a state was a function of good leadership, internal unity, and loyalty to the sovereign, and not necessarily of size. It was a time when duty and loyalty were so well developed that today's expressions describing a high degree of loyalty (e.g. "each has his own ruler to follow regardless of personal friendships") are derived from these periods. Yet loyalty and internal unity within each state were the very qualities that prevented the alliances from developing unity and dependability between states. Because loyalty was personalized, state and alliance unity usually did not survive the death of a particularly strong or charismatic leader.

To ensure alliance dependability, a guarantee was needed that the other members would respond when one party was threatened. A variety of common means were used including force, intimidation, or the exchange of such tokens as marriage between imperial families, hostages (both individuals and territory), and the posting of bond. Ultimately the most important means developed was a sense of moral obligation to maintain a reputation for upholding a principle—"To kill one's family for a principle." However, where these means were effective in enforcing unity, alliances often became too inflexible. The same unity needed to generate power to counter another alliance and thereby avoid war became the disabling element. Alliances could not redistribute power to maintain the balance. Historically those alliances that were flexible enough to accommodate the development of the approximate equivalent to the "balancer" in the European balance-of-power concept were better able to survive.[30]

Experiences of the Spring and Autumn period also produced another well known concept, "Make friends with those far from you to deal with your next door enemy." Besides the obvious advantage of presenting a two front war dilemma to your opponent, the major advantage is that your ally is not close enough to turn on you during or after the conflict.

Study of these early periods undoubtedly shaped Mao's thinking concerning the use of the united front in international affairs. During these periods the most successful states often aligned themselves with unfriendly and preferably distant neighbors to deal with a greater common threat. Such alliances were practical and relatively reliable, having been enhanced by tokens of good faith or intent, but were nevertheless transitory. Neither side assumed the alliance to be interminable, as the defeat or change in status of a common threat changed the conditions that originally justified the alliance. Similarly the "unified front" was practical, temporary, and focused on the greatest common threat. By ranking opponents according to their relative degree of common threat, and coopting all others to assist, Mao concentrated his resources in an effort to gain the preponderance of power offensively. While practical, the concept also remained true, in the long run, to the ideological purpose of communism since such practical compromises are situation specific and last for relatively short periods. If the USSR was the number one threat, efforts were largely focused to counter the Soviets until they were either eliminated, neutralized, or another threat became more dominant. Bolstered by a Sinocentric view of the world, such practicality is reminiscent of the classic 19th century British admonition that there are no permanent friends or enemies, only permanent interests.

Thus influenced by history and their own experience with alliances, the PRC's leaders began to move toward closer relations, though not a formal alliance, with the United States in 1972. By 1978, this flexible relationship, more perception than substance, appeared to the USSR as a united front by its major opponents against its interests. Having fostered this two-front image, yet pressured by the United States to further enhance the security relationship, the PRC began to recover some of its flexibility by controlling the pace at which the relationship with the United States developed and by attempting to repair a few bridges with the Soviet Union. A basic framework for cooperation has been established with the United States, communication links are in place, tokens have been exchanged, and the effectiveness of the relationship as a psychological deterrence to the USSR appears to have been proven. The PRC will continue its efforts to improve people-to-people relations with the USSR throughout the decade as a conduit of understanding, especially in the areas of culture and economics. State-to-state relations also will improve slightly through such means as border negotiations. But Beijing will not move so close to the Soviet Union as to disrupt the current anti-Soviet alignment with the United States that is needed to counterbalance Soviet expansionist activities. There may even be a slight swing back toward the United States as the PRC tries to maintain a solid but not overly dependent geopolitical relationship with the United States. This view will probably persist over the decade (1) if the Soviets continue their preoccupation with Europe and the Middle East; (2) if forces facing China's border are not enhanced excessively in response to the PRC's modernization efforts; and (3) if the administration in Beijing is not dramatically changed.

A more left-oriented administration would probably be less flexible and more likely to play down the importance of a "united front" with the United States. On the other hand, there are other leadership elements that have expressed an interest in further strengthening the relationship with the West and the United States. This difference is only in degree, however, for even those with a pro-West orientation would agree that it is difficult to conceive of any leadership faction, which once in power, would or could be willing to develop a dependent relationship with the West.

Warfare—Strategy and Tactics

The ultimate tool of national security policy is the use of military force, the threat or fear of which is the basis of deterrence. It strengthens a negotiator's hand, and justifies alliances. How military force is used—strategy and tactics—is an important factor in how China's leadership perceive the role of its military force. A debate has occurred within the top echelons of the PLA and the Party concerning the relevance of People's War to the modern battlefield and whether the concept should be changed. Personal experience, past victories, and Mao Zedong Thought have been supporting arguments for both sides of the debate. The critics of People's War have argued that it is a form of guerrilla warfare that is not adaptable to the modern battlefield of nuclear weapons, missiles, airplanes, tanks, huge logistics requirements, and major investments in training. The proponents argue that, quite to the contrary, People's War is a flexible framework for activating all the resources of China to include modern weapons.

Mao stressed the flexibility of People's War in December 1936 when he wrote, "All the laws for directing war develop as history develops and as war develops; nothing is changeless."[31] People's War is an active and total defense strategy based on the PRC's strengths of size, geography, manpower, and organization. It is a total war concept in which everyone, not just the professional soldier, has a role. The professional's role, as the principal combatant, must be supported with intelligence, logistics, personnel replacements, and guerrilla warfare. These roles can be carried out largely by paramilitary organizations, to the extent that the organizational framework exists or is functional. For example, crossborder operations in Vietnam and Korea revealed the limitations of PLA military operations based on People's War where there is no Chinese population base. The debate has reconfirmed the role of People's War while making explicit the formerly implicit principles of continuous adaptation and modernization. The institutionalization of these principles is signaled by the change in the title to "People's War under modern conditions."

People's War, as a concept, is not dependent on a specific level of technology, thus it can and will be adjusted to make maximum use of modern weapons. Like all developing nations that must make choices concerning the allocation of resources, the real argument is over how much to commit to defense modernization, by what process (ranging between foreign purchase and self-reliance), and in what areas (e.g. nuclear versus conventional; air, land, or naval systems; technical, tactical, or leadership training; logistics; etc.). Further differences arise because the requirements of limited war differ from those of general war, as do the requirements for combat in the jungle covered mountains of the South versus the vast deserts of Xinjiang, or the mountains and plains of the Northeast. The problem is further compounded when a particular conflict calls for the projection of power beyond China's borders, as happened in Vietnam.

Is a good offense a good defense? According to People's War under modern conditions, the answer is yes. Without ambitions to acquire foreign territory, possessing a limited nuclear and conventional power projection capability, and faced with the enormous task of modernization, the current administration has concluded that the strategic defense of People's War remains the best way to secure China's national security interests. Like the defense of NATO, it is an active defense, in which, once attacked, the PLA tactically goes on the offensive to seize the initiative. NATO's strengths, however, are management, training, and technological superiority or parity with the USSR and its allies; its weaknesses are insufficient time, space, and population (reflected in force numbers, etc.) and a battlefield clogged with refugees. China's situation is just the reverse, with its major weaknesses being inadequate training and equipment.

Western analyses of the PLA's capability to defend against a Soviet attack in the Northeast tend to focus on quantity and quality comparisons of equipment. These comparisons reflect the Soviet's significant numerical advantage in major combat items like tanks and planes. The PLA's technological antiques fare poorly in one-on-one comparisons; and the PLA's anti-tank and air defense systems are considered inadequate in numbers and capability. To the Western mind, the Chinese will lose and thus should purchase and manufacture more and better equipment. While these are important NATO theater criteria, these analyses ignore the differences between the two theaters and underplay the importance of the other elements of war. Chinese military planners are convinced that "as water seeks the low ground, the PLA will seek the weaknesses" of the Soviets. By getting close to the Soviets, they will minimize Soviet use of nuclear weapons; by converting cities into "Stalingrads," they will bleed Soviet forces of their momentum; by crippling the Soviet supply lines, they will hamstring the Soviet offensive; and by enduring, the PLA will ultimately be victorious. Yes, the cities of the industrial Northeast are important, but they are not the indispensable "pots and pans" some have described in the West. The cities are not more important than China's security or the ability to act independently. And any defense other than an active defense would require large foreign purchases of military equipment and a logistic dependency that the PRC is unable to accept.

Having assessed their own strategic capabilities in terms of the current international alignment of forces, the PRC's leaders believe that their limited second strike capability (nuclear) and conventional force capability present enough of a deterrence to a Soviet attack that there will be no conflict in the next five to six years. They also believe that their process of gradual modernization will continue to raise the threshold of opportunity costs so as to continue to lower prospects for conflict within the decade.

Other options, ranging from the use of guerrilla warfare and the passive defense to the strategic offense, were debated in the reassessment of People's War. Consideration in each case was given to a realignment with the Soviet Union or to a defense agreement with the West. These options either would not take full advantage of China's strengths or they would recast China in a dependent role. An offensive strategy and association with the West would have resulted in intense pressures to rapidly modernize with Western equipment at the expense of the modernization of China in all other areas. Furthermore the result would have been a dependency on the United States equivalent to that of the PRC on the USSR in the 1950s. Guerrilla warfare and a passive defense overemphasized the Chinese strengths of time, space, and population. The resultant active defense has the advantage of minimizing the expense of a quick fix while maximizing use of China's advantages.

Force Modernization

Defense ranks last in priority in the Four Modernizations program with respect to the investment of scarce fiscal resources. However, it would be a mistake to conclude that defense similarly ranks low as a national objective. The inability of China's economy to supply the necessary input for the defense of China was probably the common denominator that made agreement on the PRC's evolving economic development plan possible. Consequently the PLA's modernization requirements have received considerable attention from the central leadership, in addition to that given to development of the transportation and communications infrastructure. Hard political decisions have been made concerning manpower issues such as competency based promotions, leadership and training, force reductions and reorganizations, research and development (R&D) and procurement of equipment, and strategy and tactics. Considerable diplomatic energy and innovation have been exerted in support of defense requirements ranging from cooperation with the United States in reducing the Soviet threat to dealing with Israel's defense industries, and from opening negotiations with the Soviets to pressing the United States to agree to the sale of Coordinating Committee restricted equipment from Europe. Also difficult were the decisions to pursue joint ventures and compensation trade for their minimum capital investment requirements. The importance of these concepts to self-reliance in defense production undoubtedly facilitated agreement over their acceptance. The central leadership is convinced that the long range benefits to defense of this approach are many times greater than a large capital investment in specific foreign military hardware over the next few years.

Manpower. Mao often emphasized that men, not materials decide the outcome of a war, and that China can mobilize the masses to defeat the enemy.[32] Although these ideas are frequently cited in the West as the justification for the human-wave tactics of the Korean War, Mao's meaning is far more complex. Xu Shiyou, former Canton Military Region commander, used similar tactics early in the 1979 invasion of Vietnam, which may explain his retirement—despite his close association with Deng.[33] The PLA's superior numbers were a significant factor in China's strategic victory in Vietnam and will be in any future war, but the PLA's leadership has moved with alarm to correct: the conditions that led to their heavy troop losses, the poor performance of its younger leaders, deficiencies due to poor training, as well as the equipment failures and logistic inadequacies. Mao never advocated an underequipped army or indifference to human life. Rather, a well-trained, properly led, disciplined, and highly motivated army, fighting in China and supported by the populace, can defeat a better equipped army that is not as well led or motivated—a maxim he demonstrated several times.

Mao reportedly emphasized individual motivation. Highly motivated troops with ingenuity can defeat an opponent with more modern weapons, albeit with heavy costs as in Vietnam. However, motivation has been a problem because the Cultural Revolution stripped much of society, particularly the intellectuals and the managers, of its initiative and faith in the Party. Leaders at all levels, including the PLA, have been cautious in their commitment to the new administration, afraid that the new order will not be self-sustaining, that some inevitable change will reverse the course of present policy with accompanying wholesale leadership replacements. Furthermore, unit readiness and initiative have tended to be degraded by the excessive training time spent in political (motivation) training (which accounted for 40 percent of available time prior to Vietnam). While political training continues to be strongly stressed, more training time is being devoted to military skills. Now, only time and success can restore commitment and motivation.

The PLA also found in Vietnam that their communications were poor and their command structure in the field was unable to provide the kind of leadership based on experience, training, and professionalism that had been the bulwark of the PLA in the forties and fifties. Company grade officers were ill-equipped to lead and soldiers lacked the training to perform effectively. Thus in the future all cadre (officers) above the platoon level must receive a college education (PLA officer school), which means a major expansion in investment in personnel and other resources for the PLA that will continue through the decade.

In most armies the professional non-commissioned officers (NCO) are the repository of experience in the line units and conduct a majority of the individual and small unit training. The PLA lacks such a professional corps, which may be a source of many of its training problems. Thus there may be an effort to create some sort of system to better preserve experience in the unit. (Junior cadres with experience tend to be promoted out of the unit in a few years.) It has been widely rumored, that to enhance such professionalism, ranks will be reinstituted in the PLA in 1983.

At unit level, the reduction in political training, the increased time for military skills, and the enhanced leadership training mean a significant increase in the authority of the unit commander, as compared with the political officer. With the authority will come increased responsibility for his unit's performance, and thus motivation and commitment.

Training above the basic unit has suffered. Combined arms expertise is weak, as was amply demonstrated during the Vietnam incursion, and experience with joint operations is no better. These shortcomings, coupled with the internecine political conflicts of the past over the future of the militia, suggest that the ability of the PLA to coordinate and direct the activities of a large number of military and quasi-military organizations as required of People's War under modern conditions has deteriorated. Ongoing efforts to correct these deficiencies were highlighted by the largest joint training exercise since 1949 held at Zhangjiakou in September 1981.

The Vietnam war also appears to have found some of China's older soldiers not up to the requirements of People's War under modern conditions. Yang Dezhi, Commander of the Kunming Military Region and the field commander, was apparently given the credit in Beijing for China's successes instead of his superior, Xu Shiyou (now retired). Yang has since become the chief of staff of the PLA. This episode appears to highlight some of the rationale for the current efforts to develop a retirement system. A system of advisors is being implemented to allow the Long March generation, especially those over seventy, to step out of the pressure cooker of day-to-day operations and into advisory positions from which their expertise can be tapped while letting a younger generation assume the more physically demanding pressures of command. This system for allowing the senior generation to step aside gracefully without a loss of face will develop more fully throughout the decade, though not without opposition, particularly among political leaders. The benefits sought by such an arrangement are a more vigorous leadership with less of the fragmentation of responsibility that currently results from multiple deputies. A corollary result will be more promotion opportunities for the succeeding generations.

Training and education reforms, increased emphasis on profession-alism, introduction of technology, and the retirement system all have their opponents. Should the pendelum swing toward a more leftist administration, however, there would be strong resistance within the military, particularly from the emergent senior down through the mid-level leaders, to reverse the course of these reforms in any significant way. The experiences of Vietnam and the Soviet threat are too real for the military to accept anything more than a token return to the style of service that resulted in the bitter lessons of Vietnam and portend ill for conflict in the north unless they are corrected. A right or decentralized administration would likely support policies that would accelerate the current move toward professionalism and modernization.

Nuclear weapons. The nuclear weapons program will remain as always a protected area of investment. Approximately 5 percent of China's defense budget has consistently been funneled into the stra-tegic weapons program. This program, particularly the small cadre of U.S. trained specialists guiding it, has been shielded from such domes-tic upheavals as the Cultural Revolution. Despite dour predictions to the contrary, progress has been steady. The PRC now has at least four limited ICBM missiles (CSS-3) operational and a deployable and a full range ICBM (CSS-4) capable of reaching anywhere in the USSR and the United States. The ICBM completed its first over-water test while Premier Hua Guofeng was visiting Japan in May 1980. (Was the timing of the firing coordinated to introduce into the ambiance of the meeting's negotiations a hint of the PRC's growing strategic capability?) Al-though this relatively limited nuclear strike capability does not repre-sent parity with either the USSR or the United States, it does increase the opportunity costs and decrease the probability of a small conflict of interest leading to war. China's nuclear strike capability is sufficiently advanced that a Soviet first strike cannot assure that there will be no counter-strike. On the other hand, China will not have a first-strike capability at anytime in the foreseeable future. During the decade the potential cost of war with the PRC will increase for both the superpow-ers. Soviet concern is evident in their deployment of SS-20 missiles to the Far East.

Both because of its nuclear strength and weakness vis-à-vis the USSR and the United States, the PRC's declaration in 1964 that it would never be the first to use nuclear weapons has cost nothing and has gained them some political leverage. To date, however, they have rejected participation in any international nuclear arms limitations agreements. They have thus maintained their independence, and will continue do so for the next decade.

Over the next ten years, nuclear weapons developments probably will include work on MIRV technology and continued deployment of the CSS-4 as well as the initial deployment of the SLBM. According to the PRC, the nuclear submarine has completed its sea trials and successfully test fired its missiles.[34]

On the tactical level, the rumored use of simulated Soviet tactical nuclear weapons during a July 1982 exercise, raised the prospects that within the decade the PLA will begin deployment of additional tactical nuclear weapons. Currently the PRC has the ability to employ nuclear weapons in a tactical role by using fighter aircraft or an IRBM, if necessary; however, neither is as accurate or flexible as weapons specifically designed for a tactical role. The development and deployment of nuclear-capable tube artillery is the least likely approach because of the R&D costs, structural inadequacy of current PLA artillery, and, more importantly, the command, control, and doctrinal changes required. To be responsive, nuclear tube artillery must be pre-deployed in relatively large numbers over a broad front. As a result, it requires greater decentralization of authority than is needed by air delivered weapons. A likelier possibility is that atomic demolitions might be developed for use in blocking or canalizing Soviet forces. Although pre-positioned, centralized control of their use can be retained more easily. For relatively marginal costs, improved missile and aircraft delivery can be obtained indigenously with existing technological capability. Parity is not the immediate object; rather, the cost of a Soviet attack must be increased gradually so that the probability of success will continue to decrease.

Conventional forces. Because the greatest conventional threat, though possibly not the most likely conflict, is from the USSR, the PLA would have to deal with armored warfare on the plains of Manchuria and North China and possibly an envelopment through Xinjiang eastward toward Beijing. As indicated earlier, the Chinese figure that the Soviets expect to drive for the Yellow River and hold since a river crossing would be too costly. This would mean the loss of Beijing and the industrial north—an economic disaster for the PRC and its hopes for modernization. However, the cost to the USSR would be great and probably too high to justify a Soviet invasion in the next decade.

To deal with such an attack, the Chinese have committed themselves to building a "Great Wall of Steel." This allegory is more a mid-1990s aspiration than a reflection of near term capabilities. PLA forces are very heavily deployed in the northern military regions so as to outnumber any attacking Soviet force. Similarly, nearly all of China's early warning, air defense, and tank killing capabilities are deployed in support. Before taking on a conventional Soviet type tank battle, however, the PLA needs to upgrade its tank killing capability and survivability, having learned the hard way in Vietnam how vulnerable their tanks are.

"Modernization," as one PLA officer explained, "ideally would mean the procurement of NATO equipment. We like it. However, the PRC cannot afford it and, furthermore, purchases are a temporary fix that creates military dependency. China must develop its own research, development, and production capability and supplement it with joint production arrangements and occasional foreign purchases as necessary. Thus, for us, the Israeli 'junkyard army' solution of incrementally upgrading the equipment in the inventory will be our approach. Ultimately the PRC will develop its own capability to the point of self-reliance."[35] Already, for example, the PLA is reportedly considering purchasing new T-59 turrets from Vickers made of Britain's super tough Chobham armor, and seeking an indigenous joint production arrangement.[36] An interim solution mentioned in conversations is the placement of explosive charges on the outside of the tank's turret to cause anti-tank rounds to detonate prematurely.

An example of incremental upgrading is the PLA's joint production in China with the Dutch firm, ODELFT, of second generation night sights. These sights represent technology purchased by ODELFT from Vero, a U.S. firm, using a commercial license, and the PLA has explored acquiring the latest laser range-finding technology to accelerate their own research efforts and possibly to install on a small number of tanks. The PLA reportedly has also negotiated with the Israelis to upgrade some, if not all, of their T59 tanks to include optics, armor, and maybe a Belgian 90mm gun.[37] Firsthand experience with the Israeli approach to making incremental improvements to their "junkyard army" would be a major step toward institutionalizing the process.

A similar process with fighter aircraft would obviate some pressures for new aircraft. The introduction of selected metallurgical, production, and quality control techniques alone could produce significant performance improvements. Other possible improvements include the co-production of communications equipment and early warning radar. Although very strong emphasis has been placed on the training of the PLA's Red Arrow (Sagger missile) gunners to "pierce a willow leaf at a hundred paces," the PLA has expressed a strong interest in the joint production of more advanced anti-tank missiles such as TOW (U.S.)

and HOT (French). These and other incremental improvements together with the improvements in training, mobility, prepositioned logistics, and the "control of empty spaces" concept of People's War will provide the Chinese with a greatly enhanced deterrent capability in the North.

Warfare in the South or West produces other sets of problems because of differences in the terrain and the weather. The jungles, high humidity and rainfall of the South and the vast arid reaches of the West create maneuver, logistics, maintenance, and close air support problems that would call for some equipment and technology solutions different from those desired by commanders in the North. Beijing will be slower in providing resources to correct the equipment problems that are specific to regions other than the North.

There appears to be a certain amount of competition between the PLA's army, air force, and navy for the PLA's relatively limited resources. The dominant service is the army, and thus the claimant for the largest share. However, the navy and air force have a growing demand for high technology and advanced engineering and scientific education for missions that are not directly supportive of the Army's missions. The result may very well be that despite the lessons of Vietnam, there will be even greater difficulty between the services in developing combined doctrine and coordination, two requirements that will grow in importance as the services modernize. Through the decade, naval requirements for such blue-water vessels as guided missile frigates and large logistic ships will increase tensions just as the air force's need for higher performance aircraft has already. It is also in these two services that the greatest need for the import of high technology will be sharply felt, where the best foreign trained engineers and scientists will collect, and the strongest advocates for technology imports will develop.

Over the decade, China will avoid bulk procurement if it can develop the production capability by itself (though at a slower pace) or through such means as co-production and joint ventures. Second, China will avoid the development of complete new systems if it can upgrade existing systems to an acceptable level of performance through incremental modification, such as it is considering with its tanks. Some have thought that the Chinese should and possibly can be convinced to develop their procurement objectives toward a goal of NATO standardization. While the goal may seem desirable from a Western perspective, since it would be prohibitively expensive and would significantly increase China's dependency on the Western alliance, the Chinese are very unlikely to accept such an objective. The current leverage they are attempting to gain over Taiwan by virtue of the island's dependency on the United States for logistics and technology is instructive to Beijing. The goal is self-reliance. This does not preclude seeking assistance from others, but it does preclude placing the nation in the position of being too heavily dependent on another.

In 1980, while Under Secretary of Defense, Dr. Perry visited China where he was given an extensive tour of China's research, development and production facilities. His conclusion was that the PRC has excellent research facilities but that the developments in their facilities were approximately on a par with those in U.S. research labs fifteen to twenty years ago and that their production capability is likewise about twenty years behind the United States and West Europe. One member of the delegation noted that, "they do excellent theoretical work, but they are thin in experience."[38] A group from the American Institute of Aeronautics and Astronautics by contrast characterized China's technology as "anything from zero to fifteen years" behind the U.S. state of the art and may be a bit ahead in some areas.[39]

The Chinese clearly do not intend to remain fifteen to twenty years behind. Granted, the problems are enormous and will not be solved within the decade, but significant improvements will be seen. Technology is being actively pursued through direct purchase, transfers through joint production arrangements, attendance at international shows, subscriptions to foreign trade journals, and industrial theft. But the critical emphasis is on education, both domestic and foreign. Young cadres (officers) and soldiers are being sent to colleges and trade schools in increasing numbers. Self-improvement through correspondence courses, night school, and television courses is encouraged. The army is being geared to give every soldier both the ability to fight and to develop another skill. Though there are many problems, including a shortage of teachers, the PRC's leaders are determined to make China self-reliant.

SUMMARY

As calculated in Beijing, the development of a relationship between the PRC and the United States over the past decade—considerably short of a formal alliance—helped to lessen the likelihood of a Sino–Soviet war. With the United States playing a helpful strategic role with respect to the Soviet threat, domestic pressures for rapid, large scale modernization of the PLA decreased. Many of the demands on scarce national resources for expensive foreign and domestic weapon systems were deflected and those resources redirected into the building of China's infrastructure. Included are investments in transportation, communications, and China's ability to create, absorb and proliferate new technologies.

Chinese confidence in the deterrence of a Soviet attack is only partly attributable to the role of the United States. They have used their advances in strategic nuclear weapons, Soviet experiences with People's War in Afghanistan, and the PRC's successes in dealing with the United States to play on Soviet fears. The experiences of the past decade and their plans for the future have enhanced the confidence of China's leaders in their ability to cope, in however costly a manner, with a Soviet attack.

Through the decade the PRC will maintain a relationship with the United States that will be less than a formal alliance but which to the Soviets will have the potential of a united front. The USSR will not be allowed to overlook the possibility of China as a second front. Technology transfers will be sought to support direct and indirect improvements in the PLA's capabilities, but large equipment purchases will be minimal. Relations that will enhance the U.S.–PRC strategic relationship, without giving the appearance of increasing the PRC's dependence on the United States, will be cautiously sought. There will be tactical readjustments when the PRC is perceived to be getting too close to either superpower, but the basic relationship will remain essentially anti-Soviet in orientation.

APPENDIX—U.S. STATEMENTS REGARDING THE TAIWAN SOVEREIGNTY ISSUE

Shanghai Communiqué (February 1972)

"The U.S. side declared: The United States acknowledges that all Chinese on either side of the Taiwan Strait maintain that there is but one China and that Taiwan is a part of China. The United States Government does not challenge that position."

Joint Communiqué (December 1978)

"The Government of the United States of America acknowledges the Chinese position that there is but one China and Taiwan is a part of China."

Senate TRA Debate (February 1979)

Senator JAVITS. "I notice that the Chinese translation, according to our staff, of the communiqué, which is the basis for our action here uses a

Chinese word which means 'recognition' in respect of the PRC's view of Taiwan, the one-China view, whereas our translation—and I have it before me—uses the words, 'the Government of the United States of America acknowledges the Chinese position that there is but one China and that Taiwan is part of China,' and that is the language of the Shanghai communiqué—acknowledgement. Now is it going to be made clear to the Chinese that our position remains consistent? They have their interpretation. Whether Chiang Kaishek made the mistake of his life we won't know, probably, until long after I am gone. But that is their interpretation and not ours. We accept it. It is very important that we not subscribe to it either way"

Mister CHRISTOPHER. "Senator Javits, we regard the English text as being the binding text. We regard the word 'acknowledge' as being the word that is determinative for the U.S. We regard the Chinese word as being subject to that as one of the meanings of it. I simply give you assurance on that point."

Reagan Letter to Hu Yaobang (May 1982)

"Our policy will continue to be based on the principle that there is but one China. We will not permit the unofficial relation between the American people and the people on Taiwan to weaken our commitment to this principle."

State Department Explanation (July 1982)

"We have stated publicly, and to both sides of the Taiwan Strait, that we acknowledge that there is only one China and that Taiwan is a part of China. This is our position, and it has not changed since it was originally enunciated in the Shanghai Communiqué of February 1972 and the Joint Communiqué of January 1, 1979."

NOTES

1. Some Chinese observers believe that the U.S. policy is overly tied to the U.S. system of bases and possession of the latest technology. Interviews in Beijing and Washington, 1982. These interviews and most of the others cited in these notes were given on the condition of non-attribution.
2. For a thoughtful example of such a Western analysis, see Andrew R. Finlayson, "U.S. Aims for China: The Right Mix," *Joint Perspectives*, 2 (1981) 4: pp. 3–15.
3. Mu Youlin, "China's Independent Policy," *Beijing Review*, Vol. 26, no. 4 (January 24, 1983), p. 4. Also see Huan Xiang, "Uphold the Foreign Policy of Maintaining Independence and Keeping the Initiative in Our Own Hands," *Renmin Ribao*, 31 October 1982, in *FBIS-PRC*, 1 November 1982, p. A1.

4. Interview with Career Ambassador (Retired) U. Alexis Johnson, Washington, DC, April 17, 1982; Richard C. Thornton, *China, The Struggles for Power, 1917–1972* (Bloomington: Indiana University Press, 1973), pp. 220–221.
5. James Reardon-Anderson argues in *Yenan and the Great Powers* (New York: Columbia University Press, 1980) that the CCP's foreign policy (1944–1946) was not governed by ideological views but was very practical in its adjustments to political and military circumstances. A similar argument and counter viewpoints are presented for the 1947–1950 period in Dorothy Borg and Waldo Heinrichs, eds., *Uncertain Years: Chinese American Relations, 1947–1950* (New York: Columbia University Press, 1980).
6. Richard H. Solomon, "East Asia and the Great Power Coalitions," *Foreign Affairs*, 60, 3: p. 690. The Far East headquarters has also been reported to have been established in Chita in 1979. Chita is east of Ulan-ude along the Trans-Siberian railroad. *Asian Survey, 1982* (Tokyo: Research Institute for Peace and Security, 1982), p. 55.
7. Discussions at Chinese Academy of Social Science and Ministry of Foreign Affairs, Beijing, PRC, May 1982.
8. Interviews, Beijing, May 1982.
9. "Draft of the Revised Constitution of the People's Republic of China," *Beijing Review*, Vol. 25, No. 19 (May 10, 1982): pp. 27–47.
10. In the 1969 CCP Constitution, written during the Vietnam War and the close of the Cultural Revolution, China seeks "to overthrow imperialism headed by the United States, modern revisionism with the Soviet revisionist renegade clique at its center. . . ." Yuan-li Wu, ed., *China: A Handbook* (New York: Praeger, 1973), p. 783. In the 1957 State Constitution, China must ". . . oppose the imperialist [U.S.] and the social-imperialist [USSR] policies of aggression and war and oppose the hegemonism of the superpowers [U.S. and USSR]." *Peking Review*, Vol. 18, No. 4 (January 24, 1975): p. 12. After the ouster of the "Gang of Four" and the reemergence of Deng, the 1978 State Constitution stated that China must be prepared to deal with subversion and aggression against [China] by social-imperialists [USSR] and imperialists [U.S.]." *Peking Review*, Vol. 21, No. 11 (March 17, 1978), p. 6.
11. Interviews with PLA officers, 1982.
12. Interviews with Chinese officials, 1982.
13. Interviews, Hong Kong, May 1982.
14. Interviews with Chinese and Japanese officials, 1982.
15. Interviews, Hong Kong, May 1982.
16. Harlan W. Jencks, *From Muskets to Missiles: Politics and Professionalism in the Chinese Army* (Boulder, Colo.: Westview Press, 1982), pp. 76–86.
17. Samuel B. Griffith (trans.), *Sun Tzu, The Art of War* (New York: Oxford University, 1963), p. 73.
18. Griffith, *Sun Tzu*. p. 77.
19. Griffith, *Sun Tzu*. p. 79.
20. Interview with Ambassador (retired) U. Alexis Johnson, May 1982.
21. *Ibid.*
22. Senator John Glenn, "China–Taiwan Policy," *Congressional Record*, July 22, 1982, pp. S.8873–8875.
23. Henry Kissinger, *White House Years* (Boston: Little, Brown, 1979), p. 52.
24. Interview, Hong Kong, May 1982.
25. Interview with a U.S. banking representative who attended meeting, Beijing, April 1982.

26. In general the West has tended toward a more legalistic approach toward alliances with associated detailed documents and organizations. The Chinese have tended to prefer less detail and thus less legalistic and more moralistic interpretations of their commitments.

27. Douglas M. Johnston and Hungdah Chiu, *Agreement of the People's Republic of China: A Calendar* (Cambridge: Harvard University Press, 1968), pp. 266–276.

28. Johnston and Chiu, *Agreements*. pp. 230–274.

29. For example, Hoang Van Hoan says that "in accordance with the agreement between the two governments, beginning from October 1965 China's air defense forces, engineers, railway builders, logistics personnel, etc., were sent to work in North Viet Nam up to over 300,000." Hoang Van Hoan, "Distortion of Facts about Militant Friendship between Viet Nam and China is Impermissible," *Beijing Review*, Vol. 22, no. 49 (December 7, 1979), p. 17.

30. Richard L. Walker, *The Multi-State System of Ancient China* (Westport, Conn.: Greenwood Press, 1953), pp. 41–58.

31. Mao Tse-tung, "Problems of Strategy in China's Revolutionary War" (December 1936), *Selected Works of Mao Tse-tung*. Vol. 1. (Peking: Foreign Language Press, 1967), p. 182.

32. Mao more frequently discussed the qualitative input of man than the quantitative importance of numbers. For example see his discussion of "man's dynamic role in war" in Mao Tse-tung, "On Protracted War" (May 1936), *Selected Works of Mao Tse-tung*. Vol. II. (Peking: Foreign Language Press, 1967), p. 151.

33. David Bonavia, "No Talking in the Ranks," *Far Eastern Economic Review*, December 18, 1981, p. 26.

34. Edith Terry, "China's Long March has a Military Goal," *Far Eastern Economic Review*, December 24, 1982, p. 43.

35. Interviews with PLA officers, 1982.

36. Clare Hollingworth, "Massive Cuts in the Chinese Army," *Pacific Defense Reporter*, March 1982, p. 28.

37. Interview with commercial representative, Washington, DC, 1983.

38. Clarence A. Robinson, Jr., "China's Technology Impresses Visitors," *Aviation Week and Space Technology*, October 6, 1980, p. 25.

39. Terry, "China's Long March," p. 43.

Chapter 9

Taiwan: The Emerging Relationship

*Allen S. Whiting**

Despite the difficulties of forecasting, the key variables concerning how relations between the PRC and Taiwan will evolve over the decade can be identified and analyzed for their probable interaction and impact on PRC–Taiwan relations. Our main emphasis here will be initially on the internal situation, especially political, during the period 1983–1993. This discussion will be followed by an analysis of PRC policies and their prospective evolution.

This approach is justified by PRC statements concerning the conditions which would necessitate the use of force against Taiwan. As stated privately by Vice Chairman Deng Xiaoping and others, these include: (1) Taiwan's acquisition of nuclear weapons, (2) Taiwan's affiliation with the Soviet Union, and (3) Taiwan's refusal to negotiate.[1] The likelihood of the first two contingencies is virtually nil. Taiwan could not develop and deploy a viable nuclear weapons system without knowledge thereof becoming available to both Washington and Beijing at an early date. American opposition might be muted but communicated in credible sanctions, including the withholding of licenses and credits for nuclear power production. Mainland Chinese threats to use force against weapons production facilities or sites would carry considerable weight, especially given problems of feasibility in testing as well

*Professor of Political Science, University of Arizona.

as vulnerability to attack. Last but not least as a deterrent against the development of nuclear weapons on Taiwan is the recognition, explicitly acknowledged by Madame Chiang Kai-shek in recent years, that they could never be used against fellow Chinese.

The possibility of a Soviet–Taiwan connection has won greater attention from outside observers, but in neither Moscow nor Taipei is this seen as a realistic option. With a 4,650 mile border separating its most underdeveloped and underpopulated regions from China's massive society, the USSR can ill afford to provoke a potentially explosive neighbor into a posture of permanent hostility. Soviet intervention in the Chinese civil war so as to further reduce the prospect of uniting Taiwan with the People's Republic would certainly have that consequence. As for Taiwan, its dependence on good relations with the United States and Japan for foreign markets and foreign investment precludes risking their wrath by enhancing the Soviet presence in the western Pacific.

The third contingency, a refusal to negotiate, raises the prospect of eventual Taiwan independence. Such a prospect warrants close examination and has fueled suspicion in Beijing over U.S. intentions as well as anxiety over the situation that might emerge once the present leadership on Taiwan passes from the scene. The island's size, location, and economic viability make independence not only a theoretically realistic option, but depending on how the PRC develops and reacts, possibly preferable for most of its population.

Whether the PRC will indeed use force at some future time to obtain Taiwan remains open to question. In the 1950s, mass demonstrations mobilized tens of millions of Chinese vowing to "liberate Taiwan." Yet the government did nothing in the face of the U.S. Seventh Fleet interposition in the Taiwan Strait and the subsequent conclusion of an American military defense treaty. The deaths of Mao Zedong and Chiang Kai-shek have defused the original Chinese Communist Party (CCP)-Kuomintang (KMT) civil war. Virtually no hostilities between the two sides have occurred in more than twenty years. In 1975, Deng told an American delegation, "We can wait five years, ten years, or one hundred years, but reunion will finally be realized."[2] However, in 1980, he named reunion with Taiwan as one of the three national goals for this decade.[3] PRC behavior is affected by several factors, including domestic politics, Sino–American relations, and Sino–Soviet relations, but the most important factor likely to determine future Chinese actions toward Taiwan is developments on the island itself. Therefore, we must focus our attention there before addressing Beijing's possible courses of action.

TAIWAN TODAY

Under the Qing Empire, Taiwan was administered loosely from Beijing. From 1895 to 1945 it was a Japanese colony. After World War II Chinese Nationalist troops occupied the island but an oppressive, carpetbagging rule soon alienated the local populace. In February 1947, a Mainlander policeman killed a Taiwanese woman illegally hawking cigarettes. In a protest demonstration the next day at least four more died under police fire. Violence quickly spread as brutal military repression virtually massacred Taiwan's urban elite, numbering an estimated 10,000.[4] Many not killed or imprisoned fled to Japan and elsewhere. The commanding officer was sacked, but the event poisoned Taiwanese-Mainlander relations for years.[5]

In 1949 Chiang Kai-shek and his remnant regime fled to the island. A land reform program compensated the Taiwanese large landholders in part with stock in the small Japanese-developed industries. Taiwan's subsequent transformation into a major exporter of industrial products benefitted this nascent capitalist class so that today private industry is primarily in the hands of Taiwanese.[6] Nevertheless, the decisions affecting the island's economy, such as interest rates, currency evaluation, and export-import controls, are in the hands of Mainlanders, specifically the premier, the president, the governor of the Central Bank, and the ministers of Finance and Economic Affairs.[9]

Politically, Chiang imposed his national government on top of the existing provincial regime, Taiwan theoretically being only one part of the Republic of China. It logically followed that top positions were held by Mainlanders. But their writ, whether it be in foreign affairs, defense, or internal security, did not extend beyond Taiwan, the Pescadores, and small scattered offshore islands, the most celebrated of which were Quemoy and Matsu. Moreover, key local officials, such as the provincial governor, were appointed, not elected.

Gradually the demographic facts of life inevitably diluted the Mainlander monopoly of political and military power. In addition, Chiang Ching-kuo, the Generalissimo's elder son, persisted in quietly pressing for the admission and elevation of Taiwanese into the political system. First as premier, 1972–1978 (the elder Chiang died in 1975), and then as president, Ching-kuo has slowly but steadily expanded the Taiwanese presence and participation in the political system.

At the national level, Chiang's vice president and constitutional successor in case of death is Taiwanese, as are the vice premier and several cabinet officers. In recent years, the mayor of Taipei and the provincial governor have also been indigenous. More than 83 percent of the KMT's

1.8 million members are Taiwanese, although they comprise only one-third of the key Standing Committee of the Central Committee.[8]

However, the important instruments of control—the military, intelligence, and police agencies—are still Mainlander dominated. While enlisted personnel and non-commissioned officers are overwhelmingly Taiwanese, top command positions in the army, navy, and air force are held by Mainlanders. In 1980, of the island's twenty-one counties and municipalities, only one had a Taiwanese police department head.[9]

Taiwan's quasi-authoritarian rule is alleviated by elected bodies at all levels. The national bodies, such as the National Assembly which elects the president and vice-president, the legislative yuan, and the control yuan were originally chosen in 1947. Since then, their membership has steadily shrunk with death and departure, causing them to lose credibility as legitimate organs. Yet to replace them wholly with elections solely on the Taiwan base would mock their pretension to represent all China, aside from duplicating provincial bodies.

As a compromise, the legislative yuan had successive partial elections in 1969 and 1973 to replenish its ranks piecemeal. Nevertheless, from its original size of 760 it fell to under 400 by 1980, of whom roughly 100—with an average age of 75—managed to participate actively.[10] That December, 96 seats were made available for election, 69 from Taiwan and 27 from overseas Chinese constituencies. The KMT announced that its candidates could not compete for more than 49 percent of the vacancies, thereby enhancing the image of a genuinely democratic system.

The *dangwai* or "non-party" candidates, however, were formally proscribed from such practices as forming a coordinated campaign organization, while the KMT retained the benefit of various mass organizations besides the party as well as domination of the media and the armed forces.[11] Yet, despite these obstacles, the largest number of votes went to the wife of a jailed political activist. At lower levels, *dangwai* candidates won 41 percent of the votes for county and city heads, including more than 30 percent in the major city councils of Taipei and Kaohsiung and 28 percent in the provincial assembly.[12]

This gradual "Taiwanization" of the political system has not come easily. Mainlander resistance at one extreme and Taiwanese impatience at the other extreme have at times threatened the entire process as riots and repression polarize attitudes and behavior.[13] In 1977, rumors of corrupt election practices triggered local violence in the town of Chungli. The police station was burned down and a number of vehicles destroyed. In 1979, a more serious incident occurred when several thousand demonstrators in Kaohsiung attending a rally on U.N. Human Rights Day clashed with several hundred police and military personnel, resulting in numerous casualties. While the regime restrained its immediate response in both instances, military and civilian trials in 1980 levied sentence on forty-one arrested after Kaohsiung, with sentences ranging from imprisonment for life to fourteen, twelve, and six years.

The Kaohsiung incident was not an isolated affair. In February 1979, a one-year ban on new periodicals ended, opening a deliberate policy of liberalization. Several opposition journals appeared, the most prominent and ambitious of which was *Formosa,* published by a noted opposition legislator. As noted by Ralph Clough, "by, early December the [*Formosa*] group had set up ten 'service centers' throughout the island, each headed by a prominent opposition leader, and had sponsored eleven political rallies at various places at which speakers attacked the KMT. Leaders in Taipei coordinated these meetings and often took part themselves."[14]

Then in late November the publisher's office and the Kaohsiung service center were vandalized. Ten days later another center was smashed up. On the eve of the Human Rights rally, two *Formosa* representatives publicizing the affair were reportedly assaulted by police.[15] No arrests followed these incidents. Instead, *Formosa's* publisher was sentenced to fourteen years imprisonment for allegedly having secretly contacted the Chinese Communists in early 1979 to promote reunification. Moreover, one of the *Formosa* group, imprisoned after the riot, lost his mother and two daughters. They were brutally murdered at home while his wife visited him in jail. Again, no arrests occurred. In the summer of 1981, a Taiwanese professor from Carnegie-Mellon University, visiting his family, died under highly suspicious circumstances. He allegedly jumped from the library tower at Taiwan National University.

It is impossible to identify the size and composition of extremist groups operating clandestinely, possibly as *agents provocateurs,* whatever their political persuasion. Aside from the case of a mail-bomb that blew off the hand of the provincial governor and such violence as occurred in late 1979, the threat of polarization so far has been confined to relatively isolated instances. Their very occurrence, however, is a reminder of how uncertain must be our prognosis of what may occur once Chiang Ching-kuo passes from the scene.

On one point, however, most observers are confident. No single individual combines Chiang's symbolic legitimacy as inheriting the mantle of Sun Yat-sen and Chiang Kai-shek with his personal charisma and political acumen. Attention focuses upon factions and their potential for a collective leadership based on consensus rather than on a power struggle following Ching-kuo's demise. Hung-mao Tien identifies two basic coalitions. One, the "traditionalist-hard-liners," is comprised of "major military figures, . . . Party ideologues, . . . some high Party bureaucrats, . . . advocates of traditional culture, . . . and their supporters in the universities and mass media."[16] Against them stand the "technocrat-moderates," who include "senior Party leaders, . . . technocrats, . . . Western-educated and second echelon scholar-bureaucrats, . . . publishers of some major daily newspapers, . . . and an extensive network of academicians, business leaders, and professionals."

Whatever the chosen labels or the identified individuals, political analysts agree that recent years have sharpened tension in the KMT between those who would liberalize so as to increase Taiwanese identification with the government and those who would keep a tight control on any dissent or deviation from orthodox KMT rule.[17] The problem is complicated by the fiction of the government maintaining the goal of ruling China despite its loss of U.N. membership and non-recognition by all major powers. With only some two dozen small countries maintaining full diplomatic relations, the legitimacy of the ROC is damaged beyond repair. Yet its future cannot be freely discussed or debated on the island.

TAIWAN TOMORROW

In October 1949, when Mao Zedong proclaimed establishment of the PRC, no one would have predicted the survival, much less the stability of the Chiang Kai-shek regime ten years later. Asked to forecast the fate of Taiwan when President Richard Nixon shook hands with Chairman Mao in Beijing in February 1972, one might have come closer to the reality of 1982 but probably would have taken a more pessimistic course than has proved necessary. It follows, therefore, that to project the PRC-Taiwan relationship until 1993 is a highly contentious undertaking, especially because of uncertainty attending the leadership succession to Chiang Ching-kuo.

It is possible that Chiang will continue to rule throughout this period. Born in 1910, he could even live out the century. Although Chiang has had diabetes for many years, it has not become disabling. He enjoys an active but prudent lifestyle, avoiding the endless toasts and heavy banquets customary for his position. Nor is his office burdened with a high level of tension and recurring crises. Many of Taiwan's worst fears passed with the U.N. ouster in 1971, the Nixon-Mao meeting in 1972, the Generalissimo's death in 1975, and termination of American recognition in 1979 and the defense treaty in 1980. The economic shocks of the 1970s, including the OPEC oil embargo, import price inflation, and the export market recession, particularly in the United States, also have proved manageable.

Should Chiang remain in power, he is unlikely to change Taiwan's domestic or foreign policies in any dramatic fashion. Internally, he has balanced the centrifugal and centripetal elements so as to avoid any serious risk of prolonged instability or political extremism. This has been no mean feat, considering the recurring pressures for Mainlander authoritarian control as against rising demands for Taiwanese democratic self-determination, coupled with the omnipresent threat of Communist subversion and, ultimately, of attack. Compared, for instance, with the fate of Park Chun-hee in South Korea, Chiang's record offers promise of a secure status quo so long as he lives.

Externally there is little likelihood that Chiang will negotiate with Beijing. Faithful to his father's will, he has no personal incentive to betray the Nationalist heritage by abandoning the Republic of China and its anti-Communist stance. Any such personal inclination would meet strong resistance from many of his closest associates. Intimations of pending negotiations would trigger a flight of capital and people from Taiwan, including administrators, entrepreneurs, managers, and technicians essential to the island's stability. Taiwanese extremists would probably move to preempt union with the mainland through violent action, possibly supported by mass demonstrations.

Nor are the prospects for political and economic developments in the PRC so auspicious as to make union attractive in this decade. Even under the best case projections for the Mainland and the worse scenario for Taiwan, the gap in living standards, literacy, employment, and mobility is likely to remain in the island's favor by 1993. Following the death of Deng Xiaoping, the post-Mao transition may produce a stable leadership sustaining a continuously moderate, pragmatic regime. However, compared with the relative freedom from political interference on Taiwan, the Mainland still will offer a more pervasively authoritarian, Marxist-Leninist system where the dangers of extremism and repression will be a distinct possibility. Finally, Taiwan has no guarantee and no recourse should a negotiated settlement be abrogated by Beijing after a Communist takeover. The fate of Tibet, despite the 1951 agreement, provides an ominous precedent in this regard.

This does not mean that Taiwan's relationship with the PRC will remain absolutely static. It has already changed considerably since Mao's death, partly in response to decisions in Beijing, but also to decisions in Taipei. Indirect trade through Hong Kong, Japan, and Singapore, and clandestine smuggling across the Taiwan Strait, have already increased in value to an estimated U.S.$500 million. Beijing has granted amnesty to all Nationalist political prisoners. Taipei invited a PRC team to participate in an international softball tournament on the island, although conflicting positions on ceremonial symbols purportedly prompted Beijing finally to withdraw. Abroad, scholars from both sides participate jointly in fora and attend conferences without public polemics or acrimonious exchanges. On American college campuses, students from Taiwan and the PRC live together with the approval of their respective regimes. In the Taiwan Strait, the "no peace—no war" situation has stabilized to the point where Beijing has lifted military security controls from Fujian province, opposite Nationalist-held Quemoy. This opens the area, with its valuable port of Amoy, to joint ventures with foreign firms and a possible special economic zone similar to that adjoining Hong Kong.

These developments are relatively recent, but they are likely to be expanded upon. The economic complementarity of Taiwan and the Mainland augurs well for a further increase of trade. Mainland consumers can readily absorb Taiwan products that face import restrictions elsewhere, such as textiles, footwear, and electronic items. At the same time, Taiwan's need for oil may be partially met through nearby offshore reserves exploited by foreign firms under PRC contract. Other raw materials can be acquired with lower shipping costs from the Mainland than abroad. More generally, Taiwan's technological and managerial wealth, both human and material, provides a powerful inducement for the Mainland to increase economic interactions; for Taiwan there is the attraction of a one billion population market potential. Finally, the facility of doing business within a common cultural and linguistic framework contrasts with the difficulties Taiwan's industrialists experience with the loss of diplomatic recognition, fluctuating exchange rates, and the vagaries of stagflation in the world economy.

It is likely that PRC proposals for direct mail, travel, and family visits eventually will be approved by Taipei. Indirect mail already links separated families. So long as living conditions remain disparate, Taiwan does not risk loss of loyalty through such contact. Selected television films depicting life in the PRC, monitored from mainland stations, appear on Taiwan screens as visible evidence of how the two systems measure up. While the traditional pull of ancestral graves, family, and native village may counter this to some extent among the Mainlanders on Taiwan, there is little or no such attraction for the overwhelming majority of the indigenous population.

These and other links between the two sides can evolve without negotiations or any formal change in the overall relationship. Having sanctioned such developments to date, Chiang Ching-kuo has no reason to refuse further incremental moves over time. Neither side needs to take more substantive steps that would portend a qualitative transformation of the island's political status vis-à-vis the PRC.

Offsetting this likely evolution toward a closer informal relationship might be a strengthened Taiwanese orientation for the island. Without necessarily addressing the specific question of an independent Taiwan, the steady rise into higher and more powerful positions of authority of indigenous representatives might combine with the gradual atrophy of the so-called national organs to make decisions turn on Taiwanese rather than Mainlander input.

Thus, while Mainland China has adopted the *pinyin* system of transliteration, greatly simplified the written characters, and introduced a modest Latinization of the language, Taiwan adheres to Wade-Giles, maintains the highly complex traditional characters, and has made little effort at Latinization. The resulting communications gap between the two societies was highlighted in 1982 when a prominent mainland official published a letter addressed to his "old classmate" Chiang Ching-kuo as an appeal to negotiations and reunion, including an offer to visit Taiwan. The highly stylized phrases and script reportedly required explanation for Mainland readers.[18] Thus, whether Taiwan's written language remains constant or follows PRC patterns can affect the island's orientation as a separate entity.

Similarly, encouragement of a creative cultural world in arts and letters on Taiwan has nourished an intelligentsia whose sense of identity, and to a limited extent freedom, stands in a sharp contrast with its PRC counterpart. This may combine with a slow but steady erosion of symbolic association with China as a centralizing concept, the Republic of China title notwithstanding. A growing proportion of the island's younger population will have no direct memory of the regime's original orientation under Chiang Kai-shek and its incessant "Back to the Mainland!" theme.

Actually, the two trends, Mainlander-dominated and Taiwanese, can continue to coexist indefinitely, contradictory though their ultimate implications may be. Much will depend, of course, on how the PRC acts as well as reacts, which we will examine later. At this point, however, it must be noted that a gradual evolution toward either Mainland reunion or separate status without final resolution in either form is possible both under Chiang Ching-kuo and a successor regime should the latter emerge smoothly according to constitutional processes. A collective leadership comprised of party, bureaucratic, and technocratic figures could continue to delay the difficult decision of determining Taiwan's future simply by pursuing the policies existing at the time of Chiang's death, provided that no force within or without attempts to press the decision regardless of risk or cost.

Such an internal force, however, might emerge either from Taiwanese independence extremists or from Mainlander elements fearful of their emergence. The former is more likely than the latter, although neither contingency appears serious in the near future. While we lack the evidence to make firm judgments, the infrequency of such admittedly dramatic outbreaks as occurred at Chungli and Kaohsiung suggests the low probability of mass violence. The ubiquitous secret police apparatus penetrates those political, academic, and journalistic circles most apt to organize an opposition movement. Meanwhile, the general conditions reinforce political apathy in a populace more characterized by passivity than volatility, whether under Japanese or Nationalist rule.

Yet the prospect of Taiwanese independence activity cannot be ruled out altogether. The presence of foreign media, tourists, scholars, and business personnel provides an incentive to act out political demands for world opinion, regardless of the prospects for immediate success locally. Martyrdom at the hands of brutal police or military forces, however provoked, can be a tempting tactic for dedicated youths. This is particularly true where the United States is seen as the avowed guardian of human rights and the island as informal ward under the 1979 Taiwan Relations Act. An appeal to American principles of self-determination and anti-Communism may seem logical to Taiwanese radicals determined to forestall union with the mainland by a post-Chiang regime.

Once such action occurs, it is impossible to predict its outcome. Much would depend on its magnitude, location, and visibility to the outside world. The choices for the regime are few and painful. Restraint risks repetition. This in turn could invite PRC intervention or a credible threat thereof. Alternatively, suppression can feed underground fires of vengeance as well as rebellion, with mutual suspicion and tension permeating the society in expectation of further outbreaks. Finally, there is at least a theoretical possibility of a successful seizure of power and proclamation of an independent Taiwan.

An alternative force, albeit one discounted by most observers, lies in the Mainlander command elements of Taiwan's military organization. Conceivably, they might attempt to oust a post-Chiang regime in order to preempt an independence movement. This could be undertaken in the name of the ROC so as to perpetuate the status quo. Or it might be done to invite a Mainland takeover, perhaps with advance arrangements through secret and secure communication with the PLA. A PLA response could be immediate, given the mere 150 miles or so between Mainland bases and key air and naval points on the island. Although most of the enlisted ranks and non-commissioned officers on Taiwan are indigenous, a nighttime operation would find most of the troops asleep in the barracks without weapons at hand. By the next morning, all major bases could be under PLA control. These circumstances might permit Beijing's use of force to finesse the issue posed by U.S. insistence on a peaceful solution of the Taiwan problem. The initiative would be local and effected wholly by Chinese on both sides of the strait as advocated in the joint Sino–American communiqués of 1972, 1979, and 1982.

These scenarios range from the highly probable to the barely possible; others can also be conceived. They serve to illustrate the degree of uncertainty and instability that may follow Chiang Ching-kuo's passing from the scene. Their occurrence can be largely independent of those courses of action that would seem most logical to outside observers. The situation can appear desperate, and perceived alternatives pose a genuine dilemma. Under these circumstances, foreign rationality may not predict local behavior.

Ambassador Leonard Unger, Washington's last official representative in Taipei, summarized a hypothetical chain of events which would forcefully change the island's status as follows:

> The lack of an appointed successor and a possible leadership crisis could revive the Mainlander–Taiwanese tensions of earlier years, and could eventually precipitate a bid by the Taiwanese to take power and declare an independent republic of Taiwan, bringing an end to the minority government of the mainlanders. Most likely, this could provoke the PRC to attempt reunification militarily, a confrontation the United States could do little about without charges of interfering in China's internal affairs.[19]

PRC POLICY AND POSSIBLE ACTIONS

In September 1982, Ye Jianying, chairman of the Standing Committee of the National People's Congress (NPC), gave the fullest and most formal statement of PRC policy toward Taiwan to date. Delivered for the 70th anniversary of the founding of the ROC, it was a major expansion on the initial NPC Standing Committee "Message to Taiwanese Compatriots" issued at the close of 1979.[20] After reiterating the earlier proposal for the "exchange of mails, trade, air and shipping services, family reunions and visits by relatives and tourists as well as academic, cultural, and sports exchange," Ye declared, "Taiwan can enjoy a high degree of autonomy as a special administrative region and it can retain its armed forces. The Central Government will not interfere with local affairs on Taiwan."[21] He further promised that, "Taiwan's current socioeconomic system will remain unchanged, so will its way of life and its economic and cultural relations with foreign countries. There will be no encroachment on proprietary rights and lawful right of inheritance over private property, houses, land and enterprises, or on foreign investments." Other provisions offered economic assistance as needed and invited involvement by Taiwan's business persons in mainland activities.

This statement brought together in an official, public document various points that had been elaborated previously in private interviews. It left out the spelling of details for "talks to be held between the Communist Party of China and the Kuomintang of China." Although the Taiwan authorities quickly rejected such talks out of hand, it is possible that disavowable channels carried private exchanges of view and additional clarification. Such clarification is necessary at the very least. For example, the retention of Taiwan's armed forces can be meaningless, depending on the locus of final command as well as access to spare parts and weapons replacement. Similarly, the definition of "local affairs" could be extremely narrow. The absence of any time limit to leaving the "current socioeconomic system unchanged" together with the ambiguous "way of life" sharply reduces the proposal's credibility in view of the PRC commitment to implement Marxist-Leninist principles of Mao Zedong Thought, reaffirmed in the 1982 draft constitution.

The PRC is free to modify its proposal in any way and at any time, given the prompt Taiwan rejection. On the one hand, it might be made more attractive by defining Taiwan as a special economic zone such as already exists on the Mainland. Overseas Chinese investment might be guaranteed with generous concessionary terms. The island's economy would appear particularly sound with the logical consequent reduction of Taiwan's defense burden that currently consumes 40 percent of the budget. On the other hand, Beijing might threaten to withdraw its offer altogether if not favorably responded to with an implied or expressed ultimatum.

How Beijing moves may depend on domestic politics as well as on Taiwan developments. It is possible that the issue will lie dormant indefinitely. A stabilized leadership which survives the passing of Deng Xiaoping may be relatively immune to opposition challenge and preoccupied with economic modernization. A continuing confrontation with the USSR may require or justify accommodation with the United States and Japan, whose sensitivities on Taiwan could be aroused by assertive posturing, much less aggressive action. Under these circumstances, only a change on Taiwan would evoke change in Beijing.

But one or more of these conditions may not apply throughout the next ten years. Factionalism and attendant policy instability have characterized much of PRC history. Issues can be opportunistically exploited for their political utility, whether or not they come naturally onto the extant agenda of priorities.[22] Taiwan is particularly inviting in this respect. It is a matter of acute sensitivity, involving national unity, territorial sovereignty, and foreign interference. It has acquired salience through repeated avowals of nearly thirty-five years that "reunification of the motherland" must and will be achieved. This has become current by being officially identified as a policy of primacy for this decade.

Taiwan also represents a potentially valuable asset, provided it can be acquired intact. In addition to the technological resources already alluded to, its foreign exchange earnings have regularly approximated or surpassed those of the PRC in recent years.[23] While this ratio could change once China's offshore oil reserves come into full production, the island's net worth would still be a major addition to the mainland economy. Taiwan's access to the continental shelf would enlarge still further potential PRC oil reserves.[24]

Other considerations that may permit or cause Taiwan to become a serious issue include the possibility of a Sino–Soviet détente sufficient to permit the redeployment of military forces from that lengthy frontier to positions opposite Taiwan. This is a visible token of what may lie ahead should negotiations not eventuate. Such redeployment is not necessary for a credible threat to be posed toward the end of this decade, assuming a modest modernization of the PLA compared with the likely gradual deterioration of Taiwan's defense capabilities. Even should redeployment occur, Beijing's potential power would not be that much more impressive.

Most important, perhaps, is the possibility of change in the priority accorded to relations with the United States and to a lesser but analogous degree with Japan. In 1971–1972, the United States tie was deemed sufficiently important to justify a virtual finesse on the Taiwan problem. In the deftly crafted Shanghai Communiqué, each side simply stated its separate position while agreeing to reestablish relations, albeit at less than the full diplomatic level. In 1973, Beijing tacitly acquiesced in a "two-China" situation whereby the PRC maintained a "liaison office" in Washington while Taipei continued a full-fledged embassy for the ROC. Again, in 1978, Beijing permitted Washington to delay terminating its formal defense commitment to Taiwan by one year in accordance with the treaty's terms, while agreeing to establishing full diplomatic relations in early 1979. Moreover, the explicit disagreement over continued American arms sales to Taiwan did not prevent the completion of normalized relations.[25]

This priority to strengthening the American tie at the expense of Beijing's public posture on Taiwan appeared to undergo critical review in 1981–1982. The attention given by presidential candidate Ronald Reagan during the 1980 campaign to upgrading Taiwan's importance was followed by a major debate in Washington over continued coproduction of the F5-E jet fighter on Taiwan versus providing an improved fighter plane to succeed it. This triggered an assertive demand by Beijing that the United States drop all arms sales to Taiwan. Although this eventually was modified to call for a specific time for halting the arms sales, the resulting tension in Sino-American relations was the most serious in ten years. For a time, Beijing obliquely threatened to lower the level of diplomatic representation if the sales continued.[26]

Finally, on August 17, 1982, a joint Sino-American communiqué resolved the impasse by mutual concessions.[27] The PRC proclaimed "a fundamental policy of striving for a peaceful solution to the Taiwan question." The United States avowed "that it does not seek to carry out a long-term policy of arms sales to Taiwan, that its arms sales to Taiwan will not exceed, either in qualitative or in quantitative terms, the level of those supplied in recent years, . . . and that it intends to reduce gradually its sales of arms to Taiwan, leading over a period of time to a final resolution." The Reagan administration thereupon requested the Congress to approve continued coproduction of the F5-E. Once again the PRC backed down on its insistence that Taiwan was a purely internal affair that brooked no foreign interference.

Unfortunately, the past does not provide an assured precedent for the future. The strategic, political, and economic considerations that prompted Beijing to make these concessions may not apply over the next ten years. Perceptions of the United States as a makeweight against Soviet expansionism may downgrade the utility value of continued compromise on Taiwan, whether or not a Sino-Soviet détente occurs. The political vulnerability of the American tie may come under attack as eroding China's ideological ethos while forcing dependence on imperialist and capitalist sources whose gain comes at China's expense. The economic role of the United States and Japan in China's modernization program may be reduced as Beijing encounters difficulty in meeting its goals of growth or paying its debts for foreign assistance.

These possibilities cannot be predicted as inevitable nor can their timing be calculated confidently in advance. However, they do have their antecedents, whether over the past century of debate concerning how to utilize foreign ways while preserving the Chinese spirit or during the past three decades with debate over dependence on the USSR, the United States, or self-reliance. These recurring themes in Chinese politics link domestic and foreign policy inextricably with the questions of national security and economic modernization. Thus the Taiwan issue can come to the fore as a function of domestic and foreign politics independent of what happens on the island itself, assuming that no negotiations between the two sides have been begun at the time.

Ultimately, however, calculations of feasibility and risk will determine how long Beijing acquiesces in the status quo should it continue on Taiwan. Alternatively, should developments on the island raise independence as a real prospect, the issue will be forced for the PRC. In either case, the choices for action are relatively limited with the likelihood of success directly corelated with the degree of cost.

At the lowest end of the scale, Beijing could try to squeeze the Taiwan economy by pressing foreign investors and firms involved with mainland trade to embargo all further intercourse with the island. This might have a varied response, but on the whole it is unlikely to force all foreign business off Taiwan, much less force the regime to negotiate on Beijing's terms. Much would depend on the size of the firm, its relative position on the Mainland as compared with Taiwan, its dependence on governmental aid and advice, and its anticipated role in the region.

At a higher level, Beijing could announce the closure of all Taiwan ports as an administrative measure for unspecified reasons of "national security." This step is within its sovereign prerogative as de jure ruler of the province and differs from a formal blockade which legally concedes the belligerancy of a separate state. The effect, however, is the same, and requires the interdiction of shipping if it is to be enforced.

But before interdiction actually occurred, the initial impact of such an announcement might already serve Beijing's goal of destabilizing the Taiwan economy so as to pressure its regime to negotiate. Insurance costs would immediately rise for shippers, deterring some and forcing others to raise their prices. Some would avoid testing the PRC will and simply suspend operations until the situation clarified. Others could offload in Hong Kong, Manila, Singapore, or Okinawa, for transshipment by Taiwan freighters, but this would be cumbersome as well as costly. During this time, anxiety on Taiwan and abroad would rise. The flight of capital and personnel might begin. Stock market prices would plummet. Without Beijing having fired a shot, the demand might emerge, particularly among mainlanders on the island, for negotiation to begin. The actual stoppage of shipping to Taiwan is a complex but not impossible task. Shipping lanes from the mainstream east of Taiwan are relatively short, facilitating convoys escorted by the Nationalist navy. The minesweeping of harbors is also possible, depending on the technology of PRC mines. Anti-submarine warfare is Taiwan's weakest defense against the mainland's most potent threat. However, a submarine attack risks the loss of foreign lives and ships, with serious consequences for PRC relations, so it is not likely to be a preferred tactic except as a last resort. The more complicated the interdiction effort, the more important become Taiwan's air bases. This in turn raises the question of PLA attacks on airfields, thereby involving the island in direct hostilities. While not wholly inconceivable, it would also appear to be a final option.

Coincidental with or alternative to the announced port closure, Beijing could declare the offshore islands of Quemoy and Matsu closed to all outside contact. Unlike 1958, this would not involve bombardment of the islands, but, as in 1958, it would require their total interdiction. Since then, both sides have improved their respective capabilities for a prolonged confrontation of this type. Without going into details, the advantage will almost certainly lie with the PLA, given its markedly expanded sea and air power as compared with that of Taiwan.[28] The major change from 1958, of course, could be the possible absence of American military support for the Nationalist side. Beijing's objective would not be the immediate collapse or the eventual capture of the islands, but rather the raising of pressure on Taiwan for negotiations. With perhaps 100,000 troops held hostage, the majority of whom would be Taiwanese, it is not difficult to imagine the reaction of immediate family, relatives, and friends. While perhaps not significant at first, concern would increase as weeks went by without contact with or word from beleaguered husbands, fathers, sons, or brothers. Throughout this period, the reactions of the United States, Japan, and other countries could prove important. However, this lies beyond the prescribed purview of this paper.

It should be noted that Beijing's professed terms for reunion are not, on the face of it, necessarily tragic or traumatic for most of Taiwan's inhabitants. Indeed, they may appear better with time should political and economic conditions in the PRC improve. As expressed by Taiwan's premier Sun Yun-suan on June 10, 1982, "If the political, economic, social, and cultural gaps between the Chinese Mainland and free China *continue to narrow*, the conditions for peaceful reunification can gradually mature. The obstacles to reunification will be reduced naturally with the passage of time."[29] While Beijing's proposals might not be accepted freely and simply, their negotiation under duress, expressed or implied, is conceivable, at least to Beijing's strategists. If they should miscalculate, it will not be the first time in their handling of Taiwan.

In the past, miscalculation has ended in tactical flexibility. Thus, in mid-1950, an imminent invasion was abandoned rather than challenge President Truman's order that interposed the Seventh Fleet in the Taiwan Strait, despite the fact that all nominally available U.S. ships were involved in the Korean War.[30] The blockade and bombardment of 1958 ended after successful U.S.-Nationalist countermeasures including "every other day" shellings, ostensibly designed to facilitate supplying the offshore islands. As for Taiwan itself, neither mass demonstrations vowing to "liberate" it nor dire warnings to the regimes in Taipei and Washington have ever resulted in aggressive action against the main island.

In the face of this record, it would be presumptuous to pretend certainty on how Beijing might respond to failure at the specified levels of military pressure. But the critical variable that could tip the odds in favor of escalation as compared with backdown would be the perception that failure under these circumstances would mean the permanent separation of Taiwan from the Mainland, with all that would entail for the regime at home and abroad. Having undertaken these steps after decades of waiting and winning withdrawal of the U.S. defense commitment, the PRC leadership could ill afford to admit it was too weak to force compliance on one of its own provinces with less than twenty million inhabitants. Thus, in the final analysis, direct attack would seem to be the only realistic alternative.

Here again, however, preparation may not require implementation. As the visible buildup of forces opposite Taiwan accumulated momentum, Beijing could count on direct and indirect probing for negotiation. Intermediaries in Japan, Hong Kong, and elsewhere might be anxious to play a role, both to avoid unnecessary bloodshed and to advance their personal ends in facilitating a settlement. Individual defectors from Taiwan would join a mainland chorus appealing to "our kith and kin" for a peaceful reunion. After Chiang Ching-kuo's death or incapacitation, the absence of a powerful central leader on the island would invite the fragmentation of government and society as different interests struggled to assert conflicting views. Meanwhile, Taiwan's appeals for international support to preserve the status quo would win little substantive support and none commensurate with the threat of a PLA attack.

OTHER OUTCOMES

For outsiders to divine Chinese thinking or to devise Chinese solutions is somewhat fanciful, if not foolish. Foreign analysts may serendipitously strike on something not already conceived by those most closely and emotionally involved. They also may raise aspects that are repressed by the immediate participants but which deserve attention. Basically, however, outsiders have neither the time nor the incentive to think through Chinese problems to the same extent as those whose lives literally depend on it, nor do they possess the information or the opportunity to quietly test their ideas in exploratory probes.

Another serious limitation lies in the Western penchant for explicit, formal, and contractual agreements to resolve differences between contesting parties. This insistence on a legalistic approach contrasts with an Asian preference for tacit understandings that deliberately leave ambiguity for time to resolve. For example, the absence of a formal peace treaty in the Korean peninsula more than thirty years after the conclusion of hostilities is an anomaly in Western terms. However, the stability of the DMZ and the behavior of both sides probably has not been seriously worsened by the existing armistice agreements.

The Taiwan Strait provides an excellent example of how mutual accommodation can be informally arrived at, even between historically antagonistic civil war opponents. Communist and Nationalist forces recognized the need for a tacit ceasefire if fishing, essential to both sides, were to flourish without fear of attack. Arrangements that emerged while the Seventh Fleet nominally patrolled the area survived its removal in 1969 as well as termination of the U.S. defense commitment ten years later.

These instances caution against concluding that the PRC-Taiwan relationship must be resolved in a hard and fast manner during this decade. The future of Taiwan can remain in limbo indefinitely so long as the island does not become expressly independent. The ability of Chinese on both sides of the strait to live with ambiguity and uncertainty on this question has been amply demonstrated over more than thirty years.

Publication of the PRC draft constitution in 1982 is suggestive in this regard. The preamble solemnly states, "Taiwan is part of the sacred territory of the People's Republic of China. To accomplish the great task of reunifying the motherland is the sacred duty of the entire Chinese people, including our compatriots in Taiwan."[31] This leaves unspecified the time or manner of achieving this goal. Article 30 declares, "The state may, where necessary, establish special administrative regions [*te bie xing cheng qu*]. The rules and regulations in force in special administrative regions shall be stipulated by law according to specific conditions." This is a new article, absent from previous constitutions. It thereby differentiates "administrative" from "autonomous" regions which are defined in Article 29 as comprising "nationality areas."

The terminology "special administrative region" of Article 30 is identical with the nine-point proposal offering Taiwan "a high degree of autonomy." This suggests the provision was deliberately designed for Taiwan, and possibly for Hong Kong and Macao as well.[32] In fact, leaders of a Taiwan organization in Beijing called specific attention to the linkage of language in the two documents as evidence of the "government's sincerity in seeking to resolve the Taiwan issue."[33]

Conceivably, Beijing could unilaterally declare Taiwan to be a "special administrative region" where the "rules and regulations" prevailed "by law according to specific conditions" that applied to the island at the time. The Taiwan authorities would be free to ignore this declaration. Alternatively, they could devise a reciprocal formula which acknowledged that "specific conditions" that prevailed over the mainland permitted a separate "system" to function there. Neither side would have formally renounced its traditional position or changed its actual practice, but each could maintain that an agreed concept of "one China" had theoretical sanction. In this regard, recent attention on Taiwan to the concept of "one state, two systems" suggests a softening of positions analogous to that occurring on the Mainland.

Whether this or some other artifice would satisfy all elements in both capitals cannot be determined at this juncture. But it is not beyond the realm of possibility that Chinese on both sides of the Taiwan Strait, as specified in the Shanghai Communiqué, can move from agreement on one China of which Taiwan is a part to tacit understandings that will avoid the worst case outcome of renewed warfare. The incentives not to use force against Taiwan are powerful. Its economic value could be sharply reduced if the prospect of war became serious or, worse, reality. The fratricidal human losses would weigh heavily on the PRC image abroad as would the military losses at home. Meanwhile, Taiwan would have no hope of winning a prolonged war of attrition or surviving an airborne barrage targeted on the island's concentrated population and transportation systems.

Those considerations do not guarantee a peaceful resolution to the Taiwan issue. They reinforce, however, the likelihood that formulas will be evolved by both sides that can postpone and perhaps obviate a time of reckoning. With this in mind, it is incumbent on outsiders, especially other governments, to avoid any steps that lessen this likelihood or seek to impose solutions to this essentially Chinese problem.

NOTES

1. For a careful and thorough review of PRC statements on the matter, see Frank S.T. Hsiao and Lawrence R. Sullivan, "The Politics of Reunification: Beijing's Initiative on Taiwan," *Asian Survey*, XX, 8: 789–802.
2. Deputy Prime Minister Deng Xiaoping to U.S. World Affairs Delegation, October 11, 1975, cited in John H. Knowles, *China Diary*, The Rockefeller Foundation, October 1976, p. 81. I accompanied the delegation. Deng repeated this statement on

October 25, 1978, at a Tokyo press conference; see Hsiao and Sullivan, *op. cit.*, p. 790.

3. Hsiao and Sullivan, *op. cit.*, p. 790.
4. Parris H. Chang, "Beautiful Island", *The Wilson Quarterly,* Autumn, 1979, reprinted in *Taiwan: Yesterday and Today,* The China Council of the Asia Society, p. 13. Graphic and detailed reports were dispatched to the Department of State, by George H. Kerr, U.S. consul in Taiwan at the time; see his *Formosa Betrayed* (Boston: Houghton Mifflin, 1965).
5. During my residence in Taipei, 1953–54, it was extremely difficult to make Taiwanese contacts without KMT surveillance. However, residence down-island in Taichung, 1974–1975, was wholly free of restraints in this regard.
6. James Hsiung in Taiwan: *One Year After United States–China Normalization: A Workshop,* sponsored by the Committee on Foreign Relations, United States Senate, and Congressional Research Service, Library of Congress, June 1980 (hereafter *Workshop*).
7. Ralph Clough, *Island China* (Cambridge: Harvard University Press, 1978), p. 48.
8. Parris H. Chang, "Politics in Taiwan: Challenge to Legitimacy," (Cambridge: Harvard University Press, 1978), p. 21.
9. Parris H. Chang, *ibid.,* p. 46.
10. *Far Eastern Economic Review,* August 8, 1980.
11. Hung-mao Tien, "Uncertain Future: Politics in Taiwan," in *Taiwan: Yesterday and Today,* The China Council of the Asia Society, p. 65.
12. *Asian Wall Street Journal,* November 18, 1981.
13. The Chungli and Kaohsiung incidents are examined from various perspectives in *Workshop, op. cit.* Additional details and post-trial commentary are in Tien, "Uncertain Future."
14. Ralph Clough, *Workshop,* p. 10. Clough visited Taiwan in November and December and was in Kaohsiung when the incident occurred.
15. *Ibid.*
16. Tien, *op. cit.,* p. 68.
17. This was the consensus of those participating in the Taiwan workshop.
18. For the Chinese text, see *Renmin Ribao,* Liao Chengzhi letter to Chiang Ching-kuo; also *Beijing Review,* 25 (1982) 31.
19. Leonard Unger, "Derecognition Worked," *Foreign Policy,* No. 36 (Fall, 1979): pp. 114.
20. For analysis of the 1979 statement and its aftermath, see Hsiao and Sullivan, *op. cit.*
21. Xinhua News Agency, September 30, 1981, in *Beijing Review,* 24 (1981) 40: .
22. For the radicals' exploitation of the policy of foreign plant imports to be paid for by raw material exports, including oil, as a means of attacking Zhou En lai in 1974–1975, see Allen S. Whiting, *Chinese Domestic Politics and Foreign Policy in the 1970s,* Michigan Papers in Chinese Studies, 1979, pp. 53–76.
23. *Asia 1981 Yearbook,* pp. 124–125; p. 253.
24. Selig Harrison, *China, Oil, and Asia* (New York: Columbia University Press, 1977); also Harold Hinton, *The China Sea* (New Brunswick, N.J.: Transaction Books, 1980).
25. Richard H. Solomon, "The China Factor in America's Foreign Relations: Perceptions and Policy Choices," in Richard H. Solomon, ed., *The China Factor* (New Jersey: Prentice-Hall, 1981), p. 37.
26. For an extended discussion of this problem in the larger context, see Special Commentator, "Where Does the Crux of the Sino–US Relationship Lie?", *Beijing Re-*

view, 25, 15. A more harsh and blunt analysis which called the arms sale issue "a time bomb" is in Commentator, "He Who Ties the Knot Should Untie It," *ibid.,* 25 (1982) 19.

27. *The New York Times,* August 18, 1982.
28. *The Military Balance, 1981–1982,* International Institute for Strategic Studies, pp. 73–75 and 79.
29. Premier Sun Yun-suan, "The China Issue and China's Reunification," address to the 11th Sino–American Conference on Mainland China, June 10, 1982, official text.
30. Details on PLA preparations in June 1950 may be found in Allen S. Whiting, *China Crosses the Yalu* (Calif.: Stanford University Press, 1968), ch. IV.
31. *Beijing Review,* 25 (May 10, 1982) 19: p. 29, unofficial translation. For Chinese original, see *Renmin Ribao,* April 28, 1982.
32. For speculation in the Hong Kong press on this point, see *Hsin Wan Po,* April 29, 1982, and *South China Morning Post,* April 30, 1982, in *Daily Report: China,* FBIS, April 30, 1982.
33. Lin Liyun, president of the All-China Association for the Promotion of Friendship among Chinese Compatriots, in Beijing Xinhua Domestic Service in Chinese, May 12, 1982, in *Daily Report: China,* FBIS, May 31, 1982; also Cai Xiao, Chairman of the General Office of the Taiwan Democratic Self-Government League and member of the constitutional revision committee, Beijing Xinhua Domestic Service in Chinese, May 7, 1982, in *ibid.,* May 14, 1982.

PART IV

U.S. Policy Evolution, 1983–1993

Chapter 10

Domestic Considerations

Robert G. Sutter*

The American reconciliation with China begun by President Richard Nixon and developed by succeeding U.S. presidents has won wide bipartisan support in the United States as one of the most important breakthroughs in U.S. foreign policy since the Cold War. President Nixon made the initial overture to China, while President Jimmy Carter's decision to normalize diplomatic relations with the PRC opened the way to extensive Sino–American cooperation in economic, strategic, and cultural relations. The two powers have enjoyed a relationship based on a foundation of opposition to the expansion of Soviet power in Asian and world affairs; both have benefited from important bilateral economic ties; and growing cultural, educational, and tourist exchanges have bound the two peoples more closely together.

In broad terms, each American administration, from Nixon's to Reagan's, has sought better relations with China in order to position the United States favorably in the US–Soviet–Chinese triangular relationship; to stabilize Asian affairs, secure a balance of forces in the region favorable to the United States and China, and foster a peaceful and prosperous future for Taiwan; to build beneficial economic, cultural,

The views expressed in this paper are those of the author and do not represent the views of the Library of Congress or the U.S. Government.

*Specialist in Asian Affairs, Library of Congress's Congressional Research Service.

and other bilateral ties; and to work closely with the PRC on issues of global importance such as world food supply, population control, and arms limitations.

The major force behind American policy has been the search for strategic advantage. During the period of U.S.–Soviet détente in the first half of the 1970s, the United States sought to use improved relations with China not only to prepare for the U.S. exit from Vietnam, but as a means of eliciting positive Soviet foreign policy behavior regarding U.S. interests; and it also sought to use improved relations with Moscow as a means of eliciting positive Chinese foreign policy behavior. American planners sought to gain a position in which the United States would develop good relations with both Communist countries, having better relations with them than they had with one another.[1]

In the face of the expansion of Soviet military power and political influence in such Third World areas as Angola, the Horn of Africa, Afghanistan, and Indochina, and the continued steady growth of Soviet strategic and conventional forces, American interest in détente with the Soviet Union declined in the late 1970s. American policy was also affected by a rising U.S. concern over American military preparedness to meet Soviet and other foreign challenges seen following the collapse of the U.S.-supported governments in Indochina; the fall of the Shah and capture and detention of the American hostages in Iran; and the acrimonious debate over American strategic preparedness during U.S. Senate deliberation over the SALT II treaty.

As a result, the Carter Administration, especially in its last two years, shifted away from a policy of "evenhandedness" that had characterized the American approach to the Sino–Soviet powers in the past. Improved relations with China increasingly came to be seen as an important source of regional and global power and influence for the United States, useful to America and its allies in the developed world as a means of countering what came to be seen as the major strategic problem for the next decade—the containment of expanding Soviet military power and influence in world affairs. Officials in the Reagan Administration came to agree with this basic position. In an effort to consolidate ties with China, Secretary of State Haig traveled to Beijing in June 1981 and announced that the United States, for the first time, was now willing to consider the sale of weapons to the PRC.

But the progress in Sino-American relations has failed to obscure persisting serious disputes in the United States over China policy. Presidents Nixon and Ford managed to avoid seriously exacerbating domestic tensions over China policy while developing and maintaining U.S.-China relations. President Carter used a different approach. His administration repeatedly pushed the China relationship forward despite sharp resistance from some Americans in the Congress, the administration, and elsewhere. Ronald Reagan also prompted a major public debate over U.S. policy concerning the sensitive issue of Taiwan during the presidential campaign of 1980. Beijing responded with strong public pressure and new demands for further U.S. compromise over the Taiwan issue—a stance that has led to the recent slowdown in U.S.–China relations.

Debate and controversy, deeply rooted in the history of American China policy, have been substantially influenced by changing international and domestic forces affecting American policy; they have also taken on a life of their own that is unlikely to fade quickly. As a result, the next decade will probably see continued political controversies in the United States over sensitive aspects of American China policy. The record of public discord over recent U.S. policy shows that the main areas for debate will focus on Taiwan, U.S. military and economic relations with China, and the high level of secrecy that has surrounded American-Chinese relations.

FUTURE POLICY DILEMMAS

In the period ahead, U.S. policymakers face a series of decisions that are likely to bring to the fore major divisions in the United States that continue to complicate American China policy. Chinese pressure has forced Americans to focus attention on the Taiwan issue. When and if Beijing reduces pressure on this question and allows for greater development in U.S. cooperation with China in military, economic, and other areas, dilemmas concerning the U.S. defense ties and assistance to China and the covert nature of American policy, would likely come to the surface.

Taiwan

Americans sympathetic with Taiwan's interests against the Mainland tend to favor what they call the "full" implementation of the Taiwan Relations Act. This would involve improved contacts of an unofficial nature between Taiwan and U.S. representatives, the opening of more Taiwan offices in the United States, and most importantly, the continued provision of U.S. weapons for sale to Taiwan. This position would not be bound by the qualitative and quantitative limits placed on U.S. arms sales to Taiwan as a result of the August 17, 1982, U.S.-PRC communiqué.

The United States could go further and formally recognize the "reality" of Taipei as one of two governments existing in China—an option favored by some of the most outspoken supporters of Taiwan in the United States. This would be similar to U.S. policy toward the two German administrations, and would presumably involve the reestablishment of some sort of official ties with Taiwan. Another option that favors Taiwan against the Mainland would involve U.S. efforts to use American influence with China in order to obtain a PRC commitment not to use force in dealing with Taiwan.[2]

The main advantages of these approaches are that they would help to discharge honorably the American commitment to Taiwan, would underline U.S. reliability and dependability in support of longstanding allies and friends, and would enhance American ideals of peace and nonuse of force in international politics. (Of course, each of these objectives enjoys wide support in the United States.) They also would meet with favor in Taiwan and would presumably enhance economic and political stability on the island, according to American proponents.

The main disadvantage concerns the likely reaction of the PRC. Thus, any sustained U.S. effort to demand a renunciation-of-force agreement from China over Taiwan or to re-establish official contacts with Taiwan would likely lead rapidly to an unraveling of the Sino–American reconciliation of the past decade. And U.S. implementation of provisions of the Taiwan Relations Act—especially the sale of weapons to Taiwan—is also offensive to the PRC, though it is hard to judge what countermeasures or retaliation Beijing would carry out. Of course, any major failure in U.S.–China relations could easily become a significant issue in American partisan politics.

Other Americans urge that the United States follow options that favor the PRC interests vis-à-vis Taiwan. Thus, the United States could try to reduce or eliminate the Taiwan issue as an impediment in U.S.–PRC relations by gradually cutting back American support, especially military support, for Taiwan. This would represent an indirect but unmistakable signal to the Taipei leaders that they should adjust to the new situation in U.S.–China relations and begin efforts to achieve an accommodation with the Mainland. U.S. leaders could speed this process by adding political pressure on Taipei leaders to come to terms with the PRC, and perhaps, in so doing, establish the United States as a formal mediator between the two Chinese sides.

The main advantage of this approach is that the United States would ease tensions with the PRC, opening the way to smoother cooperation in U.S.–Chinese relations. A solution to the Taiwan issue would remove the most serious impediment to closer U.S.–China relations.

The main disadvantage of this approach is that it could easily be portrayed as a victory of expediency over principle in U.S. foreign policy, since the United States "sold out" Taiwan for the sake of U.S. interests vis-à-vis the Mainland. It also might so alienate the Taipei leaders that they might adopt policies that would undercut the possibility of any deal with the Mainland and jeopardize U.S. interests in the region. These include developing relations with the USSR, producing nuclear weapons, or declaring Taiwan an independent state.

Between these contrasting approaches lie many Americans who seek a still unclear middle ground that will allow the United States to sustain its interest vis-à-vis Taiwan while avoiding any retrogression in U.S.–PRC relations. Members of this group judge that Taiwan's future can be best secured under conditions of improving U.S. relations with the PRC.

U.S.–China Military Ties

Americans will almost certainly continue to disagree strongly about the proper U.S. policy regarding developing military cooperation with China.[3] Support for such cooperation is likely to build so long as U.S. relations with the Soviet Union remain characterized more by hostility than by consultations; U.S. relations with China develop more closely; and Sino–Soviet relations remain cool. However, Beijing's present stance on Taiwan has placed an impediment to what many see as the next logical step forward in U.S.–China military ties, the sale of American weapons to China. If and when this impediment is removed, American policymakers are likely to be faced with the difficult task of satisfying conflicting American views on this sensitive issue.

Diverging American assessments of the wisdom of closer military cooperation with China have depended heavily on conflicting views of an underlying, broader strategic question in U.S. foreign policy—how far should the United States go in trying to improve relations with China in order to strengthen the American international position against the Soviet Union? In particular, Americans who are deeply concerned with what they see as U.S. and allied weakness vis-à-vis Soviet military power, and who view China as strongly opposed to the USSR and favorable to the United States, tend to support increased U.S. military cooperation with China. In contrast, Americans who are sanguine about U.S. power vis-à-vis the Soviet Union or who are skeptical of China's reliability or strength tend to oppose such ties.

Thus, for example, many Americans concerned with global military strategy have shown particular worry over what they have seen as the relative decline of U.S. military power vis-à-vis the Soviet Union in recent years. Dissatisfied with allied efforts to help redress the balance, many view U.S. military cooperation with China as a useful source of leverage that could help remedy that decline. In contrast, Americans interested in arms control with the USSR frequently are concerned with restoring enough trust in U.S.–Soviet relations to facilitate conclusion of important agreements on SALT, MBFR, and nuclear arms control in Europe. They see U.S. military moves toward China as contrary to this objective and of marginal utility to the United States when compared to the importance of major U.S.–Soviet arms accords.

Americans interested in Soviet affairs are divided into two general groups on this issue. Some see Sino–American military cooperation as contrary to what they judge should be the primary U.S. goal of establishing an international order based chiefly on a Soviet–American *modus vivendi*. Many others, however, see the USSR as a newly emerging great power and believe that the United States should work closely with other sources of world power—including China—in order to preclude more Soviet expansion. They see U.S. military cooperation with China as useful in this context.

American observers of China are also divided. Many are concerned with the negative impact of a U.S. refusal to increase military cooperation and transfer military supplies would have on Sino–American bilateral relations. Several judge that the United States might seriously disappoint the Chinese leaders by not following through with military supplies, after having given the Chinese the impression during visits and other interchanges that such equipment would be forthcoming. Some of them add that the supply of limited amounts of weapons and weapons-related technology represents an effective way to consolidate relations with the Chinese leadership.

But many others worry about the potential negative consequences of closer military cooperation with China for future Sino–American relations. Some worry about leadership stability in China or voice concern over Chinese intentions toward their neighbors. U.S. military ties might identify the United States too closely with only one group in the Chinese leadership—a group whose tenure may be limited and whose successors may not be favorably disposed to the United States.

Of course, not all views of U.S. military cooperation with China are governed by the U.S.–China–Soviet triangular relationship. Thus, for example, many Americans with an interest in East Asia have reflected the uneasiness of the countries of that region over U.S.–China security ties. Their concerns focus on China's irredentist claims and its potential as a destabilizing force in the region—factors that are seen as possibly more difficult to deal with if the United States appears to defer more to

China's interests in Asian affairs. Americans with particular interest in Taiwan have an obvious strong interest in blocking military ties with China. Americans with strong interests in other non-communist Asian areas have also been wary of closer U.S. cooperation with China, especially military cooperation, that appears to signal greater U.S. support for a stronger—and potentially expansionist—PRC strategic role in the region. Meanwhile, those interested in increased trade with the PRC have sometimes favored improved military ties as a means of showing American good faith toward China, of insuring a fruitful economic relationship with the PRC, and of building China's sense of security.

U.S.–China Economic Relations

There has been some recent controversy in the United States regarding normalization of U.S.–PRC economic relations, as Chinese leaders sometimes complain about U.S. restrictions on PRC imports and U.S. slowness in transferring technology to the PRC. From time to time, moreover, U.S.–China economic ties have been linked with the debate over American strategy in the U.S.–Soviet–China triangular relationship. Thus, for example, a dispute accompanied Vice President Walter Mondale's visit to China in August 1979. He pledged to provide China with U.S. Export-Import financing of up to U.S.$2 billion on a case-by-case basis over the next five years; he offered to submit to the Congress before the end of the year the previously negotiated Sino–American trade agreement which offered Most-Favored-Nation tariff treatment for Chinese goods entering the United States; and he promised Chinese leaders that the Carter administration would seek congressional action to provide investment guarantees of the Overseas Private Investment Corporation for American investors in China. Since none of these benefits were planned for the Soviet Union, critics at the time argued that Mondale's remarks clearly altered—in favor of China and against the USSR—past "evenhanded" U.S. policy in the triangular relationship.

Following the Soviet invasion of Afghanistan in December 1979, such charges had little impact in U.S. policy councils; U.S. economic relations with the PRC developed relatively smoothly. China began to receive Most-Favored-Nation tariff treatment and was made eligible for Export-Import Bank loans and investment guarantees. However, the United States did little to follow up Mondale's pledge for up to U.S.$2 billion in loans.

Officials in the Reagan administration and the Congress have proposed changes in U.S. laws in order to reduce or eliminate residual legal barriers imposed during the Cold War on economic interchange with China. For the most part, the remaining barriers are minor irritants. A notable exception concerns the Foreign Assistance Act, which prohibits the United States from giving aid to China. Once this law is changed, U.S. officials will confront a new and much more controversial series of questions on aid to China.

Many Americans favor American aid to China in order to promote economic relations, increase levels of American trade and investment in China, and solidify political ties with the PRC. But others are more skeptical.[4] Assuming PRC receptiveness to American aid, they argue that the result could be an open-ended U.S. aid program that would have several significant disadvantages for the United States.

For one thing, it could identify the United States closely with the current four modernizations program in China. If those programs do not succeed—and U.S. specialists tend to agree that they will be only a partial success at best—Chinese leaders might portray the U.S. aid effort as a major cause of the failure. (The Chinese followed a similar practice in the late 1950s when they blamed alleged inadequacies in the major Soviet aid effort for the failure in China's economy at that time.)

U.S. officials might commit the United States to backing economic development projects in China that later might appear ill-advised. This scenario is especially likely because the Chinese still appear to have no clear program for modernization and development, and have been changing repeatedly their economic priorities. A case in point is Japan's major commitment in 1979 to assist China's multibillion dollar steel mill at Baoshan, near Shanghai. At the time, the commitment was hailed by both sides as a paradigm of foreign efforts to help China's modernization, but within two years, China so changed its economic priorities that it came to view the Japanese-aided plant as an enormously expensive white elephant sucking scarce economic resources away from China's modernization. As a result, in 1981 the Chinese tried to cancel contracts with Japanese suppliers of equipment for the plant, leading to strong Japanese protests and serious friction in Sino–Japanese relations.

U.S. leaders may also make aid commitments that will fail because of changed circumstances in the United States. Thus, for example, because of serious American budget constraints, the U.S. Export-Import Bank has been unable to meet the financial commitment made by Vice President Mondale in 1979 regarding loans for Chinese purchases of U.S. equipment.

Perhaps the greatest potential danger is seen regarding possible U.S. military assistance, as opposed to commercial sales, to China. Such assistance could take many forms, including foreign military sales credits or grants. As the United States ends legal restrictions on assistance to China, in theory, it will be able to develop an arms relationship with China well beyond its current, largely symbolic importance. At present, China can afford to buy few U.S. weapons. Recent large-scale American offers of military aid to other countries in Asia (Pakistan, for instance) and elsewhere that are deemed important to U.S. competition with the Soviet Union also appear to some to set a precedent for larger military aid offers to the anti-Soviet Chinese. As noted in the previous discussion on U.S.–China military ties, any large-scale American military relationship with China would almost certainly prompt major debate in the United States.

Secrecy Versus Openness in U.S. China Policy

Ever since the beginning of the Sino–American reconciliation, U.S. policymakers have found it easier to develop relations with China behind a veil of secrecy, rather than to consult broadly and build strong understanding and public support for Sino–American relations. Such an approach has been favored by some Americans because it prevents leaks that could offend Chinese sensitivities, avoids signaling U.S.–PRC intentions to the USSR, and allows the United States to deal with sensitive issues like Taiwan free from pressure and interference from partisan groups in the United States. It also allows the administration to hide from public view internal differences and mistakes over China policy.

Critics have argued that there are serious disadvantages to such a covert approach. (It is important to note that there has been little public outcry about secrecy in U.S. China policy. Most complaints have come from the Congress.) In particular, critics say that it has led to distorted American perceptions and expectations of China, precluded the building of a solid popular consensus on China policy, and contradicted basic American ideals of democracy and representative government. Thus, by restricting access to information about China, U.S. policymakers, in an effort to win support for forward movement in relations with China, have been said to cover over negative aspects of China and instead to accentuate China's positive accomplishments and compatibility with U.S. interests as a "friend" of the United States. Such practices reportedly overemphasize the positive aspects of China and the community of Sino–American interests, and do little to prepare the American people and their government representatives for the frictions, disputes, and disappointments that may arise in Sino–American relations in the future.

Meanwhile, because secrecy has made the implications of China policy poorly understood in the United States, support for U.S.–China reconciliation has been potentially unstable—a development vividly seen at the start of the Reagan administration. If China policy were more open and better understood among the American people and their government representatives, critics argue, it seems highly unlikely that any U.S. president would have been able even to consider endangering the entire substance of the U.S.–China relationship for the sake of a political gesture of re-establishing official ties with Taiwan.

Finally, secrecy in China policy is also seen as antithetical to the important ideal in American government that the American people, through their representatives in both the Executive and legislative branches, should be informed of the major implications of new policies like the developing relationship with China, and should have some say in the formulation of those policies. Such a popular representative role seems all the more appropriate at a time when the United States is considering spending U.S. tax revenue to improve economic relations with China; and after ten years of gradual U.S. efforts to build up a strategic relationship with China—a commitment that may have to be backed in the future by the use of American military personnel.

CONCLUSION

American policymakers will continue to confront differences in American domestic opinion over China policy as they strive to manage the relationship with Beijing in the decade ahead. Of course, the salience of one issue or another will be subject to change, depending on international and domestic pressures. For example, continued pressure from the PRC for more American compromises over Taiwan will have the effect of focusing American attention on this issue in U.S.–China relations, while blocking forward movement in U.S.–PRC military cooperation that could, in turn, prompt American debate over the proper U.S. policy in the U.S.–Soviet–Chinese triangular relationship.

At the same time, a shift in the current, strong anti-Soviet posture of American foreign policy toward a revival of past emphasis on arms control and détente cannot be ruled out (especially given the strong divisions on this issue recently evident in the United States.) If U.S.–Soviet relations were to improve, it follows from one line of reasoning that American interest in establishing closer ties, especially security ties, with China would decline. Of course, increased U.S. confrontation with the USSR could well push the United States even closer to China, provided the PRC appeared to be a useful partner in containing Soviet power and was willing to cooperate with the United States. Such confrontation would probably weaken substantially the influence of those Americans who oppose closer cooperation with the PRC over strategic and economic issues and Taiwan.

American perceptions of China at the elite and popular level remain potentially volatile. In the years following diplomatic normalization, U.S. leaders tried to make the case that China should be considered as a friend of the United States. This was supported by a spate of favorable American media reporting on China, depicting the PRC as a country trying to throw off the binding shackles of the past and open itself to foreign, especially Western, contacts as part of a major pragmatic drive toward economic and technical modernization. Its foreign policy was seen as dominated by strident anti-Sovietism and an increasingly close alignment with the West. If such trends continue, they will help undercut the arguments of those Americans who are wary of closer ties with China and who oppose accommodation with the PRC over Taiwan. But if China were seen to alter substantially these programs, revert to policies of strong internal control, and reorient its foreign policy in directions more critical of the United States and less antagonistic to the Soviet Union, American enthusiasm for developing close ties with the PRC could be substantially reduced.

American interest in developing an increased trade and aid relationship with China could also run up against predicted slow economic growth in the United States in the years ahead. As a result, Americans might be even more reluctant than at present to allow large increases in Chinese imports in such sensitive areas as textiles, where the PRC enjoys an international, comparative advantage; such imports are thought to be essential if the United States expects China to earn enough foreign currency to increase its purchases of American exports. Foreign aid—never a popular political issue in the United States—is also thought likely to be especially unpopular in a period of poor economic growth; projected curbs in government spending on social welfare have also made spending programs overseas even more unwelcome.

The penchant for secrecy in the conduct of American China policy will also probably continue to confront resistance, especially from the U.S. Congress, whose influence in American foreign affairs has grown substantially since the Vietnam War. Congressional demands for broad consultations on significant changes in U.S. foreign policies—and the willingness of the Congress to legislate requirements for such consultations—will pose problems for administration officials who might otherwise have preferred to leave the delicate details and controversial implications of American China policy behind a shroud of secrecy.

It goes without saying that American leaders will be tested by these domestic complications as well as by changing international conditions as they strive to manage and develop the Sino–American relationship over the next decade. Nevertheless, amid these conflicting pressures has emerged a general trend in U.S. policy toward China that has governed American behavior over the past decade and is likely to remain the major line of development for the foreseeable future. That is, American policy has tended to move in the direction of meeting Chinese demands and conditions, and solidifying the Sino–American relationship, while gradually compromising or accommodating American ideological, political, economic, or security interests that could complicate smooth U.S.–PRC relations. The most graphic case in point has been seen in the decline of U.S. support for Taiwan by four U.S. presidents—both Republican and Democratic—in order to meet incremental PRC demands and maintain a good relationship with China.

This trend is likely to continue as China will almost certainly remain important in U.S. calculations of American strategic and other interests in world affairs. (A modest realignment of Chinese foreign policy toward a less pro-Western, more independent foreign posture probably would not undermine American interest in China appreciably, though a reaffirmation of the close Sino–Soviet relationship of the 1950s would obviously upset U.S. calculations.) During a period of expected relative decline in U.S. military and economic influence in the 1980s, American leaders will be compelled increasingly to broaden American political links and relationships with more international actors in order to promote world stability and protect American interests. Increasingly they will be unable to risk alienating such an important world actor as the PRC for the sake of domestic American political differences or other considerations regarding such issues as Taiwan, arms sales to China, or secrecy in the conduct of American foreign policy. Of course, American domestic political tensions may sometimes become severe, and unexpected developments could pose a threat of a possible sidetracking of U.S.–China relations for a time. Accordingly, it would appear wise for American statesmen to pay more attention to cultivating and managing American opinion about China in the Congress, the press, and the public realm at large in order to build a more solid consensus on the improved U.S. relationship with the PRC.

NOTES

1. For background, see Richard Solomon, ed., *The China Factor* (Englewood Cliffs, New Jersey: Prentice Hall, Inc, 1981).

2. For a discussion of these kinds of options, see Hungdah Chiu and Robert Downen, eds., *Multi-System Nations and International Law: The International Status of Germany, Korea, and China* (Baltimore: School of Law, University of Maryland, 1981).

3. For a review of diverging American opinion on this issue, see U.S. Congress, Senate, Committee on Foreign Relations, *The Implications of U.S.–China Military Cooperation* (Washington, D.C.: U.S. Government Printing Office, 1982); and U.S. Library of Congress, Congressional Research Service, *Increased U.S. Military Sales to China: Arguments and Alternatives*, Report No. 81-121 F. Washington, D.C. May 20, 1981.

4. See U.S. Congress, Senate, Committee on Foreign Relations, *United States-China Economic Relations: A Reappraisal* (Washington, D.C.: U.S. Government Printing Office, 1982).

Chapter 11

U.S. National Interests And Objectives

Helmut Sonnenfeldt*

The fundamental national interests of the United States are to secure the physical safety and integrity of its peoples and territories, to ensure the material well-being of the country, and to preserve, and adapt as necessary, the institutions and values on which the nation rests and that shape its essential character.

For much of the early history of the United States, the pursuit of these interests required relatively little involvement with the outside world. Except perhaps with regard to its material well-being (i.e., its economy), the country evolved, for the most part, without having to give much attention to threats to its fundamental interest emanating from abroad. The continental expansion of the United States did not so much result from fears that the national integrity was threatened as from a national consensus born of a variety of domestic pressures, impulses, and even controversies. Only when significant groups in the country came to believe that the nation's safety demanded outposts beyond its continental limits (and perhaps even some foreign entanglements) did serious disputes arise about the proper American role in the world and about the definition of American security interests. Those debates have existed for more than eighty years; since World War II, however, the dominant view has been that defense of the nation's physical integrity cannot be effectively conducted from a fortress America.

*Brookings Institution Guest Scholar.

259

This wider view of American national interests has also been influenced by the growing interaction between the economy of the United States and that of the world at large, though heavy involvement in international economic relationship is a relatively recent development. It is worth noting that, contrary to the Marxist shibboleth, economic imperatives (such as the need for markets) have on the whole played a smaller role in the expansion of American security interests than other factors. Nonetheless, the concern with economic security, especially with assured access to vital raw materials, has increased substantially in recent years as has the danger that hostile and predatory forces might seek to control and manipulate the sources of these raw materials to our detriment.

Despite the universalist language of the Declaration of Independence, the preservation of American institutions and values has not, historically, required their spread elsewhere. Americans have often shown sympathy for the oppressed in foreign countries and revulsion toward their oppressors, as if the United States enjoyed immunity from the contagion of tyranny. Despite some precedents, the emergence of the view that the American domestic order could be undermined from abroad resulted largely from the postwar appearance of the Soviet Union as the first persistent challenger to America's physical security interests, values, and political principles. Consequently, legislative and other measures have been taken to encourage international observance of human rights, not only for their own sake but in the belief that this would advance wider American security and political interests. Whether such policies have in fact benefited fundamental interests is, in turn, challenged by many.

FUTURE CHALLENGES AND OPPORTUNITIES

The single most severe challenge to the physical safety of the United States will continue to emanate from the Soviet Union. Only the Soviet Union has the capacity to devastate the United States or pervasively disrupt America's communication lines with the rest of the world. In the next decade there may well be an increase in individual challenges to American interests, but only the Soviet Union will likely be able to achieve cumulative accretions in power and geopolitical position in relation to that of the United States. The Soviet Union will not be the source of all instabilities and all trends adverse to American interests in the next decade. The Soviet Union, however, more than any other single actor in the international stage, will have the capacity and perhaps the incentive in its quest for superpower status to exploit such instabilities and trends in order to induce a retraction of American power and, if possible, a contraction of American interests.

Even when defending its interests, the Soviet Union prefers to advance its purposes without resorting to war, albeit with an ever-present threat of the use of force. Well aware of the potentially catastrophic consequences of nuclear warfare, the foreseeable Soviet leadership will seek the fruits of war without engaging in war. This will not preclude selected military action or the encouragement and support of others whose use of force would accrue to Soviet advantage. But the Soviets will engage in such undertakings only when they can confront the United States with disadvantageous military options and thus deter a U.S. military response.

The overall challenge of the Soviet Union is much more complex, for, apart from its military power, the Soviets have few assets with which to threaten the United States and they have many vulnerabilities that have the effect of both encouraging and inhibiting Soviet assertiveness. The Soviet political system and economic order probably will continue to lose much of their earlier appeal, in part because of the succession struggles that will occur. While the Soviets make selective use of military aid, political support, and economic instrumentalities and will continue to employ propaganda, agitation, and amenable foreign Communist parties and other groups, the principal means by which the Soviets can hope to affect political alignments will be by shifting the balance of military power in their favor. The United States therefore faces the unavoidable imperative of maintaining adequate balances geographically and in various categories of military power as well. But if this is done and sustained, there should be scope for the United States and others to exploit the weaknesses of Soviet economy, the stagnation of its society, and the tensions among its nationalities. The combination of military equilibrium, Soviet vulnerabilities, and Soviet need for external economic support will possibility lead to explicit or tacit arrangements to reduce the severity of Soviet threats to American interests. Chances are however, that American interests will continue to require active defense against Soviet encroachments during the next decade.

The possibility of nuclear war will continue to dictate the utmost care in contemplating the use of military power in situations where a direct American–Soviet clash could occur. Yet avoidance of war cannot be the sole determining factor in American policy, since the United States would then be open to Soviet pressure and blackmail. Fear of nuclear war, present though it undoubtedly is on both sides, has not proved to be an adequate basis for potential modus vivendi. Caution in the potential use of force must therefore continue to be combined with a posture that credibly conveys a readiness to employ force when crucial interests are threatened.

If in the coming ten years American policies can contribute to persuading the Soviets to shift some of their energies and ambitions to domestic affairs, threats to American interests and the danger of open warfare may be reduced. This certainly should be among the primary objectives of American policy.

Disillusionment about the prospects of postwar cooperation against the USSR and concern about Soviet expansionism were among the motivating forces behind the American decision to break with tradition and to participate actively in a system of alliances and other institutions including the indefinite deployment of American forces abroad, commitments to come to the defense of foreign countries under attack, and the association of the American economy more explicitly with the external world.

Thus, the territorial integrity of many countries in Europe, Asia, the Middle East, and Latin America has become an American interest second in weight only to the territorial integrity of the United States itself. (To say this is not to derogate from the American commitments under NATO and other treaties but simply to take account of the American constitutional processes in the event of an attack upon an ally and the War Powers Act, which controls various potential uses of military force abroad.)

The economic well-being of other nations (notably, but not confined to, the industrial democracies) affects American economic conditions and vice versa. Americans clearly feel more comfortable if nations with which the United States is intimately associated enjoy libertarian forms of government. The precise extent to which America's association with other nations should be controlled by the internal order prevailing in such nations remains, and is likely to remain, a matter of controversy. But Americans still remain essentially united behind the proposition that open or covert Soviet efforts to influence or change the domestic order of U.S. allies or other countries would be contrary to American interests.

These broad American interests concerning the security and general condition of allies and certain other countries are not likely to change dramatically over the coming ten years. What are in flux are the strategies and policies that would best serve to safeguard these interests, and there is controversy also about the costs. In this context, it has to be pointed out that while the most fundamental interests of nations may not be subject to great change (except perhaps over extended periods of time) the more derivative interests may come to be adjusted in the light of developments. For example, persistent domestic economic

difficulties and discord in economic relationships among the industrialized democracies could sap cooperation in military matters. Or, fester-
ing disputes about military policies and postures could undermine efforts in the common defense. Or, differing perceptions of interest in
regard to various Middle Eastern issues could over time produce disso-
nances within NATO or between the United States and Japan that
would have adverse effects on military relationships. Even though the
fundamental American interest in the security of allies might not be
affected by such frictions, the public consensus behind the exertions required to protect these interests might well erode.

The challenge of the next ten years is to find and maintain a balance
between national and multinational interests within the pluralistic international institutions to which the United States is a party. These
institutions and the relationships that surround them are historically
unique; there has been no prior experience in the construction and
maintenance of peacetime institutions of indefinite duration among
pluralistic, democratic societies. The American interest in the continued survival and vigor of these institutions and ties is evident. What is
at stake is the capacity of diverse and often geographically distant nations to demonstrate the feasibility of these nonhegemonic international institutions and the ability of these institutions to better satisfy
the needs of the individual members than will the alternatives. Therein
lies the opportunity for the next decade, for the alternative to the kinds
of institutions that have emerged in the last three and a half decades is
either international anarchy or alignment under the hegemony of a Soviet regime based chiefly on raw power.

INTERNATIONAL TRADE

In the course of the last several decades, Americans have come
to see a broad compatibility between their own economic well-being and
an open international economic order. Generally speaking, they have
been convinced that free enterprise was more likely to generate satisfactory economic conditions than various forms of controlled economies.
Under conditions of mounting economic stringency, however, American
commitment to an open international economic order has become diluted. Many Americans question the commitment of other trading nations to a truly open system. American administrations of both major
parties have continued to resist protectionist pressures and have remained committed to increasing freedom in the trade of goods and services, but the position will be harder to maintain.

If world trading relationships (especially those involving industrial nations that are security allies) become increasingly subject to restrictions or to manipulation designed to benefit particular economic sectors in particular countries, such developments will adversely impact on political and security relationships. Such highly nationalistic economic policies would not disrupt multinational political and security arrangements all at once, for the process would be gradual and not without resistance. But, in a period when perceptions and specific interests have come to diverge on a range of issues, predatory trading practices and domestic economic policies that disregard their impact on other countries would add a highly disruptive element to America's alliance relationships.

Thus, the objective American interest in the period ahead calls for continued efforts to liberalize the international trading system or at least to hold at bay the pressures for restriction and manipulation. Whether this can in practice be pursued is a crucial issue for the next decade.

SUPPLY SECURITY

This issue is fairly recent for the United States, despite certain historical antecedents. The question is not only one of physical access to needed resources but of access under reasonable conditions and at reasonable prices. The possibility of physical disruptions of supplies or of efforts by suppliers to impose onerous or unacceptable political and economic conditions was a generating factor in the U.S. perception of danger to its interests and to the future cohesion of its alliances from the resource supply dependency that appeared possible from the Western Europe–USSR pipeline project and the Japan–USSR energy projects. Western Europe and Japan, in turn, stressed (1) the danger of their own excessive dependence on energy supplies from such crisis-prone areas as the Middle East; (2) the consequent need to diversify their sources of supply; and (3) that reliance on Soviet supplied energy would not be dangerously high. They also contended that the Soviet peacetime need for hard currency and the Soviet interest in retaining a reputation as a sound business partner make disruption or manipulation of energy supplies unlikely.

These same concerns resulted in far-reaching unilateral commitments by the United States to prevent Soviet or other hostile dominance over the Persian Gulf, on whose oil the United States is considerably less dependent than are Western Europe and Japan.

American interest in international supply security also calls for policies that help supplier nations to obtain reasonable returns and other benefits for their own economies. By the same token, it is not in the American interest to acquiesce in price-gouging and other pressure tactics.

Besides assisting others to avoid being supply-dependent on the USSR, the United States is interested that the Soviet Union's role as a supplier should not facilitate Soviet military programs and should not ease the strains that these military programs and the Soviet system place on the overall Soviet economy. These two considerations argue strongly for finding common policies and approaches that would limit Western resource relationships with the USSR to present or near-present levels while alternatives to meet the economic requirements of the nations concerned are developed. Thus, resource policy is at once a major challenge and opportunity for the United States and its allies in the next ten years. It is both a challenge to reduce the actual and potential vulnerabilities and resultant tensions in the West and an opportunity to strengthen collaboration and mutual support.

THIRD WORLD

This term has been used to refer to countries and areas that are neither part of the Western industrialized world nor are they under Soviet domination. Because the diversity in this so-called world is so great, it is virtually impossible to make useful generalizations about it. Nonetheless, the United States has the negative interest of seeing no portion of the Third World fall under Soviet domination and of encouraging those states that are currently in some measure beholden to the USSR to reduce that measure. These interests derive naturally from the broader American interest in halting and, where possible, reversing Soviet geopolitical aggrandizement, especially in those regions that play a significant role in the security and well-being of the United States and its allies. The United States, however, need not intervene in all instances where Soviet influence might be expanded. Not all Soviet influence threatens significant American interests; indeed, any eventual modus vivendi with the USSR must inevitably allow for a certain Soviet influence and presence beyond the borders of the USSR. (Soviet staying power has proved deficient in a number of client states, often because the country involved sooner or later rejected Soviet encroachment.)

Positive American interests include the encouragement of economic and social advancement consonant with the needs and the special character of the societies involved, genuine nonalignment where this is the choice, political independence, peaceful settlement of disputes, and the steady growth of just and orderly government under conditions of expanding individual freedom. As these interests are served, the fundamental American interest in a world environment congenial to American values will be served as well. But the mere recitation of these interests highlights the difficulty of advancing them; many are beyond the effective capacity or the reach of the United States (at least in the short run), although this should not deter the United States from proclaiming them.

Not every country or region is of equal importance to the United States. The pursuit of American interests thus requires selectivity both as to country and region and as to the policy means employed. Because of the global role and weight of the United States, however, the focus of American concerns cannot be altogether fixed. Areas seeming to be of less urgent interest could acquire significance for the United States if they became either engulfed in conflict or catastrophe, the object of Soviet ambition, or a major factor in the world economy. Such shifts will almost certainly occur again in the decade ahead. To use a pertinent example, China was for almost two decades in the Soviet orbit. While the United States was not indifferent to fluctuations in Soviet–Chinese affinity, no important American interest seemed sufficiently affected by such fluctuations to warrant major adjustments in American policy. Once it became clear that the Soviet–Chinese relationship had been fundamentally transformed, the American interest in seeing this transformation endure became palpable. Although with pain and hesitation, American policy adjusted to serve this interest. There are many frictions and divergences in the American–Chinese relationship, but the American interest in Chinese independence will henceforth endure not merely in the form of a wish but as an operational objective of American policy.

In neither the Third World not elsewhere are American interests always in harmony with each other. Thus, a number of results could occur; namely, economic advancement in a country could take a form that actively conflicted with American economic interests; American commitments to certain countries could burden relations with others; American concern for human rights could alienate a regime whose support the United States values in other respects; U.S. support for social progress and modernization could undermine political stability in certain societies; and the need for a crucial resources could produce affinities to regimes with which the United States otherwise has little in common. Such tensions and contradictions can be cited, although most cannot be readily resolved and many produce domestic controversy over policy choices (if not over the very definition of American interests).

Chapter 12

U.S. Military Strategy And Force Development

David E. McGiffert* and Franklin D. Kramer**

The U.S. Navy is fond of reminding us that U.S. military strategy must be global in scope. It is true that the oceans are everywhere and that the resulting temptation to plan naval forces independently of prioritized contingencies is great. In contrast, the limitations imposed by geography on land warfare tend more clearly to force the choice of priorities, a choice which necessarily underlies and sets limits on any global defense strategy. That choice critically affects the composition of our armed forces and their peacetime deployment. And that choice has been critically affected by the People's Republic of China (PRC) and its relationship with the Soviet Union and the United States.

The importance of China in the strategic equation is not likely to diminish in the next decade if for no other reason than that the U.S.–Soviet relationship will remain intensely competitive. Fortunately, the Soviets have not proved to be adept at competing politically, economically, or socially: the Soviet economic system is arthritic and its political and social systems have little magnetism. In military competition, however, the Soviet Union is a formidable opponent. The Soviets have sustained a steady increase in defense expenditures for fifteen years at

*Covington and Burling.
**Shea and Gardner.

a rate of 2 to 5 percent in real terms annually. A fundamental assumption of this paper is that the Soviets will continue to make a comparable investment in their military capabilities over the next ten years and that, against the backdrop of substantial and increasing military power, the Soviet policymakers will continue to look for external targets of opportunity that they can prudently exploit to expand Soviet influence and diminish that of the United States.

U.S. DEFENSE POLICY

Fundamental U.S. defense policy has remained substantially constant for a long time. Vis-à-vis the Soviet Union, that policy has at least three major elements:

1. deterrence of nuclear attack by maintaining strong, invulnerable, and versatile nuclear forces
2. deterrence of non-nuclear military attack by maintaining conventional forces of considerable size and mobility, backed by the threat of escalation to nuclear warfare
3. containment of Soviet power by being prepared to defend forward in Europe and Northwest Asia, necessarily implying a policy of collective defense (i.e., reliance on allies for a major military contribution in Europe and East Asia)

Whether the post-Vietnam United States has, or is perceived to have, the will to use military force far from its shores in defense of vital national interests is not clear. Nor is it clear that there is an American consensus as to what interests should be deemed vital. But it can at least be said that there is no compelling suggestion in the statements of post-Vietnam administrations, in post-Vietnam military budgets, or in opinion polls that the United States should adopt a different set of fundamental defense policies—for example, a policy of continental defense or of reducing forward-deployed conventional forces to a nuclear trip wire role.

These basic defense policies are unlikely to change in the next ten years because the underlying global conditions for American security and for the security of its allies are not likely to change fundamentally in that period. The United States and the Soviet Union will remain in serious military competition. The alliances on each side, though buffetted, will probably hold together if prudently managed—the U.S. alliances because their members will continue to see their security as better protected by association with the United States, and the Warsaw

Pact because its members have little choice. Third world instability will continue. The globe will become a more dangerous place in a way that calls for greater defense effort but not in a way that compels a fundamental defense policy reorientation.

GLOBAL DEFENSE STRATEGY

Within the policy framework outlined above there have been changes in strategy that have flowed from the major changes in strategic context over the last twenty years. Those changes in context include the development of parity in strategic nuclear weapons;[1] the Sino–Soviet split and U.S.–PRC rapprochement; and the emergent dependency of the industrialized democracies on Persian Gulf oil coupled with a greater threat to that oil due to the British withdrawal from the area, the collapse of Iran, the Soviet invasion of Afghanistan, and Soviet footholds in Ethiopia and South Yemen (significantly offset by the loss of the Soviet foothold in Egypt).

The "2½ war" criterion of the 1960s represented a planning assumption (which implied both a strategy and a force sizing standard) that the United States should be prepared to fight simultaneously a conventional forward defense of NATO against the Soviet Union, a defense of Southeast Asia or Korea against a full-scale attack by the PRC, and a lesser contingency elsewhere. This criterion assumed that absent preparations of a kind that would allow U.S. allies time to fully mobilize, the Soviet Union could not mount a major attack simultaneously in two major theaters, nor could the PRC effectively attack Korea and Southeast Asia at the same time.

The "1½ war" approach enunciated in President Nixon's first foreign policy report to Congress in 1969 envisaged general purpose forces adequate to meet simultaneously either a major Soviet attack in Europe *or* a major Chinese attack in Asia, to assist against non-Chinese threats in Asia, and to meet a minor contingency elsewhere. This change was motivated by the view that, in light of the Sino–Soviet split, a coordinated attack by Russia and China was unlikely and that, in any event, such an attack could not and should not be met with ground forces in both theaters.

Avoiding the "1½ war" label, PRM-10, the early Carter administration's analysis of defense strategy, concentrated on the forces necessary to defeat the Soviet Union in a global conflict, with the first priority (after defense of the United States) given to the defense of Europe while still providing some forces to defend against a Soviet attack on Northeast Asia. These latter forces were mainly air and naval because it was postulated that the United States would not insert ground forces on the Asian mainland sufficient to stop a Soviet conventional attack. In addition, PRM-10 provided for some additional forces necessary to deal with a smaller regional conflict involving a third country (e.g., in Korea). When the follow-up analysis of the putative regional conflict was made, however, the analysts assumed a Soviet invasion of Iran. Thus, the major-minor war approach tended to merge with the new (for strategic planning purposes) concept of a global war with the Soviet Union and that war was postulated on three major fronts (Europe, East Asia, and the Persian Gulf) rather than two. The pre-Carter administration assumption of a Chinese attack in Asia entirely disappeared.

Of course, since U.S. and allied forces could not deal with a major Soviet attack in all three areas at once, planning assumed a sequential response, with the priority of effort directed to Europe while engaging, insofar as possible, in a holding action elsewhere. That U.S. and allied forces could not deal with a major Soviet Attack in three theaters at once was considered ominous only to the highly debatable extent that the Soviets could mount such major attacks simultaneously.

All the strategies outlined above had in common the assumption that it is desirable to limit the conflict geographically as much as possible and at the lowest possible level of destructiveness. However, the strategy supported by some in the current administration suggests that the best deterrent to a Soviet attack (e.g., in the Persian Gulf) is "horizontal escalation"—to expand instead of limit the conflict geographically, and to raise, rather than try to contain, its destructiveness. Critics of this approach argue that the United States and its allies are more vulnerable to horizontal escalation than is the Soviet Union. Perhaps reflecting this view, the national security advisor has said that it is in the interest of the United States to limit the scope of any conflict. While "the capability for a counter-offensive on other fronts is an essential element of our strategy . . . it is not a substitute for adequate military capability to defend our vital interests in the area in which they are threatened."[2]

Indeed, if subsequent press reports are reliable, the Reagan administration appears to have set strategic planning priorities for a worldwide war with the Soviet Union that in fact differ little from the Carter administration. (1) defense of the United States, including Alaska and Hawaii and contiguous areas (Canada and the Caribbean Basin); (2) defense of NATO and the preservation of lines of communication to NATO; (3) assurance of access to oil in Southwest Asia; (4) defense of U.S. allies in the Pacific and the lines of communication thereto; (5) defense of friends elsewhere.[3]

FORCE STRUCTURE

What of the forces to implement this strategy? A quantitative comparison of today's force structure with that immediately preceding Vietnam suggests that the permutations in U.S. military strategy over the last twenty years have, in some respects, been paper exercises of theoretical interest but little practical effect. The numbers of army and marine divisions in the active forces and the overall tactical airforces have, for example, remained relatively constant. Some would say, indeed, that the shift from the 2½ to the 1½ war criterion was designed less to reflect realities abroad than to narrow the difference between JCS stated requirements and actual capabilities by eliminating the basis for a significant portion of the requirements. On the other hand, it can plausibly be contended that the change from 2½ to 1½ wars exerted downward pressure on the overall capability of active U.S. land forces. For example, although a comparison of the number of Army divisions in 1964 (sixteen active, twenty-three reserve) and 1983 (sixteen active, eight reserve) does not reveal the fact, a substantial amount of ground combat support capability was shifted to the reserve components during this period, resulting in a relatively less capable active Army almost 20 percent smaller than in 1964 (972,000 versus 784,000). Yet, expansion in strategy to include a forward on-land defense of the Persian Gulf area has not resulted in reversal (nor, indeed, any official proposals for a near-term reversal) in this decline in active U.S. ground forces.

Of course, U.S. forces have been modernized and are far more capable than twenty-five years ago. But the same is true of Soviet forces, which have, in addition, narrowed their technological disadvantage. The point is that the Soviet threat now covers three major theaters and is greater than the Sino–Soviet two-theater threat of twenty years ago. Yet U.S. forces have not been commensurately expanded.

REGIONAL STRATEGIES—EUROPE
AND THE PERSIAN GULF

This strategy-force mismatch is likely to continue for the foreseeable future, for to presume that steady, sustained, and major increases (3 to 5 percent per year after inflation) in the U.S. defense budget, which would be needed to offset Soviet gains, will occur in the face of competing domestic demands and the volatility of the U.S. political process is to ignore experience. The mismatch will tend to affect both peacetime overseas deployments and the orientation of the strategic reserve in accordance with strategic priorities. Hence, before East Asia is considered, some discussion of strategy and force levels for higher priority theaters is needed.

NATO continues to adhere to a strategy of forward defense and flexible response. The viability of that strategy is, however, increasingly doubtful because the Soviets' military build-up has eliminated NATO's advantage in strategic nuclear capability, has increased Soviet superiority in longer-range theater nuclear weapons (and will, before long, presumably close the gap in shorter-range systems), and has made greater qualitative improvements in conventional forces that already had a large quantitative advantage. By so doing, the Soviets have reduced the credibility of nuclear forces as a deterrent to conventional attack, making that aspect of flexible response less meaningful, while at the same time exacerbating the difficulties of defending forward with conventional force at or near the inter-German border.

These developments clearly imply the need for a greater NATO conventional force capability. Whether this greater capability necessarily means (or should mean) a large increase in U.S. forces earmarked for NATO defense depends on an evaluation of the feasibility and effectiveness of the following:

> expanding the reserve forces of the European allies
> technological advance (e.g., weapons lethality and availability of tactical intelligence on enemy rear areas)
> doctrinal change (e.g., greater emphasis on maneuver warfare and attacks on reinforcing Warsaw Pact echelons)
> the more efficient use of NATO resources through standardization and interoperability of weapons systems
> arms control efforts, such as MBFR

It seems safe to say, however, that none of these developments separately or in combination is likely to reduce U.S. force requirements significantly, but rather, given the fiscal constraints and the resistance to change within the alliance, some increase in those requirements is likely.

As for the Middle East/Persian Gulf, there seems to be a reasonable consensus that U.S. deployment of conventional forces should be large enough to make clear to the Soviets that aggression will lead to confrontation and therefore that the appropriate strategy lies somewhere between a nuclear trip-wire approach and a full forward defense near the Soviet frontier. Whether one plans to defend with several divisions along the Zagros mountain line or with a lesser force using the Gulf as a natural barrier, the need, as is the case of NATO, is likely to be for more U.S. forces to carry out the regional strategy than are now available.

REGIONAL STRATEGY—THE PACIFIC

The United States has vital political, economic, and security interests that call for an East Asia that is stable, peaceful, and much more closely associated with the United States than with the Soviet Union. Strategically, it is important that the Japanese be pro-U.S. rather than pro-Soviet or neutral. Similarly, it is important that the Soviet Union see China as a potential threat, thus tying down major forces that might otherwise be available elsewhere. Finally, it is important that there be a political and military environment in the ASEAN region compatible with maritime freedom of movement, which is particularly important for U.S. naval vessels with their added mission in the Persian Gulf area.

U.S. defense goals in the Pacific logically follow from these interests: protecting the United States, most prominently Alaska and Hawaii, supporting commitments to allies, and maintaining maritime access.

Containing the outreach of Soviet military power serves all these goals. And the strategy to accomplish such containment is, in essence, a coalition strategy in which the major formal players are Japan, South Korea, and the United States in Northeast Asia; Australia, New Zealand, and Thailand in Southeast Asia; and the Philippines, which has a pivotal role in both cases.

To implement a coalition strategy, the United States has urged Japan to devote more resources to its defense forces, has pressed the Koreans to do the same, and has maintained a military assistance program to Thailand and the Philippines as well as to South Korea and others. It has also modestly increased the capability of U.S. forces.

This coalition strategy has some obvious problems. Its foundations are imperfect. For example, the Japanese are obligated to participate only if Japan is attacked. Second, in at least one instance—the defense of South Korea against a *Soviet* attack—the strategy is heavily reliant on a nuclear response with all the attendant problems of credibility and the risks of escalation. Third, it is subject to preemption by higher priority needs. As already indicated, the clear thrust of U.S. strategic planning is to put Europe and Southwest Asia sequentially ahead of East Asia, even though, paradoxically, our last two wars were fought in East Asia. Consequently, the distribution of U.S. forces (except for the Navy) is heavily weighted toward Europe and Southwest Asia, and even the Navy's peacetime deployment patterns have been adjusted so that the Pacific fleet spends a significant number of ship-days in the Indian Ocean. Moreover, the demands for U.S. forces in those other theaters will, if anything, grow—with negative implications for force enhancement in the Pacific.

In these circumstances, the significance of China to U.S. strategic interests is particularly acute. This may be readily seen by cataloguing the benefits that the United States has so far accrued from the Sino–Soviet split and the normalization of U.S.–PRC relations and by imagining what the demands on U.S. military strategy and forces would be were those benefits neutralized or reversed.

First, the United States has been able to drop China as a putative military adversary. Second, U.S. forces have greater flexibility; the fleet need no longer patrol the Taiwan strait, for example. Third, Sino–Soviet antagonism has tied down about 25 percent of Soviet ground forces in East Asia alone. These forces are largely add-ons to the Soviet force structure, rather than involving draw-downs of forces in Europe; however, there is no assurance that they would be eliminated in the event of a Sino–Soviet rapprochement. Fourth, the Sino–Soviet split has removed any possibility of Soviet naval or air bases along the Chinese coast or Soviet access to Chinese ports for repairs and refueling of naval vessels. To the Soviet Pacific fleet, this denial only reinforces the daunting possibility that it could be bottled up in the Seas of Japan and Okhotsk. As long as a large part of the Soviet Pacific navy must return through the gauntlet of the straits north of Japan to obtain major overhaul and repairs, its power projection capabilities will be correctly seen as limited by the nations of the region. Fifth, the Chinese have undoubtedly exercised a restraining influence on the North Koreans. And finally, while Vietnam's fear of China has led it into a security relationship with the Soviet Union, that same fear may inhibit Vietnam from permitting the Soviets the degree of basing rights (e.g., a major naval facility or a forward base for Backfire bombers) that would pose a significant threat to the maritime lines of communication in Southeast Asia.

POLICY EVOLUTION

U.S. military strategy and forces in East Asia and the western Pacific are thus a function of Soviet military capabilities *and* Chinese orientation. To the extent that the lower strategic priority accorded East Asia does not reflect the view that U.S. interests are less vitally involved than elsewhere but rather the conclusion that the military threat is relatively less demanding, the Sino–Soviet split is mostly responsible. Ideally, U.S. defense policy should therefore evolve in a way that reinforces that condition. This, in turn, requires a perception of U.S. commitment to a forward military defense of its interests in the area, a commitment to deter Soviet expansion by maintaining a balance of military power.

If this perception is to be nourished, it is important that significant quantitative reductions in U.S. forces in the area, or publicly earmarked for the area, either be entirely avoided or very cautiously handled, with full consultation. This hold-the-line precept applies almost regardless of the excellence of the military justification for reduction. For these forces are symbolic to an extraordinary degree; their drawdown is likely to have political consequences that undermine a coalition strategy and thus may be self-defeating.

Second, the United States needs to maintain its forward military base structure, which now centers on Japan, Korea, the Philippines, and Guam. For purposes of being better able to deal with Southwest Asia contingencies, it may be desirable to base another carrier group forward, for example, in Australia, and to be able to utilize Thai airfields. But the minimum requirement for continued U.S. military credibility in East Asia is to maintain at least a forward basing capability of roughly the same order of magnitude as that of today. For example, loss of Clark and Subic would seriously erode U.S. forward defense capabilities; special attention to the Philippines will therefore be needed, probably including continued military assistance.

The reverse side of this coin is denial of basing opportunities to the Soviets. This is a goal to be achieved primarily by political and diplomatic means, although showing the flag as a reminder of U.S. military strength is helpful as is security assistance in certain cases. From the perspective of base-denial, a political solution in Southeast Asia reducing Vietnam's dependence on the Soviet Union would be especially desirable. Similarly, U.S. political relationships with the other countries of Southeast Asia and the archipelagic nations of the Pacific basin will critically affect Soviet opportunities.

Third, selective U.S. force enhancements will need to be made for both symbolic and military purposes. To ensure the viability of the coalition strategy, the United States msut do its share to offset steadily increasing Soviet military capabilities. Since U.S. strategy assumes that Chinese forces offset Soviet ground forces (or that in any event available U.S. ground forces are insufficient to mount a conventional defense against the Soviets on the land mass of Asia), the principal force enhancements probably should emphasize naval and air capabilities. However, if the North-South balance of forces on the Korean peninsula shifted dramatically in the North's favor, the United States might want to increase its ground forces in South Korea.

Fourth, although it is not clear what they should be, some decisions will need to be made about theater nuclear forces. If, as happened in Europe, the Soviets' enhancement of their theater nuclear capability by deploying the SS-20 produces a demand by U.S. allies and friends for redressing U.S. deployments, then some augmentation of U.S. theater nuclear capability would be difficult to avoid, politically if not militarily. Almost certainly, however, given the Japanese nuclear neurosis and the potential problem of overrun in Korea, any increased theater nuclear capability should be seaborn.

Fifth, credit or grant security assistance programs will need to be continued—in the Philippines if necessary to assure continued use of Clark and Subic, in Thailand as a contribution to Thai deterrence of Vietnam's adventurism and as evidence of the U.S. commitment to Thai security, perhaps in South Korea for symbolic reasons, and in other countries, such as Indonesia and Singapore, that border the key straits of Southeast Asia.

Finally, the United States needs to have a positive defense relationship with China, although it is far from clear what the dimensions of that relationship or the pace of its expansion should or could be. Some argue that the view that Chinese forces "tie down" major Soviet forces is misplaced and that therefore U.S. military assistance to the PRC is irrelevant. Of course, what is necessary to tie down Soviet forces in the event of a U.S.–Soviet war will depend on circumstances. And it is true that Soviet forces seem much larger than necessary to contain a China that will not have a significant capability to wage offensive war against the Soviet Union in the next decade. Indeed, current Chinese strategy recognizes that a successful forward defense is not feasible and relies heavily instead on trading space for time.

There do not, moreover, appear to be compelling reasons why, in the event of conflict in Europe, the Soviet Union would want to tie down their forces by opening a second front against China; to the contrary, it would probably wish to achieve its wartime goals in Europe first and be tempted to swing some of its counter-Chinese forces to other fronts for this purpose. Since Chinese weakness suggests that the Chinese would not wish to provoke Soviet countermeasures by initiating an early attack, the degree to which a swing of forces would appear prudent to the Soviets would presumably depend on the risk of later Chinese attack (e.g., following an exhausting stalemate in Europe or a U.S.–Soviet nuclear exchange) and its probable weight (as well as the speed with which particular types of Soviet forces could return). From this perspective, it is in the U.S. interest to encourage gradual improvement in China's military posture, particularly in its ground and air forces, even if it is unlikely that this will create a credible threat to the Soviet Union of an early second front.

Appropriate encouragement could in theory include: (1) political and diplomatic signals; (2) official defense consultations, intelligence and information exchanges, and exchange of naval visits; (3) technology transfers; (4) weapons sales—perhaps including coproduction; (5) PRC collaboration with and assistance to U.S. forces in Asia; and (6) joint defense planning. The emphasis in U.S. policy is currently on signals and on official consultations, with some technology transfer and an expressed willingness to consider arms sales on a case-by-case basis.

Joint military planning or force coordination would be unnecessarily provocative to the Soviet Union and almost certainly unacceptable to the PRC. Technology and weapons transfer should continue, recognizing that it is a matter not only of content but of pace: to proceed too slowly risks souring the relationship now; to proceed too fast risks souring the relationship later because room for further steps has been exhausted.

Moreover, it is important to proceed cautiously avoiding exaggerated expectations and recognizing that the political component of such an assistance program is more significant than its military contribution. For it is probably not practically possible, even if it were politically wise or feasible, to provide military aid that would do more than marginally affect Chinese capabilities vis-à-vis the Soviets in the next decade. The gap is too wide. Chinese military technology is about a generation behind. Chinese weapons are based largely on Soviet designs. Chinese hard currency is limited. Chinese industry cannot quickly absorb quantum advances in technology. Chinese priorities emphasize the civilian economy. Thus, while U.S. policy should favor an increase in Chinese military capabilities, the bilateral defense relationship is likely to be characterized more by political symbolism than by large and rapid substantive contributions to that goal. From the U.S. perspective, the strategic contribution of Chinese forces and the degree to which they tie down or offset Soviet military power are not likely to expand greatly in the next decade.

NOTES

1. Strategic nuclear forces are not discussed beyond noting that time has eroded the basis for the postwar strategy of relying on superior U.S. strategic nuclear forces to offset the Soviets' geographic proximity to areas critical to U.S. security and the

Soviets' conventional force superiority. It is assumed that rough parity in strategic nuclear forces will be maintained over the next decade.
2. Remarks to the Georgetown Center for Strategic and International Studies, May 21, 1982.
3. Washington *Post,* June 2, 1982, quoting from Department of Defense Policy Guidance. Southwest Asia was first made a significant priority in President Carter's 1980 State of the Union address; the Carter administration did not make an explicit priority choice between Southwest and Northeast Asia, however.

Chapter 13

Trade And Technology Transfers

Leonard Sullivan, Jr.,* with Ellen L. Frost,**
and David S. Holland‡

It is by no means obvious that, over the decade, unlimited increases in civil or military trade and transfers between China and the
United States—and other Western nations—are either practical or desirable. Before the United States embarks on any ambitious exchange
program, several questions need to be addressed:

What are the implications for China, the United States, the Western
Alliance, and others of trade and technology transfer and of its
withholdance?
What are some of the problems in asymmetric partnerships?
What are China's realistic prospects for economic development?
What are the potential foundations for developing China's military
strength, and what specific military development objectives might
be established?

In addressing these questions, additional issues are raised that point

*Defense Policy Consultant, Systems Planning Corporation.
**Director of Government Programs, Westinghouse Electric Corporation.
‡Sr. Vice President, Pennzoil Exploration and Production Company.

out the need for a clearer understanding of both U.S. and Chinese national objectives and the vast asymmetries between us.

IMPLICATIONS OF EXPANDING TRADE

There are several reasons for the United States to be interested in maintaining and increasing trade with China. Within our free enterprise private sector, there are the normal economic motivations to gain access to a seemingly endless commercial market, as well as to a variety of affordable and genuinely needed Chinese commodities. We believe that such trade will expand and be mutually beneficial in future years.

At the governmental level, increased U.S.–China trade could strengthen political bonds with the corollary reduction in any Chinese tendency to restore political or economic ties with the Soviet Union. In this respect, new U.S. mechanisms might be desirable to produce trade, regardless of economic gain. Such mechanisms are available to the governments of centralized economies such as the Soviet Union; the United States, however, has seldom tried to use trade controls for purely political purposes in other than exceptional (and negative) cases. Hence, while we have frequently withheld trade to express displeasure with the immediate course of events (Russia, Poland, and Argentina are recent targets of U.S. constraints), our democratic government exercises little positive control of market forces for political influence with specific allies or clients. To the extent that our objective is to perpetuate the Chinese–Soviet alienation, it is sufficient that we encourage Chinese trade with the West—not just with the United States.

Furthermore, a significant governmental benefit of continuing trade is to draw nations into closer societal and cultural partnerships. Who would doubt that the Japanese movement towards Western culture and society has been accelerated by the extraordinary commercial trade ties that have built up between Japan, the United States, and Western Europe? While we have no strong urge to assure the rapid development of Chinese baseball and jazz clubs, we would certainly like to encourage Chinese national preferences that would make communism less palatable in the long run and thereby would further institutionalize resistance to stronger bonds with their major continental neighbor. Any notion of modeling China in our own cultural image, however, would appear neither plausible nor desirable. The West would do well to strengthen its cultural-societal bonds with China at a very measured pace out of respect for the potential for counterproductive reactions.

IMPLICATIONS OF TECHNOLOGY
TRANSFER

The implications of encouraging or discouraging technology transfer between the United States and China are perhaps somewhat more subtle and far-reaching. While trade can be a short-term instrument of national persuasion, technology transfer tends to require a longer-term perspective—both towards benefits and possible consequences. Possibly the most trivial reason for encouraging technology transfer is for private industry to reap the benefits associated with the sale of the technology. Under some licensing conditions, these transfers can bring modest income to some beneficiaries in the private sector. Under current world technological conditions, however, the ability to *sell* U.S. proprietary technology around the world would appear to be declining. In many areas Beijing will continue to find it more beneficial to *buy* that technology elsewhere. The United States has not yet come to grips with the fact that technological superiority is not an inalienable right for Americans. U.S. industry has, on many occasions, appeared to "sell" its technological edge at a very low price and now seems to be seeking protection from the natural consequences of its eagerness. While we have not yet lost our technological advantage to the Soviets (other than in many military equipment areas), there are a decreasing number of areas where we can claim technological advantage over other members of our Western Alliance.

On a government-to-government basis, the U.S.–PRC Science and Technology Agreement was signed with China in 1979, and, as of May 1983, there are twenty-one protocols being exercised, varying from cancer research and earthquake studies, to hydroelectric power generation and space technology. In mid–1982, talks were begun on the possibility of an agreement on nuclear cooperation that would enable American companies to sell nuclear power plants and components to China.

Such accords should not be tickets of admission, but should reflect a basic national policy decision to enhance the self-sufficiency and competitiveness of the recipient nation. An outstanding case of this has been between the United States and the Republic of Korea (ROK) involving efforts to stimulate the scientific and engineering capabilities of South Korea first for strictly commercial industrial applications and subsequently (and to a lesser degree) for indigenous weapons development and manufacturing capabilities. While the United States should not try to take credit for the ROK's rapid increase in industrialization, GNP, and world trade, neither should we pretend that we had no hand in it. Technology transfer can lead the horse to water: only national ambition, diligence, and honest hard work can make it drink up the rewards. Whether or not the South Korean experience could be readily repeated elsewhere is by no means obvious. Equivalent access to technology in Greece and Turkey, for instance, has not produced an equivalent economic boom.

Technology transfer can also encourage a country to make what it may not be able to buy. Limitations on the availability of foreign exchange and credits place upper limits on the effect of technology transfers on the rate of growth of national development. And, there are advantages in restrained rates of growth, and in "bootstrapping" one's way up in the world. Unfortunately, few countries have governments patient enough to wait for several more generations to catch up on a century or more of missing progress. An excessive appetite for sophisticated technology, particularly in the face of social and religious incompatibilities, could prove equally indigestible. Consequently, it will benefit the United States to encourage the Chinese to seek only deliberate progress, and it will behoove the Chinese to demonstrate some of their renowned patience in the pursuit of their objectives. Chinese retrenchment from their overly ambitious ten-year plan appears to be a very sensible step in this direction.

Technology transfer can also benefit countries by allowing them to develop capabilities that we might be politically, ideologically, morally, or even economically unable or unwilling to provide for them. Pharmaceutical facilities, for instance, might allow the Chinese to produce means for population control that we in this country might be unwilling to condone as a direct transfer. Other technologies that do not meet U.S. regulatory standards might also be transferred at the generic level without raising the level of consternation that would accompany the sale of finished products. For instance, it may be more productive to improve Chinese coal-fired boiler efficiency than to worry about scrubbing the resulting stack gases to minimize pollutants. Moreover, there are many items of military hardware that we might be unwilling (or unable) to sell in quantities sufficient to equip a very large Chinese force—well over twice the size of our own forces. A single one-time technology transfer becomes one means to avoid the perpetual revisiting of the quantitative issues. Whether this is a virtue or a sin depends on one's perceptions of the practicality, desirability, or acceptability of "controlling" another country's warfighting potential.

Technology transfers have also developed a psychological and political symbolism that in many cases far outweighs their functional utility. The technology gap between the more- and less-developed countries somehow personifies the inequities between rich and poor, north and south, and the unfair exploitation of the backward through imperialism, capitalism, or just plain competence. It is becoming a moral imperative, then, for the successful to bestow their technological gifts on the underprivileged. Refusing to confer such largesse when requested can certainly be construed as a significant international insult. It is on this basis that the headstrong government of South Vietnam ended up with an operational research nuclear reactor in Dalat in the early 1960s, even though the University of Saigon turned out to be unable to keep the laboratory's roof rainproof. Soviet technicians are currently restoring the reactor to operational condition.

Even more fundamental is the fact that technological prowess has become a symbol of national standing and an important factor on the scorecard of East-West competition. After all, communism promises economic superiority, and that economic superiority is to be gained through technological success. At least in the eyes of the Soviet Union, then, technological competition in weaponry, space, medicine, the means of production, and so forth is fundamental to the Marxist credo. Since technology for technology's sake is also a major Western fetish, it cannot be surprising that the rest of the world looks to technology as the key to the improvement of its standard of living. For better or worse, then, technology has become a factor in all four aspects of the correlation of world forces: economic, military, political, and ideological.

It should be fully understood, however, that once technology transfers reach a certain level the process is no longer reversible. Perceptions of stability in "technological parity" can be very misleading. Technological parity can lead inexorably to a substantial foreign advantage through differences in national governmental practices not directly related to technology itself. Americans in general do not realize the fragility of our currently perceived technological lead. We may similarly underestimate the capacity of other countries to entertain national ambitions of their own that could impinge upon the U.S.-accepted status quo. The United States will do well to accept the words of DoD Directive 2040.XX on the *Control of International Technology, Goods, Services, and Munitions Transfers* that states that it shall be DoD policy to:

> Treat defense related technology as a valuable, limited national security resource, to be husbanded and invested prudently in pursuit of national security objectives.

Perhaps the most extraordinary example of shifting the military technology balance has been achieved between the United States and Israel. Over the past decade we have created in Israel a military technological capability that, for all intents and purposes, exceeds our own.

They have had access to our latest research and development efforts. Due to their small bureaucracy and high motivation, they can field special purpose weapons and support equipment much faster than we can. The Israelis apparently used sophisticated weaponry in their attacks against Soviet-supplied Syrian military equipment in Lebanon, which is more advanced than anything in American inventories. Their ability to use these high technology systems is also enhanced by the close operational relationships between their technical industries and their citizen armies. Moreover, the Israelis now have considerable operational warfighting experience with the latest U.S. aircraft and missile systems that U.S. forces lack. If a scenario could be envisioned, for instance, where U.S. naval carrier forces were required to fight against land-based Israeli forces, it is by no means clear that U.S. forces would prevail.

A somewhat similar situation appears to exist on the commercial side with the development of electronic microcircuitry for computers, word processors, electronic games, and the like. After a decade of total access to U.S. technology, the Japanese now appear destined to move out ahead of the United States in the development of "fifth generation" components by the end of this decade. Having caught up with us in the development and production of "fourth generation" devices, their margin of advantage for the future lies in governmental financial support for Japan's civil sector R&D. While U.S. federal funds are plowed into our common defenses, the Japanese are spending some of their federal funds to subsidize the cooperative progress of their key industries. The United States may thus lose a major market unintentionally. In fact, the U.S. government makes no attempt to enhance or control the transfer of civil technology solely to protect future commercial markets for our own commercial industries. Whether the competitive American industry can police itself against this relatively new threat remains to be seen.

IMPLICATIONS OF WITHHOLDING ARMS AND TECHNOLOGY TRANSFERS

The advantages to the transfer recipient are generally presented as the major reasons for denying technology transfers to potential economic, political, ideological, or military adversaries. Such concerns have become increasingly important as the technology gap closes between friend and foe along any of the vectors of the correlation of forces. On the economic side, the fear of creating potentially threatening new competitors cannot be overlooked. On the military side, there is always the fear that the weapons potential provided will be used against an ally or, worse yet, turned against us by the recipient. There are also the fuzzyheaded views that weapons somehow cause wars and that, conversely, the absence of them prevents wars—a thesis for which there is no evident proof.

There are others who believe that it is possible to dispense technology so selectively that the recipient can be encouraged to develop certain military capabilities while ignoring others. Although this may be possible in certain starkly special areas (tactical nuclear warheads, secure communications, precision weapon guidance systems, etc.), it is not practical to be as selective as some would prefer. One cannot encourage a civil aircraft capability or tactical airlift without laying the groundwork for a strategic "power projection" capability. One cannot provide weapons that are capable of killing only military and not civilians, or adversaries but never friends. In this respect, politicians often assume a degree of selectivity that does not exist in the technology transfer game. It would be sheer folly to assume that we could assist the Chinese to become both militarily and commercially more capable at zero risk to the economies or security of neutral or Western-aligned nations nearby.

Moreover, the fears that either the technology or the actual weapons may be turned against the provider are not baseless. The British must, in retrospect, wonder about the weapons sold to the Argentinians. The United States itself was given pause for thought in trying to penetrate Iran during the hostage rescue attempt in the face of late-model U.S. weapons and technology in the hands of the revolutionary forces. But the greatest concern relates to the possibility that technology provided to third countries will soon make its way to East Europe and the Soviet Union. There is extensive evidence of Soviet attempts to gain U.S. technology, and there are elaborate in-place governmental procedures (which work poorly at best) to delay the transfer of Western technology into Comecon hands. In many areas, the Soviets may be no worse off without our vaunted technological capabilities. However, as the military balance continues to shift away from the United States in terms of both quality and quantity of nuclear and conventional weapons, it may serve our purposes to perpetuate the Soviet technological inferiority complex as a deterrent.

Arms transfer constraints are made all the more tricky by the aura of prestige accompanying the bestowal of the latest commercial or military technology. Experience certainly indicates that there is tremendous resistance to settling for less than the most capable machinery.

The Egyptians tested our newly restored friendship by demanding the latest available F-4 fighters, even though they had virtually no experience operating aircraft of equivalent complexity. Three years later, they have now transferred these aircraft to the Turks, who have demonstrated a greater ability to operate these very complex aircraft. The Egyptian Air Force will now try the simpler, but newer, F-16s.

The urge to have the latest capability even reaches down to weapon system designations. The F-5G, for instance, is an almost totally redesigned aircraft, powered by one new engine rather than two considerably older engines and equipped with all-new avionics. Nevertheless, sales have not materialized because many countries do not perceive it as a "new" aircraft. The new F-20 designation is likely to help increase sales. In fact, the more conservative designation was originally bestowed on these aircraft in the hopes that China would not object to their sale to Taiwan because of their similarity to the earlier F-5s already coproduced there.

The granting or withholding of arms transfers to achieve short-term political leverage has become too frequent to quantify. South American countries accused of human rights violations (including Argentina) have been denied U.S. arms purchases. Jordan has been denied certain arms primarily to point up its failure to participate in the Camp David process. Israel has had weapon deliveries held up when it has exasperated its American mentors. Aid to Turkey was long held back in retaliation for its invasion of Cyprus. Iraq and Libya have been denied arms on the basis of their support of terrorist operations. On the other hand, military sales to Morocco, Oman, Kenya, and Somalia have accompanied new basing agreements for the possible support of U.S. rapid deployment forces. In addition, Pakistan has been urged to resist Soviet hegemony in Southwest Asia through a very large new aid package.

The Soviets have similarly used arms transfers for political leverage by supporting various radical elements (such as those now in power in Ethiopia, Angola, and South Yemen) while withholding assistance to show displeasure (in the case of Iraq). They are also making at least temporary inroads into India with extensive military modernization programs. There are some Western cynics who believe that such Soviet assistance should be encouraged as a means of demonstrating the limits of Soviet competence and finesse. It is difficult to find countries outside the Warsaw Pact that have enjoyed a sustained, satisfactory relationship with Soviet arms purveyors. Nonetheless, threatening to take one's business to Moscow has become a popular inducement to gaining broader cooperation from the United States.

West European nations are also increasing their presence in both civil and military technology markets abroad. For Britain, France, and Germany, these sales appear to be based primarily on the desire to improve their own economic posture and to help defray the costs of developing their own technical capabilities. Nevertheless, each country places different political constraints on its willingness to enhance third world commercial and military capabilities. Needless to say, they do not correspond with each other, or with our own ever-changing criteria for such transfers. The recent Alliance differences over assisting the Soviets with their ambitious gas pipeline construction is an outstanding case in point.

Finally, it should be remembered that excessive or unsuccessful technology transfers may have a serious and lasting impact quite different from that intended. If the recipient is unable to absorb the new technology, there is a very serious potential source of embarrassment. Furthermore, if the recipient is unable to assimilate the advanced equipment, it may try to blame the failure on the donor: this can produce undesirable political backlash or require the donor to provide the personnel and management to keep the system working over the long run. Neither eventuality is healthy for a long-term relationship. Additionally, once a technology transfer has been made, it can be neither withdrawn nor soon supplanted with yet more largesse. Despite the pressures to satisfy client requests, there are powerful reasons not to progress too far too fast in the technology transfer arena.

CHINESE TECHNOLOGICAL CONSTRAINTS
(Ellen Frost)

U.S. export constraints aside, China has a limited ability to assimilate foreign technology and finance its development. There are pockets of the economy where technology is at a high enough level to permit the effective adoption of sophisticated Western know-how. Chinese scientists also keep up with the literature. Yet, if China is to make optimal use of foreign technology, many experts feel that it will first have to solve or improve a host of political, institutional, economic, managerial, and logistical problems. These include technical difficulties (such as translating research results into mass production and unfamiliarity with precision instrumentation and testing equipment), personnel problems (notably a shortage of trained scientists and engineers), difficulty in diffusing technology from one project to another, and political rivalries between those leaning toward radical nationalism and self-sufficiency and those leaning toward foreign technology acquisition and learning from abroad. Considering the many articles in both economic journals and popular newspapers discussing the new role of foreign technology, China's leaders are aware of these limitations. Much space has been devoted to learning the "lessons from importing equipment."

One of the most highly publicized examples of Chinese mismanagement and unrealistic expectations has been the licensing venture conceived in 1975 between Rolls Royce and China for the Spey turbofan engine, which was intended for use in a domestically produced Chinese aircraft. The contracts involved purchasing sophisticated machine tools and test equipment for the manufacture of fifty Spey engines as well as close-support technical assistance by Rolls Royce personnel. By 1981, only four of the engines had been tested. The Chinese did not meet their original goals. Furthermore, the Chinese apparently have no airframe within which to mount the Spey engine. The latest word is the project has been totally suspended. Both the Chinese and the British agree, however, that the "learning" aspects of the project have been appreciable and that from this experience the Chinese have developed a better understanding of the importance of management in the production process.

Reacting to the haphazard acquisition of technology, the Chinese have begun to investigate Western methods for evaluating technology purchases. A new "science" called "techno-economics," which calls for a scientific, rational plan for adopting technology, was founded in 1979. For the first time, the Chinese are considering opportunity costs and feasibility studies. Although these techno-economists have been gaining official favor and their studies are getting serious attention, their work often runs counter to the aspiration of local administrators. The acquisition of advanced technology that gains prestige for local managers or bureau administrators often pushes through unnecessary projects. Politics, family ties, and personal rivalries often cloud the decisionmaking process. An example is the sale of an American laser-equipped road-grader to Jiangxi province in the spring of 1982. The deal was aided by a relative who worked in the provincial government bureaucracy. The American who made the sale confided, "Actually, they really don't need something that advanced here."

It is difficult to assign a meaningful figure of merit to current Chinese technological capabilities. There are cases where major forward leaps in technology have failed. There are others where American businessmen claim to have proof that Chinese products reflect technologies beyond those that the U.S. government is willing to export. Furthermore, the United States has no major systematic study of Chinese technologies and scientific development, despite extensive efforts by the U.S. government relative to the Soviet Union.

It is virtually impossible to make a general judgment concerning the overall technological capabilities of a billion Chinese. While we assume that Chinese Mainlanders are as capable of assimilating high technology as the populations of Hong Kong, Singapore, and Taiwan, the task of educating the entire population appears insurmountable. Thus, we expect that in certain urban areas, Chinese technological capabilities will improve rapidly in utilizing modern Western technology. In more agrarian areas, technological advances are likely to come more slowly, resulting in a dual economy for many decades to come. Judgments reached on the basis of average national capabilities will be essentially worthless.

DIFFICULTIES IN CONTROLLING
TECHNOLOGY TRANSFERS (Ellen Frost)

The United States maintains a number of controls on exports, each of which is administered by a different agency and governed by a different law. Exports of arms, ammunition, and "implements of war" are subject to the Arms Export Control Act and to a licensing process controlled by the Department of State. Exports of peaceful nuclear materials fall under the Nuclear Non-Proliferation Act and the Nuclear Regulatory Commission. Commercial exports, including technology, may be restricted for reasons of national security, foreign policy, or short supply under the Export Administration Act (EAA) and the licensing process of the Department of Commerce. Few Chinese (and not many Americans) understand these systems.

By contrast, the United States has neither a positive export policy nor a comprehensive technology policy, even though technology is widely considered to be a national asset. There are many scattered government R&D programs, but there is no long-range forecast or "vision" comparable to those developed by the French and Japanese governments. The most clearly articulated policy affecting technology is a negative one of control particularly of "dual-use" exports—so named because they consist of goods and technology intended for peaceful civilian purposes but capable of being diverted to military use. These exports are governed by the national security provisions of the EAA and the corresponding licensing system, as described below.

In particular, dual-use exports to China are visible politically. First, they are a component of virtually all the civilian industrial projects for which China has sought Western or Japanese participation—from microelectronics to oil exploration. Even basic industries, such as steel and automobiles, use such restricted items as numerically controlled welding machines and computers. Second, there has been a tendency in the past decade to use the approval or denial of dual-use exports for purposes of political "leverage"—as a reward or "punishment." Third, they may (if diverted) contribute to the ability of China or its friends to wage war. Thus, decisions concerning the licensing of dual-use technology transfers are important to Chinese–American relations.

Background: The Licensing System

The Export Administration Act assigns responsibility to the Commerce Department for administering the dual-use export licensing system. The interagency review process operates essentially by consensus. Besides Commerce Department, the key agencies are the Departments of State, Defense, and (depending on the export in question) Energy. The CIA participates in an advisory capacity.

Of all of these agencies, the role of the Department of Defense is particularly forceful. Under an amendment to the Act offered by Senator Jackson in 1974, the President must report to the Congress whenever he overrules the Secretary of Defense on an export control matter. This unwieldy and awkward process has never been applied in practice, but it lends the Pentagon a kind of veto authority.

In the international arena, dual-use exports to controlled countries (the Warsaw Pact and China) are subject to unanimous approval procedures within the so-called Coordinating Committee, or COCOM. The lead agency for representation in COCOM is the Department of State, but its decisions are subject to the same basic interagency process as the domestic licensing process. Indeed, U.S. exports falling above certain levels of technology must be approved in COCOM before a license is issued. Other countries' exports submitted to COCOM review pass through a similar process.

COCOM itself is a voluntary, nontreaty organization with no enforcement powers. It consists of the NATO allies (except Iceland) and Japan. It has been meeting regularly in Paris for more than three decades. Broadly speaking, COCOM controls can be thought of as a series of periodically updated thresholds. These thresholds are defined in a series of lists: munitions, nuclear energy, and industrial products and associated know-how. Every few years these lists are revised through international negotiation.

Most of the work of COCOM centers on reviewing proposed exports of items on the industrial list. These fall into such categories as computers, microelectronics, signal and image processing, lasers, fiber optics, guidance and navigation, acoustical and electro-optical sensors, cryogenics, and high-precision measuring instruments and machine tools. Also included is the know-how to make these items; the United States is currently trying to broaden this category to include technology not strictly caught by the existing list (e.g., software).

Defining the technical thresholds between uncontrolled, "gray area" or discretionary, and embargoed items has never been easy. Nor does this division necessarily correspond to "sophisticated" versus "obsolete" technology. In theory, where to draw the line is supposed to take into account the strategic lead time—a concept that measures not only the state of the art in the West and Japan, but also the corresponding state of the art in the controlled destination. If Western technology developed in the late 1960s and now considered obsolete would mean a revolutionary advance in the receiving country, its transfer can be and sometimes is denied.

Strategic lead time cannot be applied, however, in isolation from other judgments, or else the level of items approved for the Soviet Union would be much higher than the level for China. High-performance computers would be approved for Moscow while hand-held calculators would be turned down for Beijing. Other factors must obviously prevail, such as the suitability of the technical configuration to the proposed end-use, the accompanying inventory of spare parts, the likelihood of reshipment to other destinations, and the particular military impact of any diversion.

History of Licenses for the PRC

During the 1950s and early 1960s, the United States maintained a virtual embargo on trade with China. Its Western allies did not. Great Britain, which to this day prides itself on its long-standing and pragmatic relationship with Beijing, moved out early and steadily in developing commercial ties. High technology transfers to China, however, were few and far between. In fact, for years the Allies maintained stricter COCOM controls for China than for the USSR (i.e., a reverse "China differential"). It was primarily the British government that persuaded Washington to abandon this differential and to place China on a par with the Soviet Union for export control purposes.

During the Nixon and Ford administrations, the first steps were taken toward treating China on a de facto preferential basis. Again, the British forced the issue by persuading the president to approve the Spey engine project over the objections of the Defense Department. This step was consistent with the Nixon/Kissinger "opening to China," which was proceeding at the same time. But the momentum for large-scale high-technology exports from the United States was only beginning to pick up steam.

During the Carter administration, there were sporadic efforts to liberalize COCOM controls for China. These efforts generally centered around a trip. (Foreign policy is often made in response to travel plans, as top officials search for some offering to take with them.) On several occasions in 1979 and 1980 visiting American officials apparently told the Chinese that they would get special treatment in COCOM. They were also offered high-performance computers that would have been denied under the old policy of treating exports to China as precedents for approving identical exports to the Soviet Union.

This forthcoming approach foundered on several icebergs. First, the more liberal approach favored by the China policymakers had not been fully aired within the bureaucracy, which remained unsure of what the policy really meant. In the absence of strong vertical leadership, they tended to postpone controversial decisions, thus frustrating the China hands. Second, was the reluctance of at least one major ally to single out China for preferential treatment for fear of Moscow's reaction. The State Department apparently sympathized with this same view, as opposed to the National Security Council staff. Where China was concerned, this tension was never resolved. Third, staff-level reviewers feared that what was not a precedent for the USSR today could become one tomorrow. In their eyes the result could be a major unraveling of controls affecting the entire Soviet bloc. Although this concern was probably ill-founded, no one seemed to be able to put it to rest with any authority.

A fourth obstacle centered on China itself. Many people, especially in the military departments, continued to believe that China is not just a potential adversary but a hostile power. These officials resisted the very notion of high-technology exports to "Red China." Some remembered Korea, others were sympathetic to Taiwan, and still others resisted relaxing controls for a country still professing communism. Over time, however, as the military services came to see the value of a stronger China in tying down Soviet military resources, their resistance eased.

Finally, even those who agreed with the policy shift did not know exactly what it meant to be "more forthcoming" towards China as compared to the Soviet Union. How much more forthcoming? Where should the upper line be drawn? And were all fields of technology to be treated equally, whether the technology at issue had potential application to "offensive" weapons or not? Thus ensued a series of half-fulfilled promises and a good many recriminations.

The export of oil exploration equipment illustrates the slippery nature of the policy questions at issue during the Carter administration. In the late 1970s, several major oil companies sought permission to conduct exploration for China's offshore oil. The technology in question could help detect oil lying underneath the ocean floor, but it could also pick up passing submarines. In other parts of the world the oil companies had carried out this work without significant host country participation, but the Chinese insisted on access to both the shipboard process and the resulting data. They wanted to lease and eventually buy the equipment. The U.S. Navy objected vigorously. The Energy Department intervened at a high level in support of the sale. The State Department remained relatively passive. The resulting bureaucratic struggle pitted security goals (protecting antisubmarine warfare technology) against both energy objectives (diversification of oil supplies) and political goals (signaling the Russians and "rewarding" the Chinese). In the end, a compromise was adopted permitting a limited degree of data-sharing and training.

Recognizing the ambiguity of the Carter era "liberalization," the Reagan administration tried to put its own liberalization policies on firm ground with a policy published in the Federal Register on December 29, 1981, including the following commitment to potential exporters:

The export licensing policy resulting from this review will permit approval of export licenses for commodities at significantly higher technical levels than allowed previously. In general, there will be a predisposition for approval for products with technical levels twice those previously approved to China.

Products with technology levels above that "double threshold" guideline were to be considered on a case-by-case basis. Licenses were no longer to be denied merely because the end-use was military or the end-user was engaged in military activity, although approval would not be likely if the technologies in question would make a "direct and significant contribution to nuclear weapons and their delivery systems, electronic and antisubmarine warfare, and intelligence gathering." (These are long-standing concerns in the Pentagon.) Nor should the equipment "substantially exceed" the requirements of the stated end-use. Continued uncertainty resulted in a presidential directive in May 1982 instructing that there should be disposition for approval for products *above* the double threshold unless there is a clear and demonstrable risk to our national security.

Despite these statements, some observers argued that export control practices continue to fall short of stated policy. Approval of exports above the double threshold required high-level and time-consuming review. It was jarring to those Americans who expected a radically different outcome, and it aroused Chinese resentment over the apparent gap between actual and stated policy. Indeed, some observers believe that Beijing's leaders exploited the disagreements over technology transfer, endowing them with a political and symbolic importance beyond their actual economic significance and putting U.S. officials on the defensive. Others disagreed, citing the role of high technology in key sectors of the Chinese economy and expressing sympathy with Beijing's frustration.

While in Beijing in May 1983 for a meeting of the Joint Commission on Commerce and Trade, Secretary of Commerce Baldridge informed the Chinese of the administration's intent (trip diplomacy?) to resolve this issue by transferring the PRC from the Export Administration's regulatory category "Country Group P" to "Country Group V." Under Group P there was concern that, despite the December 1981 policy, China was still considered a "potential adversary." By placing China in Group V with the NATO countries, India, Yugoslavia, and others, China's friendly, nonaligned status in U.S. policy was affirmed. However, as of this writing (June 1983), the regulatory guidelines that will determine what is approved have not been completed.

Paradoxically, the decision to liberalize U.S. policy on the export of arms to China was far less contentious, as key Pentagon licensing and policy officials were involved in the decisions from the beginning (unlike the decision on dual-use technology). Furthermore, the arms decision was more concrete, leaving less room for doubt. Even now there remains a degree of ambiguity suggesting that while China should not be treated as harshly as the Soviet Union, neither should it qualify for the same kind of treatment as our NATO allies and Japan.

Controlling technology transfers is at best a difficult and imprecise bureaucratic problem. Technology transfer to China will continue to pose some extremely awkward questions, reflecting the basic dichotomy facing any U.S. administration. On the one hand, the administration has made it clear that it wishes to nurture and promote a strong, secure, and "friendly" China—at least from economic and political standpoints. On the other hand, the continued existence of strategic trade and transfer controls certainly implies concern about China's ability to solve its problems of peaceful succession and maintain a "moderate" course. To the extent that high-level government officials must still wrestle with this fundamental dichotomy, the results are likely to continue to involve frustration, disappointment, and delay. There will almost certainly continue to be a pattern of inconsistency that may be more harmful to U.S. short term foreign policy interests than the technology at issue. This will be reflected not only in our relations with China, but with our Western allies as well.

WESTERN ALLIANCE PERSPECTIVES (Ellen Frost)

From the perspective of the Western alliance, economic relationships with the PRC pose frequently divisive questions. No two allies have exactly the same perspective on economic relationships in a national security context. For example, the West Germans worry far more about the effect of a "China differential" on their relations with Moscow than the British, whose stake in détente is considerably smaller. Those with long memories remember that "moderates" have been in power in China before only to disappear. Their cautious and moderate approach to trade and technology transfer conflicts with the school of thought that says that "the enemy of my enemy is my friend." Washington, of course, contains all of these views—within the same administration.

The national security context is important because China is a major power that has not solved the problem of peaceful succession. Moreover, Beijing has posed a threat to its Asian neighbors before and may again. To the extent that trade and technology transfer either strengthen China's military-industrial base or alter the pattern of resource allocation, they are factors in the national security equation.

At the narrowest end of the security spectrum, the allies agree on the need to control (but not necessarily to prohibit) the export of goods and technologies to China with direct and tangible application to the production of arms, ammunitions, and instruments of war. Controls on the export of those items are the main raison d'être for COCOM.

At a different place on the security spectrum are "dual-use" goods and technologies. In general these are not controlled by COCOM. Sometimes these technologies are defined as necessary to "the defense industrial base." As applied to the Soviet Union, examples include large industrial projects designed to produce high-quality steel and other specialty metals, high-performance vehicles, and other projects contributing to the readiness, mobilization, and sustainability of military operations. However, since the distinction between defense industrial base and the industrial base in any country is artificial, the Allies have resisted the extension of export controls to large industrial projects for the Soviet Union. They would almost certainly do so if Washington were ever to apply the same logic to China.

Yet Washington is right. Economic relationships not subject to CO-COM controls may be clearly "strategic" in the sense of both strengthening military capabilities and creating potential dependencies that could be exploited for political or military purposes. Moreover, financing these projects takes on strategic dimensions as well. As the case of Poland illustrates, it is the debtor who has influence over the creditor, and not vice versa. These worries are premature in the case of China, but they may not be ten or fifteen years down the road.

The absence of a coordinated, alliance-wide policy on technology transfer to the Soviet Union received widespread press attention during the recent controversy over Western participation in the Soviet gas pipeline. The need to adopt consistent policy toward China is less spectacular but equally important in the long run.

There are at least two factors inhibiting the development of an allied consensus on technology transfer to China. The first is that policies toward China are bound up, to a greater or lesser extent, with corresponding policies toward Moscow. Political sensitivity on this point is acute. Reasons may vary (Bonn versus London), but any sign that U.S. policy may be playing the "China card" primarily to annoy the Soviets breeds resistance. Fortunately, the Reagan administration's expressed interest in Taiwan has tended to preclude this kind of rhetoric. Nevertheless, the more public the search for a consensus on China, the more difficult it will be for our allies to agree on a common policy.

The second obstacle stems from trans-Atlantic attitudes toward exports. Although perspectives are changing, Americans have tended to downplay or ignore the importance of exports, treating them sometimes as if they were a favor to another country. Consequently, a variety of policies ranging from nuclear nonproliferation to human rights tend to find expression in export restraints, much to the irritation of American businessmen.

As mentioned, Washington's policymakers have repeatedly used controls on dual-use technology transfer for purposes of short-term political "signaling" or leverage because of their flexibility. Unlike other instruments of foreign policy, export licensing decisions do not require congressionally approved budget levels. They are not subjected to a congressional review period or veto. With a few exceptions (e.g., engines for Iraq), congressional interference is rare. There are no amendments comparable to those prohibiting Export-Import Bank loans to the Soviet Union for energy development. The law that governs export licensing, the Export Administration Act, is a relatively open-ended piece of legislation. As a consequence, export licensing decisions appear to offer the policymaker a simple "yes-no" decision. Delay is also a real option, since statutory licensing deadlines are not taken too literally and delay itself can be a signal of sorts.

In Europe and Japan, by contrast, governments resist short-term interference with exports. Given the importance of exports to European economies and record-high levels of postwar unemployment, both industry and government leaders go out of their way to promote an image of reliability as suppliers. Moreover, Europeans are skeptical about the effectiveness of an on-again-off-again approach to exports as a tool of foreign policy leverage. To the extent that they believe at all in using trade and trechnology transfer as instruments of foreign policy, they think in positive and long-range terms—for example, that steady nibbling at the trade "carrot" will give the targeted country an incentive to behave peacefully.

What irritates our allies most is when Americans appear to be restraining European exports while promoting our own. Europeans find it hard to believe that American foreign policy is not motivated by commercial gain. The very appearance of a double standard arouses deep-seated commercial suspicions and severely undermines other goals that Washington may be trying to achieve. This is an example of what Secretary Haig called "turning an Eastern failure into a Western one."

Conversely, American businessmen perceive that Europeans often bypass or ignore export controls, thereby leaving U.S. businesses at a competitive disadvantage. They complain that their European and Japanese rivals do not have to go through a lengthy, two-step hurdle—first a domestic review, then a COCOM review. Differences in reexport control policy are also an issue. Commercial tensions continue to fester.

Forging a durable alliance-wide policy toward technology transfer to China will require sensitivity to differing priorities and needs, including legitimate commercial aspirations. Great care must be taken to ensure that U.S. policy initiatives do not revive fears of the "China card" syndrome. Similarly, technology transfer policies must rest on relatively consistent political and security perspectives. Technology transfer to China cannot—and should not—be turned on and off like a faucet. (Secretary of State Shultz calls this "lightswitch diplomacy.") For Americans, this means forswearing the use of export licenses for short-term leverage or signaling purposes. This in turn implies elimination, or at least greatly scaled back use, of the foreign policy controls authorized by the EAA. This is certain to be an issue in the 98th Congress.

In conclusion, technology transfer to China poses difficult questions. While they may appear technical on the surface, at their root they are basically political. For they symbolize, in a sense, how much we can "trust" China not to become an adversary—not just now but in the future, when current technology transfers bear fruit.

This perspective suggests the need to distinguish between short-term and long-term effects of trade and technology transfer. Since the current leadership shows signs of relative stability, exports whose benefits can be more or less predicted should (other things being equal) be approved. A steel plant might be such a project. But it is not necessarily wise to foster in China a state-of-the-art microelectronics industry whose output is less easily tracked. Why not sell limited numbers of chips instead? Or, since the Chinese are likely to insist on as much technology as possible, why not hold on to the relatively small "black box" component for as long as possible?

A different but not inconsistent approach is to identify particularly sensitive areas of military technology and measure dual-use exports against diversion into those fields. This is more or less what the Pentagon has been doing for some time. For example, if a proposed export could be diverted for use in nuclear weaponry or antisubmarine warfare, its chances of approval are dimmer than if it could be applied to anti-armor capability. This selectivity reflects a judgment that unbridled military strengthening in China is not automatically in our interest even if it does tie down more Soviet divisions.

On the positive side, a modestly equipped army and a diversified industrial base can be stabilizing for China. Cooperative relations can help foster the "strong, secure, and friendly China" envisaged in the Reagan administration's policy announcement of December 1981. Technology transfer is a limited—even marginal—instrument in the context of China's vast economy, but it has a constructive place.

Additionally, it must be recognized that American commercial business enjoys a degree of independence from governmental influence that is practically unparalleled elsewhere in the world. More and more, this is becoming a mixed blessing. American businessmen are becoming increasingly aware of the benefits accruing to their industrialized competitors that have accepted a cooperative partnership with their governments. In addition, the objectives of these other governmental-industry teams are overwhelmingly directed toward strengthening their economic positions both at home and abroad. The influence of national security implications, as well as the short-term control of international events, are seldom if ever evident. To the extent that virtually all of our allies derive a greater fraction of their GNP from international trade, this positive and protective long-term cooperation between governments and their industries is not surprising. Rather, the inescapable question is whether or not U.S. business interests continue to be well served by a hands-off, management-by-exception, relationship with its government. At the very least, this loose approach is certain to give rise to appearances of inconsistency and lack of organization in the market place. Furthermore, it tends to leave positive trade initiatives to the vagueries of individual corporate decisions, while focusing discontent on the negative role of governmental regulations and proscriptions. The absence of such a partnership has already given rise to substantial frustrations between government and private participants in our trade relations with China. China must learn to recognize and tolerate the inherent inefficiencies of the American business/government culture and avoid drawing inappropriate inferences concerning national policy inconsistencies or affronts.

U.S.– CHINA ECONOMIC PROSPECTS

As Bob Dernberger pointed out, China faces serious economic difficulties. To what extent can trade, about 16 percent of China's GNP, improve its prospects? The prognosis is mixed. On the one hand, imports of Western and Japanese goods and technology can serve to postpone needed reforms. Despite efforts to modernize the economy, there is little evidence as yet that underlying patterns of industrial ownership and incentives will be fundamentally altered, although abolition of communes could herald a major change in effectiveness in the agricultural sector. On the other hand, pockets of growth in key sectors, such as coal and oil, can generate hard currency while "pulling" supporting sectors forward. China's total trade still amounts to only a relatively small fraction of its lagging GNP, although it has grown over the past decade at a better rate (7 percent) than all East Asian less-developed countries other than South Korea and Singapore. The Chinese have also been able to maintain a reasonable balance of payments and have hardly begun to use the total credit lines now available to them from Western nations or the World Bank. The United States awarded China "Most Favored Nation (MFN)" status in February 1980.

Chinese exports presently consist mainly of agricultural products (38 percent); fuel (11 percent); chemicals, minerals, and metals (10 percent); and manufactures, of which textile fibers and finished clothing represent 23 percent. The United States already imports several strategic materials from China (tantalum, titanium, and vanadium), and others (such as cobalt) may follow. U.S. imports of Chinese textiles are already a source of concern to American manufacturers. If the Chinese can continue to develop their energy resources (coal and oil) and promote more efficient energy use, they will find eager markets abroad for any surpluses.

Chinese exports are now growing slightly faster than their imports. Not surprisingly, imports of machines, equipment, and other manufactured products account for over 60 percent of their imports—a fraction likely to continue to grow. Raw materials and fuels account for another 16 percent. Iron and steel products comprise roughly one-third of the manufactured imports. These will probably continue to be needed in view of the recent Chinese decision to go slow on the development of their own heavy industries while favoring creation of more light industries that are less capital intensive. Food imports are currently about 12 percent of the total, as the Chinese export rice, meat, fruit and vegetables, while importing other grains such as wheat. Although unlikely, it is not inconceivable that China could become a net food exporter within the next decade as population growth tapers off, and food production becomes more efficient. China has increased its fertilizer production tenfold since the early 1960s and now imports less than 20 percent of its total usage.

The total licensed exports from the United States to China rose rapidly from $18 million in FY78 to $479 million in FY79 and dropped back to $443 million in FY80 and to $419 million in FY81, indicating possible limits in China's current purchasing power. During the same time period, technical data licenses rose from 10 in FY78 to about 60 in FY79 and FY80 and then up to 126 in FY81. This trend towards limited imports coupled with increasing technology transfer is to be expected.

During the three years from FY79 through FY81, total U.S. exports to China topped $9.1 billion. By comparison, U.S. exports to the Soviet Union during that same time period amounted to roughly $7.6 billion. Excluding foodstuffs, these recent export levels to China are much higher than those to the Soviet Union. They are vastly larger than total U.S. exports to the East European countries of the Warsaw Pact. Clearly, China has already achieved a trading status well beyond that which it could enjoy as an ally of the Soviet Union.

All in all, the Chinese are developing exports that the United States can use, while we produce a variety of commodities of interest to the Chinese. How much they can afford to buy will probably depend on their ability to generate foreign exchange. How much we are willing to buy may depend on their increased production of oil and other raw materials, as well as the acceptability of their light-manufactured goods.

In response to these opportunities, many Western and Japanese firms are devising medium- and long-term commitments designed to get around China's hard currency shortage. These include deferred payment in kind, offsets or buybacks, coassembly and/or coproduction, and leasing arrangements. Most of these deals have the effect of forcing an up-front investment and hence limiting a company's flexibility. Firms whose payment consists of the output of a finished project cannot easily abandon the project halfway through.

Given the sheer dimension of China's needs, even a stepped-up program of trade and technology transfer will have only a marginal impact on China's economic development. Moreover, the West has very limited resources at its disposal: World Bank assistance, export credit subsidies, and very little bilateral aid (e.g., disaster relief). Far more important will be how the West treats China's exports. Here the precedents are not reassuring from Beijing's point of view.

One example of a trade problem that will almost surely surface in the future is subsidies. Right now consumers are delighted to find exquisitely made Chinese basketry selling for very low prices at the local five and dime store. If all goes well in China, baskets and handicrafts will soon be accompanied by inexpensive light-industrial goods. Imports from China might even be eligible for duty-free entry under the system known as Generalized System of Preferences (GSP), if, as expected, Beijing joins General Agreement on Trade and Tariffs (GATT). But even without them, imports from China could rise to a formidable level in precisely those sectors of Western economies that are already declining. For any items not consumed in China, lengthy and contentious countervailing duty investigations could possibly ensue. China is now wisely establishing an appropriate cost accounting basis.

One precedent applicable to Socialist economies is the case of Polish golf carts. Thus, Poland decided to make golf carts to sell in the West. (Apparently no one used them in Poland.) A U.S. manufacturer charged that Poland was subsidizing its exports and demanded countervailing duties. Since Poland did not sell golf carts at home and since prices were hopelessly distorted anyway, there was no domestic index with which to calculate the "real" cost of producing golf carts. In order to determine what a reasonable price might be, U.S. investigators had to construct a hypothetical model for the manufacture of golf carts in a third country.

It is also easy to conclude that China's grasp of copyright, patent, royalty, and licensing practices may be less than perfect, perhaps deliberately so. A U.S. manufacturer hoping to capture a billion Chinese consumers might be forced to transfer proprietary data, only to find out that Chinese export concerns were suddenly competing with him in third markets. Many firms, aware of this danger, are taking their time about signing contracts. But even when their lawyers are satisfied, which court of arbitration board will Beijing recognize for the settlement of disputes? China is now working on the final draft of a Western-style patent law, having established a working group under their China Council for the Promotion of International Trade (CCPIT). If adopted, this should also allay some fears of unfair business practices.

There is also the question of debt rescheduling. So far the Chinese have been extremely conservative about borrowing from abroad. But as development proceeds and a new generation comes to power in Beijing, Western bankers could conceivably rush into the same pitfall that they fell into in Eastern Europe. One only hopes that both sides will look coolly at repayment prospects and debt service ratios before extending financial commitments.

PROBLEMS IN ASYMMETRIC PARTNERSHIPS

In matters of trade and technology transfer, it would be a mistake to underestimate some of the problems and issues arising from large asymmetries between the trading partners. Many of these would appear to be too obvious to mention, but yet they seem to arise from time to time. Language barriers, for instance, may have a far more important influence than we are willing to admit. Recently there was a telling comment from a participant in the ongoing debate with the Japanese concerning the possible "unfairness" of the present trade between the countries. The Japanese noted that he was not surprised that 10,000 English-speaking Japanese all over America were selling more effectively than 100 English-speaking Americans holed up in Tokyo hotels. He made it clear that it was optional to buy in the seller's tongue but virtually essential to sell in the buyer's tongue. Given the reluctance of Americans to learn any language other than their own, while the Chinese appear anxious to learn English, one might expect the trade balance to soon favor the Chinese!

There are of course many other barriers to easy trade or technology transfers. There may be some ideological, philosophical, or even religious barriers—as we have found to our embarrassment for American Jews trying to do business with many Arab countries. There are also educational and cultural barriers that can unwittingly impede the development of close economic ties. Many of these problems may not arise if the purpose is to sell American products, as is, to the Chinese. On the other hand, if we wish to enter a Chinese market (the way the Japanese entered our automobile market), then we may find it particularly difficult to sell what we want rather than what they want. This will be even tougher if we find that American product standards exceed their own specifications and are therefore unnecessarily expensive or complex.

In some cases, these problems may be diminished by the transfer of technology, rather than the transfer of finished hardware. In finished hardware, it may be too late to accommodate to local preferences. By transferring technology, the translation to indigenous usage is accomplished within the recipient's domain. The more asymmetric the partnership, the more the trade or transfer may benefit from concentration on unfinished bulk materials or generic technologies.

Asymmetries in national wealth can also cause difficulties. With the United States well above the average of the developed nations and with China well below the average of the developing nations, a discrepancy of roughly 30:1 in GNP per capita exists. This cannot be overlooked as an indication of the vast differences in standard of living, industrialization, consumption patterns, personal aspirations, and the like. While such differences need not inhibit trade, they do suggest that there will be substantial differences in the types of commodities being exchanged and possibly in the procedures involved. For instance, refrigeration technology for food processing and storage may be far less practical than advances in more primitive drying or canning techniques. There must be scores of American (and West European) technologies for which there is little practical Chinese use, even though they may admire and covet them. And in some cases we can no longer provide what they can afford. At one end of the spectrum, the United States no longer manufactures nonelectric typewriters. At the other end, we have not produced a nonnuclear-powered submarine for over twenty years! In both the military and the consumer worlds, one suspects that some of the simpler devices from the Comecon nations may be more appropriate than those from the West. Moreover, it will surely be in our best interest to encourage multilateral trade so that China can earn dollars that can then be used for purchases in the United States. In fact, Chinese trade already shows this balance: exports go primarily to Comecon countries (North Korea and Vietnam) and to the Third World (including Hong Kong), while imports are mostly from the industrialized countries of the West.

American efforts to provide suitable military and civilian equipments to the Vietnamese were noticeably hindered by our failure to understand some of their geographic, climatic, and physiological differences. U.S. equipments sometimes failed to work in the very hot humid surrounds of Southeast Asia. Possibly more important, we did not recognize or accomodate to the differences in physical stature. American boot lasts were by no means comfortable for the Asian foot: Vietnamese could not see out of American bulldozers when seated to drive them, so they solved the problem by having a driver and a separate observer. While there may be fewer physiological differences between the Chinese and us, geographic differences could introduce new problems. For instance, U.S. military radios are "optimized" for short distance, high density communications in Europe and could well prove inappropriate for the greater distances on the Chinese Mainland. It is also quite possible that Chinese roads and bridges may not accommodate the weight and size of U.S. equipment.

Along the same vein, there will almost certainly be major differences in military strategy, doctrine, and tactics that will make it somewhat dubious whether American military equipments are matched to their methods of fighting. If they are not, then our equipments will only be fully effective if the Chinese can be made to change their own preferred approach to warfare. Doctrine embodies culture, which is difficult (if not impossible) to change lightly or quickly.

EVOLVING U.S. COMMERCIAL RELATIONS WITH THE PRC (David S. Holland)

For many years, Chinese and U.S. industry viewed each other as *terra incognita* as far as potential business dealings were concerned. Trade between the United States and China was slow to get off the ground during the early 1970's, compared to the PRC's trade with Japan and Western Europe. Japanese industry and government were particularly aggressive in approaching the opening China market and soon established a leading position in that market. American companies were initially less aware of the business potential of the new relationship with China. The U.S. government was bound by trade restrictions, export controls, and negative attitudes toward China that dated back to the Korean War. Only gradually were official restrictions eased, and indeed some are still in place today.

Fortunately, during the period of political limbo prior to the establishment of diplomatic relations in 1979, there were pragmatic leaders in the PRC and in the United States who found nonofficial means of conducting commercial relations. For ten years the PRC's China Council for the Promotion of International Trade (CCPIT) and the U.S. National Council for U.S.–China Trade have provided information and guidance to the U.S. business community in dealing with the Chinese.

Since 1979 the role of the Department of Commerce with respect to U.S.–Chinese commercial relations has increased. Due to the historical development just outlined, the functions of the National Council and the Commerce Department may be expected to overlap to some extent as time passes. It will be a task of leadership in each to ensure that interaction between them remain on a constructive basis that is supportive of the commercial interests of the nation.

In addition to the contributions of the CCPIT and the National Council, Pullman Kellogg, Boeing, Western Union/RCA, and Baker Trading are important early pioneering firms in the Chinese way of doing things, an experience that they shared with other firms. In those early years, the Chinese invited interested firms to give presentations in a seminar format. These for the most part were primarily of benefit to the Chinese. The Americans conveyed a great deal of information regarding their company products and technical procedures without any assurance that they would receive a contract or establish any type of business relationship. It was the Chinese way of doing business and necessary for becoming "old friends."

Another important result of these early contacts was the identification of issues where the Chinese commercial and legal structure gave rise to technical problems for U.S. industry. These included the lack of a comprehensive tax system that could be meshed with the U.S. system, the need for a legal framework for joint ventures, and licensing, trademark, and patent protection and techniques for technology transfer. The tax creditability issue became a critical problem for offshore oil exploration, a problem which appears to have been resolved by a flexible Chinese attitude and careful attention to the precise provisions of Chinese tax law. Some of the other problems have not yet been solved, but at least they have been raised and addressed. Progress in dealing with these technical issues obviously posed complex problems for the Chinese bureaucrats who had to find ways to supplement their own legal system to accommodate the foreigners.

Senior Chinese officials unexpectedly called temporary halt to their expansion program in early 1981 when they realized that spending was exceeding funds available and that many purchases had been ill-considered. Thereafter, in an effort to compensate for inadequate capital for expansion, the Chinese began a rapid experiment with alternative forms of business arrangements such as "coproduction" and "compensation trade." The National Council in commenting on these efforts has observed that ". . . it is perhaps surprising that a strong vote of confidence in the strength of the capitalist system should come from China."

Flowing from what may be considered a period of mutual business education, commercial relations have prospered in particular in the following categories: banking and financial services, construction equipment, mining equipment, heavy industrial equipment, petroleum equipment, commodities trade, general imports, and tourism. In addition, recently there has been constructive interest in pursuing new forms of trade such as feasibility studies and high technology guidance.

The key element of China's modernization program for the next decade could well be the offshore petroleum program. The success of this program could not only satisfy the PRC's own domestic needs for hydrocarbons but also provide a surplus for export with which to finance its modernization projects. After a decade of largely fruitless efforts to explore for oil on its own, the Chinese Ministry of Petroleum concluded that cooperation with foreign oil companies would greatly speed the process. During 1980, forty-eight foreign oil companies participated in broad-gauge seismic surveys along vast sections of the Chinese continental shelf in the South China Sea and Yellow Sea. Two French oil companies and a Japanese consortium were granted contracts for exploration in large blocks located in the Bohai Gulf and the Tonkin Gulf. From the Chinese perspective, there are many advantages to joint exploration for offshore oil, including an increased ability to satisfy the domestic demand for petroleum products, export of surplus oil to finance the modernization program, the externalization of much of the exploration risk, and the introduction of advanced offshore exploration technology into the domestic oil industry.

Xinhua, the Chinese news service, announced on December 30, 1981, that "a host of data from geological surveys and drilling indicates that there are widespread and thick sedimentary rocks with mature oil-bearing layers and that more than 400 possible oil-bearing structures of various types have been found in these [offshore survey] regions. Both the Chinese and foreign geologists unanimously believe that oil reserves in these waters are very rich, [offering] good prospects for oil exploitation." Based on current projections, drilling may begin in some of these new areas by early 1984.

The best prospects for oil and gas are believed to be in the Pearl River Mouth Basin, which is south of Hong Kong and between Hainan Island and Taiwan. The basin covers about 58,000 square miles and a sedimentary section that is generally several thousand meters thick but reaches over 10,000 meters in the center of the basin. Major oil accumulations are believed to be in sandstones in or associated with structural and/or stratigraphic traps.

Published reports so far indicate that offshore China will probably not be as productive as the Middle East, but it could some day rank as one of the world's major producing areas comparable to the North Sea. Estimates of potential recoverable reserves by Western sources range from 20 to 50 billion barrels.

Expenditures for exploration and development will be large, with estimates as high as $20 billion. Large oil accumulations that have wells capable of high flow rates must be found to justify expenditures in the hundreds of millions of dollars for individual field development. Return on the investment for development will not begin for six to eight years from the issuance of the contracts. It is not likely that a foreign company would recover its total investment for some years after that.

It is a reality of petroleum exploration that "the presence of hydrocarbon within the postulated reservoir and trap must await the penetration of the drill bit." Accordingly, caution is necessary in anticipating what China's offshore potential will be. However, the fact that fifteen

U.S. oil companies as well as a number of foreign companies invested several hundreds of millions of dollars in extensive seismic work and are willing to invest billions of additional dollars in exploration and development can be taken as strong evidence that their combined judgment is that China has high potential for major hydrocarbon production.

The importance of this major resource in China's economic develop- ment cannot be over stated. Additionally, the international implica- tions of having another major oil-producing area in the Far East ob- viously are great, including those of a strategic nature. In particular, the creation of an alternative to Middle East oil dependency for the countries of Northeast Asia—and for U.S. forces in the region—could diminish a major current vulnerability.

The nature of the offshore industry and the role of U.S. companies with respect thereto reinforces the importance this particular area will have for U.S. trade in the decade ahead. Much of the expertise and technical equipment needed to accomplish China's objectives with re- spect to oil and gas development will come from the United States. Our nation and its economy should benefit greatly from our involvement in assisting in development of such an unexplored region. A governmental objective, therefore, should be to insure that U.S. commerce is able to achieve the advantages that potentially should accrue to the nation if this relationship is administered wisely.

The financial implications of a large offshore development program warrant particular consideration. Because of the structuring of the pro- duction contracts, the PRC will require billions of dollars to finance its share of the development costs of the offshore effort. Oil companies owned or subsidized by foreign governments could have a substantial competitive advantage over U.S. companies if they are able to include as part of their bid submittals a government-backed loan at subsidized interest rates.

U.S. policymakers will need to monitor carefully these developments to ensure that U.S. firms are not displaced or disadvantaged in the off- shore oil program by such an intervention by foreign governments and that the strategic importance of a strong offshore China development is dovetailed with U.S. global policies. Such dovetailing must occur be- cause the United States has reached a point in its economic history where the government cannot afford to ignore the effect of its own poli- cies on the success of U.S. firms in competing in international com- merce, which in turn is necessary for a healthy domestic economy.

Commercial relations are inhibited if they are subject to random in- terdiction and disruption because of the vacillating political attitudes of administrators. The Chinese may be expected to view negatively an investor or a commercial partner from a host nation where political attitudes vary from time to time. There must be a long view of how the United States perceives a potential trading partner so that investors can proceed with some confidence that they will not be compromised by sudden shifts for political or arbitrary reasons.

This will be especially important from the standpoint of decisions relating to the level of technology that can be sold to the PRC. Policy decisions relating to the export of specific items should be processed and approved expeditiously in the executive branch unless there is clear and demonstrable danger to U.S. national security. To this end, government agencies should review and amend regulations that constitute impediments to such rapid decisionmaking.

Not only must government personnel act affirmatively to avoid impeding the ability of U.S. firms to compete, they should be educated on what is happening in the international marketplace to a point where they will understand the need to facilitate the efforts of the U.S. private sector in international trade at least to the extent of offsetting the activist role of foreign governments in support of their trading companies. Fortunately, the Department of Commerce has indicated that it recognizes the importance of such reinforcement of U.S. firms and has assigned senior personnel to its Beijing office to deal with the offshore program and other major commercial opportunities that are arising.

As an aspect of the effort to allow trade to fulfill its potential as a strengthening element in relations between the two countries, we need to be particularly mindful of those areas of U.S. technological development that coincide with those China needs for its development. Our agricultural skills and our energy industry are without parallel. Our light and heavy industry have much to offer. U.S. expertise in renewable energy sources would be applicable to remote areas of China. There are many, many others, and our government should be aggressive in identifying and encouraging U.S. firms with such expertise.

At the same time and as a concomitant to our interest in developing the China market for our goods, we must be sensitive to China's need to also have export markets to balance its trade. Unfortunately, protectionist efforts in this country have already surfaced. The International Trade Commission (ITC) has dealt with complaints involving ceramic tableware, canned mushrooms, and textile piecegoods. Additional cases may be expected. The National Council has noted that "China's nonmarket economy, its low wage rate, and its lack of cost accounting make it particularly vulnerable to charges of unfair trade practices." The other side of the commercial coin that must be borne in mind by U.S. policymakers was articulated recently by the president of the National Council in testimony before the ITC. "The United States has maintained a considerable surplus in bilateral trade with the Chinese since trade resumed in 1971. . . . our exports to China exceed our imports from China by two to one. Last year alone, we enjoyed a trade surplus of $1.7 billion with China. . . . If the PRC is to continue buying large quantities of American products, there is a clear need for Chinese products to have fair access to the U.S. market to earn the foreign exchange necessary to finance exports."

In sum, China's desire to modernize was a major aspect of its political turn to the West. The importance of U.S.–PRC commercial relations warrants continuing attention and sophisticated understanding by senior U.S. officials. We must seek to develop to the fullest advantage of both countries those elements of trade where the United States has technology or experience needed by the PRC while being mindful of the importance of maintaining an equitable balance of trade. With regard to China's offshore petroleum effort, both commercial and strategic issues should be considered in the global context of U.S. national interests.

MILITARY DEVELOPMENT

If the development of civil trade and technology transfers with the Chinese will be difficult, such difficulties may be almost insurmountable on the military side. U.S. forces (hopefully) represent the maximum achievement of top-quality equipment. It is through this device and this perception that we hope to achieve a military deterrent to Soviet expansion. But the Chinese represent the flip side of this objective. They have a potential to deter aggression on their own continent through the development of large quantity forces that simply cannot be overwhelmed. In short, we represent opposite extremes of the quality verses quantity quandry. It is by no means evident that we can put ourselves into the appropriate frame of mind to visualize unique Chinese military needs. Consider these Chinese requirements for simplicity as compared with typical U.S. design objectives:

Chinese	
ease of production	planned product improvement
decentralized production	long storage life
low cost (by Chinese standards)	redundant operation
very easy to maintain	operation by reservists
austere parts resupply network	augmentation by citizenry
easy training	exportability
"living off the land"	arsenal approach/evolutionary
high reliability	development
long design life	

United States

maximum unit effectiveness	electronic sophistication
minimum weight	U.S. regulatory constraints
air transportability	technological superiority
high levels of automation	U.S. physical parameters
personal convenience	competitive private industrial
high individual survivability	sources
least manpower	

These differences are so extreme that it appears clear that many real-world military equipment solutions should probably be of non-U.S. origins. The comparisons between the Soviet AK-47 and the somewhat lighter but less rugged M-16 rifle come immediately to mind. The American soldier in Vietnam was reminded several times a day over Armed Forces Radio to keep his rifle clean to assure that it would work. As a natural follow-on to this concern for simplicity, it is probable that there often will be non-U.S. technologies and non-U.S. designs that would be more compatible with the Chinese military and economy. Moreover, there are other cases where it might be far more appropriate to transfer our older, more mature technologies rather than those on the leading edge of modern science. Moreover, the United States has devoted more and more of its energies to developing a force that can hold its own when outnumbered. All common U.S. infantry manuals start from the presumption that our soldiers must learn to prevail from a position of numerical inferiority. It is by no means clear that we are in a position to provide meaningful advice in obverse situations. An effective program to modernize Chinese forces requires an inversion of the American culture that produced our Vietnamization program only a decade or so ago.

The magnitude of the problem associated with the equipping of Chinese forces can be described statistically in gross terms. Chinese forces are perhaps 10 percent larger than Soviet forces and are almost 2.5 times as large as American forces. Yet Chinese defense spending is estimated to be roughly one-third of U.S. spending and less than a quarter of Soviet spending. If anything, Chinese estimates may be on the high side. In any event, Americans spend roughly $55,000 per year on each person on active military duty, while the Soviets spend roughly $35,000 per man. Even our wealthier NATO allies spend about $44,000 per man, while the non-Soviet Warsaw Pact nations spend about $21,000. By comparison, the Chinese appear to be able to spend between $6,000 and $9,000 per man (based on ACDA's estimate of 1979 defense spending rates). There are of course countries that spend considerably less than China. Brazil, Egypt, South Korea, Taiwan, Thailand, and Turkey all appear to spend between $3,000 and $5,000 per man, while India and North Korea are below $3,000.

It is of some interest that the average per-soldier spending of the less wealthy NATO nations (Greece, Italy, Portugal, Spain, and Turkey) is roughly the same as that estimated for China. It is quite possible that if successful initiatives can be developed to effectively arm Chinese forces at lower cost, these same techniques might prove useful even for some of our NATO allies.

Recognizing that Chinese forces can accomodate to a substantially more spartan standard of living than can Western forces, there still appears to be a need for the Chinese to equip their forces with weapons and support equipment roughly one-quarter as expensive as Western equipment—but with the corollary assumption that they should generally expect to outnumber their adversaries in individual battles. This would be a challenging, but by no means impossible, objective. Across the spectrum from fighter aircraft to antitank missiles, cost differences of a factor of three exist among many Western weapon systems between the simplest and the most sophisticated. Further cost reductions may be possible with greater standardization and simplification, accompanied by less automation and versatility. Whether designs can be adjusted or reworked to match more limited Chinese production techniques and materials would require thorough study. It would also remain to be seen whether the American defense community would be capable of creative initiative so foreign to our own post-World War II design culture. Other countries may in fact be better suited to the task. It is not clear, however, whether the Chinese defense community would be prepared to adopt a unique approach to their military needs.

There is certainly no reason to assume that the Chinese are inherently incapable of developing, producing, or operating modern weapons of war. Chiang Kai-shek's troops adopted American weapons during World War II with considerable success, although in many cases their training periods had to be somewhat longer. Chinese forces on Taiwan have continued to be equipped almost exclusively with American weaponry, and have also become involved in the coproduction of some reasonably sophisticated aircraft, such as the F-5. Chinese personnel also operated extensive maintenance and repair facilities on Taiwan for American equipment worn down and damaged in Vietnam.

By the same token, Mainland Chinese military have been able to adapt, produce, operate, and maintain Soviet-made military equipment. As is the Chinese custom, they have been able to redesign Soviet equipment to make it even simpler to operate in several instances. It is Soviet practice to "downgrade" the sophistication of the weapons they transfer to other countries outside the Warsaw Pact. In the main, however, the Soviets have been reluctant to turn over the logistic support of these weapons to the host nations. Like Egypt and Somalia, China found itself with a great deal of inoperable Soviet military equipment shortly after the Soviets withdrew their political support. It would appear to be a substantial testament to Chinese technical development that they have been able to restore that equipment to operating condition, to develop and produce their own derivatives of that equipment, and, in some cases, to "reverse engineer" and manufacture their own version of complex foreign equipment for which they do not even have the blueprints. The "Chinese copy" of the Boeing 707 has taken over a decade to build and to certify for use by Chinese airlines. While some critics claim that this is an indication of Chinese backwardness, the engineering community is more likely to look with some admiration on this feat.

There is also a tendency to overlook the fact that the Chinese have developed, largely on their own—and with the help of Western-trained Chinese scientists (one of whom taught this author theoretical supersonic aerodynamics at M.I.T. before returning to China in 1951)—both nuclear weapons and long-range rockets for their delivery. They also design, build, and multiple-launch their own satellites. Like the Soviets, there is a large spread between the technical capacity of its highly educated professionals and the average rural Chinese who might be expected to operate complex weapons within the military. Like the Soviets, the Chinese will have to emphasize operational and logistic simplicity in recognition of the limited skills of their military inductees. As a matter of fact, the American defense community would do well to acknowledge the growing gap between our own designers and operators.

In short, there is no apparent reason why the Chinese cannot develop, adapt, produce, operate, and maintain weapons and other military equipment of contemporary effectiveness. The trick will be to find the means to economically equip very large, dispersed forces with simple, reliable weapons that, when used in large numbers, can match the effectiveness of opposing forces. To do so may well be within the Western technological state of the art, but it certainly has not been the primary design objective of the American defense community for the past several decades. A joint multinational effort might well produce the best results for the Chinese.

SUMMARY AND CONCLUSIONS

Trade and technology transfer to China over the next decade will inevitably be heavily influenced by political and security considerations—and vice versa. U.S. policies in these areas can best be formulated if the Western alliance (including Japan) will come to grips with the following basic issues:

1. Is China's economic development in the long-term security interest of the United States and its allies?
2. Assuming either (a) no further, or (b) a limited Sino–Soviet rapprochment, what are the opportunities and dangers posed by China's economic future?
3. Are there particular sectors and technologies whose development would run counter to Western security interests? If so, can we develop coordination between arms transfer policies, export control policies, export financing policies, and other policy instruments affecting these sectors and technologies?
4. To the extent that there is conflict between economic and military definitions of security, how can the Alliance best reach agreement on the appropriate tradeoffs?
5. In the light of these concerns, how can economic instruments best be applied? What are their limits? Are means and ends proportional—that is, is what we want from the Chinese attainable and controllable with the instruments we have at hand?
6. What, in fact, do we want the Chinese to do and become?
7. What, in fact, do the Chinese want to do and become?

In general, China's economic development is in the long-term security interests of the United States and its allies. In fact, China's economic development is of far greater importance than either its political or its military development. For the foreseeable future, whatever dangers might be posed by a rapidly improving economic future are far outweighed by the advantages of assisting China to join the ranks of stable, independent, self-confident, developing nations.

Nonetheless, despite the strategic advantages of assuring that China continue to "tilt" towards the West, there is no firm basis to conclude that China is no longer a "potential adversary," either by returning to some Soviet-led coalition or by actively contesting vital U.S. interests elsewhere in the region (vis-à-vis the Republic of Korea, for instance). From this standpoint, then, our assistance in the economic, political, and military development of China must proceed if not with caution, at least with prudence.

This in turn suggests the need to develop trade and joint development projects in the economic sphere rather than engaging in excessively ambitious and premature technology transfers. As long as the United States remains somewhat uncertain about its own ultimate objectives—or China's—the extent of technological transfers should be constrained since they are nonreversible.

While the United States would encourage the development of certain arms transfers, it is quite reasonable to restrain the extent of these sales with a strong emphasis on defensive rather than offensive capabilities—at least to the extent that it is practical to differentiate between the two. Again, direct or indirect arms sales are probably preferable to open-ended technology transfers.

Although these conclusions are easy to draw, they will be difficult to implement in practice. American governmental processes do not create the impression of a well-orchestrated, positive, long-term program for civil sector economic assistance and cooperation, either nationally or internationally. We do not seem to fully recognize the strategic importance of promoting economic development or the dangers of neglecting the strength of the "potential *economic* adversaries" among our highly competitive industrialized allies. We are likely to appear ambivalent and inconsistent in our purely commercial trade due to the separation of government and private enterprise and due to government reluctance to control or promote U.S. industry's role in the civil market place. We are likely to appear disorganized and incoherent in the licensing of "dual-use" technology, as different elements of the national bureaucracy trade off the conflicting policy objectives of "fostering a strong, friendly China" and preventing militarily significant technology from falling into the hands of a "potential adversary." We are likely to appear less positive and less aggressive than many of our closest Western allies because of the unwillingness of our government to conspire with our private business sector and because we will place international security above national economic gain. Unless China takes the trouble to understand the limitations and inefficiencies of our American governmental processes, there will be plenty of room for misunderstanding both our capabilities and our intentions.

Additionally, there will be plenty of room for Americans to misunderstand Chinese capabilities and intentions. If we believe that we can coerce China into becoming subservient to the political and strategic interests of the West, then we will find ourselves at odds with China's own objectives for national growth. On the other hand, if we seek to discover China's own national objectives, it is likely that we will find them both reasonable and acceptable, since China seeks a position of strength, stability, and independence in the community of responsible nations. The United States should support and reinforce those objectives, despite China's communist form of government.

There are major asymmetries in the economic and cultural positions of our two societies that will make it difficult to work together in restrained but mutually beneficial ways. The tendency of Americans—and other Western nations—to mirror-image and to see others as actual or potential replicas of ourselves can only make these dealings even more difficult.

Moreover, on the military side, we stand at opposite ends of the quality versus quantity spectrum, and it is difficult to imagine that our normal military institutions would be capable of transcending the fundamental differences in needed approach. In fact, we may be unable to accomplish our objectives primarily because we cannot translate them into terms that the intended beneficiary can accomodate. It is important that our aims with regard to the Chinese over the next decade recognize these basic impediments to cooperative actions.

Despite these asymmetries, however, there can be little question that China holds a substantial latent potential for influencing the long-term strategic balance economically, politically, and militarily. Whether this influence evolves as favorable or unfavorable to basic Western interests may well depend on our collective capabilities to transcend these asymmetries. The extent to which the United States can play a decisive role in the outcome depends in considerable measure on our own abilities to transcend the awkwardness implicit in our democratic, capitalistic, free enterprise system.

Our major near-term opportunities to assist China's development along compatible lines are in economic cooperation and growth, the area in which we could benefit most directly but for which we are least well nationally organized. Over the next decade and beyond, the major "China challenge" for the United States will center on our own ability to orchestrate prudent public and private economic interests in trade and technology transfer involving both civil, "dual-use," and military applications. We sorely need to improve our collective understanding of both the extent and the limits of our own national interests, of our common interests with the Chinese, and of Chinese capabilities to assimilate and benefit from our assistance. We also need to develop and sustain a unified, consistent, efficient, and demonstrably reasonable mechanism for implementing appropriate economic programs with China (and elsewhere, for that matter). If we continue our current laissez-faire procedures, we will run the risk of losing out not only to our friendly economic adversaries but also to our real political and military adversaries as well.

Chapter 14

Taiwan: The Emerging Relationship

*Robert G. Sutter**

INTRODUCTION

The normalization of U.S. diplomatic relations with the PRC announced by President Carter and Chinese Premier Hua Guofeng on December 15, 1978, settled some major outstanding issues concerning the Taiwan question in American foreign policy. The United States finally decided to recognize the PRC, to break its official ties with the Chinese Nationalist administration in Taiwan, and to terminate the U.S. defense treaty with Taiwan. The administration also reaffirmed U.S. adherence to the principle of one China, seen originally in the Shanghai Communiqué signed by President Nixon during his visit to China in February 1972. Thus, it acknowledged the Chinese position that there is but one China and Taiwan is part of China and recognized the PRC as the sole legal government of China. In an accompanying statement, President Carter also emphasized the U.S. expectation that the Taiwan issue would be settled peacefully by the Chinese people, and the administration made clear that the United States would continue to sell defensive weapons to Taipei. To the Chinese and to many international observers, the normalization communiqué signaled that

The views expressed in this paper are those of the author and do not represent the views of the Library of Congress or the U.S. Government.
*Asian Affairs Specialist, Library of Congress Congressional Research Service.

the United States expected Taiwan to be reunited eventually with the Mainland.

No sooner, however, had the normalization agreement been announced than American officials in Congress demonstrated strong differences over U.S. policy toward Taiwan, especially in February and March 1979, when they considered the Taiwan Relations Act (TRA).[1] Congress added a series of amendments to the bill proposed by the Carter administration, which dealt with U.S. pledges of protection for Taiwan, arms sales to the island, and other matters. The resulting legislation seemed to contradict the thrust of the normalization as it clearly implied that the United States expected Taiwan to remain separate from the Mainland and under U.S. protection for the foreseeable future.

Beijing protested what they perceived as the contradiction in U.S. policy even before the Act was passed.[2] The Carter administration attempted to assuage PRC concerns, while it avoided doing serious damage to U.S.–Taiwan relations or directly challenging Congress over the TRA. The administration pledged to carry out the Act in a way consistent with the principles of the normalization agreement. Such carefully crafted ambiguity was required in order to maintain the delicate balance of American interests in the seemingly zero-sum game of U.S. relations with the PRC and Taiwan.

The general American goal in this area has remained clear: the United States wishes to maintain and develop improved relations with the PRC, but at the same time it wishes to sustain close ties and safeguard important interests in Taiwan. Implementing such a policy has been complicated repeatedly by the intense rivalry between the PRC and Taiwan and by the antagonism between their respective supporters in the United States. In broad terms, U.S. policymakers have continued to be confronted with difficult decisions regarding Taiwan. In each instance they must decide whether to tilt U.S. policy toward helping the people on the island to remain free of PRC control or to tip the scales in the other direction, facilitating PRC efforts to gain control of the island.[3]

U.S. INTERESTS IN TAIWAN

American strategic interests in Taiwan have changed substantially as the United States has come to view the PRC more as a friend than a foe to U.S. interests in East Asian and world affairs.[4] The demise of the U.S. containment system against China, the implementation of the Nixon Doctrine, and the developing concordance of Sino–American interests in maintaining a favorable balance of power in Asia against

Soviet "expansionism" have severely undercut the arguments of those who have maintained that an American pullback from Taiwan would have a detrimental impact on U.S. strategic interests in East Asia.

The United States does maintain a strong and growing stake in Taiwan's vibrant economy. Bilateral trade in 1982 was valued at $13.2 billion, more than double U.S. trade with the Mainland. American investment has also grown; private American direct investment averages around $200 million per year.

Perhaps the strongest and most widespread American interest in Taiwan concerns what some have called "moral" considerations. Taiwan has long been viewed positively by a majority in the United States because (1) its government has sustained a longstanding friendship with the United States dating back to World War II; (2) the economy is seen as a model of development, and (3) the people enjoy close professional and personal relations with thousands of Americans and show no apparent interest in affiliation with the Mainland government. As a result, a large group of Americans oppose as "immoral" and "unconscionable" any U.S. policy toward China that would not leave room for continued U.S. support for Taiwan. According to this view, the United States should not subject the people in Taiwan to PRC military pressure or intimidation and should not force them to come to terms on reunification with Beijing.

Faced with continued strong PRC pressure and criticism in the United States, President Reagan adopted a more ambiguous policy toward Taiwan after taking office than that suggested by his campaign speeches. He continued to voice support for the TRA but stopped short of restoring official contacts or granting major weapons sales to Taiwan. At the same time, he began to reaffirm U.S. commitments made in the normalization communiqué and pledged repeatedly to strive to improve relations with the PRC.

This approach defused the U.S. domestic tensions in U.S.–PRC–Taiwan relations for only a short time. By late 1981, U.S. policymakers were faced with sharply conflicting pressures concerning the issue of U.S. fighter aircraft sales to Taiwan.[7] Taiwan leaders and many in the United States argued strongly that the United States should decide soon to sell more advanced fighter aircraft to Taiwan in order to enhance the security and stability of the island. In contrast, leaders of the PRC and many commentators in the United States warned repeatedly that such sales would run the risk of prompting a hostile Chinese reaction that would jeopardize important American interests in relations with China. The debate focused less on the strictly military implications of the possible arms sales to Taiwan than on their broader political implications for U.S. relations with the PRC and Taiwan. Most notably, the arms sales options most favored by Taiwan and American advocates of stronger U.S.–Taiwan relations were almost invariably those most firmly opposed by the PRC and many American supporters of closer U.S.–PRC ties.

The Reagan administration announced on January 11, 1982, that it had decided not to sell Taiwan jet fighters more advanced than the F-5E then in production in Taiwan, but it reaffirmed its commitment to sell arms (reportedly including more F-5E fighters) to the island. The administration did not specify the number of U.S. planes to be sold or the duration of the sales.[8] The decision was widely hailed in the United States as a sign of sensible moderation in American China policy. Meanwhile, the administration sent a diplomatic mission to Beijing to discuss the subject with the PRC.

China remained dissatisfied with the U.S. stance. After several months of reportedly delicate negotiations with the PRC, the Reagan administration announced in April 1982 that it was going to sell a package of military spare parts to Taiwan, the first sale of military equipment to Taiwan specifically announced by the Reagan government. The Chinese did not downgrade relations because they said that the package did not involve weapons, had been agreed to by the United States and Taiwan prior to Chinese demands for a gradual cutoff of all arms, and—in the PRC view—the United States had agreed not to consider military sales to Taiwan while Sino–U.S. discussions on the issue continued.

After several months of further talks, the United States and the PRC on August 17, 1982, issued a joint communiqué that established at least a temporary compromise over the arms sales question. As a result, two days later the administration was able to announce, without prompting a major, hostile PRC response, the proposed sale of 60 F-5E/F aircraft to be coproduced in Taiwan from 1983 to 1985. Reaction in the U.S. Congress was mixed. Critics tended to focus on the possible negative implications of the communiqué and related PRC demands for the future U.S. relationship with Taiwan. Those who spoke out in sup-. port of the agreement stressed the achievement of the communiqué in avoiding a rupture or downgrading of relations with the PRC without, in their view, compromising Taiwan's future or U.S. relations with Taiwan.[9]

IMPLICATIONS FOR FUTURE POLICY

The Reagan administration appears to have succeeded to manage the 1981–1982 debate over arms sales to Taiwan and to reach an understanding with the PRC that avoided a downgrading in the U.S.–

PRC relationship while the United States continues the sale of fighter aircraft and other weapons to Taiwan. Unfortunately, the record of friction and discord surrounding U.S.–PRC–Taiwan relations in recent years holds out little hope for a permanent resolution to this and other sensitive aspects of the Taiwan question in American foreign policy. It seems likely that the best that can be expected for the foreseeable future is for American policymakers to continue to try to manage the sharply conflicting pressures they feel from the PRC, Taiwan, and American domestic policies.

The broader shift in China's foreign policy in 1982 toward a more independent, less pro-American foreign posture is thought to reflect several important considerations, including:

1. A political maneuver designed to offset potential criticism by political opponents of Deng Xiaoping and other reformers in the PRC for allegedly having "sold out" China's interests vis-à-vis Taiwan for the sake of improved relations with the United States.
2. China's recently more sanguine view of the Soviet "threat" to Chinese security.
3. Beijing's perceived need to take extraordinary measures to block what it sees as a trend in Taiwan favoring a future status for the island separate from Mainland control.

Taiwan's Policy

Taipei's policy has been largely reactive up to the present. Well aware of their relatively small position in American strategic plans, especially when compared with the strategic importance of the PRC, Taiwan leaders have attempted to highlight their economic importance to the United States and to strengthen the longstanding U.S. ideological and sentimental ties to the island. The latter effort has been compromised to some extent by bad publicity in the United States caused by continued martial law on the island and reported human rights abuses (such as the unexplained death of an American-employed Taiwanese professor in July 1981) and by Taipei's public refusal to respond positively to persisting PRC overtures for talks, even on such relatively minor matters as postal communications and fishing. Taipei leaders remain caught on the horns of a dilemma regarding PRC overtures. If they respond positively in order to counter the PRC initiatives or to win favor in the United States, they run the risk of prompting instability in Taiwan on the part of the majority Taiwanese population. Many among this eighty-five percent of the population in Taiwan are said to fear that the minority Mainlander group, which controls the levers of government power in Taiwan, might be tempted to make a deal regarding re-unification with the PRC at the expense of Taiwan's future autonomy and Taiwanese political rights.

U.S. Domestic Politics

Political tensions in the United States over policy toward Taiwan reached high levels in 1978 and 1979, when Congress and the Carter administration were at odds over the normalization decision and the Taiwan Relations Act, and in 1980, when Ronald Reagan's campaign statements prompted major public controversy. They appeared to sub-side briefly as the Reagan administration entered office.

More recently, however, as the administration attempted to accom-modate strong PRC demands on the issue of U.S. arms sales to Taiwan, some conservatives in the Congress and the Republican Party became strongly vocal in opposition to meeting the PRC demands and criticized harshly the alleged pro-PRC bias of some officials in the administra-tion, including former Secretary Haig. Thus, President Reagan has faced a domestic political dilemma. If he does not follow the conserva-tives' advice, he risks fostering a split in his own political constituency. But if he acquiesces to the conservatives' pressure and takes actions in regard to Taiwan that prompt a downgrading in relations with the PRC, Democratic leaders could be expected to point to the incident as a "failure" in the administration's foreign policy.

PROSPECTS FOR THE DECADE

The United States will likely continue to seek a balance in its China policy that will allow for the maintenance of close unofficial ties with Taiwan while maintaining cordial relations with the PRC. Achievement of this goal is by no means certain. For each scenario of U.S., PRC, or Taiwan policy trends favorable to U.S. interests, there is a scenario that works against American objectives.

Among possible positive developments, one of the most important would be a reduction in PRC pressure over continued U.S. relations (such as arms sales) with Taiwan. Beijing may come to believe that it would be unlikely to obtain reunification with Taiwan without the sup-port of the United States, since a continued hard line on U.S.–Taiwan relations could seriously alienate American opinion from China and jeopardize chances for reunification with Taiwan.

The PRC domestic political situation may stabilize to a point where Chinese leaders would be capable of reaching a compromise with the

United States over Taiwan without risking damaging political repercussions inside China. And the development of private contacts between the PRC and Taiwanese may reach a point where mutual confidence is sufficient to allow for some meaningful discussions of peaceful
contacts and relations, perhaps leading to a tenuous association of Taiwan with the Mainland, possibly along the lines of Hong Kong. This
trend would be complimented by the development of a more representative government in Taipei that would act as the spokesman of the Taiwanese majority as well as the Mainlander minority on the island.
Such a regime may have more flexibility in reaching an understanding
with the PRC than the current Taipei government because it would not
have to worry as much about hostile Taiwanese reactions to fears of a
"sell out" of Taiwanese interests by Mainlander authorities in talks
with PRC leaders.

The specific problem of U.S. arms sales to Taiwan should be reduced
as Taiwan continues recent efforts to become more self-sufficient in
arms production. The island already has developed a capability to supply major ground force equipment; key weaknesses are in sophisticated
air and naval defense. Considering Taiwan's growing investment in
R&D and recruitment of U.S.-educated Chinese scientists to work in
Taiwan, the capability to produce weapons comparable to the F-5E may
be developed within the next ten to fifteen years.

Meanwhile, American divisions over Taiwan policy could fade over
time. Memories of past commitments to Chiang Kai-shek and hostility
to "Communist" China are gradually being undermined by the more
positive evolution of U.S.–PRC relations during the past decade. Americans and their government representatives could become even more
positive regarding the PRC, thereby reducing the perceived need for the
kinds of guarantees and military relations with Taiwan called for in the
TRA.

Of course, future trends could work against U.S. interests. Beijing
may remain intransigent against U.S.–Taiwan relations, or it may up
the ante in applying pressure on the United States. Thus, it could not
only press for a cutoff of U.S. arms shipments to Taiwan, but it could
also demand that the United States explicitly recognize PRC sovereignty over Taiwan, actively support PRC proposals for reunification,
and apply pressure on Taipei to come to terms with the Mainland. If the
United States refused, the Chinese could respond not only by downgrading diplomatic relations with the United States but by shifting
Chinese policy away from the United States and confronting American
interests more directly in sensitive areas, notably Taiwan. Beijing
could threaten to retaliate against American companies that supply
Taiwan with products useful in developing military equipment, or it

could demand that American and other foreign shippers to Taiwan first get approval for their shipments from Beijing.

Beijing also might adopt more extreme domestic or foreign policies that would alienate American opinion. Thus, PRC leaders could launch a major crackdown on the relatively more free individual expression in China since the death of Mao, could sharply cut back on economic interaction with the West in favor of a more autarchic approach to development, or could establish improved relations with the Soviet Union as part of a more even-handed Chinese posture toward the two superpowers. Any of these trends, especially if combined with a harder PRC line on Taiwan, could make it more difficult for American leaders to justify compromise over Taiwan. In contrast, they could presumably increase the influence of those Americans who argue that U.S. benefits in relations with China are potentially unstable and ephemeral and are insufficient to justify jeopardizing longstanding American interests vis-à-vis Taiwan.

Taipei may respond to increased PRC pressure for peace talks and declining American military support with extreme domestic or international policies contrary to American interests. Thus, Taipei leaders may attempt to cope with their difficulties by exerting greater political control on the island, leading to a major crackdown on dissidents and a reversal of the evolutionary progress toward more representative government. It may judge that self-sufficiency in defense requires the development of nuclear arms or that Taiwan's international viability can only be secured by means of seeking an alignment with the Soviet Union or formally declaring Taiwan an independent state. Such radical options are not only likely to alienate American support; they also risk prompting PRC military reaction. In the event of renewed PRC military pressure on the island, the United States would face the difficult task of choosing between its strategically important Asian partner and its longstanding island ally.

Policy toward Taiwan also could again become a major partisan issue in American politics, complicating U.S. ability to achieve a proper balance in U.S.–PRC–Taiwan relations. Thus, for example, the Reagan administration may manage to accommodate PRC demands by cutting back on military and other ties with Taiwan and by softpedaling past American commitments made in the Taiwan Relations Act. Conservatives would have a tough time accusing Ronald Reagan of being "soft" on Taiwan, but they presumably would have an easier time in attacking his aides who have been prominently involved in China relations. Meanwhile, if the Reagan administration fails to accommodate Beijing and relations with China are downgraded, Democratic leaders could be expected to exploit this evidence of the administration's "mismanagement" of U.S. foreign policy.

SOVIET POLICY

Apart from U.S.–PRC–Taiwan considerations, longer term American foreign policy could be influenced heavily by shifts in U.S. and/or PRC perceptions of Soviet policy. According to this view, as the United States or China sees greater need to cooperate with the other against suspected Soviet expansionism, it would be more willing to accommodate over Taiwan. If the Soviet threat were seen by the United States as growing more dangerous and the U.S.–China connection were seen as useful in countering Soviet power, strategic pragmatism would appear to override considerations in U.S.–Taiwan relations and push the United States into favoring the PRC over Taiwan.

Under these circumstances, the United States would presumably be more willing to cut off military supplies to the island, would recognize PRC sovereignty over Taiwan, and would pressure Taipei to join peace talks with the PRC. Arguments against such action would continue to focus on the "moral" American commitment to Taiwan's well-being and U.S. economic interests on the island, but their relative importance in U.S. calculations would fade in comparison with broader U.S. strategic interests, depending on how threatened the United States felt in the face of Soviet expansion and how useful China appeared to be as a partner against the USSR.

The same line of reasoning holds that a decline in U.S.–Soviet tensions and/or a reassessment of China's utility and reliability against the Soviet Union could reduce American incentive to compromise over Taiwan. The likely strategic benefits of accommodation with the PRC over Taiwan would not, in this case, outweigh the disadvantages to American interests vis-à-vis Taiwan.

Similar logic suggests that a major reason for Beijing's recent intransigence over the Taiwan issue is because it is more confident regarding the Soviet threat. The Chinese reportedly see the USSR confronted by a major international front led by a strongly anti-Soviet American government and bogged down in various international adventures that sharply reduce the Kremlin's ability to take actions against China's interests. As a result, the Chinese see no immediate need to join more closely together with the United States against Moscow and can afford to maintain a hard line on Taiwan.

Amidst these conflicting domestic and international pressures affecting U.S. policy toward Taiwan and the PRC, one general trend appears to stand out as the dominant feature in American policy over the past decade that is likely to remain the major line of development for the United States in the foreseeable future. That is, American policy has tended to move in the direction of meeting PRC demands and conditions, while gradually cutting back contacts and accommodating U.S.

ties with Taiwan for the sake of better relations with the PRC. Placing strong emphasis on maintaining and building good relations with Beijing, American Presidents—Republican and Democratic—have been willing to cut back slowly on U.S. interaction with Taiwan in an effort to accommodate PRC demands. While there have been some twists and turns in this trend and unforeseen future developments could change its course, there is ample reason to expect it to continue to govern American China policy for some time to come.

China continues to loom large in American calculations of strategic interests in East Asian and world affairs. By contrast, American strategic interest in Taiwan has declined markedly as the United States has come to view the PRC more as a friend than as a foe to U.S. interests. As a result, U.S. officials have repeatedly attempted to accommodate these interests to PRC demands concerning U.S.–Taiwan relations to pursue what they presumably judge as a more important goal of developing Sino–American friendship in an era of global uncertainty and challenge to American interests from antagonistic international forces, notably expanding Soviet power. In view of the deep and widespread concern in the United States over the need to check and contain Soviet expansion and given the continued Chinese policy of opposition to the Soviet Union, it seems likely that U.S. leaders will continue to try, wherever feasible, to accommodate American interests in relation to Taiwan to the need for meeting PRC demands in the broader interests of preserving and developing a closer Sino–American relationship.

NOTES

1. See in particular U.S. Congress, Senate Committee on Foreign Relations, *Taiwan,* February 5, 6, 7, 8, 21, and 22, 1979 Hearings (Washington, D.C.: Government Printing Office, 1979).
2. Beijing's protest is replayed in the U.S. Foreign Broadcast Information Service Daily Report, *China,* (March 26, 1979).
3. For a comprehensive assessment of American policy and options regarding Taiwan, see Ralph Clough, *Island China* (Cambridge: Harvard University Press, 1978). See also U.S. Congress, Senate Committee on Foreign Relations, *Taiwan: One Year After U.S.–China Normalization* (Washington, D.C.: Government Printing Office).
4. For a recent review of American statements of interest regarding Taiwan, see U.S. Congress, House Committee on Foreign Affairs, Subcommittee on Asian and Pacific Affairs, *The New Era in East Asia* (Washington, D.C.: Government Printing Office, 1981).
5. These disputes are reviewed in U.S. Congress, House Committee on Foreign Affairs, *Executive-Legislative Consultations on China Policy, 1978–79* (Washington, D.C.: Government Printing Office, 1980).

6. The statement is replayed in the *Congressional Record* (August 28, 1980), p. E 4112–E 4113.

7. For a discussion of this debate, see A. Doak Barnett, *The FX Decision* (Washington, D.C.: Brookings Institution, 1981). See also Michael Gordon, "No Tigersharks for Taiwan," *National Journal* (January 16, 1982).

8. *Washington Post* (January 12, 1982).

9. See discussion in Library of Congress, Congressional Research Service, *Taiwan and the U.S.–PRC Communiqué,* Issue Brief 82093 (periodically updated).

Chapter 15

The Atlantic And Pacific Alliances

Terry L. Deibel* and Gen. Russell E. Dougherty**

Since signing the North Atlantic Treaty in 1949, the United States has relied on a variety of security partners to support its national defense. In peacetime, their explicit links with this country help deter Soviet aggression, while in war their added military capability might well make the difference between success and failure. Particularly in a time of budgetary stringency, the services provided by American allies are to the defense of U.S. interests.

Nevertheless, with all their benefits, alliances are hardly an unmixed blessing. Their costs include reciprocal American promises and expenses, as well as substantive adjustments of U.S. foreign policy. In addition, alliances are means of policy, not ends, and are destined (as relations with Ethiopia, Taiwan, and Egypt show) to change with American interests and shifts in the balance of power. Consequently, tension is inevitable between the need for U.S. reliability as an ally and the flexibility in alliance policy that the accelerating pace of change demands.

The views expressed in this paper are those of the authors and do not represent the views of the National War College or the U.S. Government.

*National War College.

**Executive Director, Air Force Association.

In fact, the character of American alliances has dramatically altered since John Foster Dulles negotiated binding treaties with scores of nations around the globe.[1] Today three types of U.S. security relations might be loosely termed "alliances." Those of the immediate post-World War II era were *formal,* based on treaty promises designed to build allied confidence and deter enemies. Some eventually included physical commitments, such as stationing troops abroad, forming combined commands, or building common infrastructure. Most U.S. relationships in Asia are of this type, including those with Japan, Australia and New Zealand, South Korea, and the Philippines.[2]

Since the 1950s, however, U.S. commitments[3] have generally been less intense. Instead of treaties, *semiformal* relationships are based on bilateral documents (e.g., the Rusk-Thanat communiqué) or on unilateral statements of intent (e.g., the Taiwan Relations Act) buttressed by defense cooperation and military sales. Other ties are completely *informal,* with the United States searching out access to facilities and territory abroad and offering, in exchange, military and economic assistance backed by executive branch statements of intent to defend (as in Saudi Arabia or Kenya). Though less stable for both sides, these arrangements are more acceptable to the post-Vietnam United States and to our new friends, who often fear the domestic and foreign policy consequences of identification with the United States. Such relationships are also more flexible and more attuned to present needs as well as to the tradition of action that prevailed in U.S. foreign policy before World War II.

TRENDS IN U.S. COMMITMENT POLICY

The heyday of formal U.S. alliance formation in the 1950s was radically different from the current world scene. Soviet exhaustion from World War II, the U.S. atomic lead and American postwar prestige made the acquisition and maintenance of allies far less difficult than it is today. Similarly, overwhelming U.S. economic strength and the lack of Soviet power projection capabilities meant that support of our allies was a relatively small burden and risk for this country. Changes in these conditions have severely undermined the ease with which the United States can attract and hold allies, with important effects on the future U.S. commitment posture in the Pacific:

1. The decline in U.S. power during the decade before 1978 was accompanied by a reduction in American commitments, especially in the Pacific. For America's industrialized allies (Japan and the

ANZUS powers), these changes were relatively minor, but for the Southeast Asian states, Korea, and Taiwan, the impact was dramatic.

2. Since at least 1979, however, this reduction of U.S. commitment has been checked and somewhat reversed.

3. These cyclical swings in American policy were quite a bit stronger in the Pacific than they were in the Atlantic, although NATO experienced a lesser slackening of support and resurgence of U.S. attention (e.g. the "year of Europe," contrasted with the 1979 theater nuclear forces modernization decision).

4. Commitment changes have often not been the result of the careful adjustment of American alliance systems to changed international conditions or U.S. interests. Instead, they seem to be *ad hoc* reactions to unrelated domestic events (e.g., Watergate) or unintended regional developments (such as defeat in Vietnam).[4]

These conclusions suggest, at a minimum, that the current U.S. concern for Pacific defense may not last. If another cycle of commitment reduction begins, history indicates it will affect Southeast Asia and the Philippines more than Japan and ANZUS. Both conclusions favor extreme care lest American policy get ahead of what long-term public opinion and available resources will support, particularly regarding China (where our policy has also been cyclical over the decades)[5] and the smaller Asian states. Any other policy risks undercutting regional perceptions of American steadiness and reliability and are a major factor in both allied confidence and enemy deterrence.

Exactly how long the current official American focus on Asian security will persist or how far it will go is difficult to predict. Pressures for *both* the expansion and contraction of U.S. security relationships can be expected in the years ahead. On the side of expansion is the likely continued growth of Soviet military power, unconstrained in the short run by SALT II or Pacific arms control agreements, as well as continued U.S. dependence on energy, raw materials, and markets that mandate parallel growth in American world interests. If the economic constraints of the past decade continue, security partners will become even more important to U.S. defense. Add to that a stiffened public attitude toward protecting U.S. interests overseas, and one has a powerful mix of pro-commitment factors.

Conversely, the growth of Soviet power may persuade many Americans that the primary goal must be to avoid confrontation.[6] Public and congressional skittishness about additional commitments will be reinforced by the fact that new security partners are likely to be relatively unstable, governments in dangerous parts of the world with which

Americans have little cultural affinity. Resource scarcity and expanding U.S. commitments will make it increasingly difficult to support these generally poor and weak countries with American aid. Moreover, unless American resources available for defense are seen to be expanding, U.S. credibility as an ally must decline to some extent with each additional commitment we undertake.

The most likely result of these conflicting forces will be continued flux in American alliances in Asia and elsewhere. Policymakers will be hardpressed to manage the process of change. Political sensitivity in the United States and among potential security partners will require discretion in establishing and maintaining security ties; the time for signing formal alliance treaties has probably passed. U.S. decisionmakers will have to keep relationships flexible and minimize commitments to states where there is no compatibility in security interests but only a U.S. need for facilities access or overflight rights. They will find that making the deterrent real (and U.S. allies really defendable) will be far more difficult than in the past, and that the combination of over-the-horizon forces, facilities access, and expensive sea- and airlift is far less effective militarily than the old-fashioned base structure with resident American forces of days gone by.

EAST MEETS WEST: THE ATLANTIC AND PACIFIC ALLIANCE SYSTEMS

Within the parameters set by the general trends sketched above, the two-front character of U.S.–Soviet competition poses complex dilemmas for American allies in Europe and the Far East. On the most basic level, the Atlantic and Pacific communities are tied together psychologically by the knowledge that the prime external threat to their security and the major defense against it come from the same sources—respectively, the Soviet Union and the United States.

The nations on each side of the Soviet military giant appreciate the value of multifront deterrence, and each front would find belligerence on the other critical in case of general war in its region. But each also appreciates that the United States has limited defense capabilities and might have to choose between theaters in a global war. Although the U.S. choice is a matter of speculation, the traditional European emphasis in American diplomacy, the relative nearness of the Atlantic threat, the deeper U.S. commitment to NATO, and America's strategy in the last two global wars all point in the same direction. Moreover, no matter in which theater U.S.–Soviet global conflict began, nations in the other would probably value preservation of the peace in their own region more highly than whatever help the United States could offer them. Offsetting the advantages of two-front deterrence, then, is the Soviet option of a two-front threat to the United States at allied expense.

Other factors further differentiate Atlantic and Pacific. Europe is physically nearer and culturally, politically, and sociologically more like this country. Whereas the Pacific region is composed of a variety of countries at different stages of economic development, the allies in Europe are all industrialized economic powers. Even U.S. bilateral interests vary considerably by country in the Pacific but are more constant and intense across Europe.

The defense problem is also very different. Pacific defense is a naval and air job, more easily accomplished for any individual nation than in Europe, though more difficult over its vast area for all. The European theater is concentrated so close to Soviet power that its land defense lacks critical room for fallback and maneuver. Massed U.S., European, and Soviet power means a more intense conflict than in the Pacific, but it also means less likelihood of war.

Consequently, the two alliance systems are also quite different in the following ways:

Legally, the Pacific treaties include weaker reciprocal commitments than does the North Atlantic Treaty, both in their characterization of the *casus foederis* and the response the allies promise to make. Unlike NATO, in the Pacific an attack on one is not legally considered an attack on all, and the treaties make no reference to the use of armed force in response.[7]

Politically, NATO is a single alliance framework with a politico-military forum (the NATO Council), whereas the Pacific nations (with the exception of ANZUS) operate independently, without any political framework or planning organization such as that in Brussels.

Militarily, NATO has a collective force, including a combined command and common infrastructure, but the Pacific allies can field only a collection of forces whose total weight might not be as great as the sum of its parts.[8] Though NATO has its Greek-Turkish problem, the breadth of the Pacific region and its relative distance from Soviet power also allow for many more inter-nation disputes detrimental to a common defense effort.[9]

In sum, the United States is probably less prepared for general war in the Pacific than in Europe (given the lower level of threat) but has more freedom of action in the Pacific than it does in Europe.[10] Militarily, the Pacific demands that choices be made concerning the defense perimeter and who is to be defended both before and after the opening of hostilities. Politically, U.S. flexibility is enhanced by the breadth, diversity, and political fluidity of the Pacific region and the relative weakness of U.S. alliances there.

Still, the limitations on American policy sketched earlier apply with special force to the Pacific. The difficulty of attracting and holding allies is compounded by the area's cultural and physical distance. The expense of a credible defense there in this era of reduced budgets and limited basing is extreme, given the distances involved. The problem is thus one of protecting moderate interests in a region where establishing credible local deterrence is extremely difficult and expensive. Such difficulties can be finessed as long as the level of threat remains low, but the recent growth of Soviet Far Eastern military capabilities (both in the North and out of Vietnamese naval bases) makes continuation of that state of affairs increasingly problematical.[11]

THE FUTURE OF U.S. PACIFIC ALLIANCES

Can U.S. alliances do more to provide credible deterrence and defense at reasonable cost in the face of a growing threat? Should the United States increase its commitments to Asian states? Can it persuade them to increase their commitments to us? How would either of these things be done?

The formal commitments between the United States and its Pacific allies, mostly inherited from the 1950s, are surprisingly homogeneous and reciprocal, given the diversity involved. All these treaties define the *casus foederis* as "armed attack . . . on either of the parties" (the Manila Pact refers to "aggression by means of armed attack"), and all specify that each party will "consider the attack dangerous to its own peace and safety" and respond to "meet the common danger in accordance with its constitutional processes." They differ regarding the geographic area wherein the triggering attack must take place. The Japanese and Korean treaties limit the area to "the territories under the administration of Japan" and (for Korea) those "under [the parties'] administrative control." The ANZUS, Philippines, and SEATO treaties speak more broadly of "the Pacific area," or the "treaty area," and thus would appear to obligate the local powers to help the United States in a regional war.[12] Legally, then, none of the Pacific allies are obligated to join or help the United States in a global war with the Soviets unless such a conflict extends to their territories (for Japan and Korea) or the Pacific region (for the other powers), whereas the United States is obligated to help them if they are attacked regardless of its broader wartime responsibilities.[13] Offsetting this apparently unequal set of obligations, however, is the fact that the United States remains quite free to determine the level at which it will "meet the common danger" and to choose the means of response (troops, aid, or merely diplomatic support), even though its ally may be involved in a life-and-death struggle.

Although these mutual commitments are not identical, therefore, they are roughly proportional to each nation's ability and interests. Ways to increase these obligations might include the following:

1. *Upgrade or expand the legal commitments involved.* For example, the United States might formally pledge to provide specified assistance if an ally were attacked, or our Pacific allies might agree to treat an attack on the United States elsewhere in the world as a *casus foederis.* Given the unfashionableness of formal treaties noted above, however, this expedient is unlikely over the decade.[14]
2. *Have an ally promise informally to perform specific defense tasks if the United States were attacked.* For example, it might agree to the use of local facilities or overflight by U.S. armed forces in specified contingencies. This would be less risky than the first option but would still increase allied commitments in a public way that would alter the perceptions on which deterrence is based. Indeed, such a limited commitment might seem more credible (and therefore be more effective) than a broader one.
3. *Change the physical role played by each player in defense of the region.* The U.S. effort to persuade the Japanese to assume responsibility for local air defense and sea lane protection out to 1,000 miles from the home islands is especially apposite here. First, the resulting deployment of Japanese forces may place Japan where it is more likely to be involved in a regional conflict between the United States and the Soviet Union than it would be under the 1960 treaty. Second, Japan's upgraded association with U.S. defense efforts in the Pacific would strengthen the perception of alliance cohesion so important to deterrence. As other American allies in the region develop greater economic capacity, opportunities may develop for them to play similar expanded defense roles as well. Growth in allied military capability, however, may pose dangers to interregional peace and stability. In addition, some allies will be able to assume a greater role only after substantial further investment of U.S. aid and assistance, and expanded local responsibilities will mean some loss of U.S. control. Indeed, too great a shift of defense burdens could loosen the bonds of the alliance rather than strengthen them.
4. *Increase U.S. forces in the region (possibly acquiring new bases) and increase military and economic assistance to our allies.* This

of course depends on growth in American economic and military power and also on the interregional balance of Soviet military deployments. If we postulate that Soviet power will continue to grow (although probably at a reduced rate) during the decade and that the Reagan military modernization program will not be realized fully (in light of recent trends in congressional attitudes and the fact that since World War II, U.S. defense expenditures have never risen more than three years in a row[15]), then it seems likely that the ratio of military strength between the two superpowers will not change appreciably in the decade to come. If so, a relative increase in U.S. forces in the Pacific would presuppose a comparative drawdown in the Atlantic, difficult to justify unless the Soviets significantly change their allocation of forces or the European allies substantially increase theirs.

In fact, it is easier to imagine a dramatic escalation in the threat level in Europe or the Arabian Gulf, forcing the United States to reduce its Pacific presence, than to project significant increases in the Pacific. Such a move would definitely effect our relationship with China, which made it clear during the 1970s that it hopes to see a continuation of U.S. commitments in the Pacific as an offset to growing Soviet power there.[16] At the same time, too rapid a U.S. build-up in Asia would give the Chinese more room to maneuver between the superpowers (as their recent discussions with the USSR illustrate) and might cause American allies to relax their own defense efforts. Even in an era of unlimited resources, there is clearly some level of presence beyond which the United States should not go.

5. *Make the whole greater than the sum of its parts by introducing greater cohesiveness into the Pacific alliance structures.* Given the differences in interests among Pacific nations and the variety of threats arranged against them, any effort to create a NATO-like structure for the Pacific region would probably cause more trouble than it would cure. However, creating a loose governmental Pacific Defense Council to better coordinate Pacific defense efforts might help the United States deal with competing interests in the Far East by raising the consciousness of allied leaders about how American and Soviet actions in one part of the region affect events elsewhere. It might also provide an interchange of ideas and establish personal contacts useful for future cooperative efforts, as well as foster an image of cooperation that might add marginally to regional deterrence. On the other hand, one might question the utility in trying to interrelate subregions as diverse as North and

Southeast Asia or the wisdom in reminding local leaders of how thinly stretched American power is.[17]

The Formal Industrialized Allies

How, then, should these techniques be applied to the three obvious categories of Pacific allies? Japan, Australia, and New Zealand are not only the oldest American allies in the Pacific but they are also the ones to whom American formal commitments have remained most vital over the years. As stable, industrialized democracies with capitalist economic systems, these nations have many security interests that complement the United States and also have the greatest potential for increasing their alliance security roles. Despite their importance, these countries face rather low active levels of threat to their security, either inside or outside.

U.S. support for ANZUS defense arrangements should continue to pay dividends far out of proportion to its cost. The Frazier government in Australia has supported U.S. efforts toward a renewed containment of the USSR, offering not only diplomatic support but also staging rights for American ships and aircraft.[18] It has pledged a 7 percent defense increase over each of the next three fiscal years.[19] Moreover, Australia is a country with great natural wealth that will be of increasing value to the Western defense community in the decades ahead.[20]

Japan's sheer economic weight and dynamism make it the key strategic asset in the Pacific. Deterring an attack on Japan will continue to be the most important U.S. security task west of Hawaii. Yet Japan's low level of external threat indicates that U.S. forces remain there for broader reasons—namely, to maintain facilities that would be essential should war occur in East Asia (especially in Korea) and thereby to reinforce everyone's confidence that the United States would respond. Japan has also been forthcoming in support of U.S. positions on issues such as Iran and Afghanistan and has used its economic aid efforts to support other Asian nations of importance to us.[21]

Thus, the level of U.S. military presence in and around Japan is a matter of clear self-interest and bears little relationship to the controversy over whether Japan is doing enough for its own self-defense. The United States will doubtless continue during much of the decade to push Japan to take on more defense tasks, and recent history suggests that the Japanese will respond cautiously, gradually assuming more of the defense burden. In spite of American frustration at the slowness of the process, it is probably in the U.S. interest that it move in a manner calculated not to alarm the Soviets unduly, given the evident horror with which they view the spectre of a full-blown U.S.–Japanese–PRC alliance. Too fast a military expansion of Japan would also disturb other U.S. allies in North and Southeast Asia, not to mention China, where the decades of Japanese expansion are remembered well.[22] The essential task of future U.S. alliance diplomacy regarding Japan will be to ensure that economic frictions do not so erode the psychological foundations of commitment that the credibility on which deterrence rests is compromised.

Korea and Taiwan

If U.S. alliances with Japan and the ANZUS more than pay for themselves, the same can not be said for these two special cases, since they are of far less intrinsic value to the U.S. strategic position. Consistently ruled outside the U.S. defense perimeter by the highest national authorities in the immediate postwar years,[23] Taiwan and South Korea were made American allies in order to shore up U.S. defensive positions as a result of the Korean War. Neither country has a truly representative form of government or the economic weight of Australia or Japan; but each possesses a government freer than the obvious alternative and both have developed dynamic market economies with high levels of U.S. investment. Korea and Taiwan have continued to play a role in U.S. regional policy—perhaps more so than their intrinsic importance would seem to merit.

The United States faces its most serious threat in the Pacific from North Korea, given the presence of American forces on the line of attack into the South. Unfortunately, the Carter troop withdrawal effort demonstrated that the risks of reducing the American presence are far greater than those of staying put. However, in addition to the risks, the costs of staying put are considerable.[24] Moreover, aside from its intrinsic value, South Korea's role in area deterrence is an open question, despite its wartime importance to the defense of Japan. Perhaps the optimal solution over the next ten to twenty years would be a gradual "Koreanization" of the defense effort.[25] Whether the North Koreans will allow such an effort to proceed is problematical, but it should be an important policy goal for U.S. diplomacy vis-à-vis the PRC and the USSR.

Taiwan will continue to be a difficult situation for U.S. policy. On strictly legal grounds, the Taiwan Relations Act (TRA) deliberately provides a deterrent level of support. Moreover, the United States continues to provide arms to Taiwan under the TRA as interpreted by U.S.–PRC understandings of August 1982,[26] and the island remains a major U.S. trading and investment partner. These factors create an indefinable predisposition by the United States to respond to an attack on the island[27] but also strain the U.S.–PRC relationship, a matter of far greater importance to U.S. global as well as regional interests.

If there were a clear and present military threat to Taiwan (as there is to South Korea), then one could argue in favor of continued politico-military ties to the island in spite of their adverse impact on U.S.–PRC affairs. There has been no such threat, however, since at least the early 1970s, a fact demonstrated (in contrast to Korea) by the total withdrawal of U.S. combat forces from Taiwan. Hence, the argument for limiting support of Taiwan to what the PRC relationship will bear is overwhelming.[28] With the formal alliance gone, the U.S. commitment to Taiwan will gradually fade over the next ten to twenty years at no serious detriment to American economic ties, to Japanese confidence in the United States, or to broad deterrence of Soviet aggression in the Pacific.

The ASEAN States

The relationships with the states of ASEAN differ radically from the two groups already considered in three respects. First, only two of these states are really allies of the United States—Thailand under the Manila Pact, and the Philippines with its bilateral U.S. security treaty. Second, although recent U.S. support to ASEAN has been given to enhance security and deterrence in the Pacific, the Association itself is not a security pact and is unlikely to become one. Third, after the end of U.S. involvement in Indochina in 1975, most ASEAN members defined their security policies as internal resistance to insurgency rather than deterrence of outside attack. Although the recent growth in Soviet naval power in the area has attenuated this trend somewhat, many ASEAN states now feel less need for protection via external commitments, while fear of Chinese hegemony (especially in Malaysia and Indonesia) has encouraged efforts at accommodation with Vietnam and the USSR.[29]

Thailand is the only ASEAN state facing a serious external threat, but it is intermittent and thoroughly intertwined with refugee and insurgency problems. Presidents Carter and Reagan have both renewed U.S. pledges to Thai security,[30] and Thailand remains a major Pacific recipient of U.S. security assistance. Yet the level of concrete American political and economic interest is low, a fact reinforced by the American people's registered unwillingness to become involved in defense of another Asian nation so close to the scene of their recent defeat.[31] Indeed, the United States could find itself politically and militarily unable to honor its commitment in case of major attack. Until some broader regional accord can be reached, this may be a case where constructive ambiguity in U.S. policy is desirable.

In the Philippines, the problem is quite different. American bases in Clark and Subic are essential for U.S. power projection in the entire region and vital to the Pacific route to the Indian Ocean and the Arabian Gulf. Relocation of those bases would be difficult and expensive, though some dispersion of American assets to other Pacific locations might be a wise precautionary move. The threat here is internal rather than external, and that problem, like so many in the area, is one that cannot be solved but only managed.

In ASEAN itself, the United States finds perhaps its major opportunity. ASEAN remains primarily a nonmilitary organization, as indicated by the recurrent popularity among its ranks of proposals for neutralization. At the same time, most members of the organization have their own reasons for desiring a continued U.S. defense presence in the area, including the SRV/Soviet presence and various inter-state suspicions that prevent formation of an effective regional security organization. The more explicit the Soviet threat, the more likely the group will continue to welcome the U.S. presence. Conversely, any over-identification of the United States with China or appearance that the U.S.–Chinese relationship is developing into a full-scale alliance would have a negative impact on U.S.–ASEAN ties.

These subregional analyses suggest a three-track U.S. policy over the 1983–1993 period. First, the United States should improve its defense ties and presence in this area, but in a bilateral context. Second, the United States should work through ASEAN to ameliorate internal security problems by means of economic development and pressures for political liberalization. Third, every effort should be made to defuse the Vietnamese threat through dialogue, for only in that fashion can the potential danger in Thailand be reduced. In this regard, a Chinese accommodation with the Soviets over a neutralized Cambodia would be a positive (if unlikely) development for American security interests.[32]

An Alliance with China?

This final security relationship is the central concern of this study. Should the United States make an alliance with the PRC? By "alliance" is meant a strengthened relationship that carries the implication—expressed or implied—that the United States would come to China's defense if attacked and vice versa. Such a relationship would probably include military aid and cooperation, but the United States could supply military hardware without such a pledge (although at some point of military involvement a commitment might logically be inferred). The striking fact about such an alliance is that none of the other U.S. security partners in the Pacific favor it. Although Taiwan and South Korea are probably most opposed to the idea, all of America's Asian friends fear the resurgence of Chinese power and ambition such an alliance might portend. Hence, a Chinese commitment would be doubly expensive, requiring not only U.S. military assistance to China but greatly increased U.S. presence and aid to other Asian allies to balance growing Chinese military power. It may be an exaggeration to say that the United States must choose between its current Pacific security partners and an alliance with China, but progress in mutual defense with current allies would appear to be hampered by such a step.

It is not hard to forecast other difficulties with such an arrangement. Fundamental would be its polarizing effect on the politics of South and Southeast Asia, where opportunities for growth in U.S. influence (or at least a dilution of Soviet alliance-building efforts) may well become apparent over the next decade. Although the United States would consider a Chinese alliance solely in the context of its global effort to contain Soviet power, it would be difficult to persuade states like India or Vietnam that the Chinese did not intend the alliance to be directed against them. The result might be an increase in tensions on the periphery of China with serious effects on internal stability and international security. In other words, if U.S. goals in the Pacific include the maintenance of general peace and security as well as containment of Soviet power, an alliance with China might well subvert the first more than it served the second.

Is there good reason for such an alliance anyway? Would it achieve the confidence- and deterrence-building purposes of an alliance? A militarily stronger China would provide some added deterrence against a Soviet attack, but only at the cost of added insecurity for the United States. Second, whatever contribution a U.S. promise to defend might make to China's own sense of security and confidence would seem to be minor, given the enormity of internal factors affecting the same level of confidence. Third, even if a Chinese promise to treat an attack on the United States as an attack on herself were to help deter Soviet aggression against the United States, such a pledge would go far beyond the norm in U.S. Pacific alliances. It is extremely unlikely, in fact, that a U.S.–Chinese alliance could be made truly reciprocal.

Finally, it should be noted that there has not been a general war between the Russians and either the Chinese or the Americans since the nuclear age began. An attack on either would be a decision of incalculable consequence for the Soviets, and it is hard to see how the perceptual factors weighing against such a decision could be strengthened by an alliance that would be extremely provocative to the Soviets. Moreover, the history of U.S. policy toward China has never shown an American willingness to fight on behalf of Chinese territorial integrity, either against the partitioning European powers in the nineteenth century or against the Japanese in the twentieth century. Nothing indicates that U.S. public opinion could be brought to lend credibility to a Chinese alliance today.

Despite these conditions, there are those who argue that such an alliance is necessary to prevent deterioration in U.S.–Chinese relations or even an eventual PRC rapprochement with the USSR and that the relationship must continue to move forward or else slide backward. If so, this relationship would be utterly different than other international contacts that ebb and flow in response to international and internal developments within parameters set by the coincidence of their overall interests.[33] The United States and China have a fundamental common interest in the containment of Soviet power, independent of their respective foreign policies. Their "passive coalition" is likely to endure and even prosper without alliance, unless one side or the other forgets where its true interests lie and, through mismanagement, foregoes the innate advantages of today's global pattern of alignments.

CONCLUSIONS

If the United States is to overcome its off-again, on-again approach to its Pacific security partners, U.S. policy must be set at levels sustainable for the long run. Yet more is required than simply increasing or reallocating U.S. commitments and resources. Creative approaches to and dialogue with the states to be deterred are needed. Thus, the paradox of a successful commitment policy must combine increased security ties with renewed efforts at dialogue and accommodation.

These tasks can be more effectively accomplished by a cooperative rather than strident leadership style by the United States. The lower level of threat faced by the United States and most of its allies in the Pacific than in the Atlantic provides the opportunity for emphasis on the service that security commitments can provide as a guarantor of a stable environment—in which allies' economic and socio-cultural interests can be pursued. American alliance policy in the Pacific ought more than in Europe to center on the economic, political, and diplomatic instruments of policy. The road to security for the Pacific, especially for its developing American security partners, lies in good and prosperous governments. Supporting indigenous efforts in that direction may well be the most efficient contribution the United States can make to extended deterrence in the Pacific region.

NOTES

1. For an up-to-date look at these treaties, see Department of State, "United States Collective Defense Arrangements," Special Report No. 81 (Washington, D.C.: Government Printing Office, April 1981).
2. NATO, of course, was the model of this type. See Alan K. Henrikson, "The Creation of the North Atlantic Alliance, 1948–1952," *Naval War College Review* 32 (May–June 1980):4–39.
3. The various factors that contribute to the existence of a security commitment are examined in Terry L. Deibel, *Commitment in American Foreign Policy: A Theoretical Examination for the Post-Vietnam Era,* National Security Affairs Monograph Series 80-4 (Washington, D.C.: National Defense University Press, 1980).
4. *Washington Post* (June 12, 1977) suggested that Carter's foreign policy advice on Korea resulted from fears that Korea might become his own Vietnam.
5. Richard H. Solomon, "American Defense Planning and Asian Security: Policy Choices for a Time of Transition," in Solomon, ed., *Asian Security in the 1980s: Problems and Policies for a Time of Transition* (Santa Monica, Calif.: RAND Report R-2492-ISA, November 1979), p. 19.
6. For example, the Stevens amendment reducing U.S. troop levels in Europe. U.S. Congress, House Appropriations Committee, "FY 1983 Defense Appropriations Bill," Report 97–980 (December 20, 1982) 94: *Washington Post* (December 21, 1982), p. A4.
7. U.S. Congress, House Committee on Foreign Affairs, *Collective Defense Treaties* (Washington, D.C.: Government Printing Office, 1969), pp. 218–221.
8. Only in South Korea does the United States have a combined command relationship similar to that with NATO.
9. The Malaysians and the Indonesians, for example, each have sizeable ethnic Chinese populations, a fact which makes them look upon a strong Vietnam opposed to China as an important buffer state, desirable even at the expense of a loose Vietnam–USSR alliance. Richard H. Solomon, *Choices for Coalition Building: The Soviet Presence in Asia and American Foreign Policy Alternatives* (Santa Monica, Calif.: RAND Report P-6572, April 1981), p. 75.
10. Solomon, "American Defense Planning," p. 21.
11. William R. Freeney, "U.S. Defense Interests in the Pacific," *Current History* 81 (April 1962): 145–147. Indeed, one might say that defense choices are easy in the case of vital interests, especially when the costs of defense are low and relatively easy in the case of secondary interests facing little threat or defended at low cost; but they become extremely difficult when a secondary interest is faced by a high level of threat or defendable at high cost, or both.
12. See "Comparative Chart of Certain Provisions of Regional Collective Security Agreements," U.S. Congress, House Committee on Foreign Affairs, *Collective Defense Treaties* (Washington, D.C.: Government Printing Office, 1969), pp. 218 ff.
13. Harold C. Hinton believes that the U.S.–Japanese treaty is particularly asymmetrical, given the lack of Japanese obligation to defend the United States or U.S.

interests in the Western Pacific. See "The United States and Extended Security Commitments: East Asia," *The Annals* 457 (September 1981): 104.

14. Executive agreements might seem to provide a way out, but in fact no matter of such importance could be concluded without congressional approval. And on the Pacific side, the Japanese domestic reaction to two prime ministers' use of words like "alliance" and "unsinkable aircraft carrier" (in reference to Japan's defense relationship with the United States) highlights local sensitivities to closer American ties. Also, the Japanese constitution prohibits coalition warfighting.

15. Charles W. Kegley, Jr. and Eugene R. Wittkopf, "The Reagan Administration's World View," *Orbis* (Spring 1982): 241.

16. The PRC attitude included South Korea. Hinton, pp. 93, 98.

17. Perhaps with these statements in mind, former Secretary of State Cyrus Vance has proposed formation of an informal, nongovernmental " 'Pacific Roundtable'— composed of leaders and experts from the private sector across the entire Pacific" as a useful first step. See Vance, "American Foreign Policy for the Pacific Nations," *International Security* 5 (Winter 1980–1981): 13.

18. "Australia's Leader Offers United States Staging Facilities at Naval Bases," *Washington Post* (February 2, 1980).

19. Department of Defense, "Congressional Presentation: Security Assistance Programs FY 1983," p. 53.

20. Joseph M. Siracusa, "Australian–American Relations, 1980: A Historical Perspective," *Orbis* 24 (Summer 1980): 271–287.

21. Vance, p. 8.

22. John Stirling, "ASEAN: The Anti-Domino Factor," *Asian Affairs* 7 (May–June 1980): 286.

23. Ernest R. May, "Korea, 1950: History Overpowering Calculation," in *"Lessons" of the Past* (London: Oxford University Press, 1973), pp. 52–86.

24. South Korea gets more than double the FMS financing of any other Asian country and is number three in the region in IMET. "Congressional Presentation," p. 51.

25. For applicable techniques, see Deibel, "A Guide to International Divorce," *Foreign Policy* 30 (Spring 1978): 17–35.

26. Department of State, "U.S.–China Joint Communiqué," *Current Policy* 413 (August 1982).

27. Henry Rowman contends that the U.S. commitment to defend the people of Taiwan "effectively remains." American Security Interests in Northeast Asia," *Daedalus* 109 (Fall 1980): 82.

28. Just what the relationship *will* bear is a matter of debate, but Michel Oksenberg indicates that Taiwan has been one of three critical factors affecting the state of U.S.–PRC relations since 1972. "Reconsiderations: A Decade of Sino–American Relations," *Foreign Affairs* 61 (Fall 1982): 175–195.

29. Sheldon W. Simon, "The ASEAN States: Obstacles to Security Cooperation," *Orbis* 22 (Summer 1978): 415–435. See also Stirling, *op. cit.*

30. Edward Walsh, "Thailand Prime Minister Is Given Security Reassurance by President," *Washington Post* (February 7, 1979).

31. George H. Gallup, *The Gallup Poll: Public Opinion, 1972–1977*, Vol. 1, 1972–1975 (Wilmington, Del.: Scholarly Resources, 1978), pp. 468–490.

32. The PRC has apparently raised this issue with the USSR in their current "renormalization" talks. *Washington Post* (January 18, 1983).

33. For one view of the parameters of U.S.–PRC and PRC–Soviet relations, see Donald S. Zagoria, "A Triangle in Flux: Gauging the Sino–Soviet Thaw," *The New Leader* 65 (November 29, 1982): 3–5.

PART V

Perspectives Of Key Actors

Chapter 16

Africa, Middle East, And Latin America

*Jeffrey Gayner**

Since the Bandung Conference of 1955, China has been conscious of its relationship with the Third World and has gradually developed a unique tripartite analysis of the world in the aftermath of its split with the Soviet Union. In 1974, Mao tersely expressed this perspective:

> In my view, the United States and the Soviet Union form the first world. Japan, Europe, and Canada, the middle section, belong to the second world. We are in the third world. . . . With the exception of Japan, Asia belongs to the Third World. The whole of Africa belongs to the Third World, and Latin America too.[1]

This theory prominently arose at the Sixth Special Session of the U.N. General Assembly later the same year. Within the United Nations and other international forums, China has consistently attempted to speak and act as a revolutionary communist regime, an emerging world power, and a third world developing country. This has invariably led to various reactions among most of the non-Communist third world regimes. China's support on any specific issue has been welcomed by

*Counselor for International Affairs, Heritage Foundation.

other developing countries, whether in economic clashes in the North-South dialogue with the developed Western countries or in denunciations of Soviet military aggression in places such as Afghanistan. Nonetheless, China has stayed independent of leading Communist and non-Communist powers and has thus been viewed as a unique player in international relations. According to Michael Yahuda:

> China's international position suggests very much a picture of a country whose political system is perhaps one of the most autonomous in the world, and of a country which internationally is untrammeled by the kind of inter-dependencies and alliance systems which limit the freedom of manoeuvre of other major powers.[2]

As China developed a working relationship with the United States over the past decade, it concommitantly made a dramatic increase in a wide range of diplomatic, economic, and political relations with other Western countries. This substantially altered China's previous status as a unique political entity in the Third World that consciously remained very distant from both sides of the East-West conflict, at least in the years since the Sino–Soviet split. Most third world nations generally accepted China's changing status as simply a more mature role being played by Beijing in the world. Also, at least in terms of growing economic relations, it coincided with the growth of trade and economic transfers between Western nations and nearly all third world countries.

Although many third world countries continue to exhalt their close working relations with the PRC in political rhetoric, the reality of such relations reveals little substance. In recent years most third world countries have placed less importance on their relations with the PRC and consequently are less concerned about Sino–U.S. relations.

AFRICA

Outside of Asia, China has always had its largest and most important third world relations with sub-Saharan African countries. In particular, Chinese foreign assistance programs have been directed at establishing better relations with African countries in the period of decolonization. For many years the Chinese fiercely competed with the Soviets for influence over various countries, and, in the case of southern Africa, the two Communist powers even supported warring factions.

In recent years the Chinese assistance programs have diminished substantially, as has their influence. The legacy of some of their aid programs, however, remains important. The most ambitious assistance program ever undertaken by Beijing involved the $413 million Tan-Zam railroad project that was designed to provide an alternative transportation route for black African countries to use in order to avoid commercial dependence on South Africa. Although the railroad has not functioned very efficiently in recent years, it is still hailed by leaders in the area. In July 1982, for example, President Kenneth Kaunda of Zambia expressed his continued appreciation for this project: "We cannot forget that other countries refused to bail us out in building an alternative route to the sea. But China gave and built for us Tazara, which is the pride of Africa." He also praised Chinese military assistance to Zambia during the conflict with Rhodesia: "Historians will recall that when Zambia was under siege, China gave us arms." Finally, he hailed "Chinese leadership and people in liberating themselves and their help in liberating hundreds of millions of other people. China was one of the biggest opponents of fascism, colonialism, neocolonialism, and apartheid."

China does not usually receive such lavish praise from African leaders, although they do express their appreciation for what assistance Beijing provides them. Overall asisstance from China has fallen substantially from its peak of $1,124 million in 1970 to one-tenth of that amount a decade later, with small programs in twenty-five countries. Nations have found that however enthusiastic moral support has been from the PRC in their various liberation struggles, the Soviet Union has often provided much more substantive support. In the late 1970s, the PRC lost most of her ideological struggle with the Soviets in southern Africa.

Although countries in Africa may no longer look to China to play a decisive role in their future, they nonetheless indicate a willingness to work with Beijing as a fellow third world nation. China's policy pronouncements of not interfering in the internal affairs of other countries are taken seriously in Africa. Thus, there is far less suspicion of the PRC than of the Soviet Union or the United States. Countries have been more willing to establish diplomatic relations with Beijing, for example, than with Moscow.

The limits of the Chinese role in Africa parallel the view African countries have, of U.S.–China relations. During the 1970s, nearly all African countries that had diplomatic relations with Taipei terminated them in favor of Beijing. Thus, they welcomed the establishment of full diplomatic relations between Washington and Beijing. Since 1979, most countries have not indicated any concern about the precise character of that relationship.

Only a few countries in Africa have particularly close relations with the United States *and* China. Thus, Robert Mugabe, Prime Minister of Zimbabwe (who has received significant aid from both countries), welcomes closer relations between the United States and China in the future. Tensions in U.S.–PRC relations could have a debilitating effect on Zimbabwe's efforts to avoid undue Soviet influence. Kenya, especially sensitive to potential conflict in the Horn of Africa, also appreciates the value of U.S.–PRC relations in terms of the broader East-West conflict.

The Republic of South Africa is possibly the principal African political player that takes not only cognizance but action as a result of U.S.–China relations. Although it is only a third world country in terms of per capita income and location, South Africa has established increasingly close relations with Taiwan due to the fact that both nations suffer from political isolation. Taiwan increased trade more rapidly between 1977 and 1981 with South Africa than with any other country in the world, rising from $118 million to $690 million. After the PRC displaced Taiwan in most capitals of Africa, Taipei set up formal diplomatic relations with South Africa. If the United States were to simultaneously take additional actions to threaten the continued integrity of Taiwan and were to put pressure on South Africa, the Taipei-Pretoria relationship would grow substantially. Nuclear cooperation is even possible, although both governments deny this.

MIDDLE EAST AND NORTHERN AFRICA

In North Africa and the Middle East the PRC has done a moderately effectively balancing act in dealing with the conflicting forces in both areas. It has maintained particularly good relations with key U.S. allies in the area, such as Morocco and the Sudan. The dean of the African diplomatic corps in Beijing is Ambassador Abderrahim Harkett from Morocco. He recently summarized very well the general perspective of both African and Middle East countries toward Beijing:

> The People's Republic of China and the Chinese people have always granted an effective support to the African liberation movements as well as their disinterested assistance to African countries for the development of their national economy. The government of the People's Republic of China endeavors to defend in international meetings the African cause and that of third world countries fighting for a more just and better balance new international economic order.[3]

In 1981 the vice president of Sudan, General 'Adib al-Majid Hamid Khalil, visited the PRC and signed agreements including economic, cultural, and military relations. He also praised China for bringing great strength to the Third World and indicated that Sudan and China had "identical" views on key foreign policy issues, such as the withdrawal of Soviet forces from Afghanistan and Vietnamese forces from Kampuchea. The PRC indicated its appreciation for close Sudanese relations with a $57 million interest-free ten-year loan, its largest single aid venture in recent years.

Other countries in the area that have had especially good relations with the PRC are Tunisia, Egypt, and North Yemen. On the other hand, the more left-leaning Arab states (such as Libya and Algeria) maintain cordial relations with the PRC but have more limited bilateral cooperation programs in economic and trade areas.

Saudi Arabia still maintains diplomatic relations with the Republic of China (Taiwan) and thus represents one of the most significant failures of Chinese policy in the Middle East. The Saudi relationship to Taiwan is second only in importance to Taipei's relations with Washington. Although there is little prospect of change in Saudi policy in the future, Riyadh carefully monitors U.S. China policy, and Beijing may hope that the United States will encourage a change in Saudi policy.

In general, Middle Eastern countries do not perceive China as a significant element in the years ahead. As Edward E. Azar has written, "Only during the 1963–1973 period have the Chinese played any visible role in the area, and even then that role was marginal." His conclusion about the future, written three years ago, appears as valid today: "The influence of . . . China in the Middle East will not grow significantly in the foreseeable future. Indeed. . . . [it] may even diminish further."[4]

LATIN AMERICA

Of the various areas of the Third World, the PRC has always had its most limited relations with countries in Latin America. Until the United States normalized relations with Beijing, very few countries in this area had diplomatic relations with the PRC. Even today, half of the twenty-five countries that still recognize Taiwan are in Latin America. Most Central American countries maintain relations with Taiwan.

Several important Latin American nations have indicated increasing interest in expanded trade and other economic relations with the PRC. Brazil, for example, established its first joint economic venture with the PRC in late 1981 under the sponsorship of Brazilinvest, which has an operating office in Beijing. But Brazil, like other free-market economies, has experienced problems in dealing with the PRC. When the Chairman of Brazilinvest commented on marketing possibilities, he stated, "It is very difficult, for example, to export large volumes of nonperishable consumer goods in view of the marketing method used in the PRC which does not allow direct purchase. The Chinese citizen must obtain a coupon at the shop and his name is registered on a waiting list."[5] Nonetheless, trade is projected to grow from $400 million in 1981 to $1 billion by 1985. Oil purchases by Brazil, now running about 70,000 barrels per day, are expected to rise significantly under an agreement reached in May 1982.

A similar growth in commercial relations has occurred with Mexico. Regular meetings of the Mexico–China joint economic committee take place, and trade has risen to $100 million. As with Brazil, no parallel growth has taken place in political relations.

The most curious PRC relationships in Latin America exist with two of the most disparate countries: Chile and Nicaragua. Ever since the overthrow of the Allende government and the break in diplomatic relations between Chile and the Soviet Union, Beijing has had extremely close relations with Santiago. Their common anti-Soviet attitude has led to frequent political exchanges in which they assert firm support for the principles of nonintervention and opposition to hegemonism. Despite radically differing political and economic systems, the two countries seem to reflect a deeper level of cooperation with the PRC than has any other country in Latin America. A joint Chilean–PRC commercial concern, signed in late 1981, was the first such agreement by Beijing with any Latin American country. Private Chilean businessmen will now market machinery produced by PRC state corporations throughout Latin America. From 1977 to 1980, overall trade rose by 368 percent, reaching $134 million.

On the other hand, despite the triumph of a Marxist revolutionary movement in Nicaragua, the PRC has not been able to displace Taiwan as the official Chinese representative in Managua. PRC Vice Minister of Foreign Trade, Wang Runsheng, travelled to Managua following an extensive meeting in Santiago and could only talk vaguely of improving commercial relations with Nicaragua. Thus, contact with Nicaragua has been limited to some economic relations.

In general, Latin American nations remain rather indifferent to the PRC and consequently have ignored the status of U.S. relations with Beijing. Those countries that do not have relations with the PRC (such as El Salvador and Guatemala) do not believe that Beijing can help them, particularly given China's rhetorical support for revolution. Thus, more countries in Latin America than in any other region are either indifferent to or, in some cases, dismayed by U.S. neglect of Taiwan as U.S. relations develop with Beijing.

CONCLUSION

The relationship of third world countries with the PRC is not affected by the character of U.S.–PRC relations. Once the Shanghai Communiqué was issued and the PRC was admitted to the United Nations, the United States ceased lobbying third world countries about their Chinese policies.

While China has improved relations with Washington in the last decade, it has diminished its influence in the Third World, although no connection exists between the two developments. In terms of political and military relations, China now figures much less prominently in third world affairs than it did five years ago. As indicated in this brief review, few third world leaders make pilgrimages to Beijing any more, and Chinese leaders seldom visit third world countries. Instead, political contacts are on a much lower level now.

Only in the areas of trade and other economic relations has growth continued in Third World–PRC relations. This is true even though third world countries realize that China cannot substantially contribute to the resolution of such problems. Thus, Chinese trade and limited aid are welcome but are of only marginal importance.

Overall, existing and prospective Chinese relations with the Third World (particularly outside of Asia) will remain relatively limited. In recent years, China has reemphasized relations with third world countries as a central component of her foreign policy. But at the same time third world countries have recognized that China has only a very limited capacity to influence their economic, political, or military affairs. Thus, China's role in Asia, Africa, and the Middle East will continue to be marginal and the nature of Washington-Beijing relations will have virtually no impact on the foreign policies of these third world governments.

Chapter 17

Japan

*Gaston J. Sigur**

To discuss Japanese perceptions of the emerging U.S.–China strategic relationship, we must understand that there is not just one Japanese perception but several, as one would expect in a pluralistic society. But there are certain views that seem to reflect the majority of Japanese thinking and, in particular, the thinking of those who make and influence policy in Tokyo. These are the views that will subsequently be referred to as the perceptions of "the Japanese."

Since 1952, the Japanese have had a continuing relationship with the PRC. Until 1972, this relationship was an economic rather than political one, and Japan maintained its diplomatic recognition of the Republic of China government on Taiwan. With the U.S.–China rapprochement of 1971, Japan moved rapidly to establish full relations with China and did so in September 1972.

The Japanese seemed anxious to use the improved political atmosphere in Beijing to strengthen and broaden economic ties. Japanese businessmen, like their American counterparts, were euphoric about what they professed to see as almost unlimited economic opportunity for profit in the vast China market. By 1982, a more realistic attitude

*National Security Council staff member.

had replaced this somewhat overly sanguine appraisal, and Japanese government and business, while moving ahead with economic ventures of various kinds and dimensions with China, have since then lowered their expectations of quick and unqualified successes in this area.

As the two most active free enterprise nations operating in China, the United States and Japan are naturally competitive in certain aspects of their economic relations with Beijing. Businessmen in both countries are seeking to make the most productive deals with the Chinese, sometimes at the expense of one another. But this competitiveness on the economic side does not reflect any Japanese desire to see U.S.–China relations become less friendly. Quite the contrary is true. The Japanese clearly believe that the strengthening of U.S.–China ties will contribute to the furtherance of good Japanese–Chinese relations.

Japan (as does the United States) wants to see China pursue policies that will contribute to Chinese internal stability and a healthy economy. The modernization and administrative reform campaign now underway in China is the Chinese leadership's way of moving to achieve these goals. U.S. and Japanese assistance is desirable if these goals are to be attained in the shortest possible time.

The Japanese assessment of China's prospects for success in modernization and reform is cautious. China's difficulties and problems are legion, and a long, hard road lies ahead (even if the best of circumstances obtain). For the Japanese, this means that Chinese participation and influence in regional and global affairs is likely to be of quite a limited nature, as China concentrates on putting her own house in order in the immediate years ahead.

In the long run, however, Japan is concerned about the growth of Chinese power and the possible use of this power to extend Chinese influence in the Asian and Pacific region. Japan does not quarrel with the concept of strategic cooperation with China in a global sense but has some apprehensions about how this cooperation is to be put into effect in regional terms. A powerful China could conceivably act counter to Japanese interests in East Asia and could diminish to a significant degree the role that Japan wishes to play in the region.

In this regard, Japan also takes into account the attitudes of the non-Communist states in Southeast Asia—those belonging to the Association of Southeast Asian Nations (ASEAN). These countries are especially conscious of the possible emergence of a China with the potential, the will, and the determination to assume a dominant position in Southeast Asia. What will this mean for the future of these states and for the governments that are presently in power? In political and economic terms, what effect would this kind of development have on the relations of the ASEAN states with Japan? Japan has spent a great deal of time and money to better its ties with the Philippines, Indonesia, Singapore, Malaysia, and Thailand. The Japanese intend to spend much more in the coming years. It would not be in Japan's interest (as some argue) to have to engage in a competitive or confrontational policy with an increasingly powerful China in Southeast Asia.

In the long term, the Japanese express concern over the possibility that China will seek to develop a military establishment with a major potential for offensive action. The Japanese hope that the United States will not participate in aiding such a program on the part of China. This is not to suggest that the Japanese see any indication that the current leadership of China is about to embark on such a course, for such is not the case. Nor do the Japanese believe that the United States would ever consciously help China in going down this path. Given China's enormous size, population, and raw materials base, the Japanese think that they cannot totally dismiss the possibility of a more aggression-minded and armed China in the years to come.

Of more immediate concern to Japan is the attitude of the Soviet Union toward a close strategic relationship between the United States and China. For years the Soviet Union has warned, both publicly and privately, that it will do everything it can to discourage just such a relationship from developing. The Soviets have bluntly told the Japanese on numerous occasions not to abet "American designs" in this regard. At least to show in part how serious they are in this matter, the Soviets have (as is well known) deployed great quantities of men and material in Soviet Asia. Some of these are presently in certain northern territories, the possession of which is in dispute between Japan and the Soviet Union. Whatever the reason for the Soviet land and naval build-up in Asia and the Pacific, the Japanese do not want to exacerbate what they see as an inherently dangerous situation. In other words, they want the United States to proceed with caution in its strategic relationship with China and to take into account possible Soviet retaliatory measures.

The Japanese also want the U.S.–China relationship to develop in such a manner that it does not adversely affect the U.S.–Japan alliance. The alliance with the United States is central to Japanese foreign policy. It is essential that this relationship be maintained and strengthened over the years if Japan's broad foreign policy objectives are to be attained. Japan does not want the U.S.–China relationship to detract from the U.S.–Japan one. As the Japanese see it, this latter relationship is very special and must remain so if Japanese national interests are to be best served.

In sum, Japan wants U.S.–Chinese relations to continue to improve within certain parameters, such as those referred to above. The Japanese believe that care must be taken by both the United States and China if this is to take place without unduly disrupting (but indeed serving the interests of) peace and security in the Asian and Pacific region.

Chapter 18

Southeast Asia

Leonard Unger*

For many centuries, ever since Chinese rule was extended into what are now its southernmost provinces of Yunnan, Guangxi, and Guangdong, the peoples of Southeast Asia have looked mostly with apprehension at their giant neighbor to the north. The Chinese Emperors regarded the early states of Ava, Pagan, Srivijaya, Ayuthaya, Lang San, Kampuchea, and others (forerunners of today's Burma, Indonesia, Thailand, Laos, etc.) as tributary states, even though they were permitted their independence for the most part. Vietnam, however, was held directly under Chinese rule for about a thousand years, leaving the fear of an expansionist China that has preoccupied the Vietnamese ever since. In recent centuries, European nations usurped China's role in Southeast Asia while China itself wrestled with Western intrusions.

China continued, however, to influence the ASEAN countries through the thousands of its sons (and some daughters as well) who worked the plantations and mines and provided an otherwise largely nonexistent trading element in the cities and towns of the region. Thus, the entrepreneurial city-state of Singapore is 75 percent Chinese, Malaysia with its plantations is almost 40 percent Chinese, and in Indonesia, Thailand, and the Philippines, 3 to 5 percent of the population is still identifiable as unassimilated Chinese. The Chinese population in

*Former U.S. Ambassador to Taiwan.

359

these areas is concentrated in the large cities and provides much of the personnel for each country's commercial and financial sectors.

Once the PRC was established as the government in Beijing in 1949, a new relationship opened up with what are now the five ASEAN countries. This relationship was characterized by caution and apprehension on the part of the latter as they feared the pressures a resurgent and possibly expansionist China might exert—particularly the backing that the new China was bound to give to revolutionary forces in their own homelands. They feared the Trojan Horse potential of their Chinese minorities, for each of the ASEAN countries had its Chinese and sometimes North Vietnamese-supported insurgency.

When the United States rejected the new Communist regime in China, two of the ASEAN nations, Thailand and the Philippines—those geographically closest to China—supported American policy and also maintained their relations with the government now on Taiwan. The other three broke with Taiwan and established ties with the PRC, a course of action consistent with their general "third world" and sometimes neutralist identifications. But they all continued to have their apprehensions about the Mainland giant. Thus, the establishment of U.S.–PRC relations was a welcome stabilizing development but also one which created some new concerns.

AREAS OF FUTURE MUTUAL INTEREST

Looking ahead, neither China nor the ASEAN countries want to see the Soviet Union's influence and/or presence in East Asia or the Western Pacific expanded or strengthened in any way. Real as the apprehensions of some ASEAN countries are about the PRC and its intentions in their direction, they are little tempted by the idea of the USSR as a counterweight (although this might be less true if the United States and Australia were to foreswear any security role in the region). Furthermore, the ASEAN countries would like to see Japan's security role (which they would like to see expanded) concentrated in East Asia and the West Pacific but not in the South China Sea.

Specifically, ASEAN wants to be sure that the sea routes connecting East Asia and the West Pacific with the Indian Ocean are kept open. Japan, Korea, and Taiwan, as well as the PRC, all share this objective. A substantial share of the fuels for their energy requirements must pass through the Malacca, Sunda, Lombok, and Macassar straits, as well as the substantial commerce they have with Western Europe.

The PRC and its ASEAN neighbors will continue to share the fundamental objective of keeping Southeast Asia as free as possible from any regime dominated by or heavily responsive to the Soviets. While the ASEAN nations all maintain normal and superficially friendly ties with the USSR, they are distrustful of Soviet motives. Cooperative and open relations with the Soviets would not survive if one of the ASEAN nations were to come under Soviet influence. The PRC would find this equally alarming because of the jeopardy to its own security.

As Indochina moved in recent years into an increasingly close relationship with the USSR, the PRC and the ASEAN countries (particularly Thailand) perceived their security diminished, especially as the Soviets used that relationship to establish military positions at Danang and Cam Ranh Bay. In this same context, the PRC and the ASEAN countries (particularly Thailand) will continue to press for modification of the Vietnamese-dominated regime in Kampuchea. In the United Nations and elsewhere, the PRC and ASEAN will continue to seek jointly to preserve some status for the Kampuchean elements and factions that are more responsive to their views and that are in opposition to the present Phnom Penh government.

The ASEAN countries and the PRC will continue to share another common concern about the exodus, mostly illegal, of hundreds of thousands of refugees from Indochina who arrive on their doorsteps and present difficult political and economic problems. A special group has been the Kampucheans who fled the horrors of Pol Pot and sought asylum overland (at least initially in Thailand) and by ship throughout the ASEAN area. Prior to that time and continuing to this day, there have been the hundreds of thousands of Vietnamese refugees fleeing the political and economic pressures of life in that country. Large numbers of Chinese origin went overland or by sea to neighboring China or Hong Kong while many others, as well as hundreds of thousands of Vietnamese, moved to Thailand, chiefly, and to other ASEAN countries.

The ASEAN nations are intent on accelerating their economic development, particularly in the industrial fields. Since indigenous managerial talent and financing is not presently capable of achieving this development (other than at unacceptably slow rates), the ASEAN nations look above all to Japan and the United States to help provide capital, technological knowledge, and—in the initial stages—some entrepreneurial impetus. The ASEAN nations also depend heavily on the United States and Japan to supply markets for their agricultural, forest, and mineral products and, at a growing rate, for the products of their labor-intensive industries. This is less true of Singapore, with its increasingly sophisticated industrial output, but it still depends on those same markets to significant degree.

Ideologically, China might be expected to look askance at the increasing market and capital orientation of South Asia's economic organization, the growing role of multinational corporations, and so forth. In fact, it probably derives some reassurance from this trend, as it brings about the continuing involvement of Japan and the United States in the region and is thus a built-in obstacle to the development by the USSR of significant influence in any of those countries. Perhaps Beijing also sees the strengthening and expanding of free markets and entrepreneurial groups in the ASEAN countries as giving increased support to the elements in the population who would give the strongest support to anti-Soviet positions.

AREAS OF FUTURE CONFLICTING INTEREST

The PRC will probably continue to project an image of friendship and understanding toward its ASEAN neighbors and an acceptance of the political and economic systems that prevail there, however different they may be from what China itself has chosen. On the other hand, modernization of China's underdeveloped economy increasingly will create demands for Western capital and technology as well as access to Western markets. This will compete with the needs of the ASEAN nations and will potentially exacerbate traditional differences.

Memories are long and strong in all of the ASEAN countries and particularly in Malaysia and Indonesia. Sharp and bitter experiences brought on by Beijing-supported Communist insurgents, insurrectionists, fifth columns, and the like have not been forgotten. Visits by Chinese leaders, including Deng Xiaoping, intended to demonstrate Beijing's benign and entirely friendly attitude, have had some success in Thailand but have gained only limited acceptance further south. In Malaysia, memories go back to the "emergency" of the years after World War II when it was Beijing's support of indigenous, mostly ethnic Chinese insurgents and terrorists that projected a reign of terror and widespread insecurity. For some time this threatened the successful emergence of the new, independent Malaya, later to become Malaysia. Indonesia saw its most determined Communist bid for power in 1965. The conviction remains strong there that China was primarily responsible for what occurred.

Thailand and the Philippines, although less violently affected, have faced similar threats supported by the PRC. The insurgency in Thailand's Northeast, North, and far South were given strong material and vocal support from Beijing for many years. This lasted almost until Chinese high-level emissaries and finally Deng himself made friendship visits during which they sought to identify the real villains as Vietnam and the Soviet Union. Some Thai and other officials remained unconvinced, however, that those dissident elements have been totally abandoned by their former sponsors and supporters.

In the Philippines, the earlier Huk rebellion and agrarian and urban insurgents, some still quite active today, all received more support from China than from any other source. Even today, reassurances from Beijing as to its entirely friendly intentions gain acceptance only slowly. In fact, the PRC faces a dilemma here and in some degree throughout the ASEAN region. It is one not easily resolved and one that poses real problems even for the affected ASEAN countries themselves. Should Beijing abdicate its position with dissident groups, cut off its support, and invite Vietnamese and/or Soviet-supported elements to take over?

Some centuries ago, imperial China asserted its claim to the waters and scattered islands lying within the South China Sea. This is an area bordered (roughly speaking) on the west by Vietnam, on the south by Malaysian and Indonesian territories, and on the east by the Philippines. This body of water has been important since history began as the link connecting East Asia with the "Nan Yang" or Southeast Asia and with the straits that lead to the Indian Ocean and beyond. Today tankers bring Japan around 70 percent of its oil via the South China Sea.

In the vast expanse of the South China Sea there are few significant islands, in terms of land area. There are, however, many reefs and atolls that have long been seen by outside powers, including China, as strategic points to be controlled. And, recently the expectation of finding significant offshore petroleum deposits has arisen.

Here, then, are the seeds of serious disputes among the coastal countries themselves and, perhaps, with others as well. In fact, the PRC has already asserted its rights to the entire South China Sea and has engaged in direct military action with Vietnam—albeit brief and limited—over the Paracel islands. In a political climate like that of the present, China will probably eschew such direct confrontations with the ASEAN coastal states over the decade. This includes confrontations with all of them, to some degree, although the conflicting interests are there and could escalate at almost any time.

Differences with the ASEAN states (other than Singapore) may again arise over the treatment of Chinese minorities. Tensions exist in Thailand and the Philippines, although they are not as great as in Muslim countries such as Malaysia and Indonesia, where communal tensions have produced occasional major crises. Such tensions will inevitably generate conflict with the PRC even though the latter protests that it has no intention of interfering in the internal affairs of these countries.

As we enter the decade, tensions between China and the states of Indochina will continue to run high. Similarly, the ASEAN countries are generally supportive of Thailand's concern about the security threats arising from the Indochina refugee inundations—in particular, from the Vietnamese-dominated regimes in Kampuchea and Laos and from Vietnam itself. Yet the ASEAN countries, in varying degrees, have their reservations about how ready they are to maintain the uncompromisingly hostile posture toward Vietnam that China urges them to take. They do not wish to drive Vietnam further into the arms of the Soviet Union nor to expose themselves to greater PRC pressures resulting from a severely weakened Vietnam.

Since the intentions and likely actions and reactions of the United States will be quite uncertain during the next decade (as contrasted with the much more predictable situation of the 1950s and 1960s), the ASEAN countries will be more circumspect in all regards and, for this reason also, will be reluctant to commit themselves to the extent that the PRC and United States want to an anti-Soviet, anti-Vietnamese policy.

Finally, the Taiwan question could, under some circumstances, generate tensions in ASEAN–PRC relations. While all the ASEAN nations recognize the PRC without reservation, they do have some continuing, regular communication with Taiwan. In some cases they also have important economic connections and in several cases have significant personal ties, military training arrangements, and the like. In the present relatively relaxed circumstances lines are not drawn too tightly or sharply, but if tensions should mount across the Formosa straits and some kind of military solution be threatened for Taiwan, there would be negative repercussions on the PRC's relations with the ASEAN countries.

Chapter 19

NATO Europe

Rainer W. Rupp*

To oppose a perceived anti-Chinese Soviet containment strategy in South and Southwest Asia, the Chinese have developed their own countercontainment strategy, encouraging the build-up of Japanese, American, and NATO–European defense efforts. Indeed, Chinese leaders continue to assert that the principal threat to international security is found in various regions of instability and is directed against NATO rather than against China. But despite frequent Chinese prodding of the West Europeans to be more vigilant concerning the Soviet threat, it is highly unlikely that there will ever be any NATO European government that would seriously consider establishing close cooperation with the Chinese in security or defense matters. Unlike the United States, which considers Chinese opposition to Soviet and Soviet proxy expansionism as an important strategic asset and which views its economic, political, and military relationship with China as a contribution to stability in Southeast Asia, NATO European government sources have carefully avoided making any similar statements. Recognizing Russia's sensitivity on this issue, they avoid moves that could lead to a serious deterioration of relations with the Soviet Union and East European countries.

In this context, it is of particular importance for Americans to understand that since the end of World War II, the major European countries

*Member, Economic Directorate of NATO Headquarters.

have been reduced from world powers to regional middle powers. Consequently, matters of regional security policy are given priority over global considerations. Although crucially dependent on free trade and access to raw materials and their supply security, Western Europe's worldwide trade interests are supported by responsive foreign policies, economic, financial, technical, and military cooperation, and assistance programs, but not through power projection. Unlike the United States, which is separated from the Eastern world by two oceans, Western Europe is an appendix of the Eurasian landmass, which is mostly covered by the Soviet Union. Unlike Europe, the United States as a superpower pursues its policies from a global perspective. As the most important regulatory power on a worldwide scale, a key element of America's foreign policy is power projection. For this purpose, it is also associated (by means of assistance pacts and defense cooperation agreements) with many non-NATO countries, particularly in the Pacific area.

In view of the above, it is easy to understand why European nations consider all relations with the People's Republic of China (PRC) secondary in importance to relations with the Soviet Union and Eastern Europe. With the exception of the United Kingdom's responsibilities for Hong Kong, no other NATO European country has a direct involvement in the Far East. Nevertheless, given the growing importance of the Pacific basin for world trade and the need for stability in this area, there is no NATO European nation that is not interested in the economic, military, or political development of the PRC.

Indeed, all NATO European governments are in favor of improving their economic, cultural, and political relations with the PRC. Since the opening of China to the West the benefits of increased exports to China are only too obvious. But this is not the only reason. Most West Europeans share the view that a Chinese leadership that succeeds in solving its most pressing economic problems and makes progress in the development of the country is less likely to pose major challenges to the international community in the years ahead than a leadership that fails and encounters mounting domestic problems. Therefore, Europeans consider it important to avoid any policy aimed at preventing or slowing China's economic growth. Instead, many West European governments are prepared to assist China economically and financially and thus contribute to the success of the current Western-oriented economic development policies. In view of the magnitude of China's problems, however, prospects that Western aid could make any significant contribution to China's overall development are extremely small.

When Chinese Vice Premier and Minister for Foreign Affairs Huang Hua addressed the European Parliament in Strasbourg in 1980, the occasion provided an ideal opportunity to identify the differences between

European and Chinese expectations about each other's respective role in world affairs. Speaking in flowery terms about the need for greater political and economic cooperation to oppose the common (Soviet) threat, Huang made, in essence, the following points. Although there are differing views between Europe and China about the appraisal of the current international situation, the objective conditions and the factors making for war are growing because of the insatiable (Soviet) hegemonist who threatens the security of Western Europe in particular. Because China and Western Europe are facing a common threat, Huang believes that Western Europe wishes to see a prosperous China and that China for her part wishes to see a united and strong Western Europe. Therefore, friendly relations will surely continue to grow, and China's modernization efforts offer a broad prospect for cooperation.

But Huang also stressed another reason why China would like to see a united and strong Western Europe: Europe could develop an equal partnership with the United States. This smacks strongly of the revised version of the "Three Worlds Theory" in which the "U.S. hegemonist" remains a "hegemonist" although one in decline and therefore the lesser enemy. In this context, it should be remembered that the PRC has continued to accuse the United States of "imperialist" and "hegemonist" behavior toward the Third World, the interest of which China claims to protect in the role of self-proclaimed defender. Therefore, a united and stronger Europe would not only keep the Soviets from shifting their attention to the Far East, but it would also create a useful counterbalance to the United States and reduce the room to maneuver with respect to China and the Third World.

The Europeans, however, show little interest in an increased security relationship with China. Instead, they mainly focus on the commercial potential of the China market and on the possibilities to open it further. There is also a certain wariness about the motivation of China's support for a united and stronger Europe as they fear the purpose of it is to alarm the Soviet Union and thus free China to some extent from the consequences of the growing Soviet military power.

Notwithstanding the views of NATO European nations about specific aspects of China's current and future role in the world, there is a broad consensus that developments in the world's fourth largest economy and the third largest military power cannot be ignored. Although its foreign trade is still only 1 percent of world trade, its imports of capital goods and technology are already sizable and its growing role in the world economy are potentially of great international importance.

The emergence of China and its opening to the West in the second half of the 1970s was a dramatic element in the diffusion of power that contributed to a multipolar world. Already a major regional power in

Asia, China's long-term global policy is seen to be aimed at achieving a major world power status. It will take China some while to exploit this potential role and to make active use of it, for China is still in the process of learning and gaining understanding of the workings of both the international community and its organizations and the interaction structure and administration of modern industrialized societies. Furthermore, the Chinese leadership has been forced to revise significantly its bold and optimistic plans of turning the country into an economic power of the first rank by the end of the century.

The biggest problem facing the current leadership over the decade is the task of meeting the raised hopes and expectations for a higher standard of living of a very large and poor population, which cannot be achieved if it fails to ensure economic stability and growth. Furthermore, demands of special interest groups (such as the military) are likely to lead to more social strain and dissension in the leadership. Additional serious setbacks in the modernization programs and further cuts in defense expenditures could provoke the military to seek a more active involvement in the political and economic decisionmaking process. Combined with the continued widespread resistance to "de-Maoization" among the lower- and middle-ranking cadres and possible popular discontent about unmet economic promises, this could lead again to changes of the economic and political orientation of the country. Such changes would most likely be evolutionary and would not involve a new period of political turmoil, although the latter cannot be completely discounted.

Given the higher priority of the modernization of the civilian sector and the fact that short and medium term economic prospects are not encouraging, defense modernization is likely to be further delayed. Even if China got a massive infusion of foreign defense technology and military aid, the impact on its force capabilities, in counter-Soviet or counter-United States terms, would not become apparent in this decade and probably not during the next. In view of this situation, China will continue to be unable to meet its priority strategic goal of adequate security against the superpowers, especially (under current circumstances) against the Soviet Union.

Most Europeans consider this awkward situation to be the main reason behind China's efforts to foster Japanese, European, and American resolve to hold Soviet "social imperialism" at bay. China's contribution to this process would be primarily moral and rhetorical for China, aware of its weaknesses, has always carefully avoided any action that might provoke a war with the Soviet Union. China's resources are currently focused on the hard domestic issues of economic development, which, if successful, would ensure continuity for the leadership in power. Any erosion of Western economic health or of political unity would, as perceived by the Chinese, have grave implications for China, forcing it to further increase its already heavy defense burden. Any increase of tension between NATO and the Warsaw Pact, however, is likely to ease Soviet pressure on China and Chinese interests.

In order to achieve its long-term strategic aims, China needs time and peace, at least with the superpowers. It also needs foreign assistance in building a modern economy and hence a more valid base for military modernization. For this China has adopted economic and political tactical stances that can be reversed at any time. The most dramatic tactical change had been from close friendship with the Soviet Union and enmity with the United States to a reverse of both these positions and the opening to the West in general (although the Chinese system had few affinities with Western societies). It should be kept in mind that the actual span of undisturbed relations between Moscow and Beijing was a span of only five years, 1949–1954. It is this predilection for seemingly effortless change in direction that demands caution in predicting long-term trends in China, except for the central goal of great power status. China's long-term policy could be summed up as strategic rigidity with tactical flexibility.

Despite this Chinese intransigence, there are few NATO Europeans who would want to deny China its legitimate role in world affairs. They are also prepared to assist China in its economic development but are concerned, like the United States, as to whether Western assistance through commercial and economic relations will overcome Chinese introspection and encourage greater and more constructive Chinese involvement in the international economic community. As the industrial countries increase exports to China, Beijing will exert growing pressure on them to facilitate larger imports from China, which, like those from other developing nations, compete with vulnerable domestic industries. Already the Chinese demands to allow higher imports of Chinese textiles pose certain problems in NATO countries, where they meet opposition from labor unions and business leaders of the industries concerned. Many similar problems will arise as the Chinese attempt to increase exports of labor-intensive products and as industrial nations are compelled to take into consideration the legitimate interests of other developing nations with whom China competes. If the Chinese, however, conclude that their exports are not fairly treated by Western countries, it could have an adverse effect on general economic and political relationships. China's increasing readiness, however, to take account of, and even participate in, established institutional arrangements for resolving international trade questions should lessen the scope for friction in this area.

Apart from the question of arms sales, the most complicated and politically charged issue posed by the improved economic relationship with China are those relating to sales of high technology with possible military application. There is no clear line on such "dual-use" technology, which is needed for economic modernization but also helps to enhance Chinese military capabilities and to lay the foundation for future modernization of the People's Liberation Army. Many arguments are made in favor of relaxing strategic controls on trade with China and the potential commercial advantages are obvious. Politically, such sales are also seen to help strengthen ties with China.

As concerns arms sales, most Europeans are in favor of caution, particularly if it concerns weapons or high technology that can be easily used to improve China's offensive military capabilities. Chinese interests and policies toward many areas, including potential areas of conflict in Southeast Asia, are by no means identical to those of the West or regional non-Communist powers.

The suggestion of closer military cooperation and security relationship, however, meets with a considerable degree of apprehension in Europe. The reason for this is NATO Europe's particular interest in a successful management of START, INF, MBFR, East-West trade, and so forth. For the same reason, Europeans would view with apprehension any close and large-scale Sino–American military cooperation designed to give China an offensive capability because the Soviets would undoubtedly view this as a major step toward an overt alliance against them and because it would become almost impossible to establish the degree of confidence and trust between East and West necessary to arrive at agreements on arms control to which NATO remains committed. Mainly for this reason, Europe continues to consider its relations with China, for all its strategic and economic interests, as secondary in importance to its own security and the classic East-West relationship continues to be of the most vital importance for the foreseeable future.

Chapter 20

Hong Kong

*Richard Nations**

There are two reasons why the prospects for the PRC and the United Kingdom reaching a mutually satisfactory solution to the future of Hong Kong are not encouraging. The first is that the Crown Colony (tribute ceded to foreign victors of the inglorious Opium Wars) remains a lodestone for China's latent xenophobia. The second reason is Taiwan. Permitting the British any substantial role in Hong Kong after its leases expire on the New Territories in 1997 would be difficult for Beijing to reconcile with its own reassurances to Taiwan that the PRC is capable of absorbing Hong Kong's capitalism without doing irreparable harm.

If economic self-interest were the only consideration, Britain and China could probably agree to leave Hong Kong largely as it is. The benefits to London of preserving the status quo in what has become the world's third largest financial center need no elaboration. Hong Kong is London's direct conduit into the most dynamic region in the world economy.

Beijing also has a great deal to gain from allowing Hong Kong's vitality to survive the formal transfer of sovereignty. First, since Hong Kong reflects in microcosm the tangle of legal, commercial, and monetary problems posed by China's own opening to the West, the steps taken in

*Correspondent, *Far Eastern Economic Review*

Hong Kong to settle these matters and preserve investor confidence could convincingly demonstrate the national priority China attaches to its modernization.

Second, China's trade surplus with Hong Kong has grown from HK$13,283 million in 1979 to HK$18,541 million in 1981. This trade contributes heavily to the nearly 40 percent of Beijing's hard currency income that is derived from economic relations with Hong Kong.

Third, since 1970 Hong Kong has moved from twentieth to first position in China's re-export trade, while trade in goods imported for transshipment to China has shown an even more spectacular growth in percentage terms. In 1979 Hong Kong's re-exports to China were up 514.5 percent from 1980 and only fell to 73.3 percent after Beijing's economic retrenchment. The decade ahead promises even further growth.

Fourth, Hong Kong plays an irreplaceable role as a "political filter" for trade with Taiwan, Indonesia, South Korea, Israel, and South Africa. The trade between China and Taiwan through Hong Kong grew remarkably from US$70 million in 1979 to about US$460 million in 1981, and two-way trade between China and South Korea through Hong Kong reached about US$215 million in 1981. Trade from countries with which Beijing has no diplomatic relations accounted for about 40 percent of the goods transshipped into China from Hong Kong in 1981.

Fifth, Hong Kong will continue to play a vital role in China's modernization well into the next century because China's own transport facilities—road, rail, and port—are likely to remain inadequate, despite the heavy emphasis placed on infrastructure in the Five Year Plan (1981–1986) adopted by the National Party Congress (NPC) in November 1982.

Beijing also has sunk roots deep into Hong Kong's commercial soil. Together with its twelve sister enterprises, the Bank of China is estimated to control as much as 40 percent of Hong Kong's financial market. Surrounding the Bank of China's Hong Kong branch is a mushrooming Chinese business presence involving finance houses, trade offices, emporia, property development companies, shipping houses, and insurance companies. Up to fifty Hong Kong companies are thought to be controlled by Beijing, employing tens of thousands. Chinese investments in Hong Kong continue to grow and already exceed US$2 billion, a dramatic increase in Chinese investment in Hong Kong since 1977, when a number of timely land and building purchases were made. (This was just before the market in the Colony skyrocketed.)

China's stake in Hong Kong was the long-presumed argument for preserving the status quo either by Beijing ignoring the 1997 deadline or by a negotiated settlement that would render to China the trappings of sovereignty while leaving the administration essentially in the hands of the British. This is the solution favored in proposals to Beijing by Hong Kong's commercial classes. China's sovereignty could be denoted by such symbols as the Chinese flag flying above the Governor's mansion while, if absolutely necessary, a Chinese-appointed figurehead occupied it. But to secure the all-important confidence of business, the two governments have to secure the integrity of three essential institutions—the Hong Kong dollar, the commercial code, and the administration. The first two of these could be reconciled with Chinese sovereignty by explicit statements confirming the distinctive status of Hong Kong's currency and law and by moving the final authority for each from the Bank of England and House of Lords in London to a newly created monetary authority and court of final appeals situated in Hong Kong itself.

Such a power sharing would have China assert authority without exercising control over an area it claims as an inalienable part of its territory and would oblige Britain to accept responsibility for the affairs of its distant Asian clone without the ultimate power which only sovereignty confers. It would be an arrangement without precedent, different in essentials from the international mandates that governed the free cities of the post-war settlements and far from ideal for either Britain or China. But compromise is of the essence in Hong Kong and, were economics the predominant consideration, there would be no reason to rule out such an agreement.

But 1997 is a point of intersection for broader historical forces likely to overwhelm economic rationality. The Falkland War brought home to Britain the costs of sustaining claims to sovereignty over distant colonial possessions in the face of the burgeoning nationalism of ascendant third world powers. The Sino–U.S. joint communiqué of August 17, 1982, signaled a shift in China's own national priorities away from strategic cooperation with the West and toward assertion of a new nationalism. The divergent courses the two nations were set on in 1982 seemed incompatible with any meaningful power-sharing agreement for Hong Kong.

Viewed from Beijing, Hong Kong has been only one of a host of challenges facing a regime struggling to consolidate itself after a decade of chaos. In the eighteen months before the Thatcher visit, however, a more nationalistic set of priorities matured in Beijing. In 1981 the Chinese leadership observed a favorable shift in the global balance of power. Bogged down in Afghanistan and Poland and on bad terms with the new U.S. administration, Moscow was perceived to redirect its energies toward shoring up its own crumbling perimeters rather than expanding them to encircle China. The diminished Soviet threat in turn diminished the value of "strategic cooperation" with the United States and rendered less tolerable its costs in its relations with Taiwan and the Third World. This set the state for the assertion of a new nationalism appropriate to China's future growth as a world power in its own right. Domestically, this nationalism led to further consolidation of the cautious nation-building pragmatism associated with the country's paramount leader Deng Xiaoping. It is no coincidence that early in 1982 Deng elevated the recovery of Taiwan to one of the highest national priorities for the 1980s.

Hong Kong has always been linked with Taiwan in the official Chinese mind, but the events in 1982 made Hong Kong the "model" for the solution to the Taiwan problem. In the past Chinese officials could dodge the Hong Kong question by merely asserting that Taiwan would be resolved long before 1997 need be addressed. But this became increasingly unrealistic as pressures mounted to take the Hong Kong question up in a serious fashion. First, the hopes for the September 1981 Nine-Point Program—Beijing's major initiative to negotiate Taiwan's reunification—were deflated by Taipei; and a year later, the "Shanghai II" joint communiqué with the United States dispelled what illusions may have lingered in Beijing over the prospects of an early settlement with the Guomindang (KMT). Meanwhile, 1982 was the last year that long term fifteen-year leases could be written under Hong Kong law, since Britain's own lease on the New Territories granted by the Qing Dynasty in 1898 expired in exactly fifteen years time. But the enormous costs of defending British sovereignty in the distant Falklands may have had more to do with the new urgency felt in London to clarify Hong Kong's status. By the time Mrs. Thatcher arrived in Beijing in September 1982, the Chinese had little choice but to contemplate the implications of tackling Hong Kong first.

This time factor introduces a new political imperative into the Hong Kong problem: the Chinese must resolve the future of the Crown Colony—in a manner compatible with its offer to Taiwan—if it is not to play into the hands of opponents who argue that reunification will only mean Taiwan's inevitable demise at the hands of clumsy or devious Communist *apparatchiks*. At the heart of the Nine-Point Program is an offer to leave Taiwan's social and economic life alone if Taipei will acknowledge Beijing's claims to sovereignty over the island. The third of the Nine Points reads: "After the country is reunified, Taiwan can enjoy a high degree of autonomy as a special administrative region. . . . The Central government will not interfere with the local affairs of Taiwan." This proposition was backed up in the new Constitution adopted by the NPC in December 1982. ARTICLE 30 of the Constitution states: "The rules and regulations in force in special administrative zones shall be stipulated by law according to special conditions." Hong Kong's left wing press, which often reflects Beijing's unofficial thinking, interpreted ARTICLE 30 as the legal framework for "free market zones" that would minimize damage to either Taiwan or Hong Kong. ART. 30 and the Taiwan reunification plan gained considerable prominence as reference points for the solution to Hong Kong's future after Deng Xiaoping met with "twelve left wing personages from Hong Kong and Macao" in the Great Hall of the People in July 1982.

This gives Beijing a political motive as well for taking care that the aftershocks of 1997 do not rumple Hong Kong's fragile economy. It also provides an argument bound to gain influence in China's ruling circles against any substantial role for Britain in Hong Kong's new order, however desirable maintaining the status quo may be for the sake of preserving business confidence. To share power with the British would be tantamount to an indirect admission by China that it is incapable of running a free market economy on its own. This in itself would be damaging enough to Beijing's prestige and would devalue the Nine Points accordingly. But any power sharing arrangement in Hong Kong, however artfully it transfers emblems of sovereignty to China, would be read as a tacit acknowledgement that foreign powers are also indispensible in Taiwan, where (it would be argued) the "unofficial relations" with the United States are essential to the island's own distinctive economic and social balance. However unintentional, the timing of the Hong Kong question not only turns it into an undeclared "model" for Taiwan but also saddles Beijing with a first-class paradox for that very reason: China's modernization dictates that every effort be made to preserve Hong Kong's prosperity; but the larger nationalism, which alone can make the Chinese tractable to the inequalities modernization inevitably entails, rules out the one condition—a major British role—most likely to quench private investors' fears of a Communist takeover of Hong Kong. Viewed from Beijing, therefore, the imperatives of the Hong Kong question are straightforward, if perhaps contradictory. China must obtain sovereignty over Hong Kong in substance as well as form and in a manner that will not leach Hong Kong's vitality in the process.

This may not be unacceptable to the British, who may in the long run judge that power sharing is as untenable as asserting claims over distant territories. The position Prime Minister Thatcher staked out during her China visit was criticized in Hong Kong and Britain as rigid adherence to empty legalisms and as insensitive to China's mood. But London left itself room for a graceful disengagement from Hong Kong on grounds of international law by declaring as valid in international law the two nineteenth century treaties—the Treaty of Nanking (1842) and the Convention of Peking (1860)—that ceded Hong Kong island, the southern tip of Kowloon, and Stonecutters Island to Britain in perpetuity. It is generally agreed that the administration of Hong Kong island is not feasible without control of the New Territories. The British position therefore shifts the onus for its presence beyond 1997 to an extension by China of the lease under a treaty—the Convention of Hong Kong (1898)—that Beijing has long declared it does not formally recognize. This in turn puts the British in a position to either compromise or withdraw from Hong Kong on legal principle, if it is decided that there is little advantage in taking responsibility for Hong Kong's affairs with neither the authority nor power to back it up.

Mrs. Thatcher declared that the second negotiating principle is concern for the welfare of Hong Kong's five million people as British subjects. While the Hong Kong Chinese may not be pro-British, local opinion polls conducted in May through June 1982 overwhelmingly affirm their preference for British rule and their aversion to Chinese socialism. Ninety-five percent of those polled preferred a continuation of the status quo, while well over 80 percent indicated that civil and economic liberties such as freedom of choice (86 percent), freedom of speech (83 percent), comfortable living standards (86 percent), and the freedom to make money (82 percent) are essential to the Colony's well-being. No fewer than 22 percent—mostly in the fifteen to thirty-four-year-old age group—said they would "try every means to leave" if Hong Kong were handed to Beijing. A broad swathe of Hong Kong's Chinese will find it hard to reconcile themselves to anything short of full British sovereignty after 1997. Should London decide that it is not in their interest to stay, claims are likely to be used as bargaining counters to secure the best deal possible for both the Hong Kong Chinese and British commercial interests by retaining the currency, the law, and the administration.

Hong Kong, moreover, has an immense potential for tapping the irrational depths of nationalist sentiment in China, not to mention Britain. It is an emotion that the authorities on both sides would prefer to control for negotiating purposes but one that can easily get out of hand. China's rejection of the British claims as products of unequal and therefore invalid treaties is nothing new. Nevertheless, the note of asperity that broke the surface following the Thatcher visit was nonetheless disquieting. And authoritative Chinese commentary accused the British of attempting to "reawaken memories of imperialist humiliation and aggression" by standing on treaties wrung from China as spoils of the infamous Opium Wars. To calm all anxieties, both sides nonetheless managed a joint statement affirming a "common aim of maintaining the stability and prosperity of Hong Kong." Nonetheless, there is a perverse dynamic set in motion whenever affairs of state touch on the sacrosanct matter of sovereignty: the identity of the nation itself is somehow reified in the concrete object of its policy, however trivial the original stakes. This is what galvanized the British to horrendous national exertion in defense of the Falklands, a remote island territory that was little known and of lesser value until it was cast as the surrogate of British dignity in the face of an intolerable effrontery at the hands of a minor power, Argentina. It would be unwise to rule out a symbolic displacement that renders Hong Kong instead the object of China's "sacred national mission," particularly if negotiations hit a rough patch. Such portentous overtones quickly glossed the pro-Beijing Hong Kong press late in 1982: "In history," one paper declared, "patriotic heroes have realized the principle of dying for a just cause." And another opined: "A nation's pride will never be infatuated with the stink of coppers."

Of course neither side intends to kill outright the goose laying Hong Kong's golden eggs, but the problem is how to induce the bird to stay while they quarrel over its nest. The week of the Thatcher visit triggered a panic in the local stock exchange that wiped a full 20 percent off share values listed in the Hang Seng index. Over the same period the value of the Hong Kong dollar against sterling (a better measure of the currency's weakness than the overvalued U.S. dollar) plunged from HK$10.43 to HK$10.81. The full-blown crisis in business confidence compounded the impact of the world recession to cut Hong Kong's GNP growth in 1982 to under half of the 10.7 percent averaged annually over the past five years. After hovering so long between today's profits and tomorrow's politics, faith was finally broken in the sheer energy and opportunism that have always been Hong Kong's most valuable assets. The Thatcher visit forced Hong Kong to contemplate what six months earlier would have been unthinkable—rule perhaps by local Hong Kong notables, with at best their own currency and law, certainly under Beijing's flag, but probably controlled by party officials sitting in Guangdong. Whether such a formula or any of its many variants could ultimately restore that faith is an unanswered question. Beijing no doubt wishes to assert sovereignty and preserve Hong Kong's prosperity. But, if it comes to a choice between the two, the volume of capital flight by year end 1982 attested to the Colony's fears of Beijing's choice.

Chapter 21

South Asia

Richard Nations *

For nearly four years Afghanistan has been the point where PRC and U.S. foreign policies are most compatible. Both powers agree that Pakistan should be rewarded for not accommodating Moscow's interests in Kabul (which led President Reagan early on to offer to rearm Pakistan if Islamabad does not recognize the Soviet-installed Babrak Karmal regime). Kampuchea and Afghanistan are the two places where "strategic cooperation," which drew the United States and China together over a decade ago, has actually materialized.

But the intrusion of Soviet power across the Hindu Kush has set afoot a geopolitical realignment in South Asia which may strain that harmony over the decade. By the end of 1981, the search for new power combinations was apparent as India grew increasingly wary of Moscow's friendship. This in turn gave China new incentives to pursue both rapprochement with India and détente in the region in order to encourage South Asia's latent anti-Soviet tendencies. The United States, however, has committed itself to another course. Transfixed by the threat to the West's oil lifelines, Washington seized upon Pakistan to anchor the western flank of the Persian Gulf against the anti-American crosscurrents of Islamic and third world nationalism, which it fears merely softens the area up further for Soviet advances. This in turn alienated

*Correspondent, *Far Eastern Economic Review*.

India and deepened the polarization in the Subcontinent. With China treating the region where India is preeminent as a whole and the United States encouraging the integration of Pakistan into the Persian Gulf, such divergent approaches may find Washington and Beijing on opposing sides of major South Asian issues over the course of the decade.

U.S. POLICY TOWARD THE REGION

Since the soviet invasion of Afghanistan, Washington's approach to Pakistan has been dictated by the strategic paradox it faces in the Persian Gulf. The Carter Doctrine declared U.S. intention to use force if necessary in defense of its vital interests in the Gulf, but with no bases in the region and no regime willing to offer any, the United States must rely upon the invitation of a friendly regime to put its forces into action. Until the United States develops a credible capability to project power—a key objective for the Rapid Deployment Force (RDF) in the Reagan administration—Washington will confront in the Gulf region the classic dilemma of a world power whose commitments exceed its resources.

Washington now needs the moderate regimes of Southwest Asia as much as they need the United States. Both the Carter and Reagan administrations offered Pakistan arms to defend against the threat of Soviet-backed incursions across the Afghan border. Pakistan also offered Washington the opportunity to restore its shattered reputation as a reliable patron and to demonstrate that a security relationship with the United States is not incompatible with a nonaligned and Islamic foreign policy (a message Washington is exceedingly keen to propagate in the Gulf region). Pakistan's President Mohammad Zia ul-Haq reportedly refused to offer the United States use of military facilities for the RDF, a gesture which would have been tantamount to political suicide in the febrile climate of Pakistani nationalism. Nonetheless, aligning the United States with Pakistan's security needs appealed to Washington as a step toward cultivating the political climate in the Gulf necessary to make military cooperation possible when the next crisis arrives.

President Zia had rejected President Carter's offer of $400 million as "peanuts" not merely because of its size, but because Carter failed to allay Pakistani suspicions that his commitments to Pakistan's security was deeply compromised by too solicitous a regard for Indian opinion, since he was only willing to offer Pakistan carefully selected defensive equipment and communication gear designed to reinforce the country's northern border.

The Reagan administration's $3.2 billion military sales and developmental aid package opened a five-year line of supply to modernize the Pakistani military across the board. The Reagan administration insists that re-equipping Pakistan will not upset the balance of forces on the Subcontinent. "Given the large number of advanced aircraft which the Indians already will have received from the Soviets and Great Britain," Undersecretary of State James Buckley told the House Foreign Affairs Committee in September 1981, "they will emerge six years from now with an even greater edge over the Pakistanis notwithstanding the addition of forty F-16s to the latter's inventory." Nonetheless, just to make sure there are no mistaking the Reagan administration's tilt toward Pakistan, the early 1981 decision in Washington to terminate the 1962 nuclear fuel supply agreement with New Delhi further convinced the Pakistanis of President Reagan's support.

Reagan's Pakistan package received the discreet endorsement of Saudi Arabia, which reportedly offered to contribute at least $500 million toward the $1.6 billion cost of Pakistan's military purchases. This cemented the deal between Islamabad and Washington. Aid from the custodian of Islam's holy shrines to purchase American arms is perfectly acceptable to a Pakistani public that looks askance at U.S. military assistance as redolent of the now discredited "imperialist clientship" of former President Ayub Khan. It also allowed President Zia to present the U.S. military package at home as a straight purchase with no strings attached to Pakistan's nonaligned and Islamic foreign policy. From Riyadh's perspective, Pakistan acts as a stabilizing influence in the Gulf. It is distant enough not to be embroiled in Arab politics but close enough to provide some insurance against the twin threats of internal subversion and external challenge launched by Islamic radicalism.

Encouraging informal political and military cooperation between two regimes that share an arms supply arrangement with the United States is a critical part of the Reagan administration's response to the strategic dilemma of the Persian Gulf. The idea of promoting formal multilateral security arrangements in the region was quickly discarded after President Reagan assumed office, but the Saudi contribution to the Pakistani arms deal was pointed to by Pentagon officials as an example of how the "strategic consensus" on the western flank of the Gulf was taking shape.

Pakistan may prove to be an indispensible American asset during the next Gulf crisis, but reequipping Pakistan does not define U.S. security interests in South Asia. Until 1965, U.S. administrations were willing to arm Pakistan (in pursuit of geopolitical interests outside the Subcontinent) as the "cornerstone" of two regional alliance systems (SEATO and CENTO) designed to contain the expansionism of a monolithic Communist menace. Again Washington looks to Pakistan to "anchor" its interests in the Persian Gulf. In both instances, while Washington was willing to arm Pakistan, it refused to provide it with a security guarantee against India, which, as a democracy, enjoyed far greater public support in the United States. This has left the U.S. posture in South Asia in the untenable position of providing Pakistan with enough weapons to be a threat to India but not enough to deter a conflict or ensure Pakistan's defense. When the inevitable war broke out in 1965 and 1971, the United States remained neutral, alienating both Delhi and Islamabad.

This ambiguity is reflected in the disagreements over the 1959 Executive Agreement that Islamabad has consistently interpreted as a U.S. guarantee of its borders, although the United States insists that it applies only in the event of "Communist or Communist-inspired aggression." Washington's failure to support Pakistan in 1965 and then in 1971 (after India signed its treaty with the Soviets) inspired the myth of the "American betrayal," which remains today a tenet of that country's nationalism. From the outset in 1980, Islamabad demanded that the Carter administration upgrade the 1959 Executive Agreement to a full treaty with Senate ratification as a condition for Pakistan's acceptance of U.S. aid. This demand was discreetly dropped when the Pakistanis dealt with the Reagan administration because the Pakistanis chose to consider "the credibility of the administration in power more valuable than a paper treaty," as Pakistani officials commented at the time. This, however, only recenters U.S. policy back in the heart of South Asia's contradictions, deepens the polarization in the region, identifies Washington with the weaker side, and leaves it with little choice but to repeat the "historic betrayal" of neutrality in the event of a fourth Indo–Pakistani war.

PRC POLICY TOWARD THE REGION

China strongly endorses President Reagan's support for Pakistan, but unlike the United States, China approaches South Asia as a whole. China's objective is to minimize Soviet influence in the region, contiguous with its strategic underbelly in Tibet. As Vice Premier Deng Xiaoping told a visiting Indian parliamentarian in April 1981, Sino–Indian relations "only deteriorated after Nikita Khrushchev visited India in the mid-1950s." Since the two countries exchanged ambassadors in 1976, sporadic efforts to normalize relations have been aborted by the embarrassment arising from differences over Indochina. The Indian Foreign Minister cut short his trip to China in the wake of the unexpected incursion by the PLA into Vietnam in February 1979 and Chinese Foreign Minister Huang Hua cancelled a scheduled trip to India to protest New Delhi's recognition of the Heng Samrin regime in Kampuchea in June 1980.

The prospects for a realignment in South Asia took on new life in the wake of the Soviet invasion of Afghanistan, which demoted India to the same unenviable geopolitical position that China had occupied in the 1950s—a weaker power, a military client, and now virtually a neighbor of the Soviet Union. The many promising possibilities in the new situation have not been overlooked in Beijing. Vice Premier Deng chose a visit by Indian Foreign Minister Subramanian Swami early in 1981 to woo New Delhi with the new theme that "India is no longer a client of the Soviet Union." Reflecting on their own bitter experience with Moscow, the Chinese seem confident that in time differences in national interest are bound to assert themselves now that the Soviet Union has intruded itself into what New Delhi has looked upon jealously as its domain. China's diplomatic strategy toward South Asia is aimed at reducing its differences with India, promoting détente between Pakistan and India, and encouraging anti-Soviet tendencies in the Subcontinent as a whole.

As a first step, late in 1980 Deng publicized Chinese initiatives to resolve the border problem with India by offering a "package deal" based on a swap of conflicting claims left over from the 1962 border war. China would retain the Aksai Chin region in the western sector, while Beijing, in exchange, would recognize India's claims to the McMahon Line as the legal boundary in the East. Simultaneously, Chinese media attacks on the government of Indira Gandhi ceased, and China indicated that New Delhi's absorption of the Himalayan kingdom of Sikkim early in the 1960s would not be allowed to stand in the way of improved bilateral relations. Chinese officials and press commentaries began to stress that which the two countries held in common as "the world's two oldest civilizations and most populous countries which have no conflicts on issues of world policy and stand to gain by cordial relations."

To reassure old friends, Chinese Premier Zhao Ziyang visited Pakistan, Nepal, and Bangladesh in June 1981. In Islamabad he reassured President Zia that China would not pursue improvement in its relations with India at Pakistan's expense. Nonetheless, no joint communiqué was issued at the end of his visit, and Zhao departed from past practice by avoiding even the pro forma reference to Kashmir in his banquet speeches. Such favorable nuances were not missed in New

Delhi. In Kathmandu Zhao pointed out that "South Asian countries are now brought face to face with the threat of the Soviet Union." He encouraged the nations of the region to accelerate the process of détente. By publicly endorsing the late Bangladesh President Rahman's proposal for the seven nations of South Asia to join together in a "Regional Forum," China appeared, in its own way, to be pursuing the "strategic consensus" in South Asia that the Reagan administration hoped to construct in the Persian Gulf. While China can be relied upon to continue its formal support for Pakistan, it is unrealistic to promote a regional détente in South Asia without indirectly accepting India's preeminence. Zhao's message in Kathmandu seemed to imply that China would no longer oppose India's regional ambitions to the extent that New Delhi detached itself from Moscow's orbit. To underline his keenness on a breakthrough with India and to link Sino–Indian rapprochement to the process of reducing tensions within the region, Zhao repeated Deng's border proposals from Kathmandu. The following July Foreign Minister Huang carried new proposals to New Delhi urging that the two countries delink the process of normalization from the final solution to the complex border situation and promote scientific and cultural exchanges while the border negotiations proceeded.

India has responded cautiously. If Beijing wants normalization, New Delhi insists that solid advances toward a border settlement are necessary first to placate a wary parliament embittered by memories of the 1950s, when the warmth of the "Sino-Indian Brotherhood" era, symbolized by the fraternity between Prime Minister Jawaharlal Nehru and Zhou Enlai at Bandung, was abruptly shattered by a seemingly unprovoked Chinese power play on India's Tibetan border. Beijing may well say that "there are not major issues of world policy separating the two countries," but New Delhi looks upon China as a major force fueling a new Cold War centered in the Indian Ocean and Persian Gulf. The prospect of Sino–American military cooperation is an Indian nightmare. For New Delhi, the policy of Sino–American "strategic cooperation" boils down to stirring trouble on India's flanks. India sees China and the United States colluding to increase tensions both in Indochina (by supporting the Khmer Rouge) and in Afghanistan (by arming the Afghan insurgents), a major obstacle as far as New Delhi is concerned in achieving a negotiated withdrawal of Soviet forces.

But most important, few if any in that small circle that shapes New Delhi's China policy believe that Beijing has abandoned its determination to play an independent power role south of the Himalayas. Rather, China's South Asian policy over the past two decades has been to weaken India by encouraging a national assertiveness among the Subcontinent's peripheral states.

India, however, does have reasons for pursuing rapprochement with China, including the Soviet thrust into Afghanistan. A decade ago the Indo–Soviet Friendship Treaty strengthened Prime Minister Gandhi's hand decisively in the power politics that allowed India to prevail over Pakistan in the Bangladesh war. Today Mrs. Gandhi finds her Soviet ties increasingly an embarrassment both at home and abroad. During the Nonaligned Summit Meeting in February 1981, the delegates rejected Mrs. Gandhi's draft communiqué, which focused the threat to peace in the region on the U.S. presence in the Indian Ocean and instead implicated the Soviet Union and its allies by calling for the withdrawal of foreign forces from Afghanistan and Kampuchea. The government's chagrin was compounded by its failure to induce the withdrawal of Soviet troops from Afghanistan by quiet entreaty. Indian opinion began to question whether India had lost control over events in the Subcontinent.

In mid-1981 Mrs. Gandhi moved to restore Indian influence over events by launching a full-scale diplomatic initiative aimed at striking a distance from the Soviet Union, diversifying its resources of diplomatic and arms support with new openings to Europe (particularly France), and outflanking Pakistan by simultaneously pursuing peace talks while taking India's case directly to Islamabad's friends. When by the beginning of 1982 it became increasingly clear that the Taiwan issue was seriously obstructing any real military cooperation between the United States and China and that it might even lead to retrogression in their relations, New Delhi saw increased opportunities for its diplomacy in Washington and Beijing.

In April 1982 India signed a $3 billion deal with France for the purchase of 40 Mirage 2000 under a contract that would allow India to undertake the manufacture locally of up to 110 aircraft. Paris agreed to a delivery schedule parallel to the introduction of the F-16s into the Pakistan Air Force, committing France to deliver one of its best aircraft to India at almost the same time that the aircraft was scheduled to enter service at home. The Indian press hailed the move: "The new cordiality and content in Indo–French relations and also the strengthening of links with Britain are again facets of a policy of using the European Economic Community as a counterweight of sorts against the Soviet Union."

In April 1982 Mrs. Gandhi visited Saudi Arabia for two days in an effort to convince the Saudis that India's geopolitical mass makes it a vital factor in the stability of Southwest Asia. It is doubtful that she dissuaded Riyadh from pressing its commitments to finance arms supplies for both Pakistan and the Muslim insurgents in Afghanistan, but the Saudis appeared to realize that Pakistan's value as a factor in the

Gulf equation could be neutralized altogether by a resurgence of active Indo–Pakistani hostility. Accordingly, Mrs. Gandhi was cordially received, and substantial financial contributions to Indian development projects were promised.

Then Mrs. Gandhi accepted an invitation to visit the United States, extended personally by President Reagan at the Cancun North-South summit in October 1981. She could not, however, expect to talk persuasively to Islamabad's friends while maintaining a posture of unrelenting hostility toward Pakistan itself. Once the U.S. Congress endorsed the administration's Pakistan package and continued opposition became futile, India's posture toward Pakistan changed from threats of war to proposals for peace. When Pakistani Foreign Minister Agha Shahi arrived in New Delhi in January 1982 to discuss President Zia's 1981 proposal to negotiate a "no war" pact with India, Mrs. Gandhi responded with a counteroffer of a "friendship treaty" together with a joint commission to promote Indo–Pakistani relations. The next round of scheduled talks was postponed following an all-but-predictable diplomatic flap over Kashmir, but by mid-1982 it was clear that both countries had determined that the new situation on the Subcontinent required that each engage the other—if only for tactical reasons—in an effort to achieve regional détente.

Mrs. Gandhi's first trip to the United States in a decade came at a moment when U.S.–Indo relations (which had never been cordial but never openly hostile either) hit their lowest point since President Nixon dispatched elements of the Seventh Fleet into the Bay of Bengal. The fact that she chose to curb the anti-American rhetoric and visit Washington in search of improving relations with President Reagan reflects one central reality of South Asia in the post-Afghanistan era—namely, India needs U.S. friendship more than the United States needs India's friendship.

The climate of U.S.–Indo relations is bound to improve over time as a result of her visit, but thus far New Delhi has only moved to balance, but not reduce, its Soviet ties. However embarrassing the symbolism of Indo–Soviet relations may be in the wake of the invasion of Afghanistan, Moscow still provides India with 70 percent of its arms, and most of the Indian establishment still believes that the Soviet Union remains the most reliable supplier. India continues to align itself with the Soviet Union on most international issues, recognizes and extends aid to the Heng Samrin regime in Phnom Penh, and refuses to condemn the Soviet invasion of Afghanistan.

Both Washington and Beijing can be relied upon to encourage New Delhi to seek alternatives to Moscow, but the question the Indian leadership has not addressed is what price it is willing to pay in its relations with Moscow in order to induce a comparable reduction in Chinese and

U.S. support for Pakistan. Neither power is likely to accept India's definition of its own position on the Subcontinent if it is still perceived as critically reliant on Moscow and aligned with it diplomatically.

CONCLUSIONS

The Soviet invasion of Afghanistan triggered a geopolitical revolution in South Asia that bears directly on the course of U.S.–Sino relations in the next decade. Washington now faces two broad alternatives in the region. The United States could accept India as the region's paramount power and accordingly adopt a policy of "malign neglect" towards Pakistan. Such a policy would leave Pakistan with little choice but to reach an accommodation with India on New Delhi's terms. This would align U.S. and Indian interests in South Asia, provide a sound footing for a substantive improvement in their relations, and diminish Soviet influence. Finally, it would put U.S. policy in Asia on a higher geopolitical plane because the United States would be seen as the balancing power in a new triangle formed by China and India, who will compete to become the dominant Asian power by the turn of the century. Such a policy, however, would also mean a sharp reversal of the current course, would amount to the "betrayal" the United States is frequently accused of, and would undermine American prestige and influence among Islamic and Gulf states just at a moment when it has no credible military option.

The second course is to continue to encourage the integration of Pakistan as a U.S. asset in the Persian Gulf. This promises the benefits of aligning the United States with the direction that Pakistan has chosen for itself, while at the same time consolidating pro-Western forces in a region where the United States must rely almost exclusively on political goodwill. The danger of this course is that it identifies Washington with an unstable and unpopular regime, rather than with the broad consensus of national security concerns shared by the military and civilian leaders. It is also a policy that is vulnerable to the Indian "veto" of another Subcontinental war.

For this course to succeed, the United States must balance support for Pakistan with an active policy to promote Indo–Pakistani détente. There is a rare moment now (while the power constellation surrounding South Asia is still fluid) for the United States to seize the initiative in a process in which China, India, and Pakistan—all the major powers except the Soviet Union—have engaged. Moreover, the U.S. arms package to Pakistan gives Washington renewed leverage over both parties for the first time since 1965.

Chapter 22

Korea

William H. Gleysteen, Jr.*

Despite an initial ideological jolt, the leaders of the Republic of Korea (ROK) reacted rather favorably to normalization of U.S. relations with the PRC in 1978, and they now desire a similar evolution in their own policy. They remain wary, however, about the development of real intimacy between the United States and China—especially active security ties—not only because they see the PRC as quite capable of reverting to an adversarial role but also because they fear that U.S.–PRC collaboration could occur at the expense of traditional allies and might provoke an adventuresome turn in Soviet policy.

REACTION TO IMPROVING U.S.–PRC RELATIONS

By the late 1970s, South Korean attitudes toward China had moderated from the deep distrust and hostility of the post-Korean War years to a grudging acceptance of the view that friendly U.S.–PRC relations would (to paraphrase the words of former President Park Chung Hee) serve American national interests and "probably" benefit peace and stability in East Asia. Under President Chun Doo Hwan the Korean Government has advanced its own policy to the point of urging Beijing to help reduce tensions in Korea, to develop bilateral contacts,

*Director, Asia Society.

and to work toward full diplomatic relations. Although not often articulated in public, South Korea's apparent objectives are to limit automatic PRC support for North Korea and to establish a working relationship with a major power that has some complementary economic interests as well as a role to play in any political settlement on the Korean peninsula. So far there is no sign that the Koreans seek a China connection for leverage against Japan and the United States.

While the speed of this evolution in South Korean thinking toward China may have surprised some, it is, nevertheless, a logical reaction to changed geopolitical circumstances in Northeast Asia, particularly the fissuring of relationships among the Communist countries and China's new ties with the United States and Japan. Equally important, it reflects the new self-confidence and enhanced status that have accompanied the growth of the ROK's economic and defense capabilities. A reversion to old patterns is unlikely because the new look in Northeast Asia better suits Korean interests. Koreans would not be overly concerned by occasional U.S.–PRC friction; some probably foresee such tensions as inevitable between major powers. But if U.S.–PRC relations were to revert to serious confrontation, the reaction in South Korea would be one of considerable concern.

SOUTH KOREAN POLICY TOWARD
THE PRC

The ROK has formally declared its desire to establish full diplomatic relations with the PRC, recognizing that the process may take some years to accomplish. Denigration of the PRC has ceased; indirect trade and informal contacts have been encouraged despite awareness that the Chinese are constrained by their determination not to jeopardize ties with the DPRK; potential conflicts with China (over fisheries and oil exploration) have been sidestepped; and many intermediaries have been urged to speak on Seoul's behalf in Beijing. The results so far are less impressive than the change in the ROK's posture. Yet the Chinese have become considerably more realistic about South Korea and have tolerated significant contacts of an unofficial character.

VIEW TOWARD ACTIVE U.S.–PRC
SECURITY TIES

ROK attitudes toward U.S.–PRC security cooperation are governed by strict—and to some extent parochial—considerations of how such developments affect Korean interests. Koreans acknowledge some benefit to their security from the existing U.S.–PRC relationship. They appreciate the fact that Chinese forces help offset growing Soviet military strength and that U.S. forces no longer need be deployed against China. They see these security advantages, however, as inherent in the existing U.S.–PRC relationship. Development of active security ties with the PRC would not, in their view, significantly improve the largely passive advantages of the current situation nor guarantee their permanence. Were the United States to go beyond limited military cooperation to major efforts to bolster Chinese security, Koreans doubt the PRC would respond by undertaking a larger role in countering the USSR. On the contrary, they fear such American actions would more likely embolden China in its dealings with its Asian neighbors. In short, Koreans seem convinced that active U.S.–PRC military collaboration would not help Korea's defense, and at least some of them consider Americans naive in believing that military cooperation with China would serve U.S. as opposed to Chinese interests. Expressed in another way, Koreans are more prone than Americans to worry about China's ideological orientation and historic role as Asia's preeminent power.

SPECIAL CONSIDERATIONS

Reinforcing general skepticism and occasional anxiety, South Koreans inevitably measure any particular development in U.S.–PRC relations by its potential impact on certain issues of particular concern.

Military Benefit to South Korea

ROK political leaders and military officers fear that if the United States were to supply China with significant amounts of advanced weapons or military technology, some military benefit would flow from China to the DPRK—not immediately but perhaps at a time of strain in U.S.–PRC relations. The Chinese might supply North Korea with a Chinese-made fighter aircraft enhanced by U.S. avionics or jet technology. Similarly, Korean officials worry that U.S. military assistance to the PRC would lead eventually to Foreign Military Sales (FMS) arrangements in which China by its sheer size would absorb a disproportionate share of U.S. resources. They cite the examples of Israel, Egypt, and Turkey.

Impact on Chinese and Soviet Behavior

Of greater concern to a broad spectrum of South Koreans is the potential impact of U.S. security cooperation on Chinese and Soviet policy toward the Korean peninsula itself. The conventional and hard-to-chal-lenge view is that China's support of the DPRK is fundamental and cannot be bought off by any U.S. actions, including military assistance. Even if Beijing wished to soften its stand toward Seoul, it would be con-strained by fear of a North Korean tilt toward the Soviets. Were the PRC to persist, the fear is that the Soviets would step in, possibly in-dulging the North Koreans with advanced weapons and dangerous ad-vice. But even if the USSR resisted the temptation, South Koreans doubt North Koreans under Kim Il-Sung would become more flexible if they saw China, a key ally, dallying with active security ties with the United States.

Impact on North Korea

South Koreans tend to assume that U.S. relations with China have cre-ated discomfort in Pyongyang and that active military collaboration would intensify the North's tendencies toward paranoia, inflexibility, and nationalistic preoccupation. Although this could well be the reac-tion to a sudden dramatic change involving U.S.–Sino military cooper-ation, Pyongyang might be less alarmed by a modest and gradual de-velopment. Moreover, their negative reaction might be moderated by the kind of counterarguments the Chinese probably used in 1971 through 1972 to ease North Korean concerns over normalization—for example, that better U.S.–PRC relations would increase Chinese influ-ence on U.S. policy and open opportunities for North Korea. At a mini-mum, however, Pyongyang would be uncomfortable and tempted to play harder on its Soviet connection. North Korea might also consider a nationalistic overture to the South.

Taiwan

At least superficially, South Korea's attitude toward Taiwan is incon-sistent in that Seoul appears ready to forsake its own official relations with Taipei while watching very carefully for any signs that the United States might pull the rug from under the Taiwanese. In any event, Ko-reans do not consider their position on recognition critical to Taiwan's survival, whereas U.S. arms decisions vis-à-vis both Taiwan and the PRC could be. In the unlikely event that the United States sold the PRC a sophisticated fighter aircraft while limiting Taiwan to a lesser version, the degradation of Taiwan's defense would reinforce Korean concern about the danger to South Korea. The negative reaction would probably be considerably stronger if the United States were at some future time to begin drastic reductions or termination of arms sales to

Taiwan. Koreans would be less worried about the fate of Taiwan than about a precedent that might be extended to the Korean peninsula.

CONCLUSION

Unlike the process of normalizing relations between the United States and China, the Koreans—both North and South for different reasons—would be uneasy if the United States and the PRC appeared to be developing an active security relationship. Were such a relationship to emerge it would not be the first time that either North Korea or South Korea objected to a major policy of its protector power without questioning the continued utility of the relationship. In the case of South Korea, concern would be controlled if the United States demonstratively exercised great caution in military dealings with China and sustained the quality of security cooperation with the ROK. A warming trend in ROK–PRC relations would also help. On the other hand, Korean anxieties would grow massively if they sensed that the United States were seriously contemplating either a major buildup of PRC military strength or a security entente with Japan and the PRC as a partial substitute for the U.S. military presence in Asia. Fortunately, the Koreans consider these remote prospects.

Chapter 23

The Soviet Union

William G. Hyland*

China will remain one of the Soviet Union's most critical strategic problems over the next ten years. Only relations with the other
superpower, the United States, will be as important. Yet, compared
with U.S.–Soviet relations, which are in an almost constant state of agitation (although without fundamental changes), the Soviet Union's relations with China have been virtually frozen. During the 1960s, Sino–
Soviet relations clearly and openly deteriorated to the point of a genuine threat of armed conflict in 1969–1970. A slight easing was achieved
by a Chinese tactical retreat, but the subsequent interim led nowhere.
Indeed, China subsequently outmaneuvered the Soviets by creating
the opening with the United States and thereby effectively denied Soviet policy the option of a U.S.–Soviet alliance against China. No significant change occurred in Sino–Soviet relations until the death of Mao
Zedong, when the Soviets launched new probes to determine whether
the departure of Mao could change the basic Sino–Soviet conflict.
   The sparring that followed Mao's death finally resulted in an agreement to begin formal talks. This interlude collapsed over the Vietnamese invasion of Cambodia. The wider maneuvers taken by each side
were much more important—namely, China's normalization with the

*Senior Associate, Carnegie Endowment for International Peace.

United States and its treaty with Japan and Moscow's sustained offensive in South Asia and the Gulf region. The significance of this interlude is that the worst case did not, in fact, occur: China "counterattacked" in Vietnam but Moscow remained passive. The Red Army did not move. And, in retrospect, it may be that in the winter of 1978–1979 the apogee of Sino–Soviet conflict was reached.

Relations, of course, did worsen, but not as much as might have seemed likely given the various provocations in Southeast Asia. The Chinese finally denounced the Sino–Soviet mutual assistance treaty of 1950, giving the obligatory one-year notice. But, ironically, this served to trigger a new round of negotiations. These talks in 1979 were also destined to collapse—this time as a consequence of the Soviet invasion of Afghanistan in December. The course of these negotiations in 1979 demonstrated the USSR's difficult choices.

First, the Soviets have sought a broad resolution of the conflict at the political level, which would be reflected in a joint statement of principles, thus reproducing the pattern of Soviet–American détente in the early 1970s. The Chinese have countered, however, with specific demands—for example, withdrawal of some Soviet forces from the disputed border areas and Mongolia, withdrawal from Afghanistan, and a settlement of the Vietnamese invasion of Cambodia. The Soviets have resisted all these demands. The price for some amelioration of tensions would be a Soviet military and political disengagement or, in other words, a complete reversal of Soviet policy since 1964–1965, when the Soviet military buildup in the Far East began.

Moreover, the Soviets have been faced with the prospect of either conceding a predominant Asian role to China (especially in Indochina and, to a lesser extent, in Japan) or accepting the long-term burden of increased military protection of the Soviet Far East, an area destined for much greater economic development.

The Soviets have had to choose between a policy of confrontation or one of conciliation. It seems that the Soviets have chosen the course of seeking some reconciliation: thus, the renewed Soviet offers to resume negotiations in 1981–1982. Leonid Brezhnev went so far as to concede the "socialist" status of China and called for a gradual "normalization." These talks began in September 1982, and a second round was held in March 1983. It appears that the Chinese backed down from their efforts to establish "preconditions." The talks have proceeded without Soviet agreement to Chinese demands.

As an indicator of how Sino–Soviet relations might conceivably develop in the 1980s, it is worth noting that the terms of Soviet diplomacy have also been softened. Initially, the Soviets brusquely rejected the notion of thinning out any Soviet forces, suggested "confidence-building" measures (undefined), and insisted on an agreed statement of principles (a "firm legal foundation," as the Soviets put it) that would incorporate the nonuse of force (territorial integrity, etc.). In other words, they endorsed the status quo, a position that Beijing was unlikely to accept. After proposing the resumption of negotiations in September 1981, however, the Soviets began to elaborate a new public position. Of particular importance was Brezhnev's public address in March 1982 at Tashkent, where he affirmed ("we do not deny") that a socialist system existed in China, that Moscow would not support "two Chinas" (thus ending any flirtation with Taiwan), and, in addition, he denied any "threat" to the Soviet Union. This latter disclaimer might have seemed no more than routine propaganda, were it not for subsequent Soviet policy statements. The Soviets for the first time offered to negotiate about the growing deployment of SS-20 intermediate range missiles stationed in the Far East. Even though this was prompted by increasing Western pressure on the entire SS-20 deployment in both European and Asiatic Russia, it was nevertheless the first indication that the Soviets might separate their military deployments from a political settlement. Second was the promise, made at the United Nations by Gromyko, that the USSR would not be the first country to use nuclear weapons. This too had its origins in the contest for European opinion, but the Soviets made it clear that it applied to China as well. It may well have meant an end to a first-strike policy against China's small missile force.

Thus, prior to the talks in September 1982, the Soviets had implemented unilaterally part of the program that was put forward for negotiation. In return—though not part of an explicit bargain—the Chinese agreed to resume negotiations. No doubt the Chinese have used the Soviet card to worry the United States, stressing that an opening to Moscow remained an option, especially if Sino–American relations worsened over Taiwan. Possibly indicative of Chinese thinking was a general appraisal of the Soviet situation that ran contrary to Western contentions that the Soviets were in a profound crisis. The Chinese appraisal warned against premature conclusions about Soviet weaknesses and foresaw a general balance of power between the two superpowers. The Soviets, for their part, increasingly emphasized the incompatibility of U.S. and Chinese interests and the significance of Chinese internal movement away from Maoism.

It appears that the 1980s will witness some accommodation between Beijing and Moscow. The motives are already evident. First, as far as the Soviets are concerned, the threat from China is still a real one, but it lies more and more in the future. In the early 1970s, Brezhnev predicted a major threat from China within ten years (that is, before 1982). The Soviets have had a palpable fear of Chinese encroachments in the Far East. Even the Soviet Chief of Staff joined the political analysts in warning of the danger to Soviet borders. But this theme was more prominent in the late 1970s, when it appeared that the United States would underwrite a Chinese military modernization program that would also be supported by both Europe and Japan. This has not happened. Now the Soviets must perceive that Chinese military modernization will be much slower than anticipated. Indeed, the Chinese program has been curtailed and deferred, and the amount of foreign military assistance has been minimal, as pointed out in earlier chapters.

Undoubtedly the Chinese view the Soviets as a long-term rather than a short-term threat, which probably reinforces the Chinese disposition (growing out of friction with the United States over Taiwan) to gain greater freedom of action in its foreign policy. This means rapprochement with the Soviet Union.

A Soviet motive in seeking an improvement in relations would be to encourage the Chinese estimate that the Soviet threat had indeed been reduced and that Chinese defense policy could, therefore, continue as a more modest effort. A strong incentive for such a Soviet approach is the growing economic stake in Siberia, symbolized by the construction of the Baikal-Amur rail line (BAL), which is intended to open the resources of the Far East to developmental projects. The Siberian region has received about 25 percent of Soviet investment in recent years. It accounts for about 10 percent of the overall Soviet economic output but contains about 75 percent of Soviet mineral, fuel, and energy resources. Consequently, a heavy Soviet defense investment has been made to protect this general area. Over twenty Soviet divisions face China, as well as a sizable tactical air force and, of course, the entire Pacific Fleet is stationed in ports highly vulnerable to Chinese tactical strikes. During the maneuvering and negotiating, the Chinese openly emphasized their nuclear options—in an exercise featuring a simulated tactical weapon, in a submarinelaunched missile, and in a new doctrinal emphasis on nuclear forces authored by Defense Minister Zhang Aiping. Thus, it is clearly in the Soviet interest to explore political avenues to reduce the threat to this vital region.

Finally, there is the Soviet analysis of the Chinese leadership and its future direction. Since the death of Mao, the Soviets have been intrigued by the course of domestic Chinese politics. While there have been some sharp differences in views among Soviet Sinologists, the general thinking has been that de-Maoization might carry over into foreign policy. This was more or less the line of speculation taken by Brezhnev at the last Party Congress in March 1981. Since then Soviet views have oscillated, but one school of thought still holds out the possibility of favorable evolution in Chinese positions.

In sum, there would seem to be on both sides of the frontier some valid reasons for a limited accommodation. Any such predictions, however, must be severely qualified. For both countries the leadership situation is very fluid. Brezhnev is gone, but Yuri Andropov is not likely to remain in power in the 1990s. Deng Xiaoping remains a powerful figure, and his hand-picked successors have a better actuarial chance to survive than their Soviet counterparts, but still the situation is uncertain. Given the volatile character of Chinese politics, predictions about the top leadership are hazardous.

Andropov has confirmed the effort to normalize relations with China and a second round of talks were held under his regime, following his ostentatious gesture toward China's then foreign minister, Huang Hua, at the Brezhnev funeral. Some relaxation of tensions in the Far East would seem a prudent program for a new Soviet leadership. But there is the sensitive problem of whether this requires concessions to China that a newly installed leadership will be reluctant to make, without having installed leadership at home. Of all the issues in Soviet politics, none is more sensitive than the threat from China. It is a theme that bridges the gulf between dissidents and *apparatchiks*. On this issue, the views of Andrei Amalrik and Alexander Solzhenitsyn are not too different from the fears of Ogarkov and Andropov. Therefore, unless the Chinese are forthcoming and accommodating, it may be difficult for a new Soviet leadership to translate a general objective of normalization into a concrete program.

That program indeed is complex because it involves the question of Soviet security in the Far East. Both sides continue to treat the border issue in a polemical fashion. A new exchange of charges occurred in January 1983. But the border dispute has for some time been more a symbol of the deeper struggle for power between the two Communist giants than an issue for genuine resolution. The Chinese, in effect, argue that the USSR should concede to China a leading position (at least in Asia) and that the USSR should demonstrate this concession by withdrawing or reducing its military presence and retreating in Afghanistan and Indochina. The Soviets argue that the Chinese must acknowledge the status quo—that is, they should recognize that the USSR is also a major Asian power (the Soviets cleverly turn around the Chinese slogan by proposing a mutual renunciation of hegemonism).

This is the basic contest, and it is not subject to resolution by a border settlement alone. It requires a more fundamental political accommodation.

This seems unlikely. And it follows that the limited reconciliation between Beijing and Moscow that seems to be evolving in the near term is not likely to prevail over the longer term (that is, by the early 1990s). The Soviets recognize that there is still a danger from China that will arise after the Chinese have settled their internal power struggles and adopted a new foreign policy commensurate with the growth in their basic military strength. As one Soviet analyst put it when discussing the alternative outcomes, a new conservative Chinese regime could put its

> heart into a foreign policy of expansion, especially as China would be able to rely on a more or less powerful nuclear potential and a more modern army. It is impossible to predict the direction which this expansion would take. But it would certainly created a threat primarily to all China's neighbors.[1]

In short, the Soviets still have a profound fear of Chinese ambitions. Solzhenitsyn summed it up in his famous letter to the Soviet leaders:

> For the next half century our only genuine military need will be to defend ourselves against China, and it would be better not to go to war with her at all. A well-established Northeast is also our best defense against China.

In the near term, the Soviets believe they now have more time to keep building up their position in the East while testing the potential for a political understanding with China. If and when this understanding fails, is definitively rejected, or breaks down over the next decade, the possibility of another severe confrontation seems likely if not inevitable. Much will depend, of course, on the relationship of the two powers with the other key actors, the United States and Japan.

NOTES

1. Fedor Burlatskiy, "Interregnum," *Noviy Mir*, No. 4 (April 1982), JPRS translation 80807 (13 May 1982), USSR Report, No. 1250.

PART VI

Interactions Of U.S. And Allied Views

Chapter 24

Arms Control

Joseph J. Wolf[*]

On June 11, 1982, Foreign Minister Huang Hua, speaking at the Second Special Session on Disarmament of the United Nations, restated, with minor adaptations, China's basic stance on arms control. He said that tension in the world is mainly the result of superpower rivalry and accused both superpowers of insincerity in disarmament talks. He criticized both the Russian proposal for a nuclear freeze and the U.S. proposal for reduction as means to attempt to attain supremacy. While otherwise even-handed in his general criticism of the superpowers, he criticized the Soviet Union for its deceptively peaceable words but hegemonistic actions without similar criticism of the United States. He strongly expressed understanding and sympathy for antinuclear movements abroad.

He then proposed that all nuclear states agree not to use nuclear weapons. Pending such agreement, each should undertake not to use nuclear weapons against nonnuclear states and nuclear free weapons zones and not to be the first to use them against each other. The USSR and the United States should stop the testing, manufacture, and improvement of nuclear weapons and should reduce their nuclear arsenals according to an agreed procedure. Noting the potential link between conventional and nuclear hostilities, he added that conventional

[*]Rapporteur, Atlantic Council Committee on NATO.

disarmament should be effected simultaneously, with all states agreeing not to use conventional weapons for intervention, aggression, or military occupation.

He repeated that China has already renounced first use, including use against states that don't have nuclear weapons. China now offered to stop all production and development and to eliminate existing weapons if the superpowers would agree to a freeze and to a 50 percent reduction in nuclear weaponry. Huang Hua thus once more insisted on substantial first steps being taken by the nuclear superpowers before lesser nuclear powers, such as China, should be subjected to controls.

In sum, China has adopted a position in which its policy is portrayed as purely defensive and its sympathies as being with all those concerned by the superpower arms race, while it has kept all its options open pending major progress in East-West arms control negotiations.

This should not be a source of surprise for a country in China's uncertain military position. As has been noted earlier in these studies, China's military assets (namely, great depth of terrain and vast manpower resources) are limited by problems of organization, tactics, logistics, communications, and lack of modern equipment. Its modest but growing nuclear force, with several hundred warheads, though small vis-à-vis either superpower, provides a degree of strategic deterrence as well as serving as a deterrent to major conventional attack from regional adversaries. Moreover, Beijing is now beginning to deploy nuclear systems with intercontinental reach. It is noteworthy that China's military nuclear program does not seem to have suffered the budgetary restrictions that have affected the rest of its defense establishment.

Although China is the most populous country in the world, is one of the nuclear powers, and has the third largest and most costly military establishment, its arms control policy is most likely to be dictated by very different considerations than those that affect the United States, its Western allies, or the USSR. As the most recent and least of the nuclear powers, China is the only one that, neither through its own efforts nor by relying on the assured support of a strong nuclear ally, can count on a nuclear stand-off with either superpower, at least over the next decade.

In sum, China's strengths (namely its size, population, natural resources, and nuclear weapons status) are more than balanced by weaknesses in other areas. Relative weaknesses can be remedied by the build-up of military potential at home, the potential support of other nations, the constraints affecting potential enemies, and the avoidance of changes in the balance of power, global or regional, which could adversely affect China's interests. And until those weaknesses are remedied, it can be assumed that China will be especially conscious of the risks of getting directly involved in hostilities that would jeopardize either the regime or the nation. The spectre of a preemptive strike continues to be the source of concern.

China has taken full advantage of its reopened relations with the United States, and, although the European allies at present give little mind to China's role in international affairs, the PRC naturally seeks to exploit the NATO–Warsaw Pact relations (particularly the U.S.–Moscow relationship) in its power balance vis-à-vis Moscow. Should Moscow–Beijing relations fundamentally improve, China's role in the global balance of power would once again unfavorably affect the Western alliance. The European allies, however, will tend to remain aloof from the Asian scene and, as in the past, will view a deterioration of China–U.S. ties in the light of how they affect the overall stability between East and West. A clear swing by China toward Russia and away from the United States could thus be a cause of friction within the Alliance. If the more likely course ensues, with some deterioration of China–U.S. ties and modest improvement of China–USSR relations, tensions probably would not be gravely affected. A closer relationship between China and the United States, particularly if it included a marked increase in U.S. support for China's military establishment, would be an irritant for U.S.–Soviet relations and could create problems for the alliance. In the field of arms control, China's growing intercontinental capability is not likely to have a major impact, although it can be played by each side as an asset of the other. Only toward the end of the decade is China's nuclear force likely to be of sufficient size to warrant the dedication of a significant number of nuclear weapons to its destruction and to make China's presence, like that of France and the United Kingdom, essential at the negotiations.

In the East Asian region, China will be certain to be deeply concerned at any possibility of any other nuclear weapons power emerging. The PRC explains that the nuclear powers should not use their weapons against non-nuclear powers since they would thus reduce the pressures for proliferation. This seems the most tangible expression of a real interest in any arms control measure on the part of the PRC. Otherwise, a cautious and somewhat cynical (or at least doubting) approach to arms control has marked its policy. A review of China's stand on specific issues of arms control emphasizes this position.

NUCLEAR TESTING

As the latest and least-armed of the nuclear powers, China's policy has been one of opposing measures that would foreclose its augmenting its own strength. It has denounced both the Limited Test Ban Treaty and the Comprehensive Test Ban Treaty as favoring the superpowers. China had originally said it would be ready to forego testing only when all nuclear weapons are banned and destroyed. The June 11 position softened this, although more in appearance than in prospect, by moving the date up to that of an agreed destruction of half the stocks of the superpowers. It seems most likely that China will abstain from efforts to arrive at any Test Ban Treaty, at least until its technological expertise increases greatly. While China's refusal to join in these efforts may be disappointing to the other Western powers, it seems doubtful that China's abstention is likely to move other nations also to abstain and is less likely to trouble the Alliance than the current U.S. position on testing.

NUCLEAR FREEZES

Since any freeze proposal would place China at a disadvantage in relation to the other nuclear powers, China is almost certain to reject suggestions for itself along these lines, while urging them for the superpowers. China has criticized Brezhnev's proposal for an intermediate-range missile freeze and in this respect seems to come closer to the NATO position than that of the Warsaw Pact.

NO FIRST USE OF NUCLEAR WEAPONS

China's policy has consistently been based on the right to possess nuclear weapons on the one hand (until total nuclear disarmament has been achieved) and a call for pledges of no first use. China itself has unilaterally declared that it would never be the first to use nuclear weapons but has termed Soviet statements to that effect insincere. It has considered pledges of no first use by the nuclear powers essential to effective nuclear-free zone proposals and has insisted on the need for all nuclear powers to join in the renunciation of first use.

The United States considers a no-first-use pledge totally unacceptable in the light of Soviet superiority in conventional as well as theater nuclear forces, primarily (but not only) in the NATO area. France and Great Britain even more strongly reject any such suggestion. The Federal Republic of Germany has taken the lead in flatly rejecting the latest no-first-use suggestions, and those views have been echoed in almost every NATO capital. No-first-use proposals for Europe and

Northeast Asia could have dramatic effects. They would leave the Soviets and their allies with a conventional advantage that the Western powers are unlikely to match in peacetime and would let the Soviets dominate Western Europe, Japan, and Korea by fear. To the extent that some no-first-use proposals rely on the deterrent power (as distinguished from the right) of any pledging nation to resort to nuclear weapons in an emergency, the proposals are self-stultifying. They would vitiate the effect of the no-first-use pledge, while weakening the ability of NATO's strategic forces to threaten retaliation and thereby ensure deterrence. Since the West is faced with the necessity of living with nuclear weapons, with all their risks, it seems better to make a virtue of necessity and continue to preserve, expressly and without ambiguity, such deterrent effect as can be gained from our strategic strength.

It is notable that despite its policy, China did not protest Washington's rejection of the no-first-use suggestion. Moreover, Huang Hua's linkage of conventional arms control measures with nuclear measures implies far greater support for the Western approach than heretofore and is perhaps of greater significance in terms of PRC–USSR–Western relations than it has yet been accorded.

The reactions of Japan and the Republic of Korea to a no-first-use pledge on the part of the United States would be equally sharp. The possibility of Japan, Korea, and even the Federal Republic of Germany being faced with the dilemma of becoming nuclear powers or submitting to nuclear blackmail by the USSR is a most disquieting one.

NUCLEAR FREE ZONES AND REDUCTION OF FOREIGN BASES

China's participation in Protocol II of the Treaty of Tlatelolco is fully consonant with its principal of nuclear free zones combined with no-first-use pledges. The protocol binds signatory non-Latin American states not to use or threaten to use nuclear weapons against any signatory Latin American state. (United States has signed Protocol II.)

Although Beijing has spoken favorably of nuclear-free zones in East Asia and has long pressed the withdrawal of forces from all foreign bases, China has not put forward any specific proposals along these lines since the amelioration of China–U.S. relations. It is very much a matter of speculation as to how vigorously China would push those concepts vis-à-vis the United States in view of the drastic changes in the balance of power that would result therefrom. In the absence of markedly improved Chinese–Russian relations, it would seem likely that China would consider such measures among the very last in any progression toward general, complete disarmament.

Any major withdrawal of U.S. forces or nuclear capability in the Western Pacific would raise Europe's concerns over the credibility of U.S. alliances worldwide and could well be taken by Moscow as an invitation to extend its hegemony.

INTERMEDIATE NUCLEAR FORCE NEGOTIATIONS

China's compelling interest in preserving NATO strength as a counterbalance to Soviet power is demonstrated by its interest in the INF talks at Geneva. Beijing has urged the West to hold firmly to the "double track" decision to proceed with the projected NATO intermediate-range build-up if the current negotiations do not first yield fruit. A pragmatic approach to the balance of power is clearly to be expected in this case. Hence, China can be expected to oppose strongly arrangements that would reduce Soviet deployment against Western Europe while leaving the Soviets unchecked in deployments in Asia.

Particularly as it is constrained in its own defense effort by economic limitations that dwarf the current serious economic problems of the West, China seems all the more anxious that the United States and its allies remain strong in relation to the USSR. One wonders if China talks of "playing the NATO card."

SALT AND START

China's own interests have clearly kept it aloof from any strategic arms limitation talks. It has denounced them as being spurious and of advantage only to the superpowers, while only begrudgingly admitting on occasion that they could have some limited benefit. It now urges progress between the superpowers as the essential first step and seems to support the combining of the Strategic Arms Reduction Talks (START), Intermediate Nuclear Force (INF), and Mutual Balanced Force Reduction (MBFR) talks, or at least to require related progress in all these negotiations.

Although the United States cannot negotiate on behalf of any friendly power or ally—China, France, or Great Britain—it cannot be imagined how a negotiable basis for a stable balance at reduced levels can be achieved without in some way taking into account the nuclear arsenals of these three powers. Thus, in the longer run, the attitude of the three may be at cross purposes with the superpowers.

What Beijing's stand on verification of strategic arms measures would be as time goes on remains speculative. It is by no means clear that China's support for verification by inspection will be easily arrived at, even in the far future.

NONPROLIFERATION

China (like France) is not a party to the Non-Proliferation Treaty. In earlier years, China justified its own nuclear acquisition by claiming that this sort of nonproliferation added to stability. As time has gone by, and Chinese–United States relations have improved, and China's concerns seem to have focused more on those regional nations that could threaten China—for example India and Taiwan.

Beijing will clearly not want to see another nuclear power in the East Asian region. It seems likely to remain conservative as to actions that might impel the technologically competent regional states—Japan, Korea, and particularly Taiwan—from developing their own nuclear weapons. Beijing is also likely to try to remain free to assist countries to develop nuclear forces to countervail those potentially inimical to China (e.g., Pakistan vis-à-vis India) and, above all, will try to preclude the Soviet supply of nuclear weapons or material to any regional state.

As a potential supplier of low-enriched uranium and heavy water, China, applying lesser safeguards than the supplier nations' agreed guidelines propose, has not insisted on government market exports. There is considerable belief that China is a source of supply to the Union of South Africa via the black market. There is also some concern that China may seek to use lower safeguards to gain an advantage as a supplier in the region (e.g., Pakistan).

Finally, it must be noted that U.S. sales of advanced aircraft to Taiwan may, in part, draw China's opposition because of the "camel's nose" implications for nuclear delivery capable systems that might threaten China.

CHEMICAL WARFARE AND
BACTERIOLOGICAL WARFARE

In the Geneva Committee on Disarmament, China has actively pushed controls on chemical warfare. It has adopted a position of strong support for the principles of nonproliferation and verification. China has spoken out against the Soviet employment of chemical weapons, but its charges have been vague and without specific back-up.

CONSTRAINTS ON STRATEGIC BUILD-UP

Fundamentally speaking, China's defense policy is indeed one of protecting its borders and territory. China has little credible offensive strength to move outside its own boundaries in the face of resolute opposition. Its primary strategy seems based on an ability to absorb, disperse, and defeat invasion forces.

As long as this is the case, the heavy investment required to mount a major nuclear strategic delivery system reaching toward parity may not appear to be a priority defense requirement. To the extent that China is able to play on U.S. strength as a deterrent to any Soviet exploitation of its nuclear power, the need to try to play "catch-up ball" in the strategic area is greatly reduced. This very strong policy consideration may well affect the degree to which future Chinese–U.S. relations are likely to be allowed to cool but not chill, thereby constraining both Beijing and Washington in their activities. The European allies, whose world (like that of any power) is egocentric, would welcome the diplomatic use of American strength to restrict Soviet expansionism so long as there was no increased risk of actual hostility in East Asia involving the United States.

China benefits significantly from the present bilateral arrangement between the United States and the USSR in that the resulting restraint on Soviet anti-ballistic missile (ABM) deployment establishes the credibility of China's nuclear capability in the Northeast. Should the United States withdraw from the present arrangement and should Moscow protect its major eastern cities with ABMs, China's nuclear deterrent vis-à-vis Moscow would be greatly weakened. Our European allies, as well as China, would surely oppose such a development, primarily on grounds that any benefits would protect only the United States and the USSR while exposing the other allies.

Those familiar with the French doctrine of a nuclear force "a tous azimuths" may wish to consider China's needs. If the United States is not viewed as a potential threat to China, then China's need for a large long-range intercontinental missile force is appreciably reduced. Indeed, the distance from Moscow to Beijing is only about 3,500 miles, and the Soviet industrial heartland lies still closer to western China. Moreover, the relatively few and scattered key Soviet cities and installations in easternmost Siberia are well within range of current Chinese systems, making the rather fragile infrastructure of the Siberian USSR hostage to China's intermediate-range strength in the event of a Soviet threat to employ nuclear weapons.

For at least the period of this study, it will be important to recognize that the state of China–U.S. relations may thus influence China's course of action in strategic weaponry. The deployment of a very long-range nuclear force would have serious implications on the United States.

BORDER PROBLEMS

Common borders with the Soviet Union in the Northeast and Southwest (both disputed) and, to a lesser extent, the Soviet–Chinese struggle for influence in the Indochinese peninsula provide the immediate bases for concern about increasing confrontation in these areas. Long-standing border disputes, fired by the emotionalism that is attached to irridentism and to hegemonic expansionism, have a way of getting out of control (as the Falkland Islands dispute bears evidence).

Whether the thinning out of forces on both sides and the installation of confidence-building measures would tend to defuse these problems to some extent is not yet clear. China has so far ridiculed Soviet proposals for the northeast border as pure propaganda, and its posture is to wait for deeds rather than words, especially since the Soviets have the preponderance of force there.

Chapter 25

Arms Sales

*Douglas T. Stuart and William T. Tow**

China's assessment of its security needs is based upon its overall evaluation of the world military balance—the "global correlation of
forces." At the present time, the Soviet Union is still regarded as the
primary threat to Beijing's security. In response to this threat, Beijing
is emphasizing defense modernization within the very limited confines
of its economic and technological capabilities in order to gain strategic
and tactical credibility vis-à-vis the Soviets. Current PRC modernization measures include the upgrading of personnel education and combined arms training methods, the improvement of research and development programs for specific weapons systems, the implementation of
a more unified and extensive command and control (C^3) system, the
continued development of a minimum nuclear deterrent posture
against Soviet forces that remain deployed in large numbers along the
Sino–Soviet border, and the purchase of selected weapons systems and
defense related technologies from the Industrialized Democracies
(IDs).

As several writers have pointed out already, China will be forced to
maintain clearcut priorities in its weapons and technology procurement programs throughout the remainder of this century and to concentrate its efforts upon the deterrence of the USSR. By the twenty-

*University of California School of International Relations in Munich.

413

first century, it will become increasingly difficult to adapt such traditional Chinese doctrines as "people's war" and "wars of national liberation" to new strategic requirements. The Chinese leadership may also be forced to conclude that significant improvements can only be achieved by an even greater reliance upon knowledge and technology acquired from the IDs (or the Soviet Union) in light of continuing frustrations with indigenous military modernization programs. If Chinese dependence upon outside suppliers increases, the suppliers will gain greater influence in setting the terms of trade unless the PRC can convince suppliers that they have a special stake in sponsoring China's defense modernization.

The PRC's policy of foreign weapons and technology acquisition seems to be following both a short- and a long-term pattern: for more immediate military needs, the limited purchase of systems to fill gaps and provide prototypes for reverse engineering; for long-range requirements, the development of an indigenous research and development base sufficient to compete with the United States and the Soviet Union. Even now, China is actively setting the foundation for its long-range self-defense program by selective purchases in such areas as software and electronics technology, especially from Japan.[1] These purchases have the potential to make a direct and significant impact on both China's strategic defense program, in such areas as targeting and guidance capabilities, and its conventional defense program, in such areas as ground and air interception systems, naval attack systems, and armored mobility.

It is in such areas that Sino–American arms relations might have their greatest long-term significance. During January 1980, for example, then U.S. Secretary of Defense Brown pledged that the United States and China would pursue their common geo-strategic interests by establishing a limited program of technology transfer that could be applicable to military purposes. Some eighteen months later, Secretary of State Haig extended this commitment to include possible U.S. sales of "lethal arms" to the Chinese. In December 1981, the U.S. Department of Commerce published guidelines for a liberalized American export policy toward the PRC. According to the new guidelines, most export licenses were to be approved unless ". . . the export would present an unacceptable risk regardless of stated end-use." Such risks were defined as technologies making a direct contribution to the development of nuclear weapons and their related delivery systems, electronic and antisubmarine warfare, or intelligence gathering.[2] Assistant Secretary for Trade Administration Lawrence Brady announced that the United States was adhering to the classification of China as a "P" group country, which would make it eligible for export licenses at technical levels roughly twice as high as those used to regulate trade to the USSR and its Eastern Europe satellites.[3] Washington stated that it would still block items that were found on the prohibited list of the multilateral (the NATO countries plus Japan, less Iceland) Coordinating Committee for Exports to Communist Areas (COCOM). Yet even this forum was showing signs that it was beginning to change its long-standing propensity to block the transfer of strategic goods to the PRC, as two computers—Japan's "Hitachi M-180" and the United States' "IBM 303" model—with possible applications for the improvement of Chinese ICBM targeting and guidance capabilities were approved for sale in mid-May 1982.[4]

FUTURE SINO–AMERICAN ARMS RELATIONS

As several authors have discussed, the question of how the PRC–U.S. arms relationship will develop is intricately related to both the question of Taiwan and to the actions of the political coalitions that have evolved within both China and the United States.

During his presidential campaign, Ronald Reagan emphasized the importance of interpreting the 1979 Taiwan Relations Act in ways that would not inhibit the United States from supplying the Nationalist Chinese regime with defensive weapons and spare parts, regardless of the inevitable objections raised in Beijing. In January 1982, however, President Reagan decided not to sell Taipei the advanced fighter aircraft that the Nationalists had requested and merely offered to extend Taiwan's existing coproduction agreement for the less advanced F-5E. The PRC protested the sale anyway and threatened to downgrade diplomatic relations with the United States. In April 1982, the Defense Department announced that it was selling US$60 million in military aircraft spare parts for Taiwan's 386 combat aircraft even while sensitive political negotiations about the future of such sales were ongoing between U.S. and Chinese officials. The United States assured the PRC that the spare parts package had been promised to Taiwan *before* the U.S.–Chinese negotiations about the matter had commenced in late 1981, that the sales would not involve any actual weapons, and that the United States would not consider such weapons sales while the negotiations continued.[5] During the ensuing weeks, Beijing sent repeated warnings to the United States about the damage that continued U.S.–Taiwan security ties would do to Sino–American relations, and China's Premier Zhao Ziyang warned Vice President Bush during the latter's visit to China in May 1982 that "serious obstacles" were intensifying strains in their countries' relations.[6] In some recent statements, Beijing has linked the question of Taiwan to the issue of U.S. forces in South Korea, thus making it more difficult for Washington to accommodate the PRC on the Taiwan issue.[7]

The Beijing leadership appears to have adopted this "get tough" position on Taiwan arms sales for two reasons: (1) to placate strong domestic political pressures from the still-powerful conservative faction; and (2) because they have calculated that China has considerably more leverage in its relations with the United States than at any time in the last decade.[8] The Reagan administration, for its part, does appear anxious to reach an accommodation with Beijing without appearing entirely cynical in its Taiwan arms trade policy. This is because the Reagan team's concern about the direct military threat that the PRC might pose to Taiwan has been overshadowed by its interest in the continued and increased "use" of China against the Soviet Union. Recently published excerpts from a strategic "guidance" for U.S. security policy in Asia tend to support Beijing's assessment of its negotiating leverage. The document asserts that the United States must seek to maintain a close strategic relationship with the PRC "by measured increases in its military capability."[9]

It is nonetheless quite possible for relations between Beijing and Washington to break down over the Taiwan arms sales issue. This could occur because of congressional constraints placed upon Reagan or because of Beijing's mismanagement of its pressure campaign against the United States.

If Beijing and Washington enter a period of downgraded or broken diplomatic relations as a result of the Taiwan dispute, the PRC might actively pursue a "second world" strategy—focusing its political and economic attention on Japan and the governments of Western Europe. Under these circumstances, China would opt for second world arms acquisition as well.[10] It is certainly true that many of the weapons systems and technologies that the United States has been willing to sell to China could be replaced by competitive products from Europe or Japan. But this Chinese strategy might founder on political opposition from key second world states for one or both of the following reasons:

1. Japan and the nations of Western Europe would not permit themselves to be pitted directly against the United States as competitive suppliers in an Asian arms race. The second world IDs are unlikely to engage in the sale of arms to China if the United States makes a strong case to the effect that the weapons represent a direct threat to a U.S. protectorate such as Taiwan or the Republic of Korea. The Falklands crisis offers an example of ID policy coor-

dination for arms sale restraint in the interest of conflict management. To the extent, however, that the link between China arms sales and U.S. security interests is viewed as very indirect or even nonexistent by a potential arms supplier in the Second World, there is a basis for serious dispute among the IDs over this issue.

2. Most of these second world ID governments would not permit China to politicize defense-related trade for purposes of propaganda or to threaten the USSR. A second world PRC strategy would put Japan and the Western European states in a much more politically exposed position vis-à-vis the Soviet Union. Under these circumstances, Moscow would probably increase its pressure on the second world ID states to discourage cooperation with the PRC.

Such a Soviet campaign would meet with varying degrees of success in the separate capitals of the second world IDs. Among the major western European states, there exists a continuum of support for China's "global anti-hegemony campaign." Along this continuum, we might locate Great Britain at the politically supportive extreme and West Germany at the suspicious and very cautious extreme, with France and Italy ranging between these two. This continuum might also be entitled "susceptibility to Soviet pressure." Thus, for example, Great Britain has continued to negotiate with the PRC for the sale of weapons systems in spite of personal warnings from Premier Brezhnev. Reportedly, a British defense mission was scheduled to visit the PRC in early 1983 with a variety of defense equipment scheduled to be demonstrated—including the "Sea Dart" anti-aircraft missile that could be installed on China's fleet of "Luda" class destroyers. British Aerospace will nonetheless have some difficulty convincing potential buyers of the "Sea Dart's" utility as a defensive system for destroyers, due to the sinking of two type 42 destroyers that were equipped with this weapon during the Falklands Crisis.[11] China has already developed its own radar navigation equipment to be deployed by 1984, which would naturally complement any foreign acquired naval missile technology.[12] Conversely, the Federal Republic of Germany has made it clear to the PRC that it will continue to give priority to Soviet interests and concerns when formulating its policies on trade and political cooperation with China.

But even in Great Britain there would be very little interest in a Chinese sponsored "second world" campaign that excluded the United States while pitting the Europeans directly against Moscow. Similar considerations would apply for Japan. During Premier Zhao's six-day visit to Japan in early June 1982, Japanese officials reportedly expressed concern that China's "Three Principles" for governing Sino–

Japanese relations—"peace and friendship," "equality and mutual benefit," and "long-term stability"—might be designed to exclude the United States and other third countries. Zhao reassured his hosts that this would not be the case and reaffirmed the PRC's understanding of the importance Tokyo attaches to the U.S.–Japan Mutual Security Treaty.[13] A month earlier, Japanese press reports publicized accounts of Song Zhiguang, the Chinese Ambassador to Japan; Liao Chenghai, Vice Chairman of the Standing Committee of the National People's Congress; and other Chinese officials assuring their Japanese counterparts that basic Sino–U.S. relations would remain unchanged although Japan could "help" these ties through exerting "positive influence" on Washington concerning the Taiwan dispute.[14] Upon assuming his post as Chinese Ambassador to Japan at the beginning of the year, Song expressed the conviction that Tokyo and Beijing should upgrade military contacts and interchanges, but this topic seems to have been scrupulously avoided during Zhao's later visit to Tokyo.[15]

It is therefore unlikely that China could manage a second world strategy for very long. Beijing might nonetheless opt for such a strategy in the near future as a tactical adjustment—to gain time and/or to increase its leverage with the United States. But this situation would not be conducive to the conclusion of major defense-related contracts with the second world IDs.

ARMS TRANSFER POLICY COORDINATION AMONG INDUSTRIALIZED DEMOCRACIES

During the 1950s, a serious rift developed between the West European allies and the United States as a result of Washington's attempt to sponsor a "China differential" in Western trade with the Communist bloc. Washington then favored a policy of greater trade restrictions against Beijing than against other East bloc states to exert special economic and political pressure upon China. The policy was ultimately rejected by the West European governments on the grounds that the West could only maintain a coherent trade policy if it maintained the same rules for all East bloc states. There was also a good deal of distrust of the U.S. argument that economic sanctions could be employed for purposes of political influence.[16]

At present, the United States is sponsoring a new "China differential" in its strategic trade with Communist bloc countries, but this policy accords special benefits to the PRC rather than imposing special sanctions. In less than three years, the United States has moved in its trade restrictions against Moscow and Beijing to a policy of virtually unrestrained strategic trade with China and increased trade sanctions against the USSR. James L. Buckley, U.S. undersecretary of state for security assistance, defended this new policy of "ending the discriminatory treatment [of China] based on its past cold war association with the Soviet bloc" on the grounds that such a discriminatory policy was "out of kilter with today's U.S. foreign policy objectives."[17] The United States has also modified existing legislation that prohibits the provision of foreign assistance to the PRC.

As a result of these policy changes, the United States is now in a position to make an increased contribution to China's defense modernization program by the sale of arms and defense-related equipment or even by the provision of such material in the form of military aid if the Taiwan arms dispute can be resolved. Many of America's industrialized democratic allies will continue to harbor fears about this possibility during the next decade. These fears are anchored in a fundamental debate over the proposition that arms trade with the PRC can be employed as a club against the Soviet Union. Within COCOM, this dispute has been subsumed within a broader debate over the whole issue of utilizing trade and trade restriction to coerce or punish Moscow.

Should the United States embark upon a campaign of active support for Chinese defense modernization, this policy will engender the following specific concerns among some of America's allies:

That the United States will view the China arms sale issue increasingly within the context of triangular conflict, which will serve to further undermine any chances for détente with the USSR, fuel the superpower arms race, and encourage a pattern of triangular risk taking.

That the United States will press the Industrialized Democracies for support for its policy of arming China against the Soviet Union, to the detriment of existing institutional arrangements for policy coordination (COCOM, NATO, OECD, etc.).

Conversely, that America's policy of arming the PRC will be one component of a broader pattern of U.S. unilateralism and global activism that many of these states see developing and that the United States will pursue a policy of arming China at the expense of its other security commitments in Asia and Western Europe.

By focusing upon the effect that arms transfers to China might have on the Soviet Union's calculations, the United States may fail to consider the threat that a militarily stronger China might pose for other Asian region states that are tied through treaty or through historical circumstance with certain Industrialized Democracies. For example, Great Britain may come to revise its cost-benefit calculations regarding a China arms sale policy when it begins to consider analogies between the recent events in the Falklands and the presently quiescent situation of Hong Kong.

That the United States will take advantage of its position of influence in such fora as COCOM to monopolize lucrative sectors of the China arms trade. The aforementioned competition within COCOM between U.S. and Japanese computer firms was something of a test in this regard. Japanese spokesmen accused the United States of manipulating the COCOM guidelines in the interest of the U.S. computer industry. The final COCOM decision to permit the sale of both the Japanese and American models to Beijing appears to have been a compromise designed to skirt a particularly divisive dispute. But it would appear that Washington and Tokyo will be inevitable competitors for what could well be a profitable Chinese software market notwithstanding the potential strategic ramifications of such competition for East Asia and for the global strategic balance of forces.[18]

Those allies that are concerned about the possibility of a rapidly escalating U.S.–China arms trade can take some reassurance in four factors that continue to exert a restraining influence on the Washington–Beijing arms sale relationship. First, Congress (which continues to hold considerable power in the U.S. foreign policy process in general and in the fields of arms transfers and technology transfers in particular through such instruments as the Arms Export Control Act) has influenced the pace and scope of U.S.–China trade in defense-related materials. Speeches by congressional leaders illustrate that there is still considerable disagreement within the legislative branch regarding the desirability of arming China.[19]

Second, the natural restraining influence of the bureaucracy has had an effect on the U.S.–China arms sales relationship. Evolving arms sales have been slowed by disagreements within and between the agencies and services responsible for the execution of U.S. foreign policy and by the reticence of those institutions to abandon existing procedures. Senate testimony provides several examples of the gap between U.S. public pronouncements of support for increased arms sales to China and the actual approval of such sales by the Departments of Commerce and Defense.[20]

Third, Washington continues to exhibit some (if insufficient) desire to obtain the support of its allies for its China arms sales policy. As previously mentioned, Great Britain is the only major American ally that shares Washington's view of the utility of arming China against Russia. Other European allies have encouraged Washington to exercise caution. More forceful expressions of concern have been heard from some of America's industrialized, developing, and newly industrialized allies in Asia, as Professor Harding discussed earlier.

A fourth and final factor limiting the pace and scope of U.S. arms sales to the PRC is the reticence of the Chinese to press the United States to increase significantly its sale of arms and/or defense-related technology to China at this time.

A BASIS FOR PREDICTIONS

The following summary considerations regarding demand and supply are offered as a basis for subsequent predictions about the nature and scope of PRC purchases of arms from the Industrialized Democracies during the next ten years. PRC demand for weapons and defense-related technologies from the IDs will depend on two factors in particular.

Persistence and Change in China's World View

Bureaucratic politics notwithstanding, PRC decisions relating to defense modernization will continue to be largely determined by the answers that the Chinese leadership gives to specific philosophical and instrumental questions about international relations. Key "operational code" questions for China concern (1) the identity and character of the PRC's principal opponent; (2) the role of force in contemporary international affairs; and (3) the appropriate tactics for the deterrence of threats to PRC security.[21] In this regard, the PRC leadership gives no indication that it is moving away from a world view that is built upon the identification of the Soviet Union as the primary threat to its security. A statement issued by the official Chinese press in early August 1982 asserted that while both superpowers were essentially "hegemonist," the PRC considers the USSR as being "on the offensive" and that a strong anti-Soviet stance must necessarily continue to be one of the main elements of China's foreign policy. Significantly, the statement further observed that Moscow's "deceptive behavior" in attempting to manipulate China with technical assistance during the 1950s was a key to Beijing's current resentment of the Russians and its reluctance to effect a political rapprochement with them.[22] Relatively low PRC defense spending during the last five years is the best indicator of the fact that China has not perceived Soviet military power along its borders as imminently threatening to its own survival. The DIA has reported that the PRC's state budget for 1982 includes a 6 percent increase for military expenditures as compared to a 4 percent increase in the government's overall budget, ". . . suggesting that Beijing is placing slightly more emphasis on military programs." But the report also noted that there was still no change in the overall status of China's military programs.[23]

In the absence of any strong indicators to the contrary, the authors are led to conclude that Beijing will continue to view the Soviet Union with caution and concern but not with alarm. This perspective will influence China's judgment of the priority to be accorded to defense modernization and the acquisition of expensive weapons and defense technologies from the IDs in an era of serious economic problems. The PRC will continue to monitor Soviet defense policy, however, for early identification of any major changes in Moscow's military posture that might imply a more direct and more immediate threat to China. In this regard, Beijing is currently giving special attention to the Intermediate Nuclear Force (INF) talks for any sign that U.S. and West European representatives are encouraging a major redeployment of Soviet medium- and intermediate-range ballistic missiles to the Far Eastern Military District.[24]

China's assessment of its geo-strategic vulnerability is also affected by developments in South, East, and Southeast Asia. Again, PRC expressions of concern regarding specific actors (such as Vietnam and Taiwan) and should be judged in the context of Beijing's actual defense spending. But China's bilateral relations with key Asian actors could change in direction or intensity in a relatively short time, providing the PRC with a new sense of insecurity or new opportunities. The IDs have some control over these developments and can influence China's calculations positively or negatively by their political, economic, and military initiatives in the region. French actions, including the sale of enriched uranium to India and the provision of foreign aid to Vietnam (at a time when Beijing is giving aid to the opposition forces in Kampuchea), are examples of the ways in which IDs can indirectly influence China's strategic calculus. A more familiar and important example is the current U.S.–Taiwan relationship.

Chinese Domestic Politics

To date, Deng Xiaoping's campaign to shore up his own power position and secure the dominance of the "modernists" has been more successful within the party and the bureaucracy than within the army. During the next decade, Deng's political opponents are likely to solicit much of their support from within the ranks of the old guard military cadres who have opposed Deng's defense modernization campaign and have been disenfranchised as a result. The degree of disaffection that exists within the PLA will be partly a function of the commitment that Deng and his followers make to the acquisition of arms and technology from the IDs at the expense of manpower. To counter such disaffection, the modernists must continue to increase the institutional stake of key military sectors in defense modernization and communicate the need for defense modernization and the benefits to be derived therefrom. This will require a policy of gradual and cautious introduction of new weapons systems to progressively reinforce the influence of the modernists without isolating large portions of the PLA leadership in the process.

From the demand side, then, we do not foresee Beijing embarking on a major arms purchasing campaign to support an ambitious program of comprehensive defense modernization. Deng Xiaoping and the pragmatist leadership that he represents will retain their commitment to the principle of defense modernization and continue to encourage the hopes of ID arms producers through visits and contract talks. Actual purchases will be quite limited in military or financial value, however, and will be concentrated in specific military sectors that have been given priority, such as air defense, armor, amphibious forces, and strategic deterrence—particularly intermediate and medium range ballistic missiles and command, control, and communications (C^3).

On the supply side of the PRC–ID arms trade relationship, Japan, the United States, and the Industrialized Democracies of Western Europe and the Pacific will each decide whether or not to sell weapons systems and defense-related technologies to China according to their answers to two policy questions:

What contribution would a militarily stronger China make toward the preservation and advancement of the common security interests of the IDs (collectively and separately) and at what costs and risks?

What benefits can be derived from the *process* of arms trade with China per se, regardless of the impact that such trade would have on Beijing's actual military strength? Several writers and a few government spokesmen (mostly American) have expressed interest in arms sales to China as an instrument for modifying the behavior of the Soviet Union. The threatened or actual sale of arms to China has been recommended as a means of punishing the USSR for actions in Afghanistan, deterring possible Soviet actions in Poland, and communicating new Western resolve. But using the process of arms trade with China as a means of nonverbal communication involves several risks. First, as Robert Jervis warns in his study *The Logic of Images in International Relations,* there is often a very great disparity between the sender's meaning of the message and the recipient's interpretation of that message. A special concern of some Industrialized Democracies is that signals designed to encourage Soviet restraint may be read as proof of offensive intent, precipitating defensive overreaction on the part of Moscow. Second, in concentrating upon the effect that a specific message will have upon a particular target, a sender may lose sight of the impact that the message has upon other nations.

It is particularly important for the United States to avoid such problems at a time when many IDs and many third world states see an increasing trend toward U.S. unilateralism and global adventurism. For this reason, the United States must make a special effort to coordinate its China arms policy with other IDs in existing fora such as COCOM and in high level informal meetings of heads of state so that if common positions cannot be reached on the sale of arms to China, there will at least be a better understanding of the differing security perspectives that underlie different policies toward the PRC.

NOTES

1. For specific software applications to military technology, especially in the context of Japanese technology transfers to China, see William T. Tow, "Prospects for Chinese–Japanese Regional Security Cooperation: Quasi-Alliance Politics in East Asia?," manuscript presented before the International Studies Association annual conference (March 23–27, 1982, Cincinnati, Ohio), pp. 15–22; and "Civilian Technology Diverted for Military Purposes," *Asahi Evening News* translation in *The Asia Record* 3, No. 1 (April 1982), p. B–1.
2. Paul Mann, "China Export Policy Takes Final Form," *Aviation Week and Space Technology* 116, No. 4 (January 25, 1982), p. 57.
3. Reported in *The Asia Record* 2, No. 12 (March 1982), p. 25.
4. *International Herald Tribune (IHT)* (May 24, 1982), p. 2. It should be noted that there are pro- and anti-China arms sales factions within the U.S. Defense Department with the Office of International Programs and Technology generally representing a "technical group" that sees little problem in exercising quality controls over materials and technology sold to the PRC, while the International Economic Trade and Security Office of DOD represents a "policy group" more concerned about the long-term implications of technology transfers to any Communist bloc nations. "China Awaits Export License," p. 25.
5. A report on the decision's ramifications is in Mann, "Reagan's F-5G Decision Pleases No One," *Aviation Week and Space Technology* 116, No. 3 (January 18, 1982), pp. 16–17. For definitive Chinese statements on this issue, see "U.S. Policy Toward China, Selling Taiwan Arms," *Liaowang* (Beijing), No. 4 (July 1981), p. 28, and reprinted in *FBIS, China (Daily Report)* (August 6, 1981), p. B–1; and "China Won't Accept U.S. 'Balanced Arms Sale'," *Beijing Review* 24, No. 25 (June 22,

1981), p. 11. For Western accounts of the Chinese response to the Reagan decision, see *The Asian Wall Street Journal Weekly* (January 18, 1982), pp. 1, 19; and *The Times* (London) (March 3, 1982), p. 7.

6. See Christopher S. Wren, "China Files Protest on Arms Sales to Taiwan," *IHT* (April 15, 1982), p. 1. For reports on Bush's trip, see *IHT* (May 8–9, 1982), p. 1; (May 10, 1982), p. 4; and (May 15–16, 1982), p. 3. His visit to the PRC was later termed to be "good for Sino–American ties" by the Chinese.

7. See "People's Daily on China's Unshakeable Stand on U.S. Arms for Taiwan," in British Broadcasting Corporation, *Summary of World Broadcasts—Far East (SWB–FE)* 7004/A1/1–A1/2 (April 17, 1982). The New Chinese News Agency's response to a recent *Newsweek* report that "the U.S. Government is taking measures to stem the export of American technology to China" was one of "no comment," as recounted in BBC, *SWB–FE/7075/A1/4* (July 14, 1982). See also "China Questions Legal Basis of Taiwan Relations Act," BBC, *SWB–FE/7074/A1/1* (July 10, 1982).

8. Stuart and Tow, "China's Military Modernization." See also Lowell Dittmer, "The Strategic Triangle: An Elementary Game-Theoretical Analysis," *World Politics* 33, No. 4 (July 1981), pp. 485–515.

9. An account of the "Strategic Guidance" document is in the *IHT* (June 8, 1982), p. 7.

10. The prospects for a "second world" PRC strategy are further discussed by Douglas Stuart, "China and West European Security," *Orbis* (Fall 1982), p. .

11. *The Times* (London) (July 15, 1982), p. 2. Also see a report in BBC, *SWB–FE/7075/Al/3* (July 14, 1982), which cites the Chinese naval academy preparing "studies" on the Falklands campaign in order to enhance the PRC's tactical thinking and military research.

12. *Strategy Week* VIII, No. 17 (May 3–9, 1982), p. 2. A recent Chinese report on overall naval modernization strategies is in BBC, *SWB–FE/7075/BII/1*.

13. Mike Tharp, "Zhao's Foot in the Door," *FEER* 116, No. 24 (June 11, 1982), p. 14.

14. *The Japan Times* (April 4, 1982), p. 1; (April 10, 1982), p. 1; and *The Asahi Evening News* (April 9, 1982), p. 1.

15. *Asahi Evening News* (February 15, 1982), p. 4. A burgeoning dispute between Beijing and Tokyo over Japan's Education Ministry revising accounts of Japanese atrocities committed during World War II in Japan's history textbooks by merely describing them in terms of "military advance" has had a surprising impact on the heretofore cordial political relations enjoyed between those two countries. At this writing, however, it seems likely that forces within Japan favoring the conciliation of this issue led by Foreign Minister Yoshio Sakurauchi will be successful in reinstating the original context of the accounts of the rationale that mutual interests related to high priorities between China and Japan should not be jeopardized over this issue. See the Reuters dispatch appearing in *IHT* (August 11, 1982), p. 6.

16. Stuart and Tow, "China's Military Modernization."

17. Portions of Buckley's testimony before the House Foreign Affairs Subcommittee on International Security and Scientific Affairs are recounted in *Aviation Week and Space Technology* 116, No. 15 (April 12, 1982), pp. 20–21.

18. Discussed in *The Daily Telegraph* (London) (September 22, 1981), p. 5; *The Japan Times* (October 20, 1981), p. 12. See also Tow, "Prospects for Chinese–Japanese Regional Security Cooperation," for further discussion.

19. Reginald Dale, "Reagan Move on Taiwan Adds to Right's Doubts," *Financial Times* (January 13, 1982), p. 1.

20. See testimony by Roger Sullivan in "The Implications of U.S.–China Military Cooperation," pp. 49–50.

21. For an example of a Western attempt to establish the "operational code" beliefs of the PRC leadership, see Davis Bobrow, Steve Chan, and John Kringen, *Understanding Foreign Policy Decisions: The Chinese Case* (New York: Free Press, 1979).

22. The Chinese statement is summarized in *IHT* (August 9, 1982).

23. Williams testimony, *op. cit.*, at 48–49.

24. Stefan Possony, "PRC/USSR: A Sino–Soviet Thaw?" *Defense and Foreign Affairs Daily* 11, No. 23 (February 17, 1982), p. 2.

25. Robert Jarvis, *The Logic of Images in International Relations* (Princeton: Princeton University Press, 1970), *passim*.

Chapter 26

Trade, Economic, And Financial Relations With China

*Christopher H. Phillips**

Over the decade China's economic and financial links with the West should continue to be developed. In general, this will be favorable to the West, but it will tend to create new tensions among the allies, each of which has its own interests in relation to Beijing. Despite differences, however, the allies generally agree that a secure China is in everyone's interest, and thus it is important that China's economy continues to be meshed with that of the West. This includes achievement by the PRC of long-term food and energy supplies to ensure solid economic growth and to prevent destabilization of the world's most populous nation.

Economic development and Western contact, while essential, may not always produce predictable results. The PRC's attempt to achieve a lower population growth by the year 2,000, while tending to create a more affluent, efficient, and productive society, will also create tensions in China that will directly affect China's economic relations with the West. "Corruption" of various kinds (which many Chinese blame on the influence of foreigners in the south of China and on China's rising consciousness as a "developing nation" vis-à-vis Western industrialized countries) has contributed to the pending prohibition on the import of

*President, National Council for U.S.–China Trade.

Western consumer goods in favor of the development of import-substitution industries.

The complexity of Western economic and financial relations with China will also increase over the next twenty years. As regionalism increases in the PRC, the West must also be prepared to deal with an increasingly decentralized nation whose provinces and regional authorities will further extend their links with local areas in allied countries, forming a more complex set of relationships at national and local levels than has existed before.

GENERAL INTERESTS

There are no fundamental differences among the allies on major China issues. All welcome the emergence of the PRC as an increasingly responsible member of the world economic community. They welcome the beneficial effects of China's contribution to global peace and Asian regional development and stability. The allies also encourage and appreciate China's willingness to participate fully in world cultural, scientific, and sports activities.

In its own interest, China will continue to want to avoid becoming dependent, both politically and economically, on any single Western ally. The PRC will use the competitive nature of allied relations with Beijing to its advantage.

The August 1982 joint China–U.S. communiqué on Taiwan arms sales reduced tensions over the controversial issue of Taiwan. But should the Taiwan issue continue to rankle in China's relations with the United States, domestic political forces will force Beijing to put greater emphasis on its ties with Europe, Japan, and the Third World at the expense of its relations with the United States. In any case, we can expect Beijing to have a more balanced relationship with the United States and other major nations in the future.

On a more practical level, the allies should continue to encourage the PRC to develop its legal framework for trade, economic, financial, and other matters with sound legal principles. Institutionalizing the economic environment in China will naturally encourage Western companies, if the business is profitable and they are accorded reasonable legal protections. Allied efforts to assist China's development of quality control, management, accounting, financial, and other sound business practices should continue to the benefit of all.

As China continues to expand its economy and international relationships, a number of issues will inevitably have to be managed among the allies.

FINANCING AND INTEREST RATES

As China's trade and business increases with the West, the need for Export-Import Bank and other concessional government financing will increase, especially for China's so-called backbone projects. The availability of low-cost financing from Japan and Europe (when the United States was unable to supply such low-cost rates or make specific fund allocations) has already created strains among the allies. Continuing divergence on this issue is likely because of the competitive edge that it represents. Such financing is used to open up new areas of business that tend to benefit companies from the contributing countries.

But China's real problem is not so much obtaining low-cost foreign funds (now official Chinese policy) but using those funds effectively. For example, although Japan provided low-cost loans for rail and port development in northern China, few of the projects have been implemented as of March 1982 (even though the equipment has been purchased and sent) because the Chinese have been unable to coordinate and carry out their plans.

It is in the allies' interest to encourage jointly more effective, realistic planning and project management in China. Joint efforts should be undertaken to ensure that adequate feasibility studies and planning are carried out for projects to be financed by concessional government financing. Given China's past record of plant and project cancellations, this would be particularly important—and mutually advantageous to both China and its business partners.

MULTINATIONAL AGENCIES

The U.S. intention to reduce funds to the World Bank has already produced considerable strain among the allies because of the policy it represents (i.e., let the private sector do the job), the effect it has on beneficiaries (e.g., India), and the impact on relations between allied countries and individual developing nations who look to them for assistance. China, while now receiving only a small fraction of the funds available during the current International Development Agency (IDA) cycle, will be a major beneficiary in the future if the Seventh IDA Replenishment materializes.

The effect of this development will be a sharpening of differences among beneficiaries and among donors. The addition of China as a beneficiary means other beneficiaries will automatically have less. As the U.S. share of donations diminishes, tensions will also rise among the donors who will have to shoulder more of the burden. These tensions have already manifested themselves in a recent proposal by three countries (France, Canada, and the Netherlands) for a separate special account for IDA funding that would be open only to non-U.S. companies bidding on World Bank projects.

Management of the allied effort here will become increasingly difficult to handle. The consequence could be that China, the newest member of the World Bank, will see these restraining moves as directed against it by the allies and might return to inward-looking economic policies.

EXPORT CONTROLS

Since the process of liberalizing U.S. and COCOM controls on sales of technology to China began several years ago, there has been discord among the allies on the question of export controls on sales to the PRC. While it may be in the allies' interest to liberalize controls for China (and eventually to give China the status Yugoslavia now holds), the effect of liberalizing controls on sales to the Chinese has already created pressure from the Soviets to reduce controls on sales to them. Each further liberalization of controls for China will tend to sharpen differences among the allies, given the likelihood that the United States and others would resolutely oppose any reduction in controls of technology sales to the Soviet Union and East European nations. Attitudes toward détente with the Soviets have come to differ markedly among the allies.

ECONOMIC AND TRADE RESPONSIBILITY

As China's worldwide commerce grows, it is in the allies' interest to encourage China to become a responsible member of the world economic community by joining the General Agreement on Tariffs and Trade (GATT) and participating in world industrial property conventions. As it is, China is obtaining the advantage of GATT without being obligated to observe the standards of fair trade that GATT represents, and no patent law is yet forthcoming.

Without educating China's national and provincial officials about GATT standards and without putting the provisions of the GATT into practice in China, there is no question that, over the next decade, development of trade with China will be hindered. Allied coordination is essential if this is to succeed.

Europe and Japan have already granted China the General System of Preferences status, while the United States hasn't—and cannot do so under the terms of the Trade Act until China joins GATT. Each time the United States, Japan, or the European Economic Community imposes quotas or other restrictions on Chinese imports (which they already do), China will be pressured to find other markets within the Alliance for its products. If, and as, protectionism increases, the allies should consult on the impact this will have on China's exports, which will help to determine the level of China's grain and technology imports and thus economic growth. There should be continuing allied consultation on decisions that will affect China's exports.

AGRICULTURAL DEVELOPMENT

In the interest of regional and global stability, it is essential that China continues to provide sufficient food and clothing for its people. To this end, it is important that the allies create the most stable conditions possible for enduring agricultural supplies in the PRC by means of long-term grain agreements and government-to-government agricultural protocols and cooperation and by encouraging the PRC to participate in global agricultural organizations, such as the United Nations Food and Agricultural Organization and the International Wheat Council.

China will concentrate its future efforts on nongrain crops, such as cotton and soybeans, and will put more emphasis on cash crops, such as those producing essential oils and spices. Consequently, China, in the longer term, may be less of an expanding market for Western agricultural produce and more of a factor influencing specialized world commodity markets.

While the agricultural sector is unlikely to create tensions among the allies over China, they must continue to be sensitive to the success or failure of China's harvest as a critical factor influencing world grain prices as a major consideration in arranging distribution of limited grain supplies at times of global food shortage.

ENERGY

The involvement of American oil companies in a multi-billion-dollar program for China's offshore oil development could well exacerbate differences between the United States and its European allies. Because of the huge capital and technology requirement of China's offshore program, U.S. oil companies could well dominate this offshore development. If that happens, the United States may tend to be increasingly preoccupied with relations with Beijing, while the Europeans may tend to be more preoccupied with the Soviet Union as they move ahead with the long-term Soviet natural gas pipeline project. The situation will thus need deft handling and careful management during the next ten to fifteen years.

Glossary

ANZUS	Tripartite treaty among Australia, New Zealand, and the United States
ASEAN	Association of Southeast Asian Nations
CCP	Chinese Communist Party
COCOM	Coordinating Committee
CSCPRC	Committee for Scholarly Communication with the People's Republic of China
DMZ	De-militarized zone
DOD	U.S. Department of Defense
DPRK	Democratic People's Republic of Korea (North Korea)
FMS	Foreign Military Sales
GATT	General Agreement on Trade and Tariffs
GNP	Gross national product
ICBM	Intercontinental Ballistic Missile
IDA	International Development Agency
IMET	International Military Education and Training
IMF	International Monetary Fund
JCCT	Joint Commission on Commerce and Trade
JEC	Joint Economic Commission
KMT	Kuomintang
LDC	Less Developed Country
MFN	Most Favored Nation

NATO	North Atlantic Treaty Organization
NPC	National People's Congress
OECD	Organization for Economic Cooperation and Development
PLA	People's Liberation Army
PRC	People's Republic of China
ROC	Republic of China (Taiwan)
ROK	Republic of Korea (South Korea)
SALT	Strategic Arms Limitation Treaty
SEATO	Southeast Asia Treaty Organization
SRV	Socialist Republic of Vietnam
TRA	Taiwan Relations Act

Index

Z